Getting Started with Bluetooth™

Getting Started with Bluetooth™

Madhushree
Ganguli

Premier

P

Press™

Premier The Premier Press logo and related trade dress are trademarks of Premier Press, Inc. and may not be used without written permission.

Press

Bluetooth wireless technology is a trademark of the Bluetooth SIG, Inc.

From the Bluetooth SIG:

"The Bluetooth trademark refers to a particular short-range wireless specification developed by the Bluetooth SIG. As often as practical, proper usage of the Bluetooth trade name should be immediately followed by the descriptor, 'wireless technology'."

All other trademarks are the property of their respective owners.

Important: Premier Press cannot provide software support. Please contact the appropriate software manufacturer's technical support line or Web site for assistance.

ISBN: 1-931841-83-7

Library of Congress Catalog Card Number: 2002106525

Printed in the United States of America

02 03 04 05 BH 10 9 8 7 6 5 4 3 2 1

Premier Press, a division of Course Technology
2645 Erie Avenue, Suite 41
Cincinnati, Ohio 45208

Publisher:
Stacy L. Hiquet

Marketing Manager:
Heather Hurley

Managing Editor:
Sandy Doell

Editorial Assistants:
Margaret Bauer
Elizabeth Barrett

Technical Reviewers:
Puneet Mehra and
Ashish Gupta

Development Managers:
Vikram Bhatia and Anita Sastry

Copy Editor:
Kim Cofer

Interior Layout:
LJ Graphics

Cover Designer:
Mike Tanamachi

Indexer:
Sharon Shock

Acknowledgements

Writing a book does not call for hard work from my side alone but also includes support from a large team. Here's a short list of the team that helped me complete this book.

First and foremost, thanks to my family that has been my strength, driving force, and support, tirelessly encouraging me to carry out this project. Thanks to my husband Anindya, and my kids Aneerudh and Anuradha for enduring the late nights and smiling through the innumerable lost weekends that I spent researching and writing for the book.

A special thanks to my project managers Vikram Bhatia and Anita Sastry for their support and confidence through this entire project. They managed the project meticulously and made the sailing so smooth for me. Their contribution to the development of this book is no less than mine.

I would like to thank all my colleagues at NIIT for having helped me with small, finer inputs that did matter in the completion of this book.

Thanks to my editor AVM Misra and my technical reviewers Puneet Mehra and Ashish Gupta for their valuable inputs. Thanks are also due to Priyanka Verma for the great illustrations.

Thank you Kimberly Cofer and Stacy Hiquet for their active support in all development stages of the book.

About the Author

Madhushree Ganguli has been working as a development executive with NIIT since 2000. In her two years of experience she has worked on various projects that included designing, development, testing, and implementing of Instructor Led Training (ILT) courses. Madhushree has authored several ILT courses on Adobe Frame Maker 6.0, Publisher 2000, and SQL Server 7.0. She has also developed courses on WML applications and Advanced Java and authored a book on Java Server Pages.

Her hobbies include reading and traveling.

Contents at a Glance

Introduction xix

Part I   **Bluetooth - An Overview** **1**
   1   Introduction to Bluetooth 3
   2   Introduction to Radio 23
   3   Architecture of Bluetooth 49

Part II **Bluetooth – A Technical Insight** **89**
   4   Baseband 91
   5   Link Manager Protocol 125
   6   Software Protocols 163
   7   Bluetooth Profiles 213
   8   Bluetooth Usage Models 251
   9   Bluetooth Security 297

Part III **Bluetooth – The Present and the Future**. . . . **315**
   10   Bluetooth Potential 317
   11   Future of Bluetooth 337

Part IV **Appendix** **355**
   A   FAQs 357

Contents

Introduction xix

PART I   **BLUETOOTH–AN OVERVIEW** **1**

Chapter 1   **Introduction to bluetooth.** **3**

The Advent of Bluetooth 4
The History of Bluetooth 5
The Bluetooth Industry Players. 6
What is Bluetooth?. 7
    Air Interface in Bluetooth 8
    Frequency Hopping in Bluetooth 8
    Networking in Bluetooth 9
An Overview of Bluetooth System Architecture 11
    The Hardware Framework. 11
    The Software Framework. 12
Bluetooth Devices. 13
Practical Uses of Bluetooth 15
Bluetooth and Other Competing Technologies 16
    IrDA 17
    Ultra-Wideband Radio (UWB) 17
    Wireless LAN (WLAN) 17
    HomeRF 17
Summary 18
Check Your Understanding 19
    Multiple Choice Questions. 19
    Short Questions. 20
Answers 21
    Multiple Choice Answers. 21
    Short Answers 21

Chapter 2   Introduction to Radio. 23

Some Basic Radio Terminology. 24
 ISM Band 25
 The Mechanics of Radio Transmission 26
 Radio Transmitters. 27
 Antenna. 33
 How Bluetooth Evades Interference 42
Summary 43
Check Your Understanding 45
 Multiple Choice Questions. 45
 Short Questions 46
Answers 47
 Multiple Choice Answers. 47
 Short Answers 47

Chapter 3   Architecture of Bluetooth 49

The Origin and Growth of Spread Spectrum Technology 50
 What the Spread Spectrum Technology Means 51
 Building High-Capacity Networks. 57
 Duplexing 61
 Adaptive Time Division Duplexing 65
 Revisiting the Open System Interconnection
 Reference Model 66
 Inter-System Communication Using the OSI Model 70
 The Bluetooth Protocol Stack 71
 The Transport Protocol Group. 72
 The Middleware Protocol Group 77
 The Networking Protocols 78
 The Application Group 80
 WAP 80
Summary 85

Check Your Understanding 86
    Multiple Choice Questions. 86
    Short Questions. 86
Answers 87
    Multiple Choice Answers. 87
    Short Answers 87

PART II   **BLUETOOTH–A TECHNICAL INSIGHT** **89**

Chapter 4   **Baseband.** **91**

Defining the Placement of the Baseband 92
    The Piconet Roles 95
    The Physical Channel in Bluetooth 98
    The Link Between Master and Slaves in a Piconet 103
    The Structure of a Data Packet. 104
    Packet Types 110
    The Type Field of Bluetooth Packets 112
    Link Connection in Bluetooth Devices. 114
    Device Discovery and Inquiry. 118
    Establishing Connection and Paging 119
Summary 121
Check Your Understanding 122
    Multiple Choice Questions. 122
    Short Questions. 122
Answers 123
    Multiple Choice Answers. 123
    Short Answers 123

Chapter 5   **Link Manager Protocol.** **125**

The Bluetooth Logical Channels. 126
Link Manager Protocol 128
    General Response Management 130

Security Management. 131
Time Management. 140
Mode Control and Management 142
Power Management 148
Information Exchange Management. 149
Connection Management. 152
Channel Quality-Driven Change 153
Quality of Service (QoS) 154
SCO Links. 155
Control of Multi-Slot Packets 155
Paging Scheme. 155
Link Supervision 156
Test Mode 156
Error Handling 157
Summary 157
Check Your Understanding 158
Multiple Choice Questions. 158
Short Questions 159
Answers 160
Multiple Choice Answers. 160
Short Answers 160

Chapter 6   **Software Protocols** **163**

The Host Controller Interface. 165
HCI Commands 167
HCI Events 169
HCI Flow Control. 169
HCI Error Codes. 169
The HCI Transport Layers. 170
The Logical Link Control and Adaptation Protocol. 171
Assumptions 172
Functional Requirements of the L2CAP. 173

The Scope of the L2CAP. 174
The L2CAP Channels and the Channel Identifier 174
Operation Between Devices 176
Operation Between Layers 177
Segmentation and Reassembly 178
The L2CAP Data Packet 179
Signaling 181
The L2CAP State Machine 183
The Configuration Parameter Options 192
Service Primitives. 194
RFCOMM 194
Control Signals 195
Null Modem Emulation. 196
Multiple Emulated Serial Ports. 196
The TS 07.10 Adaptations for RFCOMM. 199
Lower-Level Interactions 201
OBEX 202
Defining OBEX Objects and Protocol 204
How Does OBEX Work?. 204
Telephony Control Protocol. 205
TCS-BIN 206
AT Commands 206
Service Discovery Protocol 206
SDP Services 207
How SDP Services Are Discovered 208
The Plug and Play Mechanism 209
Error Handling 209
Summary 209
Check Your Understanding 210
Multiple Choice Questions. 210
Short Questions 210
Answers 211

Multiple Choice Answers 211
Short Answers 211

Chapter 7   Bluetooth Profiles 213

Introduction to Bluetooth Profiles 214
The Generic Access Profile 217
The Serial Port Profile 223
Service Discovery Application Profile 229
Generic Object Exchange Profile 242
Summary 244
Check Your Understanding 246
Multiple Choice Questions 246
Short Questions 247
Answers 248
Multiple Choice Answers 248
Short Answers 248

Chapter 8   Bluetooth Usage Models 251

Introduction to Bluetooth Usage Models 252
The Cordless Telephony Profile 253
The Intercom Profile 260
The Dial-up Networking Profile 264
The Fax Profile 272
The Headset Profile 275
The LAN Access Profile 279
The File Transfer Profile 283
The Object Push Profile 287
The Synchronization Profile 289
Summary 293
Check Your Understanding 294
Multiple Choice Questions 294
Short Questions 294
Answers 295

Multiple Choice Answers 295

Short Answers 295

Chapter 9   Bluetooth Security 297

Security in Distributed Technologies 298

The Internet Security Model 299

The WAP Security Model 299

Security in Ad Hoc Networks 299

Bluetooth Security 300

Random Number Generation 301

Key Management 301

Authentication in Bluetooth 304

Encryption in Bluetooth 305

Summary 307

Check Your Understanding 308

Multiple Choice Questions 308

Short Questions 309

Answers   310

Multiple Choice Answers 310

Short Answers 310

**PART III   BLUETOOTH–THE PRESENT AND
THE FUTURE 315**

Chapter 10   Bluetooth Device 317

The Initial Phase 318

The System and the Technical Challenges 320

System Challenges 321

Technical Challenges 321

Comparing the Market Requirements and the
Technological Developments 322

Market Segmentation 323

The Networking Scenarios 324

LAN Access. 324

Dial-up Networking. 327

Small Meetings 328

Ad-hoc Networking 328

The Coming Years and Bluetooth 329

Summary 333

Check Your Understanding 334

Multiple Choice Questions. 334

Short Questions 334

Answers 335

Multiple Choice Answers. 335

Short Answers 335

Chapter 11 Future of Bluetooth 337

The SIG Then, Now, and in the Future. 338

The Radio 2.0 Working Group. 340

The Co-existence Working Group 341

The Extensions and Enhancements Working Group. 341

The New Applications Working Group 345

The Scope for Additional Working Groups 347

Future Bluetooth Products. 348

Summary 349

Check Your Understanding 350

Multiple Choice Questions. 351

Short Questions 351

Answers 352

Multiple Choice Answers. 352

Short Answers 352

PART IV   APPENDIX 355

Appendix A FAQs 357

Index 361

Introduction

With the constant influx of new computing and telecommunication devices in the market, the focus is no longer limited to upgrades in software and hardware components. Connection between devices and availability of a synchronized, economical, and reliable means of data transfer is gaining ground as a new focal point for emerging technologies. Bluetooth is the latest entrant in the wireless market and has created quite a stir by amalgamating the services of the telecom and computing industries. Thousands of Bluetooth devices will hit the market in the next few years, impacting our social and professional lives.

Bluetooth is a cable replacement technology that connects electronic devices such as mobile phones and mobile PCs. The technology is an open specification for wireless communication of data and voice. Bluetooth is the technology standard that uses short-range radio links instead of cables to connect portable and/or fixed electronic devices. The standards of Bluetooth specify a uniform structure for communication between a wide range of devices with minimal user effort. In other words, Bluetooth can be described as a robust, simple, and economical technology that offers wireless access to LANs, PSTN, the mobile phone network, and the Internet.

PART I

**Bluetooth—
An Overview**

Chapter 1

Introduction to Bluetooth

This chapter is an introduction to the world of wireless communication supported by the commercially-acclaimed Bluetooth technology. The discussion begins with the intent and purpose of Bluetooth wireless communication. The later sections of the chapter trace the origin and history of the term Bluetooth. The final sections of the chapter discuss the practical uses of Bluetooth devices and the competing technologies available in the market today.

The Advent of Bluetooth

Most of us today lead a hectic life and would be heavily burdened with chores were it not for modern day gadgets and appliances. It is, therefore, not surprising that research and inventions play an important role in utilizing science and technology for the betterment of humankind. If you look around your home or office, you'll be able to list innumerable gadgets and appliances that are an integral part of life today. Inventions such as Edison's bulb, Bell's telephone, the Wright brothers' airplane, and the most recent personal computers are just a few examples of things that are taken for granted today.

You'll agree that the advent of the Internet has added to the success and popularity of the computer. Let me substantiate this statement by sharing an experience with you. A friend of mine, Joe, was invited to a seminar as a guest speaker. The notes prepared were forwarded to him by e-mail. However, Joe threw quite a fit when he realized that a few sections of the notes were missing. He immediately called his secretary, whom he asked to resend the e-mails for a quick revision during his trip. Previously, Joe would have been unable to access his e-mail while traveling. He could not be expected to carry the immobile desktop computer along for all his business trips. Today, the smaller mobile forms of the computer such as laptops and WAP-enabled hand-held devices or WAP phones facilitate computing and Internet access at all times irrespective of the location.

Therefore, it is not wrong to say that in the wired world of devices connected physically, mobile devices facilitate communication without the use of otherwise cumbersome wires. The scene at the macro level is identified by global connections that use the wireless TCP/IP protocol suite for the exchange of information over the Internet. However, at the micro level, all of us still use cable connections to connect the keyboard, mouse, and system unit to the computer.

For example, thanks to the wireless devices, today a sales executive can work on his presentation while traveling. However, to display the same presentation, his laptop needs to be hooked to the projector by using cable connections. Is there a way in which your PDA can directly send the presentation to an electronic whiteboard without using wires and cables?

Yes, there is. Bluetooth as a cable replacement technology aims to exploit the potential of wireless communication between mobile devices by using the ad hoc short-range radio frequency.

What was the intent behind this much talked of technology? Bluetooth was an endeavor toward replacing cable technology with a more efficient and advanced technique of wireless communication.

Bluetooth defines the latest technology and specification for small, low-cost, and short-range radio links used to connect mobile PCs, phones, and various other portable devices. How did this revolutionary technology acquire a name so far removed from its commercial functionality? The following section looks at the history of this technology of wireless communication that is so popularly known as Bluetooth technology.

The History of Bluetooth

Bluetooth technology owes its name to the Danish king, Harald Bluetooth I. It is hard to believe that a technology and a Danish king can have a common name. Seems like a weird connection, doesn't it? What are the similarities between the exploits of Harald Bluetooth I and the wireless technology that is set to hit the commercial market in 2002?

Harald Bluetooth I was the son of King Grom The Old of Jutland, the main peninsula of Denmark, and his wife Thyre Danebold. The second name, Bluetooth, pronounced as Blatand in Danish, is derived from two Danish words, "bla" meaning dark-skinned and "tan" meaning great man. Like most of the preceding Viking kings, Harald considered it honorable to invade foreign territories and exploit the treasures of the conquered lands. Instigated by the violent death of the Norwegian ruler Erik Blood Axe, an incident that widowed his sister, Gunhild, Harald invaded Norway. Encouraged by the success of the seizure of Norway, Harald proceeded to conquer the whole of Denmark. The proof that Harald's obsession for war centered on expansion of territory can be found inscribed in one of two Runic stones erected in his capital city of Jelling (central Jutland). The inscription on the rune stone reads:

> Harald christianized the Danes
>
> Harald controlled Denmark and Norway

After his death in 985 AD, Harald's dream of a unified Anglo-Scandinavian kingdom was realized by his son Sweyn I. By 1015, under the rule of Sweyn's son, Canute, the Anglo-Scandinavian kingdom also appropriated England and parts of Sweden.

Now here comes the connection between Harald Bluetooth I and the Bluetooth technology. Harald I successfully united the kingdoms of Denmark and Norway. This parallels the objective of Bluetooth technology, which aims to unite the computer and telecommunication industry. Utilizing the strengths of both the computer sector and the telecom sector is the very basis of Bluetooth technology. This technology has been designed to promote a technique of wireless communication between mobile devices and terminal equipment. The next section examines how a feasibility research study for cable replacement initiated by Ericsson Mobile Communications developed into a major project for standardizing a protocol for linking mobile devices.

The Bluetooth Industry Players

In 1994, Ericsson Mobile Communications initiated a study to explore the feasibility of using economized, low power, low cost, short-range radio links as a medium to tie up digital devices. The initial studies that used a transceiver chip, soon followed by intensive research, yielded a mechanism that used a radio unit small enough to fit into portable devices. During this time, Ericsson realized that it was on the brink of a sensational discovery which would revolutionize transfer of data and voice over portable digital devices. As a result, Ericsson decided to seek business associates to support and strengthen the search for a technical solution amalgamating the business sectors of hardware, portable PCs, and mobile phones. The radio chip, also known as the Bluetooth chip, surpassed the requirements of all other mobile solutions in terms of cost, power consumption, size, and capacity.

By 1998, five more companies, all stalwarts in their industrial sectors, joined hands with Ericsson to form a *Special Interest Group* (SIG) to study the possibilities of economically linking mobile devices with other accessories. The SIG consisted of the following:

◆ The first group consisted of Ericsson and Nokia, the market leaders in mobile telephony

◆ The second group consisted of IBM and Toshiba, the market leaders in laptop computing services

◆ The third group consisted solely of Intel, the market leader of signal processing technology

In May 1998, the Bluetooth SIG consortium formally announced its incorporation. Identifying the potential of Bluetooth, the consortium decided to work toward standardizing the use of software and interfaces for this revolutionary technology. As a result, Bluetooth documentation consists of specifications in the form of user models and profiles for developing products by using the Bluetooth technology. The core promoters published the first version or the Bluetooth specification 1.0 in July 1999, on the Bluetooth Web site at **www.bluetooth.com.**

NOTE

You will learn about the user models and protocol profiles of the Bluetooth specification in later chapters.

Currently, the SIG consists of almost 2,000 companies working toward defining an open standard for this technology. Companies registering with the SIG automatically qualify for a royalty-free license that enables them to develop Bluetooth products. The SIG has also defined a qualification process containing specific criteria to ensure that all Bluetooth products released for sale adhere to a universal standardized specification.

You can, therefore, infer that Bluetooth technology provides a standardized platform to integrate mobile phones, PCs, laptops, and other such digital electronic devices. This technology exploits the globally available radio frequency link to connect people without the use of traditional connections in the form of wires and cables. The introduction of wireless connectivity will also open doors for a quicker and more secure means to establish connections between digital devices.

What Is Bluetooth?

Bluetooth is the technology standard that uses short-range radio links instead of cables to connect portable and/or fixed electronic devices. The standards of Bluetooth specify a uniform structure for communication between a wide range of devices with minimal user effort. In other words, Bluetooth can be described as a robust, simple, and economical technology that offers wireless access to LANs, Public Switched Telephony Network (PSTN), the mobile phone network, and the Internet.

The use of Bluetooth technology as a medium to join handheld devices with computers and the Internet will no doubt encourage exchange of data and voice across a communication channel devoid of wires and cables. For example, traveling professionals today can hook up and transfer data from portable laptops to mobile phones without using cables for connection. Interestingly, this technology uses the already existing data networks, interfaces, and devices to create small groups of mobile connections. All you need to do is equip your portable handheld device with a Bluetooth chip or radiochip costing approximately $5.00. Almost every known digital device, such as fax machines, desktop computers, PDAs, printers, and joysticks, can be a part of the Bluetooth system.

The wireless connection between devices in Bluetooth is described as a short-range, frequency hopping, ad hoc radio link. In addition, the medium used for the transmission of data is the air interface that separates the two communicating devices. Therefore, before discussing the functionality unit of a Bluetooth system, the next section explains each of these fundamental terms.

Air Interface in Bluetooth

The air interface defines the radio frequency band used by devices to create links and transmit data and voice between various digital devices. The frequency band used by Bluetooth devices is the unlicensed *Industrial-Scientific Medical* (ISM) band of around 2.4 GHz ranging from 2400 MHz to 2483.5 MHz. Within the band, Bluetooth has 79 channels spaced 1 MHz apart. The choice of this band ensures transmission of both data and voice considering the size and power limitations of most portable devices. The Bluetooth air interface is available to any radio system and is predominantly used by microwave ovens and 2.4-GHz cordless phones.

Frequency Hopping in Bluetooth

The ISM air interface is a noisy radio frequency environment that faces major interference from other devices, especially microwave ovens. Such interferences cause interceptions in transmissions. The technique used to deal with the predominantly present, non-ignorable interference is known as frequency hopping. Frequency hopping is best suited for low-power and low-cost wireless radio implementations.

This technique is easily explained with the following example. What will you do if your friend informs you that the route you are traveling on is jammed after a mile or so? If possible, you will switch to a smoother route or take a relatively longer route to ensure you are far from the jam. A similar situation occurs when a frequency band is hit by interference threatening to break the continuity of a data or voice transfer. In such a state, the retransmission will always be on a different channel.

A frequency band is divided into virtual fractions, or hop channels. Each channel, or slot, used in Bluetooth is 625 μs of transmission. Interference protection is achieved by a pseudo random hop to another channel for 625 μs of transmission. A channel jammed by another device follows the principle of minimal probability of interference in the next hop channel. The process of frequency hopping is repeated constantly and spreads over the entire ISM band. Error correction algorithms are used to rectify faults caused by jammed transmission.

 NOTE

μs, pronounced as "mew-s," is a unit for measuring time in microseconds.

The frequency hop per time division is illustrated in Figure 1-1.

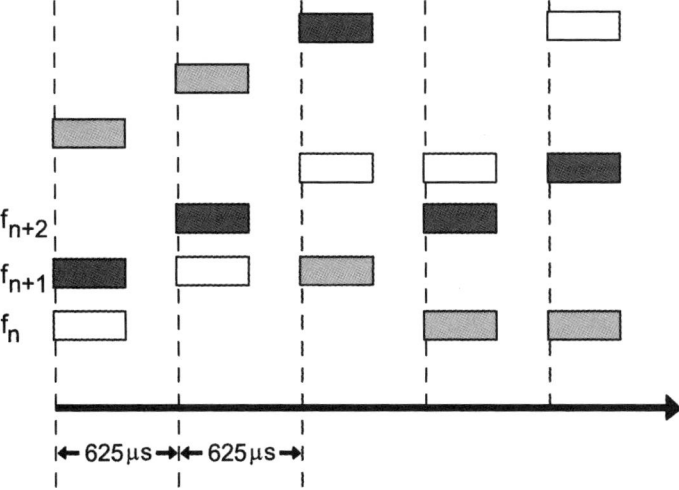

FIGURE 1-1 *Frequency hop per time division*

Networking in Bluetooth

The connection between Bluetooth devices can be either point-to-point or point-to-multipoint. The former is a connection between two Bluetooth devices, while the latter consists of several Bluetooth devices connected to each other. Either way, a Bluetooth connection creates an ad hoc network known as a *piconet*. The term *ad hoc* identifies a connection that is initiated and terminated by a single Bluetooth device that acts as the master unit. A piconet uses the same channel for data and voice transmission that is time and hop synchronized. Each piconet consists of one master-controlling unit and up to seven active slave units. The master unit's system clock and master identity (Bluetooth address) determines the phase and sequence of a hop channel during a frequency hop. The identity of the master unit determines the sequence of the hop, while the system clock determines the phase of the hop.

An offset is used to replicate the master unit's system clock among the slave units. As a result, the master unit synchronizes and ensures that all units within a piconet maintain the same time and frequency channel during a hop. The synchronized system clocks and the replicated master's identity uniquely identify each slave unit in a piconet. The software and hardware specifications of a master and slave unit are the same. However, the unit that establishes a piconet becomes the master unit controlling all traffic within the piconet.

A piconet is illustrated in Figure 1-2.

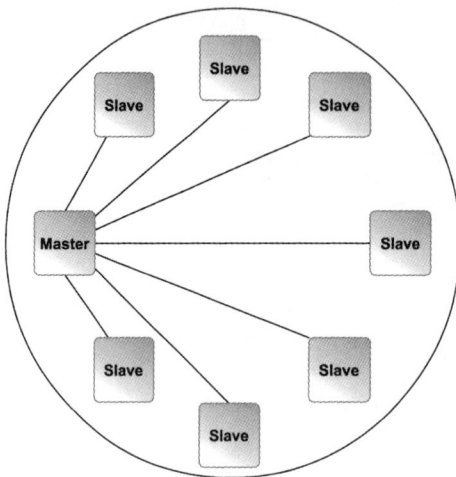

FIGURE 1-2 *Diagrammatic representation of a piconet*

The spectrum of connectivity in a piconet is increased by formation of multiple piconets in the same area. Overlapping piconets form a *scatternet*. As a result, a Bluetooth device can also participate in multiple piconets at the same time.

A scatternet is illustrated in Figure 1-3.

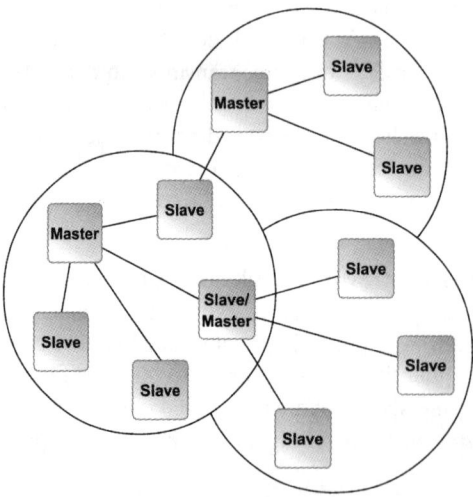

FIGURE 1-3 *Diagrammatic representation of a scatternet*

The Bluetooth system architecture consists of the hardware and software framework. Chapter 3, "Architecture of Bluetooth," discusses each of these frameworks and the Bluetooth system architecture in detail. For a better conceptual understanding of the working of a Bluetooth system, the following sections briefly discuss these two functional units.

An Overview of Bluetooth System Architecture

The system architecture in Bluetooth is segmented into several logical and independent layers. These layers can be broadly classified as:

◆ The hardware framework
◆ The software framework

The hardware framework, or the firmware, in Bluetooth consists of the radio unit, baseband, and *Link Manager Protocol* (LMP). The software framework consists of the protocol stack.

The Hardware Framework

As discussed in the preceding sections, Bluetooth uses the short-range frequency hopping radio link to transmit voice and data between devices. The use of this singular and universal radio link eliminates the need to use any physical wires for device connections. The antenna power required for the Bluetooth air interface complies with the standard specification for ISM bands at a power level of 0 dBm. The maximum frequency-hopping rate is 1600 hops/second, and the power of transmission extends between 1 mW and 100mW. The link range of a Bluetooth radio is from 10 cm to 10 m, which is extendable to 100 m by increasing the power of transmission.

The radio layer constitutes the bottom-most layer and forms the physical connection interface. The radio unit by itself is very small and can, therefore, easily fit into small and portable handheld devices. Ericsson's 1mW Bluetooth radio is about 10.2 x 14 x 1.6 mm. The radio unit consumes very little power required for transmission that is obtained from the small battery of the portable device. The maximum bit rate is 1 mbps. The estimated rate of data transfer is approximately 721 kbps.

The baseband and LMP reside over the radio layer and are meant to establish and control links between Bluetooth devices. The link control unit is responsible for digital signal processing in a Bluetooth system. The digital signal processing forms a part of the Bluetooth *Link Controller* (LC), the hardware used to perform low-level link routines.

In a piconet, the Bluetooth devices communicate using one of the following two link types:

◆ **Asynchronous Connectionless (ACL).** The ACL link supports symmetrical and asymmetrical, packet-switched, point-to-multipoint connections primarily used to transfer packet data.

◆ **Synchronous Connection Oriented (SCO).** The SCO link supports symmetrical, circuit-switched, point-to-point connections and is, therefore, predominantly used for voice transfers. The data rate for a SCO link is 64 kbps.

A typical Bluetooth system consists of a number of digital devices linked to each other. As a result, an important functional unit of this system is the one that manages the links in terms of set up, authentication, and configuration. The *Link Manager* (LM), aided by link management software, identifies other remote link managers and initiates a communication with them. The communication services provided by the LC include functions such as sending and receiving data, setting up the connection, and authenticating the other remote units.

The hardware framework also consists of the *Host Controller Interface* (HCI) layer, which functions as an interface between the hardware and software frameworks. The HCI accepts communications over the physical bus.

 NOTE

Chapter 3, "Architecture of Bluetooth," discusses the Bluetooth system architecture in detail.

The Software Framework

The devices communicating with each other using Bluetooth need not always be of the same class. For example, a PC may need to communicate with a PDA or a mobile phone may need to communicate with a laptop. The success of communication between two devices lies in their interoperatibility. The Bluetooth specification defines a number of protocols that can be used to establish universally compatible communication between two devices. The software framework consists of high-level protocols such as the *Service Discovery Protocol* (SDP), *RFCOMM* emulating a serial port connection, and the *Telephony Control Protocol* (TCS). The *Logical Link Control and Adaptation Protocol* (L2CAP), which is the bottom-most protocol layer of the software framework, functions as an interface between these high-level protocols and the baseband services of the hardware framework.

As a result, applications in remote devices run on identical protocol stacks. The functions of the software framework include

◆ Cable emulation
◆ Discovery of devices
◆ Peripheral communication
◆ Call control and audio communication

An outline of the Bluetooth system architecture is illustrated in Figure 1-4.

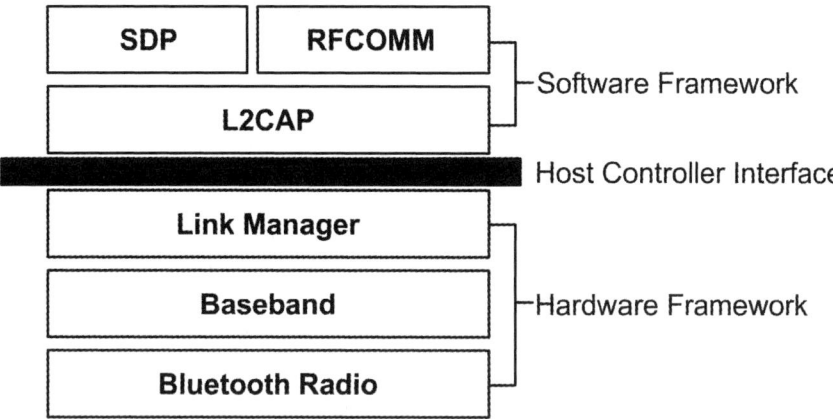

FIGURE 1-4 *Outline of the Bluetooth system architecture*

The preceding sections have provided an overview of Bluetooth technology. The next section lists a few devices that can be used for communication using the wireless technology of Bluetooth.

Bluetooth Devices

It need not be reiterated that all Bluetooth devices need to contain a radio chip to enable wireless communication. As a result, each device used for communication that uses the Bluetooth wireless technology requires certain features that are specific to Bluetooth. The following are the characteristic features of some devices enabled for communication that use Bluetooth technology.

◆ **Computers.** The Bluetooth specification defines the use of an interface containing the radio unit integrated into notebooks and laptops. In the case of desktops, a PC-card or USB containing the radio unit is attached to the computer. Some uses of notebook PCs include remote access to mobile phones, exchange of business cards between Bluetooth-enabled notebooks, handheld devices, and phones, or the synchronization of calendars between various digital devices.

◆ **Telephone.** The Bluetooth specification defines the use of an interface containing the radio unit integrated directly into mobile handsets or attached using an add-on device. Some uses of the phone in Bluetooth communication include wireless networking with a Bluetooth notebook or handheld computer, address synchronization between Bluetooth notebooks and computers, or a hands-free wireless use of a Bluetooth handset.

◆ **Other models.** The other models that can integrate the radio unit based on the Bluetooth specification are the headset, handheld and wearable devices, *Human Interface Device* (HID) compliant peripherals, and both data and voice access points.

In the course of numerous demonstrations and exhibitions through 2000, many Bluetooth-enabled products were introduced. Some product demonstrations during the year 2000 included the following:

◆ The Ericsson Bluetooth Headset, which is a lightweight, mobile phone headset containing a radio chip that connects the headset and the phone. The headset is pressed to answer calls, and voice labels are used to initiate calls.

◆ The Nokia Bluetooth Headset, which enables wireless communication over a distance of 10 meters.

◆ The Mobile Imaging Nokia 9110 communicator developed by Fujifilm and Nokia. The radio chip in the communicator receives images from a Bluetooth-enabled digital camera. The 9110 communicator is a very good example of how Bluetooth can be used to combine SMS and digital photography for mobile imaging.

◆ The Windows CE-based Auto PC device combines a computer with a car radio. It facilitates docking of mobile devices such as PDAs, notebooks, and pagers. The driver uses voice recognition technology for a wireless, hands-free communication with other digital devices.

◆ A tri-mode CDMA, which is a hands-free speakerphone from Motorola named Timeport 270. The phone fitted with a 4-way joystick will also provide headset communication that is to be introduced shortly.

The following are some Bluetooth-enabled products available on the market today:

◆ Ericsson R520 Bluetooth/WAP/GPRS/Triband

◆ Ericsson T36 Bluetooth/WAP/HSCSD/Triband

◆ Alcatel OneTouch 700 GPRS, WAP, Bluetooth

◆ TDK Bluetooth Product Range

◆ Bluetooth-enabled Nokia 9110

◆ Ericsson Bluetooth GSM Headset

◆ Ericsson Communicator

◆ 1050 from Red-M of Wexam Spings, England, which is an access point connecting Bluetooth devices to a wireless LAN

◆ A USB adapter from TDK for Bluetooth

◆ Bluetooth Headset, embedded software stack, phone module, PC-card, and protocol analyzer from Digianswer

◆ Bluetooth phone module and OdBm PC-card from Motorola

◆ Bluetooth printer adapter (11/00) from NEC corporation

The preceding sections did throw light on the various professional segments that can use
Bluetooth for wireless communication. You'll be surprised to know that Bluetooth can also
add technological magic to life at home and in society that can be experienced every day.

Practical Uses of Bluetooth

The advent of the Internet enabled people to access a pool of information without ven-
turing out of their homes. As a result, it seems like the world has shrunk to fit into homes.
Name any form of information ranging from careers to sharing recipes—the Internet has
opened a bank of information that can be accessed surpassing the barriers of location and
time. The success of the Internet was followed by mobile communication to facilitate the
concept of access to information anytime, anywhere.

The wireless technology backed by Bluetooth will definitely introduce major changes in
the way we communicate today. It's not only that Bluetooth provides for communication
devoid of wires and cables. Bluetooth also introduces wireless communication between
various types of digital devices without those tedious and burdensome cable connections.
You can change the whole setup at home. Here are a few examples of what Bluetooth can
do to change your domestic set up:

◆ You reach the doorstep, the door unlocks automatically, and you are greeted to a
  hallway with lights and soft music. The room temperature is adjusted according
  to your preferences.

◆ Your PDA can add all professional engagements to an electronic board containing your domestic engagements. In this way, you can ensure that your personal
  and domestic engagements do not clash.

◆ You do not need to reconfigure equipment added to your home security system.
  If the devices use Bluetooth technology, they'll use their omni-directional feature to recognize each other.

◆ In your car, you do not need a cradle or cable to hook up the phone. In fact, the
  phone stays in your pocket and the voice labels are used to control all incoming
  or outgoing calls.

Here are a few examples of how you can use Bluetooth technology in your office setup:

◆ You reach office and all devices, such as the desktop, portable PC, and mobile phone synchronize automatically to update the address list, e-mail messages, and calendar.

◆ You can send a presentation on to an electronic whiteboard and eliminate the need to wire a portable or desktop PC to a projector.

◆ You can transfer the attendance and record the minutes of meeting to a PDA by using the wireless Bluetooth technology.

◆ You can be notified of last-minute scheduling changes while you are traveling by using the wireless technology. The desktop PC sends the details of the changed schedule to your phone, which, in turn, automatically updates the schedule in your calendar.

◆ You can experience cordless connectivity between PC peripherals such as the mouse, keyboard, scanner, and printer.

Bluetooth will no doubt hit the market as a substitute for the cumbersome cable technology. However, there exist a few other technologies that work on the wireless technique of communication. The next section looks at the features of these technologies to understand, appreciate, and widen the perspective of Bluetooth as yet another revolutionary technology.

Bluetooth and Other Competing Technologies

Before moving on to listing and discussing the features of technologies competing with Bluetooth, let's sum up the features of Bluetooth technology. Bluetooth:

◆ Operates in the globally available 2.4 to 2.5 GHz band.

◆ Facilitates voice and data transfer.

◆ Consists of a piconet that includes up to eight devices.

◆ Provides point-to-point and point-to-multipoint connections.

◆ Uses ad hoc, frequency hopping radio links to establish connections with devices.

◆ Communicating devices need not see each other or fall in the line of sight (omni-directional).

◆ Has a range of operation between 10m to 100m.

◆ Has an estimated rate of data at 721 kbps.

◆ Costs around $10.

◆ Consumes power as less as 1mW.

The nearest and main competing technology working on a low-cost interoperable wireless technique is *Infrared Data Association* (IrDA).

IrDA

IrDA is the main contender of the cable replacement market sector that uses the infrared interface standard. This technique for wireless data transmission is limited to point-to-point connections. As a result, only two devices can communicate with each other at a time. In addition, the devices are non–omni-directional and, therefore, need to aim the IrDA beam directly at the antenna transceiver.

A new technology called Red Beamer from an Israeli company, Infra-Comm, has been able to overcome the non–omni-directional feature of IrDA. As a result, IrDA devices can now link without being in the line of sight of each other. However, the initial transmission speed for Red Beamer is rather slow at 56 kbps as compared to that of Bluetooth, which is 1 mbps.

Ultra-Wideband Radio (UWB)

The *Ultra-Wideband* (UWB) radio technology is based on radar functioning that transmits short pulses in a broad frequency range. This technology is in the primitive stages but can pose a threat to Bluetooth technology. This is because current statistics show that the UWB technique possesses far superior capacity (70m) at just 0.5mW of power consumption.

Wireless LAN (WLAN)

Both *Wireless LAN* (WLAN) and Bluetooth follow the IEEE 802.11 standard specification for wireless transmission. WLANs, however, are essentially physically configured, server-based LANs that handle high data throughput. Bluetooth intimidates the WLAN technology since both these technologies use the 2.5 GHz frequency band to transmit data. As a result, often Bluetooth and WLAN connections collide with each other resulting in the jamming of one or both connections. The foundation of the two technologies is also different. Whereas Bluetooth is used to transmit about 1 mbps of data for a distance of 10 meters, WLANs have transmission rates between 2 mbps and 11 mbps for distances that range from 15 meters to 100 meters.

HomeRF

The *HomeRF* technique is the endeavor of the *International Telecommunication Union* (ITU), a consortium founded by companies such as Microsoft, Intel, HP, Motorola, and Compaq. The HomeRF technique provides standards for an inexpensive mode of RF voice and data communication. This technology is based on the Digital Enhanced Cordless Telephony (DECT) concept that operates within the 2.4 GHz frequency band.

When compared to Bluetooth, which transmits 8 units per 1600 hops/second, HomeRF technology provides an impressive statistic of transmitting up to 127 units for 50 hops/second. However, this technology is targeted for the residential market segment and does not serve enterprise-class WLANs, public access systems, or fixed wireless Internet accesses.

It is important to understand that the essence of Bluetooth is to provide a means of communication that is mobile, re-configurable, and spontaneous. The concepts discussed so far are just an introduction to the technology of wireless communication. All the other chapters cover the technical make up and working of this technology.

Summary

With the constant influx of new computing and telecommunication devices in the market, the focus is no longer limited to upgrades in software and hardware components. Connection between devices and availability of a synchronized, economical, and reliable means of data transfer is gaining grounds as a new focal point for emerging technologies.

In this chapter, you learned how Bluetooth technology is fast emerging as a solution toward replacing wired connections with a more economical, simple, and low power consuming technique. You further learned that the core of this technology lies in the Bluetooth chip that facilitates a wireless connection between digital devices.

Undoubtedly, the advent of Bluetooth will further increase and unlock the potential of mobile communication. With the broad market support from the PC and mobile phone industries, it wouldn't be wrong to predict that the future of Bluetooth seems to be very bright.

Check Your Understanding

Multiple Choice Questions

1. State whether the following statements are true or false.

   a. The Special Interest Group (SIG) formed in 1998 consisted of three groups with a total of five members.

   b. Bluetooth devices use the licensed ISM band for data transmission.

   c. The frequency channel or slot in Bluetooth is divided into virtual fractions of 625 μs of transmission.

2. Which of the following are the high-level protocols that are interfaced by the L2CAP layer?

   a. SDP

   b. RFCOMM

   c. LMP

   d. TCS

3. Which of the following are the technologies competing with Bluetooth?

   a. LAN

   b. PAN

   c. IrDA

   d. WLAN

   e. UWB

   f. HomeRf

4. Which of the following were the promoters or original members of the SIG that was constituted in 1998?

   a. Microsoft

   b. Ericsson

   c. Nokia

   d. Sony

   e. Intel

   f. IBM

   g. Toshiba

Short Questions

1. Define ACL and SCO links.
2. Discuss the functions of the software framework in Bluetooth.
3. Write short notes on the characteristics of the following technologies:
   a. Ultra Wideband (UWB) radio technology
   b. Wireless LAN (WLAN)
   c. HomeRF

Answers

Multiple Choice Answers

1. a. True
   b. False
   c. True
2. a, b, and d. SDP, RFCOMM, and TCS.
3. c, d, e, and f. IrDA, WLAN, UWB, and HomeRF.
4. b, c, e, f, and g. Ericsson, Nokia, Intel, IBM, and Toshiba.

Short Answers

1. ACL and SCO links can be defined as:

   The ACL link supports symmetrical and asymmetrical, packet-switched, point-to-multipoint connections primarily used to transfer packet data.

   The SCO link supports symmetrical, circuit-switched, point-to-point connections and is, therefore, predominantly used for voice transfers.

2. The functions of the software framework in a Bluetooth device are:
   - Cable emulation
   - Discovery of devices
   - Peripheral communication
   - Call control and audio communication

3. a. **Ultra-Wideband (UWB) radio technology**. The *Ultra-Wideband* (UWB) radio technology is based on radar functioning that transmits short pulses in a broad frequency range. This technology is in the primitive stages but can pose a threat to Bluetooth technology. This is because current statistics show that the UWB technique possesses far superior capacity (70m) at just 0.5mW of power consumption.

   b. **WLAN**. *Wireless LAN* (WLAN) follows the IEEE 802.11 standard specification for wireless transmission. WLANs are physically configured, server-based LANs that handle high data throughput. WLANs have transmission rates between 2 mbps and 11 mbps for distances that range from 15 meters to 100 meters.

c. **HomeRF**. The *HomeRF* technique is the endeavor of the *International Telecommunication Union* (ITU), a consortium founded by companies such as Microsoft, Intel, HP, Motorola, and Compaq. The HomeRF technique provides standards for an inexpensive mode of RF voice and data communication. This technology is based on the DECT concept that operates within the 2.4 GHz frequency band.

Chapter 2

This chapter aims to strengthen the basic terminology associated with radio technology. In the preceding chapter, the term "radio" was used to refer to both the link between various Bluetooth devices and the Bluetooth chip that is a characteristic feature of every Bluetooth device.

The chapter summarizes some important components and concepts related to the radio that include transmitters, antennas, and radio waves. It also provides new perspectives and information to some topics introduced in the preceding chapter. In other words, you can read this chapter as a more detailed introduction to topics since it discusses the basics of telecommunications. A good grasp of these concepts will ensure a better understanding of the important new technology of Bluetooth.

Some Basic Radio Terminology

Each one of us, at some time or the other, has tuned in to a radio to listen to good music. The radio is a well-known broadcasting device that is linked to terms such as AM, FM, UHF, and VHF. However, most of us probably have never bothered to delve deeper into the real meaning of these terms. Every Bluetooth device, like any other wired or wireless broadcasting device, contains a radio unit to establish a link with other such devices. What the radio is made of and how it helps in communication is discussed in this chapter.

When you visualize a radio, you come up with the image of a rectangular device fitted with an antenna. The broadcasting feature of the radio is realized by electromagnetic waves or radio waves that are propagated by an antenna. Radio waves traverse through different frequencies, and that is exactly the reason why you need a radio to catch specific signals. What actually happens is that the radio tunes into a particular frequency and then picks up its signals.

Considering the number and expanse of the frequency bands, there definitely is a need to have a controlling body to manage issues related to these frequencies. The *Federal Communications Commission* (FCC) is the governing body that issues licenses to stations for specific frequencies and decides details about the rationale and usage of these frequencies.

Interestingly, the first Bluetooth devices were developed by replacing IR-based ports with radio-based wireless ports, with a range set to 10 meters. The idea was to free users from IRDA's line-of-sight requirement and also to introduce the concept of point-to-multipoint connectivity. As a result, the technology can also be described as a radio-based, wireless pico-LAN.

You now know that Bluetooth devices use the unlicensed *Industrial-Scientific Medical* (ISM) band. This frequency band is currently the center of attraction for the wireless communication industry the world over. The following sections look at the reasons why the wireless industry is so taken in by this band of around 2.400 GHz, ranging from 2400 MHz to 2483.5 MHz.

ISM Band

The primary reason for the interest in the ISM band is based on the fact that this band is widely available all over the world. Table 2-1 lists the range of the ISM band in various countries.

Table 2-1 Frequency Range of the ISM Band

Frequency Range	Country
2400 MHz to 2483.5 MHz	USA and Europe
2471 MHz to 2497 MHz	Japan
2445 MHz to 2475 MHz	Spain
2446.5 MHz to 2483.5 MHz	France

The number of available channels in USA, Europe, Japan, and Spain is 79, while that in France is 23.

In the current era, symbolized by the Internet, wireless, and handheld devices, the wide spectrum of the ISM band enables you to exploit wireless communications based on Bluetooth technology. The fact that the ISM band extends to countries listed in Table 2-1 ensures the development of a product requiring minimal changes for global acceptance.

The ISM frequency band was originally used by the high energy, high frequency, and non-communication-based applications used for industry, science, and medicine. Although these applications created interference, they were themselves insensitive to interference and could therefore use the ISM band without disturbing each other. This criterion formed the very basis for the commercial use of the ISM band by low power transmitter–driven equipment such as wireless headphones, door chimes, radio alarm systems, and even the central locking systems in cars. However, these equipments do face problems of signal overlapping and interference resulting from the unprotected and free use of the ISM territory. Have you ever experienced a sudden ebb in the volume of your headphone, just when the music gets to your favorite part? For all you know, the causative factor could be your neighbor's car lock, a doctor or an industrial worker's short wave machine, or even a stronger ham radio used by a licensed radio amateur. Quaint, isn't it? But that's the way gadgets and equipment function within the ISM frequency band. On the brighter side, there are equal chances that the equipment will continue to work without any disruptions or interference. However, with the changing trends and demands on technology, interferences would be a part and parcel of ISM frequency band equipment. The frequency hop method of transmission in Bluetooth wireless technology is a small step toward ensuring a continuous and robust link during voice and data transfer between two devices.

Bluetooth devices also use the ISM band spectrum for transmission that varies with a change in location. These devices can be made interoperable in different parts of the world by configuring them to use the same set of frequencies. With no limitations of its use within the range of the ISM band, all Bluetooth devices freely use frequency hopping to ensure continuous and uninterrupted transmissions. The factors considered during frequency hopping are as follows:

- ◆ **Synchronized timings.** The frequencies used by the transmitter and the receiver should be the same. Additionally, the time intervals of transmission should be synchronized.

- ◆ **Delivery of information.** Bluetooth technology, like most telecommunication systems, uses packets for delivering information. A single packet is contained within one to five hops.

- ◆ **Selecting a frequency.** Most telecommunication systems use a shared algorithm to select a frequency. However, in Bluetooth, the clock and the device address of the master determines the frequency used for transmission. The ISM spectrum in USA, Europe, Japan, and Spain consists of 79 channels as opposed to the meager count of 23 channels in France.

- ◆ **Hop frequency.** The hop rate (for a hop time length of 625 μs) is set to 1,600 frequencies per second.

The transmission of information in the form of voice or data begins from the transmitter at one end and is accepted at the other end by the radio receiver. Nonetheless, the terms frequently associated with a radio are radio waves, antenna, transmitter, and receiver.

The Mechanics of Radio Transmission

Consider the example of a wireless conversation between two individuals using a cell phone. Although a good amount of information is transmitted between the individuals, for bystanders the transmission of information by such a communication is invisible. How then does this information flow from one end to the other? The medium of transmission is in the form of invisible waves known as radio waves. Radio waves transmit information in the form of pictures, voice, and music over millions of miles. Here's a small list of gadgets and equipments that use radio waves for transmission:

- ◆ Radios and walkie-talkies used by the police
- ◆ Ham radios used by radio amateurs

- Wireless networks
- Cordless telephones
- Radio and television broadcasts
- Radio systems used by the aviation industry
- Systems used in communication and navigation satellites

Mostly, all wireless transmissions use and depend on radio waves for transmission. Contrary to the outward show of a highly technical and complicated working pattern, radio is actually a very simple technology. In fact, building or assembling a radio is a simple task that costs only a few dollars. All that you require to build a simple transmitter or a receiver are a few electronic components.

The transmission of voice and data from a radio is achieved by the use of continuous sine waves. Each of these sine waves uses a different frequency to transmit data. As a result, different radio signals using different sine waves are separated from each other. Each radio is fitted with a transmitter and receiver to send out and obtain information in the form of radio signals. The radio setup therefore consists of the following two parts:

- Transmitter
- Receiver

In addition, there is the antenna, which is a crucial part of any radio implementation.

Radio Transmitters

The sole function of a transmitter is to transmit information from one radio to another. This information flow between two radio units can be in the form of audio, video, or data. The working of a transmitter can be explained by building a simple battery-wire connection. How would you explain the working of a unit created by connecting a piece of wire to the two terminals of a battery? What effect would a connection such as this have on a compass? Well, basic physics explains that the flutter generated in the compass needle is due to a strong electromagnetic field created around the wire. Further, what changes would you observe if you connect a second wire parallel to the first and alternately connect and disconnect the connections to the battery? Is an electromagnetic field automatically generated in the second wire by merely connecting it to the battery? No! The electromagnetic field in the second wire is not generated automatically but is dependent on the connect-disconnect state of the first wire. Once again, the principle of an electrical generator can be used to demonstrate that a small voltage of current is generated in the second wire as a consequence of connecting or disconnecting the first wire from the battery. The course of events occurring due to the connect-disconnect state of the first wire can be summarized as follows:

- When the first wire is connected to the battery, the battery creates a flow of electrons in the first wire. As a result, an electromagnetic field is generated around the wire.

◆ When the second wire is connected (in parallel) to the battery, the magnetic field stretches to the second wire.

◆ The current and magnetic field in the first wire changes in accordance with the connect-disconnect state of the first wire. As a result, electrons flow in the second wire only if there is a change in the magnetic field of the first wire.

The change in the magnetic field due to the connect-disconnect state of the battery creates a surge and collapse in the magnetic field, which, in turn, creates a square wave of current. This can be easily explained by the fact that the current in the wire fluctuates between 1.5 volts and 0 volts corresponding to the connect-disconnect state of the wire. The wave of current created due to the connect-disconnect state of the battery is illustrated in Figure 2-1.

Square Wave

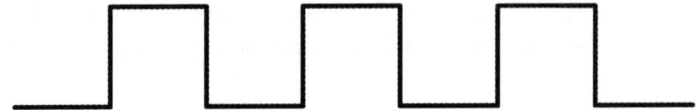

FIGURE 2-1 *The square wave created due to the connect-disconnect state of the battery*

The same phenomenon can be used to explain the working of a radio transmitter. The only difference between the battery-wire unit and a radio transmitter is that the change in current of a radio transmitter is more rapid. The continuous and rapid change in current creates a sine wave that is smoother than a square wave. The sine wave created by the rapid fluctuation is illustrated in Figure 2-2.

Sine Wave

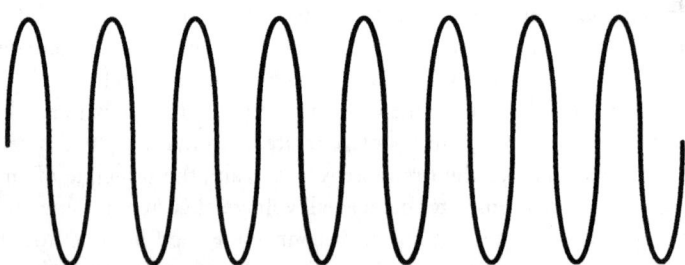

FIGURE 2-2 *The sine wave created by a rapid fluctuation in the current*

A radio transmitter is nothing but an assembly of a few electronic components such as the capacitor and the inductor that create and run a sine wave. In addition, a transistor is fitted to amplify the wave into a powerful signal. The signal is sent to the antenna, which transmits the sine wave into space. The receiver of another radio receives this wave.

The Bluetooth transmitter is no different from the transmitter discussed in the preceding sections. The singular and visibly important difference is that the Bluetooth transmitter is built to meet certain specifications. You'll recall that Chapter 1, "Introduction to Bluetooth," discussed how the SIG ensured standardization in all Bluetooth devices by creating a manual of governing regulations containing the definitions and description of adherence standards in the Bluetooth Specification. The characteristics of a Bluetooth transmitter are specified in terms of the following:

◆ Power levels

◆ Modulation scheme

◆ Symbol timing

◆ Spurious emissions

◆ Radio frequency tolerance

The following sections discuss each of these characteristics and their standards as specified in the Bluetooth Specification 1.0.

Power Levels of the Transmitter

All Bluetooth devices use the ISM band and, therefore, contain radios that do not transmit too much power. The standard for a Bluetooth transmitter is specified in terms of its power levels at the antenna connector of the equipment. A Bluetooth device without a connector uses a reference antenna with a 0 dBi gain. Based on their power output, Bluetooth transmitters are categorized into three power classes. Table 2-2 lists the three power classes of Bluetooth radio transmitters sourced from the Bluetooth Specification 1.0.

Table 2-2 Power Classes of Bluetooth Radio Transmitters

Power Class	Maximum Output Power (Pmax)	Nominal Output Power	Minimum Output Power	Power Control
1	100mW (20 dBm)	Not applicable	1mW (0 dBm)	Mandatory: +4 dBm to 20 dBm and Optional: -30 dBm to 4 dBm
2	2.5mW (4 dBm)	1mW (0 dBm)	0.25mW (-6 dBm)	Optional: -30 dBm to 4 dBm
3	1mW (20 dBm)	Not applicable	Not applicable	Optional: -30 dBm to 4 dBm

NOTE

dBi, dBm, and dBc are decibel measurements of power. These measures can be defined as:

◆ dBm is the decibel miliwatt unit of power with respect to one miliwatt

◆ dBi is the decibel isotropic unit of power with respect to isotropic level

◆ dBc is the decibels measure of power of a signal at one frequency with respect to that of a signal at carrier frequency

Class 1 devices require power control levels to eliminate an excessive emission of RF power. Power controls levels for Class 2 and Class 3 devices are optional, and are implemented only in low-power applications.

Modulation Scheme

Another characteristic feature of a Bluetooth device is the modulation scheme used for the transmission of data symbols. All Bluetooth devices are frequency-hopping systems with heavy data traffic that require the support of a non-coherent detection scheme. As a result, the binary modulation scheme is used to add robustness to the 1 MHz ISM band signals of Bluetooth transmitters. The use of this modulation scheme guarantees a data rate limit of 1 mbps. Other specifications for the modulation scheme in Bluetooth transmitters are as follows:

◆ The operating band of 83.5 MHz is divided into channels of 1 MHz with a data signaling capacity of 1 M symbols per second to obtain the maximum available channel bandwidth. The baud or signaling rate is used to define the number of symbols per second. Each symbol is represented by n bits, and has M signal states, where $M = 2n$. This type of signaling is called M-ary signaling.

◆ The modulation scheme uses the *Gaussian (prefiltered) Frequency Shift Keying* (GFSK) with a nominal modulation index of 0.3. The modulation index represents the strength of the peak frequency deviation (fd), which can be expressed as 2 fdT, where T is the symbol duration.

◆ The digital bit stream is modulated using GFSK with a *Bandwidth Time* (BT) product of 0.5. The BT product is the product of adjacent signal frequency separation (0.5 MHz) and symbol duration (1 μs).

NOTE

Adjacent signal frequency separation is the separation between modulation alphabet members or channel separation between modulated tones.

- ◆ The positive frequency deviation should be of logic one and a negative frequency deviation of zero.

- ◆ A modulation index should be between 0.28 and 0.35.

- ◆ The binary one should be represented by a positive frequency deviation and a binary zero should be represented by a negative frequency deviation.

- ◆ The minimum frequency deviation (Fmin) corresponding to 1010 sequence should be no smaller than ± 80% of the frequency deviation that corresponds to a 00001111 sequence.

- ◆ The minimum deviation should not be smaller than 115 KHz.

- ◆ The zero crossing error, which is the time difference between the ideal symbol period and the measured crossing time, should be less than ± ¹⁄₈ of a symbol period.

The modulation scheme used in Bluetooth is illustrated in Figure 2-3.

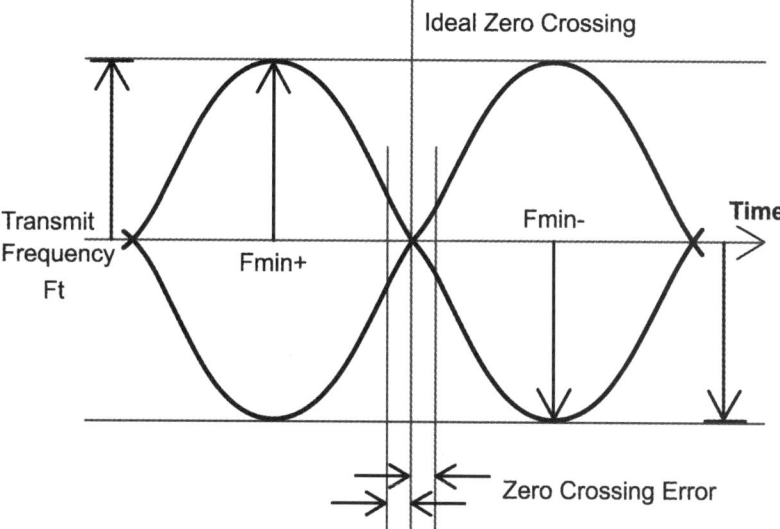

FIGURE 2-3 *The Binary Modulation Scheme in Bluetooth*

Symbol Timing

The Bluetooth Specification is firm on its demand for a symbol timing accuracy of ±20 ppm. As a result, the clock that drives symbol-processing logic in the course of its operating life should be accurate under all operating conditions. The maintenance of this symbol timing is made easier and does not call for additional costs by using the modern quartz technology, which assures the availability of 13 MHz references for GSM cellular phone applications.

Spurious Emissions

A hopping transmitter hopping on a single frequency is used to measure in-band and out-of-band spurious emissions. In other words, this indicates that the synthesizer should change frequency between the transmit slot and the receiver slot and also return to the same transmit frequency.

The in-band spurious emission specification states that within the ISM band, the transmitter should pass the spectrum mass specified in Table 2-3 and also complies with the FCC's 20 dB bandwidth. The Bluetooth Specification 1.0 for spurious emission also states that "In any 100 kHz bandwidth outside the frequency band in which the spread spectrum intentional radio frequency is operating, the radio frequency power that is produced by the intentional radiator should be at least 20 dB below that in the 100 kHz bandwidth within the band that contains the highest level of the desired power, based on either an RF conducted or a radiated measurement."

Table 2-3 The Spectrum Mass of Spurious Emissions as Specified in the Bluetooth Specification 1.0

Frequency Offset	Transmit Power
±550 kHz	−20 dBc
IM-NI = 2	−20 dBc
IM-NI 3 3	−20 dBc

In transmitters where the output power is less than 0 dBm, the FCC's 20 dB relative requirement overrules the absolute adjacent channel power requirement that is listed in Table 2-3.

The out-of-band spurious emission specification states that measured power should be in a 100 kHz band. Table 2-4 lists the out-of-band spurious emissions of various frequency bands sourced from the Bluetooth Specification 1.0.

Table 2-4 The Out-of-Band Spurious Emissions of Various Frequency Bands

Frequency Band	Operation Mode	Idle Mode
30 MHz–1 GHz	−36 dBm	−57 dBm
1 GHz–12.75 GHz	−30 dBm	−47 dBm
1.8 GHz–1.9 GHz	−47 dBm	−47 dBm
5.15 GHz–5.3 GHz	−47 dBm	−47 dBm

Radio Frequency Tolerance

The specification for the radio frequency tolerance states that the initial frequency accuracy or the frequency accuracy before the transmission of information should be ±75 kHz from Fc.

 NOTE

Initial frequency accuracy is the frequency accuracy before the transmission of any information. The bandwidth for the initial frequency accuracy of ±75 kHz excludes the frequency drift requirement.

Antenna

When you think of an antenna, you probably visualize a thin, short dipole that is very much a part of most radio units. Remember the long, thin, cylindrical, steel structure jutting out of the policeman's walkie-talkie? Or better still, the long thin steel structure in your radio, which you pull out to tune in or improve the reception of your favorite radio frequency. The dimensions of an antenna, also referred to as the *Hertzian dipole*, are measured in terms of wavelengths.

The antenna is a crucial part of the radio because it transmits and receives electromagnetic waves popularly referred to as radio waves. Antennas are resonant devices operating over a relatively narrow frequency band. For an uninterrupted transmission and reception, it is imperative to tune the frequency band of the antenna to the same frequency band as that of the radio system.

Most Bluetooth devices use dipole, microstrip, and flat panel antennas. These antennas have radiation patterns that suit Bluetooth applications in contrast to the radiation patterns of other strongly directional and more complex antennas such as multiple element dipoles, Yagis, slotted antennas, and parabolic dishes. The characteristics of the commonly used antennas are discussed in the following list:

◆ **Dipole antenna.** A dipole antenna is cylindrical in shape. It is often made out of small sections of coaxial cables. The signal feeding in dipole antennas occurs from the bottom of the device. The radiation pattern of this antenna is best from the side. Therefore, some devices are structured to facilitate the feeding of signals from the center of one side of the antenna. Half-wave and quarter-wave dipoles are preferred to ensure a relation between the length of a dipole and the wavelength of the signal.

◆ **Microstrip antenna.** A microstrip antenna is not a physical structure like a dipole but is simply a pattern on the *Printed Circuit Board* (PCB). Patterns and antenna are really very difficult to associate. The very fact that simple PCB tracks can be used as an antenna speaks volumes about the care and precision required during product designing. Even the slightest error can lead to unwanted radiating components.

◆ **Flat panel antenna.** A flat panel antenna is a square or rectangular metallic structure. The radiation pattern generated by this antenna is strongly directional and is, therefore, not suited for handheld devices. The most commonly used flat panel antenna is the *Planar Inverted F Antenna* (PIFA), which is so called due to its structural resemblance to the English alphabet F when viewed from one side. The PIFA antenna can also be made to function as a microstrip antenna by fabricating it in the form of tracks on a PCB.

◆ **On chip antenna**. An on chip antenna is an on board antenna placed in the Bluetooth module along with the baseband and radio chip. The antenna is put into operation as a four-armed, spiral microstrip placed on the top of the radio chip's package. The addition of a RF filter printed on the top of the package helps to improve the transceiver's characteristics. The on chip antenna radiates only in the hemisphere on one side of the chip. This is because of the fact that the radio chip placed within the package blocks the radio signal. The segregation of the antenna from the radio chip done away with the health concerns associated with devices such as headsets. The one disadvantage that remains with this type of an antenna is the limitation of connection to one side of the body. Although this does assure reduction of radiation levels, some Bluetooth products will require better coverage in connecting to an external antenna.

As discussed earlier, the antenna serves as a conductive medium that is used to carry electrical current subsequently released in space in the form of radio waves. The current carried by the antenna is a fluctuating current that induces an electromagnetic wave. The antenna should possess the following characteristics to ensure its efficient functioning:

◆ The impedance of the antenna should match the impedance of the transmission line connecting it. This characteristic of an antenna ensures the efficient transfer of power.

◆ The mode of the antenna should match the mode of the transmission line. This characteristic of an antenna ensures that the transmission line does not radiate energy but transfers all the power to the antenna.

◆ The antenna can also be designed to radiate in a specific direction by generating specific radiation patterns. The radiation patterns are also affected by the shielding from casings and components.

◆ Changing the polarization of the antenna can also change the patterns of radiation.

The characteristic of an antenna includes terms such as transmission lines, impedance, and polarization.

Impedance

Antenna impedance is the ratio of the voltage in an antenna at any given point to the current at that point. To ensure an efficient transfer of energy, the impedance of the radio, the antenna, and the transmission line should be the same.

The circuit of an antenna can be compared to that of a simple RLC circuit. You can, therefore, compare the inductance to the inductance of the conductors, the capacitor to the capacitance of the conductors, and the resistance to the energy lost to radiation. The short structure of an antenna contains a circuit that is governed by a large capacitative reactance and a smaller radiation resistance. As the length of the antenna increases, the inductive reactance and the radiation resistance increase while there is a decrease in the capacitative reactance. An antenna that is approximately half a wavelength long has equal capacitative reactance and inductive reactance. As a result, the capacitative and inductive reactance cancel each other and the antenna is in resonance. As the antenna grows longer (to one wavelength), the equivalent circuit is changed to a parallel resonate circuit with high radiation resistance, which is often referred to as the tank circuit. The RLC series circuit is re-established when the length of the antenna is one and one half wavelengths and when the length is at two wavelengths, the circuit switches back to the parallel circuit. The impedance pattern repeats in increments of one wavelength.

With the increase in the diameter, the reactance decreases, the radiation resistance for series resonance increases, and the radiation resistance for parallel resonance decreases. The increasing and decreasing values of the radiation resistance and the reactance lower the Q, which results in the widening of the bandwidth. Q is the quality factor that is used to measure the quality of a resonant structure, which in this case is the antenna. A typical dipole antenna will, therefore, show a resonate impedance of 100 ohms. Ideally, in order to have a broader bandwidth for transmission, the Q factor should be low, which means that the thickness of a dipole should, in turn be increased. A thick or fat dipole also needs to be cut short to avoid resonation at lower frequencies.

The impedance of a radio and the associated coaxial cable or transmission line is usually 50 ohms. Often, when antennas have impedance other than 50 ohms, an impedance matching circuit is needed to switch the impedance to 50 ohms. Radial or Larsen antennas are examples of antennas with matching impedance circuitry.

Transmission Lines

Transmission lines, as the name suggests, are lines that connect an antenna to digital devices (a radio) and help transmit information between devices. The structure of a transmission line includes two geometries. The first geometry is made up of a balanced twin conductor consisting of two parallel conductors, and the second geometry is made up of a coaxial unbalanced line consisting of two coaxial conductors. The characteristics of a transmission line are determined by factors such as impedance, loss, mode, and propagation velocity.

The preceding section discussed the factors that influence the impedance in an antenna. The impedance of a transmission line is determined by the geometry of the conductor and the dielectric constant of the supporting material. As discussed earlier, it is important for the impedance of the radio and transmission lines to match. This is because even a slight variation in the impedance can affect the amount of power transferred or result in a reflection at the discontinuity of transmission. The impedance in coaxial transmission lines is less than that in open wire, twin lead, or ladder wires.

Most coaxial transmission lines have a plastic dielectric to reduce the velocity of the signal to nearly .66 of its value in free space. This results in adding electrical length to the line, which is 50 percent more than the physical length of the transmission line.

Loss in transmission lines is mainly due to conductive loss, dielectric loss, and radiation. Both coaxial and ladder wire transmission lines have conductive losses. However, dielectric loss is more pronounced in coaxial transmission lines. Open wires are more prone to radiation losses as compared to coaxial lines. The spacing of conductors primarily dominates the tendency of open wires to radiate. On the other hand, the radiation tendency in coaxial wires is eliminated by the use of a properly fed coaxial line with matched modes.

The flow of current in transmission lines is bi-directional with a vector sum that is equal to zero. A non-zero vector sum, known as a common mode, distorts the pattern of a connected antenna due to a radiating mode. A common mode is initiated in the following two ways:

◆ By coupling to the energy radiated from the antenna.
◆ By creating a mismatch of modes. A mismatch of modes usually occurs when a balanced antenna is connected to an unbalanced transmission line. The reverse of this set-up, that is, a mismatch occurring due to a connection between an unbalanced antenna and a balanced transmission line, also holds true.

A dipole antenna is a balanced antenna, whereas a whip is an unbalanced antenna. Similarly, in the case of transmission lines, a twin lead or open wire transmission line is balanced as opposed to a coaxial line, which is unbalanced.

Often, a connection between a coaxial transmission line and a balanced dipole results in exciting a radiating common mode. What happens is that the current on the center conductor of the coaxial line flows out to the other arm of the dipole. At the same time, the current on the outer conductor flows out to the other arm of the dipole and down to the outside of the shield. As a result, a common and radiating mode is created on the cable. An interface called `balun` (Balanced-Unbalanced) is used to rectify this problem.

All through the discussion on transmission lines, I have cited the case of transmission lines with matched modes at both the ends. How does the situation change in the case of transmission lines with unmatched ends?

It is obvious that the impedance in this case will never be equal to the characteristic impedance of the transmission line. On the contrary, the impedance will vary as one moves along the transmission line but away from the mismatched termination. The value of this varying impedance can be calculated by the following formula:

$Z_T = Z_0 * Z_0/Z_L$

In the preceding formula, Z denotes the characteristic impedance of the transmission line, ZL denotes the value of the termination, and ZT denotes the extreme impedance transformation.

Radiation Patterns

The radiation pattern of an antenna can be described as the relative strength of the radiated field in all directions from the antenna. In addition, the radiation pattern expresses the receiving characteristics of the antenna and is also described as a reception pattern.

The radiation pattern of an antenna closely resembles the cross section of a doughnut. The radiation pattern is generally uniform and omni-directional. However, as the antenna grows larger, the energy radiated during transmission is distributed in time. As a result, energy from all the parts of the antenna does not reach the same point at the same time. Energy arriving at different time intervals does not compulsorily add to the phase and may result in the lowering of the signal received. This addition and subtraction creates an antenna radiation pattern, which depends on the electric size and current distribution of the antenna. Therefore, a larger electrical size of the antenna creates a more structured pattern with well-formed peaks and nulls. Similarly, a dipole antenna that is 10.25 wavelengths long will have a more directive main lobe. The wavelength dimension of an antenna consists of four lobes in one 360-degree pattern cut. For example, a 10-wavelength antenna will have 40 lobes in its pattern. The lobes are closest in the broadside dimension. The separation between the lobes at the longest dimension of the antenna is approximately 60/D, where D denotes the dimension of the antenna in wavelengths. The radiation patterns are plotted in the following two dimensions:

- ◆ **Azimuth dimension.** The azimuth dimension is a top view of the radiation pattern as seen from the top of an antenna. This pattern is in the form of a perfect circle showing equal strengths in all directions. The azimuth radiation patterns of a dipole antenna are illustrated in Figure 2-4.

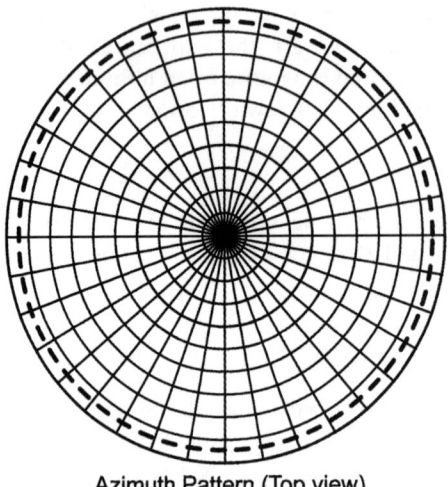

Azimuth Pattern (Top view)

FIGURE 2-4 *The azimuth radiation patterns of a dipole antenna*

◆ **Elevation dimension.** The elevation dimension is a side view of the radiation pattern as seen from the side of an antenna. This pattern shows very strong radiations with sharp droppings to nothing both above and below the antenna. The elevation radiation patterns of a dipole antenna are illustrated in Figure 2-5.

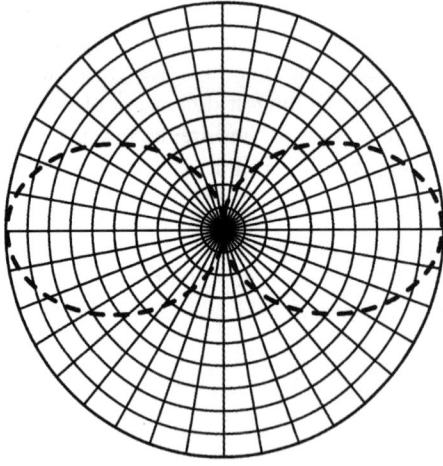

Elevation Pattern (Side view)

FIGURE 2-5 *The elevation radiation patterns of a dipole antenna*

A radiation pattern is used to picture the signal strength of a particular Bluetooth product at different angles. This, in turn, determines the placement angle and spacing between communicating devices to transmit and receive signals with optimum clarity. For example, a dipole antenna with radiation patterns similar to the illustration in Figure 2-4 works best when held upright at an angle of 90 degrees. Similarly, consider the communication between a Bluetooth-enabled laptop and a mobile phone. The clarity of the pattern at various angles can be used to estimate the placement of various devices so that they are able to catch each other's signals and connect.

The orientation of electromagnetic waves also affects the efficiency and working of an antenna. The next sections discuss the definition and effect of polarization on the transmission and reception of antenna signals.

Polarization

The electromagnetic waves present in free space consist of two elements, an electric field (E) and a magnetic field (H). The magnetic field is perpendicular to the electric field. In addition, both the electric and magnetic fields are perpendicular to the direction of propagation. The orientation of the E vector defines the polarization of a wave. The elements of polarization are linear, as well as circular. Linear waves are arranged in a plane and are, therefore, said to be vertically polarized. Similarly, circular waves are arranged in a circle and are said to be circularly polarized.

Polarization does not directly affect Bluetooth systems due to the variety of angles that are used to operate these devices. However, a radiation pattern and polarization together can be used to improve the performance of Bluetooth devices by determining the angles at which the devices should be held.

Gain and Loss

The gain of an antenna is measured in dBi and is the ratio of power in to power out. The value of dBi is gain relative to an isotropic antenna. An isotropic antenna radiates in a uniform manner in all directions, and the value of power in is equal to that of power out (gain is equal to one).

The loss of an antenna is a result of a mismatch of the feed between the radio and the antenna. A mismatch in the feed results in the reflection of the signal back to the feeder. The other reasons for loss in transmission are as follows:

◆ Material loss in the antenna due to the absorption of the signal by the propagating medium.

◆ Material loss in the propagation path due to the shielding of the casing and other components of the Bluetooth product. Most Bluetooth devices such as laptops and mobile phones contain metal screenings around internal components. These screenings block radio signals. This is the reason why an antenna is never placed inside a screen. However, antennas can be placed internally in additional pockets as is visible in the PCMCIA cards that are used in laptops.

♦ Material loss in microwave transmissions also occurs when signals pass through a strong absorbing medium, such as water or furniture.

Antenna Arrays

So far, this chapter has discussed impedance, polarization, and radiation patterns as the characteristics of single antennas. However, bear in mind that there are many types of antennas with the unique characteristics of impedance, polarization, and radiation patterns. Often, these characteristics can be manipulated to eliminate the need for building a new antenna. It is interesting to note that antennas of similar types can also be arranged in the form of an array to electronically steer and improve its gain and radiation properties. Antenna arrays can also be arranged to obtain a wide bandwidth. The most common arrangements of arrays are

♦ **Linear array.** A linear array consists of a straight row of elements.

♦ **Planar array.** A planar array consists of a two-dimensional array of elements lying in the same plane. Using fairly simple elements, this arrangement can be used to achieve higher gains. The beam in a two-dimensional array can be scanned and shaped in two directions.

♦ **Three-dimensional array.** This is a three-dimensional array where each element is treated as a planar array. Three-dimensional arrays have a wider element pattern with a complex and costly feed network.

Radio Receiver

The radio receiver should possess the following characteristics to ensure its efficient functioning:

♦ **Sensitivity level.** The sensitivity level of the receiver should be such that the raw bit error rate (BET) of 0.1 percent is met. If this specification is mapped to a Bluetooth receiver, it means that the actual sensitivity level of the receiver should be better than −70 dBm.

♦ **Interference performance.** The interference performance, as specified in the Bluetooth Specification 1.0, states that the interference performance on co-channel and adjacent 1 MHz and 2 MHz should be measured with the wanted signal of 10 dB over the reference sensitivity level. On all other frequencies the wanted signal should be 3 dB over the reference sensitivity level. Table 2-5 lists the interference performance sourced from the Bluetooth Specification 1.0.

Table 2-5 The Interference Performance

Requirement	Ratio
Co-Channel interference	11 dB
Adjacent (1 MHz) interference	0 dB
Adjacent (2 MHz) interference	−30 dB
Adjacent (3 MHz) interference	−40 dB
Image frequency Interference	−9 dB
Adjacent (1 MHz) interference	−20 dB

◆ **Out of Band blocking.** The Bluetooth Specification 1.0 states that out of band blocking should be measured with the wanted signal 3 dB over the reference sensitivity level. The interfering signal should be a continuous wave signal. The BER should be less than or equal to 0.1 percent. Table 2-6 lists the out of band blocking requirements of a receiver sourced from the Bluetooth Specification 1.0.

Table 2-6 The Out of Band Blocking Requirements

Interfering Signal Frequency	Interfering Signal Power Level
30 MHz–2000 MHz	−10 dBm
2000–2399 MHz	−27 dBm
2498–3000 MHz	−27 dBm
3000 MHz–12.75 GHz	−10 dBm

◆ **Maximum usable level.** The maximum usable level of operation of the receiver should be better than −20 dBm. In addition, the BER should be less than or equal to 0.1 percent at an input power of −20 dBm.

◆ **Receiver Signal Strength Indicator (RSSI).** According to the Bluetooth Specification 1.0, "A transceiver that wishes to support power-controlled links must be able to measure the strength of the received signal and determine if the transmitter on the other side of the link should increase or decrease its output power level. A *Receiver Signal Strength Indicator* (RSSI) makes this possible. A RSSI should have an absolute accuracy of ±4 dB or better for a receiver signal power of −60 dBm."

Table 2-7 summarizes the transmitter and receiver requirements for Bluetooth devices.

Table 2-7 The Transmitter and Receiver Requirements

Modulation	GFSK
Modulation index	0.32 ± 1%
BT	0.5 ± 1%
Bit Rate	ppm
Frequency Accuracy	Better than ± 1 ppm

 NOTE

BT is not an abbreviation for Bluetooth, but is a parameter that describes the quality of the transmitted waveforms.

How Bluetooth Evades Interference

A major difference in the operating conditions of a real transmitter and an ideal transmitter or receiver is the presence of other unwanted signals in the unlicensed ISM band of 2.4 GHz. The unwanted hostile signals create interference in the following ways:

♦ Capture the desired channel

♦ Cross-modulate information on to the desired channel

♦ Reduce the demodulated signal-to-noise ratio

♦ Lower the BER sensitivity of the radio

♦ Desensitize the radio by using large, out of band signals

It is obvious that these interferences will hamper and affect the quality and efficiency of transmission in Bluetooth devices. Some of the techniques adopted by Bluetooth devices to avoid interferences with other system signals are

♦ **Sending out weak signals.** Bluetooth devices send out weak signals of 1 milliwatt, which is very weak compared to the 3-watt signals of the most powerful cell phones.

♦ **Use of the spread spectrum frequency hopping technique.** A Bluetooth device uses 79 individual randomly chosen frequencies within the designated frequency band to hop on a regular basis at the rate of 1,600 times every second.

◆ **Automatic electronic conversation.** Two Bluetooth devices automatically initiate an electronic conversation as soon as they are within range of each other. The electronic conversation is used to determine and eliminate the need for data sharing or controlling between the two devices. If the need for data sharing or controlling between the two devices is substantiated, a *Personal Area Network* (PAN) or piconet is formed and the devices hop frequencies in unison and communicate with each other.

Before summarizing all the concepts discussed in this chapter, an explanation the working of various Bluetooth devices placed within close proximity of each other would be beneficial. The idea is to further clarify the concepts of frequency hopping and the PAN system that ensure a smooth and uninterrupted communication between the devices. Consider an example of my perception of a living room at the turn of 2002 (after the total market is captured by Bluetooth technology). Other than furnishings, the room would contain Bluetooth-enabled devices, such as a personal computer, a cordless telephone, a DVD player, a television, and an entertainment system.

Let's look at how a network initiates and the devices communicate with each other. Both the cordless phone and its base are fitted with transmitters with the address programmed into each unit. When you switch on the base unit, it sends out a signal seeking a response from the units with the address of the particular range. The handset responds to the signal and a small network is formed. The other devices placed in the room are not a part of this particular network. Therefore, signals from the other devices will be ignored. Similarly, more networks are established between the other devices that function undeterred by any interferences. Each of the devices within a particular network or piconet hops frequencies in unison and is separated from each other.

Bluetooth devices use both uni- and bi-directional communication methods for transmission. The talking and listening modes of the speakerphone are an example of bi-directional or synchronous communication. The regular telephone handset with a uni-directional communication mode is an example of asynchronous communication.

Summary

The radio is an integral part of any communicating device. The radio or the Bluetooth chip is also the core of any Bluetooth device that facilitates a wireless connection between digital devices.

In this chapter, you learned how Bluetooth devices use the 2.4 GHz license-free and noisy band for transmission of information. You also learned the specification parameters of the radio requirements that can be used to build efficient and cost effective devices. Next you learned the working and characteristics of the transmitter and receiver transmit information in the form of electromagnetic waves or radio waves. You also learned about the characteristics of an antenna that radiates patterns to assist connection between devices in any direction, at any angle.

With the inclusion of Bluetooth technology in most computing and telecommunication products, the importance of standardization during the designing of each component grows. The tight parameters used for the modulation and symbol timing ensures uninterrupted and assured transmission of data between devices. However, there is still scope for further improvisation in the system design that can be achieved with reconsideration of some of the constraints on the radio specification.

Check Your Understanding

Multiple Choice Questions

1. State whether the following statements are true or false.

    a. The radio set up in Bluetooth consists of the radio, antenna, and the transistor.

    b. A change in the connect-disconnect state of the battery creates a round wave of current.

    c. The rapid fluctuation of current in a radio creates a sine wave.

2. The wavelength of an antenna consists of _____ lobes.

    a. Three

    b. Four

    c. Five

    d. Six

3. Which of the following is the unit used to measure the gain of an antenna?

    a. dBi

    b. dBm

    c. dBc

    d. mbps

    e. kbps

4. Which of the following are the common arrangements of antenna arrays?

    a. Azimuth dimension

    b. Elevation dimension

    c. Linear

    d. Planar

    e. Three dimensional

Short Questions

1. Which are the factors considered during frequency hopping in Bluetooth devices?

2. What are the characteristics that are used to define the specifications of a Bluetooth transmitter?

3. How do hostile and unwanted signals create interference in the air interface?

4. Write short notes on the characteristics of the following technologies:

   a. Flat panel antenna

   b. Azimuth dimension

Answers

Multiple Choice Answers

1. a. True
    b. False
    c. True
2. b. Three.
3. a. dBi.
4. b, c, and d. Linear, Planar, and three dimensional.

Short Answers

1. The factors considered during frequency hopping include:

    ◆ **Synchronized timings.** The frequencies used by the transmitter and the receiver should be the same. Additionally, the time intervals of transmission should be synchronized.

    ◆ **Delivery of information.** Bluetooth technology, like most telecommunication systems, uses packets for delivering information. A single packet is contained within one to five hops.

    ◆ **Selecting a frequency.** Most telecommunication systems use a shared algorithm to select a frequency. However, in Bluetooth, the clock and the device address of the master determines the frequency used for transmission. The ISM spectrum in USA and Europe consists of 79 channels as opposed to the meager count of 23 channels in the rest of the world.

    ◆ **Hop frequency.** The hop rate (for a hop time length of 625 μs) is set to 1,600 frequencies per second.

2. The characteristics of a Bluetooth transmitter are defined in terms of:

    ◆ Power levels
    ◆ Modulation scheme
    ◆ Symbol timing
    ◆ Spurious emissions
    ◆ Radio frequency tolerance

3. The hostile signals create interference in the following:
◆ Capture the desired channel
◆ Cross-modulate information on to the desired channel
◆ Reduce the demodulated signal-to-noise ratio
◆ Lower the BER sensitivity of the radio
◆ Desensitize the radio by using large, out of band signals

4. a. **Flat panel antenna.** A flat panel antenna is a square or rectangular metallic structure. The radiation pattern generated by this antenna is strongly directional and is, therefore, not suited for handheld devices. The most commonly used flat panel antenna is the *Planar Inverted F Antenna* (PIFA), which is so called due to its structural resemblance to the English alphabet F when viewed from one side. The PIFA antenna can also be made to function as a microstrip antenna by fabricating it in the form of tracks on a PCB.

    b. **Azimuth dimension.** The azimuth dimension is a top view of the radiation pattern as seen from the top of an antenna. This pattern is in the form of a perfect circle showing equal strengths in all directions.

Chapter 3

Architecture of Bluetooth

Now that you understand the basics of Bluetooth, it is time to move deeper into a study of this marvelous new technology. This chapter begins with a brief run-through of the concepts both directly and indirectly related to Bluetooth. Chapter 1, "Introduction to Bluetooth," briefly discussed the technique of frequency hopping used by Bluetooth to avoid channel interference. This technique is actually a type of *Spread Spectrum* (SS) technology that defines the commercial use of digital radio communication. This chapter, therefore, begins with a discussion of the origin and development of the SS technology. Because networks play an important role in any Bluetooth communication, this chapter also discusses the technologies associated with the high-capacity networks used by Bluetooth devices.

The chapter moves on to discussing the skeleton of the Bluetooth architecture. Bear in mind that each of the succeeding chapters deals with individual layers of the Bluetooth protocol stack in detail. The final section of this chapter serves as a curtain raiser for hardcore Bluetooth-related concepts.

The Origin and Growth of Spread Spectrum Technology

Traveling is a part of professional life today. Therefore, it comes as no surprise that professionals prefer portable digital devices such as mobile phones and laptops as a means of communication. Do you know that there are nearly 45 million cellular subscribers in the world today? That's not all! Hold your breath for the next bit of information on cellular subscribers: Nearly 50 percent of the 45 million cellular subscribers are located in the United States alone. That does substantiate the demand and popularity of mobile phones, or cellulars as they are popularly called, as a telecommunication application. The forecasted integration of cellular systems and digital technology has been able to integrate switching and transmission, eased signaling, lowered the levels of interference, and has also met the growing market demand for these systems.

Continuous research for improving the existing telecommunication services has led to the emergence of a new and secure technology called the Spread Spectrum (SS) technology. Spread Spectrum brings the promise of a new commercial marketplace that consists of a wide range of applications from wireless LANs to integrated palmtops, radio modem devices used for warehousing, and communication systems consisting of digital cellular phones. The fact that this technology includes wireless devices substantiates its use in Bluetooth devices also, therefore this section briefly explains the basics of the Spread Spectrum technology. So, what exactly is this SS technology?

Radio communication using the SS technology has been a long-time favorite with most military organizations. A simple reason for this preference is that this technology is jam-resistant. Chapter 2, "Introduction to Radio," touched upon the subject of jamming and jam resistance in the discussion of frequency hopping in Bluetooth. I am sure you'll recollect that resistance to jamming ensures that communication is harder to intercept by the so-called enemy of all military establishments.

So immense was the potential popularity of the SS technology that before long, it gained entry into commercial development. The core of this technology lies in the fact that although SS signals are distributed over a wide range of frequencies, they are collected to their original frequency at the receiver end. In parallel, you may refer to this feature as being inconspicuous or transparent to other signals. However, this transparent and uninterrupted behavior of SS signals is not limited to the military but can also be used for commercial and industrial purposes. An added advantage is that SS signals are also unlikely targets for interruption within the same frequency. The wide-band SS transmitters use similar power levels that transmit at a much lower spectral density than narrow-band transmitters. As a result, SS signals are measured in watts per hertz. The lower transmitted power density ensures that both spread and narrow-band signals are able to share the same frequency band with minimal or no interference. It is this feature of the SS technology that has attracted immense interest and intrigued the telecommunication and wireless industry players. The following section delves a bit into this technology.

What the Spread Spectrum Technology Means

Chapter 2 discussed how the Bluetooth technology uses a wider bandwidth to ensure a better ratio between signals and noise. In addition, the use of frequency hops in Bluetooth devices maintains the continuity of communication. In this chapter, a frequency hop will be re-introduced as an easy-to-use modulation that is based on the SS technology.

Having already covered the basic technique used in frequency hops, it is rather simple to associate the two concepts.

The signals in the SS technology use code sequences that run faster than the data rate. These code sequences are not real gaussian noise and are, therefore, aptly named pseudo random or *Pseudo Noise* (PN) sequences. You can actually convert a radio fitted with a digitally controlled frequency synthesizer to a frequency hopping radio. All that this conversion needs is the inclusion of a *Pseudo Noise code generator*, more commonly known as the *PN code generator*. The PN code generator helps to select the frequency to be used during the transmission or reception of data. A uniform mode of frequency hopping over a band of frequencies is prevalent in most hopping systems. However, this mechanism of uniform frequency hopping can be done away with if the two communicating devices (the transmitting and receiving devices) know the hopping frequencies in advance.

Continuing with signal transmission using the SS technology, a practical and commonly used technique for the transmission of signals in the SS technology is the direct sequence. In a direct sequence system, the data to be transmitted is encoded by using a locally generated PN code. The data for transmission is logically added to a faster-running, locally generated PN code by using an EXOR operation called module-2. The SS receiver accepts the transmitted data and, in turn, locally generates a replica of the PN code. A receiver correlator is used to separate the actual code information from the other signals. An SS correlator of a receiver device can be tuned to recognize and differentiate specific PN codes. The SS correlator simply functions like a matching filter responding to signals encoded with PN code that match up to its own code. The SS correlator ignores all artificial or natural man-made noise and interference responding only to identically matched SS signals. The benefits of the SS technology have led to its use in the currently favored development in the telecommunication and wireless scene—the Bluetooth technology.

Because the SS technology depends on the generation of PN sequences or PN, the following section elaborates on PN sequences.

A Bit More on Pseudo Noise

As stated, the SS technology depends on the generation of non-gaussian PN sequences. PN sequences are simply codes that define the characteristics of the chip sequence, the limits for the SS system, and its capabilities. The features are governed by the type, length, and chip rate of the codes. The PN sequences facilitate interference rejection, selective addressing, error detection, error correction, and message confidentiality. Let's begin by discussing some concepts related to the codes in a PN sequence.

The codes generated in a PN sequence can be categorized as follows:

◆ **Linear codes.** Linear codes are generated by using modulo-2 additions and shift registers. The main PN sequences are linear codes that are called maximal-length or Gold sequences.

◆ **Non-linear codes.** Non-linear codes are generated by introducing a non-linear component in the feedback path. These codes are complex to implement, which is why linear codes are preferred over non-linear codes.

The preference for linear codes over non-linear codes is due to the following characteristics of linear, or maximal-length, codes:

◆ Linear codes create an auto-correlation of a maximal linear code with a phase shift correlation of −1. An exception to this characteristic is the 0±1 chip phase shift, which has a linear varying correlation from −1 to $2^n - 1$ (n being the number of shift register stages).

◆ Linear codes generate a sequence of ones and zeros in which the number of ones equals the number of zeros. Therefore, maximal-length code sequences produce zero DC current at +V and −V signal levels.

◆ Linear codes replicate the modulo-2 additions of linear codes with a phase-shifted replica of itself but with a phase shift that is dissimilar from the original.

◆ Linear codes statistically distribute the ones and zeros evenly. In other words, each repetition of the code displays the same one-zero ratio.

Once you have a clear understanding of the function and characteristics of the PN sequence, it will be easier to understand the operational modes or transmission techniques that use the SS technology. In that case, what are the various techniques of transmission based on the SS technology?

Operational Modes of the Spread Spectrum Technology

The SS technology is a transmission technique that uses modulation to spread the spectrum of a narrow-band signal with a wide-band signal. The following three techniques are used for transmission using the SS technology:

- ◆ **Direct Sequence Spread Spectrum (DSSS).** DSSS modulates by generating a PN sequence with defined properties. The modulated carrier consists of digital code sequences with a data rate signal higher than that of information signals.
- ◆ **Frequency Hopping Spread Spectrum (FHSS).** FHSS modulates by shifting the frequency of the carrier in a pattern that is ordered by the PN sequence.
- ◆ **Time Hopping Spread Spectrum (THSS).** THSS modulates by managing the timing of transmission that is based on the PN sequence.

The modulation of a carrier can also be accomplished by using a combination of the preceding three techniques (called "hybrids"). As a result, a Time-Frequency Hopping technique will determine the time and frequency of a transmission, while a Direct Frequency Hopping technique shifts the center frequency of a direct sequence signal with a PN sequence.

Before discussing the individual techniques for the implementation of Spread Spectrum, view the spectrum of DSSS and FHSS signals as shown in Figures 3-1 and 3-2, respectively.

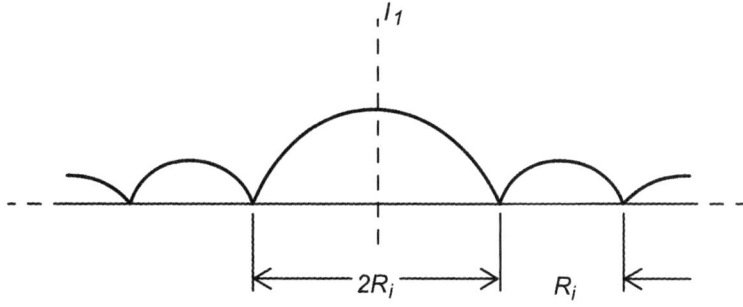

FIGURE 3-1 *Ideal spectrum of DSSS signal*

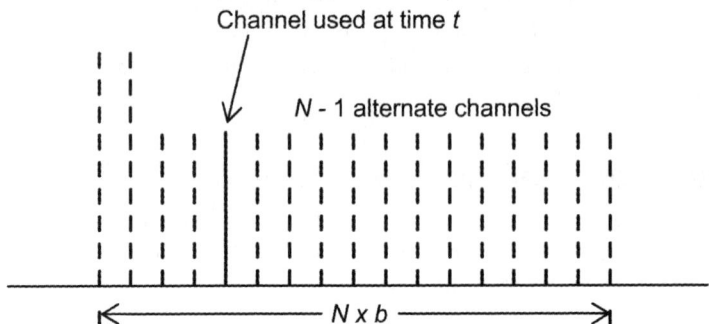

FIGURE 3-2 *Ideal spectrum of FHSS signal*

The following sections discuss each of these techniques in detail, beginning with the DSSS technique of transmission.

Direct Sequence Spread Spectrum

DSSS generates a redundant bit pattern called a chip or chipping code for each bit that is transmitted. The longer bit patterns help in the recovery of the bits that are damaged during transmission without having to retransmit the data. The statistical techniques embedded in the radio are used for the recovery of the damaged bits of data. In addition, the probability of recovering damaged data is directly proportional to the size of the data. As a result, the longer the chip, the greater the bandwidth required and the greater is the probability of recovery. DSSS seems like a low-power wide-band noise to an unintended receiver and is, therefore, rejected or ignored by narrow-band receivers.

The carrier modulation in DSSS uses the PN sequence or a digital code. Although there are two ways of generating the PN sequence, both the methods produce the same resultant waveform. The two methods for generating the PN sequence in DSSS are as follows:

◆ Multiplying the information signal with the digital code before the modulation of the carrier

◆ Multiplying the modulated information signal with the digital code

Figure 3-3 illustrates the In-phase (I channel) and the Quadrature of a DSSS implementation when the information data is multiplied with the PN code before the modulation of the carrier.

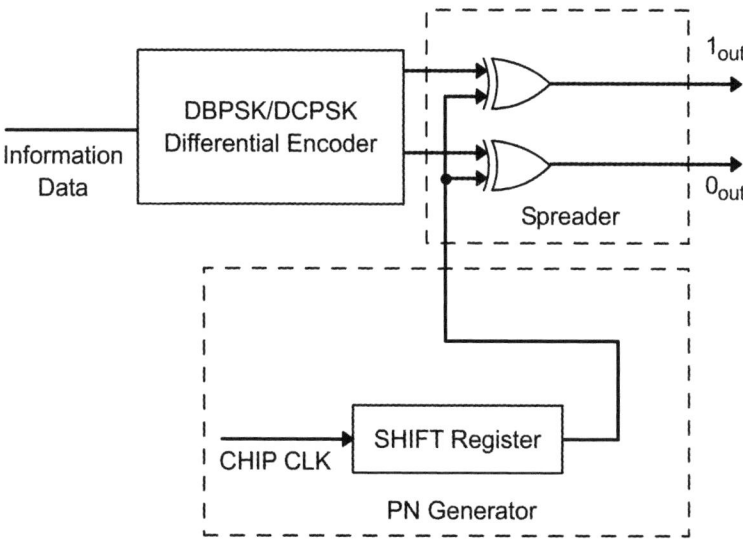

FIGURE 3-3 *Block diagram of the In-phase (I channel) and the Quadrature of a DSSS modulator*

Frequency Hopping Spread Spectrum

The concept of frequency hopping was briefly discussed in Chapter 1. This section discusses frequency hopping with respect to modulation. True to its name, a frequency hopping implementation receives data signals and modulates them with a carrier signal characterized by a frequency-to-frequency hop over a wide-band of frequencies as a function of time. As a result, due to FHSS implementation, the carrier frequency changes periodically. The aggregate frequency is low with little or no bit errors due to a reduction in interference. The data transmission between the signals from a narrow-band system and the FHSS systems do not interfere with each other because they do not transmit data at the same frequency at the same time. You may recall that in a frequency hopping radio, the carrier frequency hops over the 2.4 GHz frequency bands that ranges between 2.4 GHz to 2.483 GHz.

Similarly, two FHSS radios do not interfere with each other because of the use of different hopping patterns. If a radio encounters interference on a particular frequency, it hops on to another frequency and retransmits the data. Therefore, at a particular time, the frequency used by the two radios is always different. Such sets of hopping codes that never use the same frequency at a time are said to be *orthogonal*.

The hopping code determines the frequency and order of transmission in a radio. The transmission of data from one radio and its receipt by another radio complete a transmission cycle. It is, therefore, important that the receiver is set to the same frequency hop code as that of the transmitting radio so that it can listen to the incoming signal at the exact frequency and time. The time spent at a particular frequency during a single hop is called the *dwell time*. The FCC specifications require radios to use 75 or more frequencies with a dwell time of 400 ms. Remember that a faster rate of data transmission is prone to a greater number of errors. The nature of the modulation technique restricts the data rate of a frequency hop to 2 mbps, which curtails the number of errors occurring during transmission.

Time Hopping Spread Spectrum

Until now, THSS systems, or "Chirp" systems as they are alternatively called, have not been implemented commercially in SS systems. The advent of options, such as cheap *Random Access Memory* (RAM) and fast micro-controller chips have, however, led to the acceptance of THSS systems as a future alternative for the SS technique. Yet, despite being rarely used in commercial systems, THSS systems are often used in radar systems.

Now that you are acquainted with the basics and categorization of Spread Spectrum, the next section summarizes the characteristics of Spread Spectrum based on the discussions so far.

The Characteristics of Spread Spectrum

The enhanced capability of Spread Spectrum in transmitting data with minimal interference and errors is the primary reason for the interest and hype it has generated. The interest can be attributed to the following features:

◆ The noise-like SS signals use a wide-band for transmission and are, therefore, hard to detect. The band of transmission is intentionally made wider than the information to induce the noise-like feature in the signal.

◆ SS signals are harder to jam due to *Low Probability of Intercept* (LPI) and *Anti-Jam* (AJ).

◆ PN codes generated by the SS signals are faster than the information bandwidth or data rate.

◆ The transmit power level of SS transmitters is similar to that of narrow-band transmitters. Wider SS signals, however, transmit at a lower density than narrow-band transmitters. As a result, both Spread and narrow-band signals occupy the same band creating little or no interference for each other.

FHSS forms the framework of any Bluetooth device. The advantages of using the SS technique will undoubtedly determine the success of this technology that operates in the noisy ISM band.

The Advantages of Using Spread Spectrum

The Low Probability of Intercept and Anti-Jam features of the SS technology are the major reasons why it commanded the sole attention of military establishments for many years before its acceptance in the commercial marketplace. The advantageous features of the SS technology are described in the following list:

◆ The PN code used for the transmission of data in the SS technology makes the signals appear like noisy and wide-band signals. This behavior of signals is responsible for the feature of LPI that makes these signals hard to detect and harder to intercept or demodulate.

◆ SS signals are also hard to jam or interfere with, a feature commonly known as AJ. The energy of the SS signals or their power density is spread over a band that is approximately 100 times the bandwidth of the information. As a result, SS signals are less likely to interfere with narrow-band transmissions. The presence of the receiver's correlator integrates over a wide bandwidth to retrieve only SS signals, ensuring that narrow-band communications do not interfere with SS systems.

◆ SS systems have a tolerance level for interference that denotes the threshold, which when crossed results in the termination of any positive communication.

◆ A nagging worry during any confidential communication is the fear of signal exploitation or spoofing. Signal exploitation can be defined as the ability of an outsider, typically a non-member of a particular network, to eavesdrop into a network and use, or rather misuse, the network information. Spoofing, on the other hand, can be defined as the act of falsifying an identity to gain access to a particular network for malicious use of information. SS signals are also hard to exploit or spoof and are, therefore, a more secure means of communication.

Bluetooth technology can be described as a technology based on Spread Spectrum, which operates over a high-capacity network. The following sections discuss the two technologies that are used to build high-capacity networks.

Building High-Capacity Networks

Wireless devices opt for networking that is quick, cost-effective, and promises high-capacity connectivity. As a result, mobile operators, enterprises, and communication service providers use two basic technologies for building high-capacity networks that support multiple applications and also meet the growing demand for value-added broadband services. The following are the two basic technologies:

◆ Circuit-switched technology
◆ Packet-switched technology

Because Bluetooth uses a combination of both circuit and packet switching, the next sections discuss each of these technologies in brief.

Circuit-Switched Technology

The physical path in a circuit-switched network is acquired and dedicated to the two end points of a single connection in the network for the duration of the connection. The term "circuit" defines the route of the network that is created by the reservation of network resources all the way from the sender to the recipient even before the start of the data transfer. In that way, the reserved resources are dedicated to the circuit during the entire process of data transfer. The predetermined route or path is also called a logical channel or a virtual circuit. A network based on this technology is called a *connection-oriented network*.

Both wireless and wire line networks apply circuit switching for the transmission of data and voice. They are ideal for transmitting real-time data such as live audio and video, where the data must be transmitted quickly while retaining the order of the transmission at both ends of the network.

A ubiquitous example of the circuit-switched technology is the ordinary voice phone service. You'll be able to map the circuit-based working of this network by simply re-creating a telephone conversation. Have you ever wondered why an ongoing conversation is not ended abruptly on receiving another call? What actually ensues is that a specific physical path is reserved to your number for the entire duration of the call. As a result, no other physical line is drawn in by anyone else through the duration of the call. Can you imagine the chaos and confusion if telephones worked otherwise?

The advantages of using a circuit-switched network are as follows:

♦ Transmission of large amounts of data

♦ Guaranteed transmission capacity

♦ Separate control signaling and transfer of payload data

♦ Execution of control information processing and control signaling (routing) mainly at circuit setup and termination

Although the features of a circuit-switched network provide support for the transmission of real-time data, it also has certain disadvantages, which are as follows:

♦ A reduction in the capacity of the network due to a short-lived connection in which the setup delay forms a major part of the total connection time. Such situations are usually encountered during the transmission of short messages.

♦ A reduction in link utilization because the reserved resources of even an inactive circuit can't be used by other users.

The circuit-switched technology is often contrasted with the packet-switched technology, which is discussed next.

Packet-Switched Technology

Packet switching was developed as a more robust and effective mode of data transmission to overcome the limitations of circuit switching apparent during bursts of random traffic. In other words, transmission by packet switching can withstand some delays, which is characteristic of e-mail messages and Web pages. A packet-switched network refers to that mode of data transmission in which a message or data stream is divided into packets before being sent. Each packet consists of the following information:

- ◆ The address of the destination
- ◆ The size of the packets
- ◆ The sequence of the packets
- ◆ Error-checking information
- ◆ Payload data

The packets so created are sorted and directed by specific packet switches or routers and then transmitted individually to the destination along different routes. When the packets reach the destination, they are reassembled to form the original message.

Contrary to circuit-switched networks that are connection-oriented, packet-switched networks can be based either on the connection-oriented or connectionless technology. The technology behind *connection-oriented* networks was explained in the preceding section. The singular path of a virtual circuit in a connection-oriented network is segmented into nodes. How, then, is the continuity of the transmission maintained to ensure that the packets reach the correct destination? Each packet header of a connection-oriented, packet-switched network, such as *Asynchronous Transfer Mode* (ATM), contains a channel identifier with the preserved order of the packets that is used at the nodes to guide the packet to the right destination.

 NOTE

ATM is a technology that attempts to combine the guaranteed delivery of circuit-switched networks with the robust and efficient delivery of packet-switching networks.

The scene in a connectionless network such as *Internet Protocol* (IP) is quite different. The packets are transmitted independently and, therefore, individually contain complete information regarding the destination. Although the packets of a connectionless network are destined for the same destination, they take different routes for transmission. Therefore, there is no need to preserve the order of the packets.

An X.25 network is a good example of a packet-switched network with virtual circuit switching characteristics too. In a virtual circuit-switched connection, the physical path of the dedicated logical connection is shared among multiple virtual circuit connections. In addition, a good number of other modern WAN protocols such as *Transmission Control*

Protocol/Internet Protocol (TCP/IP) and Frame Relay are also based on the packet-switching technology.

Let's examine the working of the packet switching technology using the example of Internet services. Consider a rather common Internet task of downloading wallpaper consisting of both text and graphics. Let's trace the network journey of the wallpaper's text and graphical content. Because Internet services use the packet-switching technology, the downloaded text and graphical content of the wallpaper is divided into packets. The packets take various paths over available, free, or shared connections. On reaching the destination, the unordered packets are first recompiled and put back into their original order before being delivered to your computer. Seems very simple, doesn't it? All the way through, the information in the header is activated at the nodes to ensure that the packets are not lost.

Even though the packet-switching technology is a more robust and efficient technology as opposed to the circuit-switched technology, the former technology does have certain disadvantages. If you re-create an image of the transmission of data on a packet-switched network, you'll realize that this network is a network of queues. A queue of incoming packets is lined up at each node before being sent out on an outgoing link. Bear this point in mind while briefly touching upon the drawbacks of a packet-switched network:

◆ In situations where packets from several incoming links share the same destination link, the rate of packet arrival at a node is greater than the rate of packet transmission. As a result of this mismatched rate of arrival and transmission, there is an increase in the length of a queue. The long and growing queue causes delay in transmission and queue overflow, aptly referred to as congestion. Congestion in networks causes loss of data packets. An attempt to recover the lost packets by retransmission only adds to the congestion leading to under-utilization of the network. A sheer waste of the core concept behind the robust and efficient working of a packet-switched network!

◆ To support real-time data transmissions, packet-switched networks require advanced control mechanisms to handle the buffer and the directional capacity of the packet switches and routers at the nodes. As a result, with an increase in the transmission capacity, there is also a sharp increase in the computer power that affects and complicates the ability of information processing.

What has been discussed so far (the basics behind the SS technology and the working of high-capacity networks) pertains to a behind-the-scenes glimpse of the technologies involved in successful data transmission in Bluetooth and other wireless devices..

The basic communication network during a TV transmission or the transmission of an alarm is a simplex service that provides one-way communication. However, another mode of communication that provides a two-way data transmission, as in telephones, is known as duplex communication. The following section discusses the schemes that facilitate such a two-way exchange of information between two devices. The schemes are called *duplexing* and include frequency division duplexing, time division duplexing, and adaptive time division duplexing.

Duplexing is a word used in engineering to define a system consisting of two independent sets of equipment, each having the ability to interact with the other in case of a system failure. The concept of duplexing is discussed in the context of telecommunications.

Duplexing

The past few years have seen significant changes in the way we access a network. To keep abreast of these changes and to maintain data connectivity, the need for higher bandwidth connections has intensified. Adding to the challenge is the call for mixing the frequency traffic containing video, voice, and data in a single infrastructure. In addition, network communication, like any other mode of communication, is a two-way cyclic mode that involves an incoming and outgoing exchange of information. However, a major drawback arises from the fact that a radio transreceiver cannot transmit data while it is in the receiving mode. In fact, this phenomenon is easy to comprehend by a simple example. All you need to do is answer this question: "During a conversation, do you talk and listen at the same time?" You don't, right? Radio transmission and reception works on similar lines. A radio, at any given time, is either transmitting or receiving information.

Continuous research by system designers and network architects developed a scheme that enables a two-way simultaneous exchange of information between two devices. This scheme, rightfully called duplexing in the world of telecommunications, is defined as the operation of transmission equipment such that there is a two-way communication or exchange of messages between two points.

The two types of duplex systems available for implementation of two-way, simultaneous communication are

- *Frequency Division Duplexing* (FDD), the traditional approach method, which divides the frequency for transmitting and receiving data.
- *Time Division Duplexing* (TDD), the access method for future broadband wireless devices, which uses the same frequency but divides the time for transmitting and receiving data.

The following sections explain each of these methods in detail.

Frequency Division Duplexing

The traditional implementation of duplexing in wireless devices carrying analog traffic used dedicated and separate frequency bands for upstream and downstream frequency traffic. This technique that transmits data by the orthogonal division of a frequency channel is called Frequency Division Duplexing.

An unused frequency block called the guard band divides the two equal up link and down link frequency bands. The up and down link segregation provided by the guard band ensures the smooth functioning of an FDD system. Figure 3-4 illustrates the band segregation in FDD.

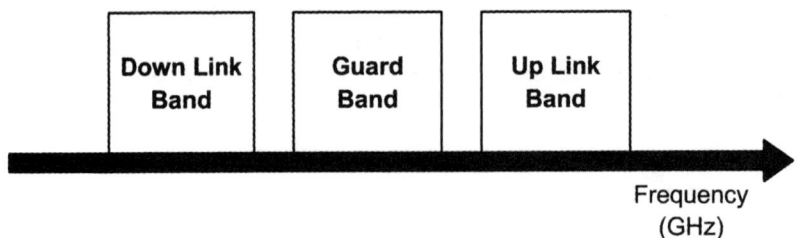

FIGURE 3-4 *The band segregation in FDD*

You'll recall that the allocation of frequency for wireless communication is the job of the FCC. How is the process of allocation different in the case of FDD implementation? Does the FDD framework consist of two links, one up and one down, along with an isolating band allocated under a single license? The prevalent practices for the allocation of bands to an FDD system are as follows:

◆ One of the methods used for band allocation is best explained by the example of the LMDS B band. This band consists of two 75-MHz blocks that are separated by a guard block measuring 150 MHz. The license allocated for the guard band, in this case, is separate. The advantage of this method of licensing is to have a guard band of one service provider function as the usable spectrum for the up and down link bands. This scheme, however, works only when there is a spatial separation between the two systems, a characteristic of point-to-point radio deployment.

◆ Another method is the one used by the *Conference of European Postal and Telecommunication Administration* (CEPT) that implements a totally different licensing method for the allocation of the guard and the up/down link bands. The licenses of multiple carriers are coordinated such that the guard band of each license pair is allocated to other carriers.

◆ Yet another method is that of block allocation. In this method, the carriers or service providers obtain licenses for blocks of frequencies for radio communication. However, for FDD implementation during two-way communication, the carrier is forced to dedicate a good portion of the allocated band for the guard band. Most of the time, these guard bands go unused. As a result, the block allocation method is a sheer waste of spectrum.

The multiple access scheme of fixed channel allocation in FDD is illustrated in Figure 3-5.

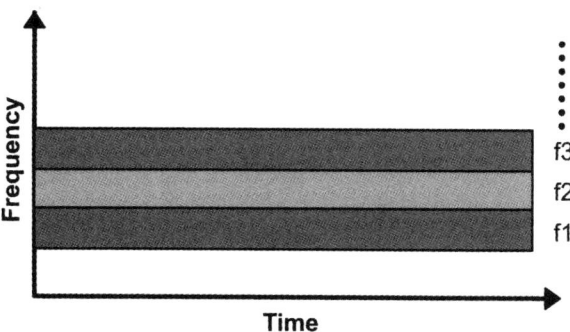

FIGURE 3-5 *The fixed channel allocation in FDD*

The next section discusses the advantages and disadvantages of using the FDD method. A study of its disadvantages will substantiate the strengths of the alternative technique of TDD, which is better accepted.

Advantages and Disadvantages of Using FDD

The advantages of using FDD are as follows:

◆ It uses narrow-band channels and not the channels of ISI.

◆ It shows low complexity.

◆ It allows continuous channel estimation and time transmission.

The disadvantages of using FDD are as follows:

◆ It requires multiple radios at the base station.

◆ It requires dedicated channels that mostly result in the wasting of idle ones.

◆ It requires the allocation of multiple channels per user.

FDD provides a simple duplex method for the transmission of a two-way signal for most applications designed for wireless voice communications in point-to-point, cellular, PCS, and satellite environments. However, the traditional approach of FDD loses out in the current mode of mixed (video, voice, and data) access between multiple points. An alternative to overcome the inefficiency of FDD is the emerging broadband wireless access method of *Time Division Duplexing* (TDD), which is discussed next.

Time Division Duplexing

The simultaneous two-way communication provided by duplexing can also be performed in time. This technique that transmits data by the orthogonal division of time, with different time slots assigned to different users, is called Time Division Duplexing. The transmitting and receiving of data in this technique operates on the same frequency channel but at different times at fixed intervals. The switch between the two functions is fast enough to preserve the simultaneous, two-way communication.

The multiple access scheme of high peak power in TDD is illustrated in Figure 3-6.

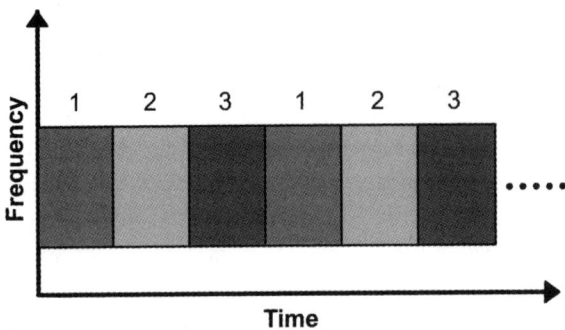

FIGURE 3-6 *The high peak power in TDD*

The low-cost, low-power platform support provided to carriers for base stations and Consumer Premise Equipments (CPEs) has indeed ensured the commercial acceptance of TDD. Therefore, it comes as no surprise that the technique used by TDD has been adopted in most communication systems throughout Japan and Europe. A very good example of such an implementation can be cited in *Personal Handyphone Service* (PHS) of Japan and *Digital European Cordless Telecommunications* (DECT).

TDD, by virtue of its advantages, has been able to perform well in the commercial wireless environment of mobile telephones. However, while discussing the advantages, you should also learn about a few disadvantages of using TDD.

Advantages and Disadvantages of Using TDD

The advantages of using TDD are as follows:

◆ It uses common radio equipment for all the users at the base station.
◆ It reduces power consumption and facilitates handoff due to non-continuous transmission.
◆ It allocates channels to multiple channels/users easily.
◆ It does not need a duplexer.

The disadvantages of using TDD are as follows:

◆ It requires synchronization.
◆ It uses multiple paths that destroy the orthogonality of slots.
◆ it requires ISI mitigation.

◆ It has the possibility of wasting idle channels.

◆ It makes equalization and dynamic resource allocation more difficult due to short transmissions.

Although TDD is, to a certain extent, an established technique for deployment in communication systems, there is abundant scope for further optimization of this technique for the delivery of video, voice, and data in fixed access methods. A more sophisticated application of TDD is the next generation broadband wireless access method, *Adapting Time Division Duplexing* (ATDD).

Adaptive Time Division Duplexing

Network access depends on the frequency traffic that is asymmetrical and varied in the case of broadband wireless devices. As a result, the adaptability of TDD for broadband wireless access can be increased to a large extent by implementing variations in the upstream and downstream bandwidth depending on the type of traffic. The Adaptive Time Division Duplexing (ATDD) method, developed by Ensemble communications based on the *Media Access Control* (MAC) protocol, made TDD more adaptable to varied frequency traffic. The sophisticated MAC protocol uses a MAC layer to automatically adjust the time spent by a link in transmitting and receiving information. The crux of this implementation is the capability of the MAC layer to maintain the appropriate amount of upstream and downstream traffic as required by a user. The operative algorithm used for this implementation tracks the patterns of the current traffic and the requests for new sessions. The up and down capacity of the bandwidth is then automatically adjusted to meet the requirements.

The advantages of using ATDD are as follows:

◆ **Reduces system cost.** The mechanism of maintaining a ratio of up-down traffic is implemented in the software. This largely helps to minimize the cost of the system.

◆ **Eliminates need for guard bands.** The implementation of ATDD does not require guard bands to segregate the upstream and downstream frequency traffic. Recall from the preceding discussion that the allocation of 200 to 300 MHz of spectrum for the guard band is a sheer waste of spectrum. In the case of block allocation for LMDS A and B bands, the use of ATDD can ensure substantial additional frequency saving.

◆ **Simplifies system design.** The radio frequency and modem components of the transmitting and receiving channels operate at the same frequency but at different times. As a result, in an ATDD system, components such as mixers, filters, and synthesizers are reused to eliminate the unnecessary complexity in design created by the frequency isolation approach (the guard bands of FDD systems). In addition, the ATDD system uses less expensive switches instead of the duplexer that reduces insertion loss.

◆ **Provides flexible systems.** ATDD systems do not need to adhere to any design specifications for the transmitting and receiving capabilities. In addition, because the need for guard bands is eliminated, these systems can be easily used for the allocation of different frequencies. If you were to implement the FDD technique for the allocation of different frequencies, the per-unit cost of each FDD system would increase. This is because each allocation would call for R&D changes and multiple systems would be needed for a particular license. Therefore, ATDD systems are more flexible systems that can cater to a large market segment with a single design.

Each of the concepts discussed so far constitutes a small but important part of the foundation for the implementation of the Bluetooth technology. In other words, it can be mapped to a string of pearls, in which each bead of pearl is an individual associated concept that together gel perfectly to form a string. Further on, you'll learn about the basic concepts that pertain to the data movement within a network during inter-computer communication. These concepts map to the functioning of any networking system except for changes in terminology and specification. The next section begins with a discussion on the *Open System Interconnection (OSI) Reference Model*, which is the primary architectural model for all inter-computer communication.

Revisiting the Open System Interconnection Reference Model

The design complexity of modern computer networks is greatly reduced by structuring the flow of information from one computer to another. This structuring is achieved by organizing the networks into a series of layers that are built vertically on top of each other.

The purpose and intent behind the OSI Reference Model is evident by mere expansion of the abbreviation. The OSI Reference Model specifies the standards for interconnection between open systems. The term "open system" refers to a system that is open to communication from all other systems that follow similar standards.

The International Organization of Standardization (ISO) developed the OSI model in 1984. On the lighter side, it is indeed a coincidence that OSI is simply spelling ISO backwards. Although an abstract model, ever since its inception, the OSI Reference Model earned acclaim as being a structured and practical introduction to easily explain the otherwise complicated concept of computer networking.

Understand that as information moves from one computer to another, various types of tasks are executed. These tasks can be further divided into seven manageable groups, each of which forms a layer of the OSI Reference Model.

The OSI Reference Model, therefore, consists of seven self-contained layers with specific tasks that can be implemented independently. The seven layers of the OSI Reference Model are

- **Layer 7 (L7), or the Application layer.** This layer makes up the user interface for providing various application services.
- **Layer 6 (L6), or the Presentation layer.** This layer provides conversion alternatives to eliminate differences in data representation.
- **Layer 5 (L5), or the Session layer.** This layer structures and organizes non-communication issues between application processes.
- **Layer 4 (L4), or the Transport layer.** This layer controls the transfer of data between systems by providing an end-to-end information exchange.
- **Layer 3 (L3), or the Network layer.** This layer relays and routes data between the users in a network.
- **Layer 2 (L2), or the Data Link layer.** This layer corrects transmission errors between adjacent nodes.
- **Layer 1 (L1), or the Physical layer.** This layer functions as the procedural mode for data transfer between network entities.

The seven layers of the OSI Reference Model are illustrated in Figure 3-7.

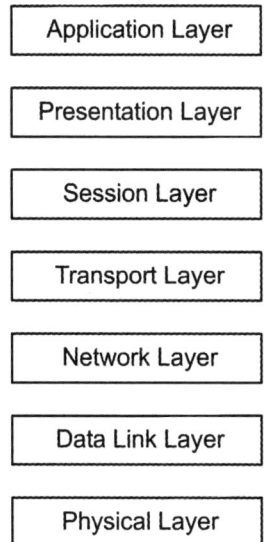

FIGURE 3-7 *The seven layers of the OSI Reference Model*

The following sections briefly discuss each of these layers.

The Application Layer

The functioning of the topmost layer or the Application layer is application-specific. In other words, the Application layer defines the level at which an application accesses the network services. The services provided by this layer are file transfer, network software services, e-mail, database access, and popular services such as Telnet and FTP.

The Presentation Layer

The Presentation layer is concerned with the syntax and semantics of the transmitted information instead of the transfer of bits from one computer to another. The Presentation layer provides services such as data encryption and compression for secure, authentic, and faster data transfer across the network.

The Session Layer

The Session layer helps to establish a session between the users on different machines. During a session there is a two-way traffic between the terminals. The Session layer provides dialog control by regulating and tracking the transmissions. It also synchronizes data by providing checkpoints in a data stream. Each of these checkpoints serves as a pointer to eliminate the need to repeat the entire process of data transfer in case of a crash.

The Transport Layer

The Transport layer primarily functions as a repackaging unit, accepting data from the Session layer, fragmenting it into packets, sending it over the network, and repackaging the packets at the receiver end. The receiving Transport layer also sends receipts signaling successful transmission. An added service provided by this layer is error recognition and data recovery.

The Network Layer

The Network layer controls the subnet network operations, such as determining the route from the source to the destination, managing traffic problems, and controlling network congestion. The Network layer also provides services such as message addressing by translating the logical message address and the name into the physical address. This service facilitates connections and data transfer between heterogeneous networks.

The Data Link Layer

The Data Link layer transforms raw transmission into a logical and structured line devoid of any transmission errors. This task is achieved by fragmenting the data from the sender into frames of a few hundred bytes, transmitting the frames sequentially, and providing acknowledgement frames from the receiver for successful transmission.

The Physical Layer

The Physical layer transmits and regulates a stream of raw bits over a communication channel. The intent behind this design is to ensure that for a transmission of 1-bit of data from one side, the receipt on the other side is also 1 bit and not 0 bit. The Physical layer is typically the domain of an electrical engineer concerned with issues such as the choice of the physical transmission medium and the mechanical, procedural, and electrical interfaces lying below the Physical layer.

Based on the issues handled, the seven layers of the OSI Reference Model can also be broadly categorized into the following two categories:

◆ The Upper Layers, consisting of the Application layer, the Presentation layer, and the Session layer. The upper layers are implemented in the software and, therefore, relate to all application issues. Of the three layers, the Application layer is closest to the end user.

 NOTE

The higher layers of the OSI model are also, sometimes, referred to as upper layers. The only difference lies in the context in which the term is used.

◆ The Lower Layers, consisting of the Network layer, the Data Link layer, and the Physical layer. These layers primarily handle issues related to the transport of data. The Physical layer and the Data Link layer are implemented in both the hardware and software, while the Network layer is implemented only in the software.

The OSI model is the conceptual architecture of the communication framework used during inter-computer communication. However, bear in mind that this architecture is not the method used for communication. In fact, a formal set of rules governs the exchange of information over a network. This set of rules called protocols defines a common technical language for standardizing communication. Most of the protocols used in networking can be identified as

◆ The LAN protocols that define communication within a *Local Area Network* (LAN) and operate at the Network and Data Link layers of the OSI model.

◆ The WAN protocols that define communication within a *Wide Area Network* (WAN) setup and operate at the lower layers of the OSI model.

◆ The routing protocols that determine the path for packet transmission, are responsible for traffic switching, and operate at the Network layer of the OSI model.

◆ The network protocols that are upper layer protocols and exist in the form of a protocol suite.

Inter-System Communication Using the OSI Model

The information that is transferred between the computers within a network essentially passes through each layer of the OSI model. As an example of the flow of information through the seven layers of the OSI model, consider a detective agency that needs to send confidential data to its counterpart operating from London. Each movement of the data from one office to another, including all the check posts it passes, represents the functioning of a layer of the OSI model. For this reason, the example uses numeric addressing in the form of first floor, second floor, and so on to represent the OSI model layers.

The message leaves the seventh floor (the location of the detective agency), which can be associated with the user terminal or the Application layer that denotes the source of the information. On the sixth floor, the Presentation layer, the message is translated to an intermediary language, compressed for faster delivery, and encrypted to maintain its confidentiality. On the fifth floor, the Session layer, the message is checked for completeness and checkpoints are created in the message to ensure that no part is lost during transmission. In addition, at the receiving end, the checkpoints can be used to verify the receipt of the entire message. Next, on the fourth floor, the Transport layer, the size of the message is analyzed to find out if it can be appended to another message for the same destination. If the message is too big despite compression, it is broken further into smaller packages or packets. Such a methodology facilitates faster transfer of a message by using multiple personnel for the packets to be reassembled at the client end. On the third floor, the Network layer, the address of the destination is checked and suggestions are drawn for the fastest route of transmission. On the second floor, the Data Link layer, the message is put into a tamper-proof special pouch or packet. The information in the pouch consists of a slip (the header) containing the message and the IDs of the sender and the receiver. On the first floor, the Physical layer, the packet containing the message is handed over to Mr. X for its journey to London. On reaching London, the entire process of the message movement is reversed and it is finally handed over to the destined addressee. In London, the flow of information will obviously begin from the first floor and end at the seventh floor. Seems very simple, doesn't it? Actually, it is the simple structuring of the OSI model that helps to easily explain the complex inter-system communication.

The layer-wise transfer of data in the OSI model is illustrated in Figure 3-8.

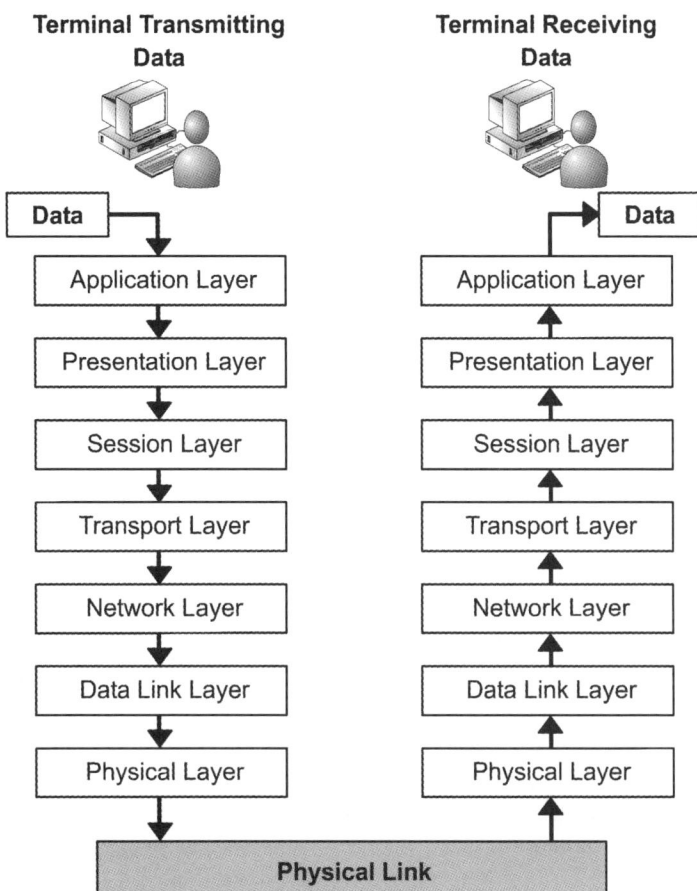

FIGURE 3-8 *The layer wise flow of information in the OSI model*

From the preceding discussion, you'll easily understand that the architecture for data transfer in Bluetooth technology also consists of layers. These conceptual layers can be used to easily explain the structure and design of communication in Bluetooth devices. The strongest feature of Bluetooth technology is its capability to facilitate communication between devices from different manufacturers. The radio is not the only element within the system that assists in communication between such diverse devices. In fact, a Bluetooth system also defines a protocol stack that helps to identify other Bluetooth devices.

The Bluetooth Protocol Stack

Just like the broad classification of the OSI model into upper and lower layers, the Bluetooth protocol stack can be logically partitioned into the following groups, each containing different protocol layers:

◆ **The transport protocol group.** The transport protocol group facilitates the identification of other Bluetooth devices. It also configures and manages the physical and logical links, allowing the higher protocol layers to transmit data through these layers.

◆ **The middleware protocol group.** The middleware protocol group provides additional transport protocols that help new and existing applications to operate over Bluetooth links. It consists of both third-party and industry standard Internet–related protocols and the protocols defined by the *Special Interest Group* (SIG) for wireless communication in Bluetooth devices. The third-party and industrial protocols include protocols such as PPP, IP, and TCP, while the protocols defined by SIG consist of three protocols. The first, a serial port emulator called RFCOMM, allows legacy applications to operate effortlessly over the Bluetooth transport protocols. The second, a packet-based telephony control signaling protocol, facilitates advanced telephony operations. The third, a service discovery protocol, as the name suggests, helps Bluetooth devices to ascertain the services available on other devices to decide on the mode of access for those services.

◆ **The application group.** The application group includes the actual applications that use Bluetooth links. This group may consist of the applications aware of the Bluetooth wireless communication such as those using the telephony control protocol for the control of telephone equipment. Another group of applications could include the applications that are unaware of Bluetooth transports, such as a Web browsing client.

For better conceptual understanding, the following sections briefly discuss the features and specifications of each of these layers as a quick preview to understand the functioning of the different layers in Bluetooth.

The Transport Protocol Group

The organization of the protocol groups in the transport protocol layer developed by SIG facilitates the movement of voice and data traffic between Bluetooth devices. The layers of this protocol group support the transmission of both synchronous and asynchronous data. Based on the placement of the different protocol layers, the transport protocol group can be further categorized into two groups. The first group or the lower transport protocol group consists of the radio, the baseband, the Link Controller (LC), and the *Link Manager* (LM). The second group or the upper transport group consists of the *Host Control Interface* (HCI), and the *Logical Link Control and Adaptation Protocol* (L2CAP). As is evident from the explanation in the preceding sections, during inter-system communication, the direction of the transmitting traffic is routed from the upper layers to the lower layers. On the receiving end, the traffic movement is reversed and flows from the lower layers to the upper layers. The layers of the transport protocol group work together and form a virtual pipe that is used to transport data from one device to another.

The next chapters primarily discuss each of the individual layers of the transport protocol stack in detail, which logically defines the Bluetooth architecture. Before moving further, study the illustration of the Bluetooth protocol stack, shown in Figure 3-9.

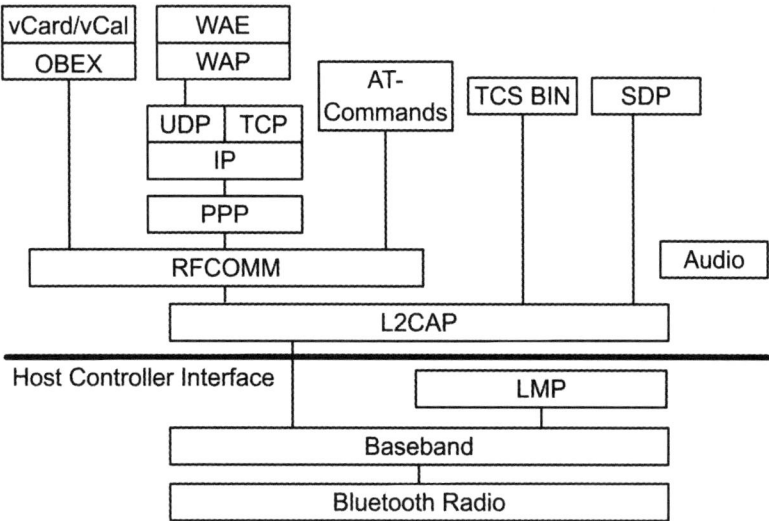

FIGURE 3-9 *The Bluetooth protocol stack*

Radio inside Bluetooth

Chapter 2 discussed the features, the requirement specifications, and the working of the various elements of the radio. This section, however, discusses the specification of the Bluetooth radio. The specification for the Bluetooth radio is mostly in the form of design specification for the transreceiver, such as its in-band and out-of-band spurious emissions, inter-modulation characteristics, frequency accuracy, and adjacent and co-channel interference. The intent of such a design specification is to ensure the development of a transreceiver to comply with the global 2.4 GHz ISM band regulations.

Because DSSS systems are relatively costlier for the low-cost requirement of Bluetooth radios, the Bluetooth radio is mostly an FHSS radio system. The ISM frequency available for the 2,400.0 to 2,483.5 GHz band specified for the Bluetooth radio operates over 79 frequency channels.

The key operations in a Bluetooth radio include a pair of logical interfaces to carry the following:

◆ **Data.** The data includes the transmitting and receiving information.

◆ **Control information.** The control information includes the information that controls the behavior of the radio. When transmitting data, the control information contains the carrier frequency that the transmitter needs to tune to before transmitting the bit stream. It also includes the power level to be used for the transmission. On the other hand, when receiving data, the control information contains the carrier frequency that the receiver needs to tune to before receiving the bit stream. It also contains the strength of the receiving signal, which is an optional inclusion.

The key operation of a Bluetooth radio helps the manufacturers to determine the best solution for the integration of the radio with the rest of the components and to design the Bluetooth chip so that it is a low-cost, power-efficient system. Table 3-1 lists the key operational parameters of the Bluetooth radio.

Table 3-1 The Key Operational Parameters of a Bluetooth Radio

Parameter	Specification	Additional Details
Transmit power	Class 3: 1 Mw (0 dBm)	Specification for a typical Bluetooth radio, optional power control that is below −30 dBm
	Class 2: 2.5 Mw (4 dBm)	Optional power control that is below −30 dBm
	Class 4: 100 Mw (20 dBm)	Requires power control of at least 4 dBm and optional power control that is below −30 dBm
Receiver sensitivity	A Bluetooth receiver should have a raw bit error rate 0.1 percent with input signal level of −70 dBm or lower.	A sensitivity level of −70 dBm should be achieved for an input signal generated by a compliant Bluetooth transmitter.
Frequency hopping rate	1,600 hops per second	Specification for a typical Bluetooth radio with residence time of 625 µsec/hop.
Modulation	Gaussian Frequency	Modulation index of 0.28 to 0.35 Shift-Keying (GFSK)
Symbol rate	1 Msymbol per second	Achieved by using the binary GFSK translating to a 1 mbps raw link speed with a bit transmission time of 1 µsec

NOTE

The suggested lower power limit (P_{min}) of < 30 dBm is not mandatory.

The radio in a Bluetooth system helps to transmit and receive data over the air. You know now that communicating Bluetooth devices form a PAN or a piconet during a communication session. Which layer of the Bluetooth protocol stack is responsible for functions such as piconet and device control? And what about details such as maintaining information related to the transmitted data, the details of the carrier frequency, and the strength of the transmission power? Well, these are the responsibility of the baseband protocol and the *Link Controller* (LC). Because of the rather ambiguous use of these two protocols in the Bluetooth specification, I would at this point first like to bring out the not so explicitly demarcated difference between the baseband and LC protocols. The LC protocol executes the low-level link routines and processes related to the baseband communication protocol. The baseband protocol, on the other hand, serves to provide specifications for the digital processing of the LC and performs functions that are discussed next.

Baseband

The baseband layer is responsible for the determination and instantiation of the air interface by defining processes to identify other devices and establish connectivity between them. In other words, once a session between two devices is established, the key functions performed by the baseband include connection creation, selection of a frequency-hopping sequence, timing hops, operations related to power control and security, and packet functions such as polling, packet processing, and the selection of link types.

The baseband provides channels for the transmission of frequency traffic consisting of voice and data. It also supports one asynchronous data link and a maximum of three synchronous voice links.

Link Management in Bluetooth

The Link Manager (LM) performs all the functions related to link management. These functions include operations such as supervising device pairing, link setup, link authentication, and link configuration. Communication is established between two LMs when they discover each other. The LM uses the services of the LC to establish such a communication aided by the *Link Manager Protocol* (LMP). The LM defines the properties of the Bluetooth air interface between the devices. To mediate the functioning between the LM and the LC, the LMP, in turn, uses the underlying baseband services to aid the LM in establishing a connection with other remote LMs.

Some other essential functions performed by the LM include authentication, initiating an inquiry to obtain a remote device's link address, requesting the name of a remote device, determining the packet-to-packet frame type, and negotiating the type of connection and limit to be set (ACL or SCO).

Host Controller Interface

The radio, the baseband, and the LM are mostly packaged together into a module that is attached to a host device. A device fitted with such a module is able to communicate wirelessly using Bluetooth protocols. The host, in turn, contains the L2CAP layer and some layers of the higher protocol. The physical interface between the host and the module, called the host transport, includes layers such as _Universal Serial Bus_ (USB), _RS-232_, and _UART_. Most LC hardware contains a firmware layer, the Host Controller Interface (HCI), which segregates the baseband layer and the LM from the host transport protocols. As a result, the HCI acts as a standard interface between a Bluetooth application and the transport protocols.

Developed to aid interoperability between host devices and the Bluetooth module, the HCI layer functions as a standard interface allowing the higher layers of the protocol stack access the baseband layer, Link Manager, and other hardware registers. However, the advantage of using the HCI is that the Bluetooth application can access the Bluetooth hardware without involving either the Transport layer or other hardware components.

The Logical Control and Adaptation Protocol

The L2CAP layer shields the higher protocol layers from the operational intricacies of the lower protocol layer. L2CAP supports the sharing of the air interface between multiple protocols and applications, a technique known as _protocol multiplexing_. It is also responsible for the segmentation of large data packets into smaller ones and the reassembly of these packets by the receiving device.

Bear in mind that the LM uses the LMP to set up an ACL link that is always available between a master and a slave within a piconet. This link provides a point-to-multipoint link that supports the transfer of data over both an ACL and an SCO link. The L2CAP, like the LMP, uses the baseband services to operate over an ACL link. An inevitable question that will cross your mind is How does the baseband differentiate between an LMP packet and an L2CAP packet? Contrary to the L2CAP packet, the ACL payload of the LMP packet contains a bit in the header and is always sent as a single slot. In addition, the priority set for LMP packets is always higher than that of the L2CAP packet. This identification method ensures that the integrity of data is always maintained during data transmission.

L2CAP transmits data in the form of packets over L2CAP channels, which in turn provide various services to the upper-level protocol layers. Each L2CAP channel contains two end points called _Logical Channel Identifiers_ (CID). As a result, each CID may represent a channel end point for the following three types of channels to facilitate a connection between a local L2CAP entity and a group of remote devices:

◆ **Signaling channels.** Signaling channels are bi-directional commands carrying signals that are required between two L2CAP entities before a communication begins. An L2CAP entity, therefore, has one signaling end point with a reserved CID of 0X0001 that is used by all signal channels between the L2CAP entity and remote devices.

◆ **Connection-oriented channels.** The connection-oriented channels are for point-to-point, bi-directional connections. A connection-oriented channel contains a dynamically allocated local CID. All connection-oriented channels should be connected to a single channel, configured before the start of the data transfer. On the initiation of data transfer, the connection-oriented CID is bound to a specific upper-level protocol to establish and negotiate a Quality of Service (QoS) agreement for each configured channel. A QoS includes negotiations for parameters such as data flow (peak bandwidth determination) and the transmission type (best effort, guaranteed, or no traffic).

◆ **Connectionless channels.** Connectionless channels are unidirectional channels for point-to-multipoint connections that are used to form groups. A single outgoing connectionless CID is dynamically allocated and is usually connected to several remote devices, which together form a logical group. Each L2CAP entity contains a single incoming connectionless CID for all the incoming data that is fixed at 0X0002. Because these channels are connectionless and do not need to be configured, all configuration-related information from the upper-level channels is passed as a part of the data packet.

The Middleware Protocol Group

The protocol layers of the middleware protocol group define a standard protocol for establishing direct communication between the layers of the high-level and low-level transport protocols. The layers of the middleware protocol group include the following:

◆ The RFCOMM transport protocol that provides serial data transfers

◆ *Service Depository Protocol* (SDP) that locates the needed services and also describes the available services

◆ A set of IrDA protocols of the IrDA standard that facilitates the use of IrDA-enabled applications

◆ A set of networking protocols such as *Telephony Control Protocol* (TCS), TCS-BIN, telephone control AT commands, and other adapted protocols

The layers of the middleware protocol group are discussed next.

Cable Replacement Protocol (RFCOMM)

The protocol stack of Bluetooth defines a protocol called RFCOMM that provides an emulation of serial port communication. The RFCOMM protocol is a subset of the *European Telecommunications Standard Institute* (ETSI) standard TS 07.10 with certain adaptations that are specified in the Bluetooth RFCOMM specification. As a virtual serial port to applications, RFCOMM facilitates the easy migration of applications developed for cable communication into the new and fascinating domain of wireless serial communication.

The RFCOMM protocol is capable of up to 60 simultaneous and implementation-specific connections between Bluetooth devices. Like a standard wired serial port, applications can use RFCOMM to carry out functions such as synchronization and dial-up networking. The RFCOMM protocol can, therefore, be used by serial port-based legacy applications to use Bluetooth transports.

Service Depository Protocol

Traditional networks such as LANs and Ethernets establish network services by using static configurations that are managed by the system administrator. However, Bluetooth links between devices are created spontaneously and, therefore, require a more dynamic method of configuration service to establish and determine the services available to the devices. The Bluetooth Service Discovery Protocol (SDP) comes across as a boon in disguise for the dynamic ad hoc networks created by Bluetooth wireless communication. SDP defines a standard method for Bluetooth devices to determine the services available on a particular device.

A Bluetooth device can work as an SDP client querying for services, an SDP server providing services for requested services, or as both an SDP client and an SDP server. A single Bluetooth device can have a single server but may be a client to several remote devices.

The Networking Protocols

The network topology in Bluetooth wireless communication is a peer-to-peer network rather than a LAN network. In addition, dial-up networking and connections via network access points are used for connections to larger networks. The accessed network, usually an IP network, uses standard Internet protocols such as TCO, UDP, and HTTP to create interactions between devices within the network.

In addition, a device may use a network access point described in the LAN access using *Point-to Point Protocol* (PPP) profile to connect to an IP network. In such a case, the Bluetooth device first connects to the network access point, which in turn connects to a larger wireless network. The Internet PPP is used to connect to the network access point.

The next sections explain some of the protocols used for creating networks in Bluetooth.

Bluetooth Telephony Control (TCS) Specifications

The *Bluetooth Telephony Control* (TCS) specifications support all telephony functions such as call control and group management. TCS is used to specify the call parameters and is compatible with the International Telecommunications Union-Telecommunication (ITU-T) Q.931 specification. The TCS protocols use binary encoding and are, therefore, referred to as TCS-BIN. During the development of the specification by the SIG, a second protocol, the TCS-AT, was defined to specify a protocol flowing through the RFCOMM layer to perform modem control functions using the AT commands. AT commands of the middleware protocol stack are used to establish a connection to a network using dial-up networking. Although some devices do use applications that define the AT commands over RFCOMM, there is no separate definition for TCS-AT in the Bluetooth Specification 1.0.

The TCS-BIN protocol facilitates call control functions, group management functions, and call signaling functions. The method used for call signaling in Bluetooth exchanges call signaling information without having to make a call connection.

Audio communication in Bluetooth takes place at a rate of 64 kilobits per second. Bluetooth audio traffic is asynchronous and uses a bi-directional route to and from the baseband layer. Bear in mind that this audio traffic does not go through the upper layers, such as the L2CAP layer. The audio traffic is transmitted in special baseband packets called *Synchronous Connection-Oriented* (SCO) packets.

TCP/IP

The TCP/IP protocol suite was developed by a group of researchers of the *Department of Defense* (DOD) during its research on ARPAnet. The research was aimed at connecting diverse networks designed by various vendors to the Internet. The success of this project was primarily due to the offered services such as file transfer, electronic mail, and remote logon.

The TCP/IP protocol suite consists of two protocol layers: the *Transmission Control Protocol* (TCP) and the *Internet Protocol* (IP). The TCP/IP protocols facilitate resource sharing across computes in a network. The TCP protocol is used for reliable network communications. It keeps track of the information that flows within a network and is, therefore, responsible for functions, such as retransmission in case of non-receipt of data and resegmenting large packets into smaller packets. The IP protocol, on the other hand, provides basic services to ensure that the data packets reach their destination. The primary functions of the TCP and IP protocols can be summarized as follows:

- ◆ **TCP.** The primary function of the TCP layer is to ensure that data is delivered from the source (client) to the destination (server). Because the chance of data loss during the transmission is high, TCP facilitates detection of data errors and triggers retransmission so that data is successfully received at the destination.

- ◆ **IP.** The primary function of the IP layer is to support data transmission between the nodes of a network. Each data packet is identified by a 4-bit destination address called the IP number.

The Application Group

The application group includes the software that is located above the middleware protocol stack, as defined by the SIG. This software is supplied by manufacturers or software vendors and is primarily used to instantiate Bluetooth profiles. A profile instantiation helps to drive the protocol stack and carry out functions such as file transfers, dial-up networking, and headset communications. Although the SIG does define the specifications for the transport and middleware protocol group, there is no defined specification for the programming interface or the API. However, a Bluetooth device does need such interfaces to define the usage scenarios (profiles) for wireless communication. As a result, an application code was added to the underlying protocol stack that together define the application protocol.

The profiles defined by the application protocol define the baseline for the use of the protocol stack and, therefore, make devices interoperable. This is particularly true in the case of Bluetooth, which uses a variety of devices operating on different platforms. The application protocol layer provides the programming API for a whole range of products irrespective of their make or operating platform.

The SIG has currently chosen profiles to serve as guidance for developing applications on Bluetooth-relevant platforms. Because the incorporation of technology on a platform calls for the use of APIs, it is best to have platform experts develop the APIs rather than have them developed by technology experts. This is the very reason why SIG has chosen to define the profiles as guidelines for the development of APIs instead of developing APIs for Linux, Windows, or Symbian.

In the 1960s, an interesting development in the computing scene was the advent of the Internet, which brought into our lives the concept of information being available anytime and anywhere. With the demand for making verbal communication also available at anytime and anywhere, what followed was the concept of the wireless mobile phone. This was subsequently followed by the introduction of the *Wireless Application Protocol* (WAP), which amalgamated the services of the Internet with that of the mobile phones. Although not directly related, Bluetooth and WAP share the same thought and intent of wireless communication. A lot of concepts in both WAP and Bluetooth show parallelism, which is why this session ends with a quick run-through on WAP and the structure of its protocol stack.

WAP

Mobile telecommunication needs no introduction. Most people carry mobile phones for improved accessibility and availability to communication while traveling. WAP is a communication protocol that allows wireless devices, such as mobile phones, *Personal Data Assistants* (PDAs), and two-way pagers to connect to the Internet. WAP is the result of the efforts of the *WAP Forum*, which includes companies such as, Phone.com (originally called Unwired Planet), Nokia, and Ericsson. In 1997, the WAP Forum came out with an open standard defining an industry-wide specification for developing applications over wireless communication networks. This specification, like the Bluetooth specification, defines a set of protocols to help manufacturers, operators, and service providers of WAP to meet the challenges in advanced wireless communication.

The WAP architecture consists of the following components:

◆ Protocol stack

◆ Bearer service

◆ Other services and applications

◆ WAP gateway

Figure 3-10 displays the various components of the WAP architecture.

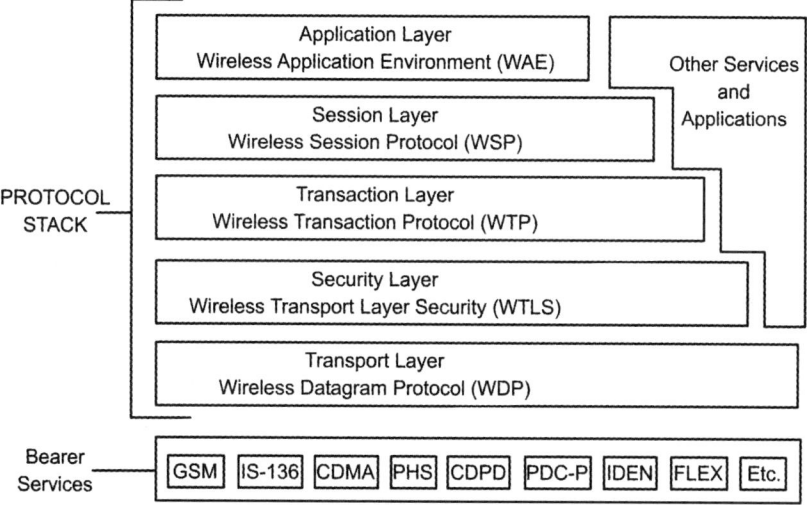

FIGURE 3-10 *The components of WAP architecture*

These components are discussed next.

Protocol Stack

WAP protocols are designed to overcome the constraints of wireless devices such as narrow bandwidth, low memory space, and low battery life. It is a layered communication stack in which each protocol in the stack is accessible to other protocols above or below it. The protocol stack consists of the following layers:

- *Wireless Application Environment* (WAE)
- *Wireless Session Protocol* (WSP)
- *Wireless Transaction Protocol* (WTP)
- *Wireless Transport Layer Security* (WTLS)
- *Wireless Datagram Protocol* (WDP)

Wireless Application Environment

WAE is the application layer that includes all the elements required for the development and execution of WAP applications. WAE forms the *Application layer* of the WAP architecture. It includes a software environment that enables developers to build interactive WAP applications. The main aim of WAE is to provide an interoperable environment to build efficient and platform-independent applications and services.

Wireless Session Protocol

WSP is the session layer that provides exchange of data between applications. The WSP forms the *Sessions layer* of the WAP architecture. This layer allows organized exchange of data between the client and the server. It links WAE to the following two session services:

- Connection-oriented session service that operates over Wireless Transaction Protocol (WTP). Session services are the functionalities that set up a connection between the client and the server. These session services provide facilities to manage a session and transmit reliable data between the client and the server. Reliable data is that which confirms a request or receipt for a particular service. In other words, the client as well as the server receives an acknowledgment for a request sent and received.
- Connectionless session service that operates above Wireless Datagram Protocol (WDP). The connectionless session service provides unreliable, non-confirmed services, for which the acknowledgment of data transfer is not provided.

Wireless Session Protocols offer services that are most suited for browsing applications. Some of the common features of this layer are long-lived sessions, a common facility for data push, capability negotiation, and session suspend/resume. The protocols in the WSP family are optimized for low-bandwidth bearer networks with relatively longer latency.

Wireless Transaction Protocol

WTP is the layer that provides reliable transmission of WSP data between a client and a server. WTP forms the *Transaction layer* of the WAP architecture. This layer runs on top of the WDP layer or an optional WTLS layer and is responsible for delivering higher-layer messages. WTP offers the following three classes of transaction service:

◆ Unreliable one-way requests

◆ Reliable one-way requests

◆ Reliable two-way requests

Transaction services define how messages are to be transmitted and received. In an unreliable one-way request, no retransmission of messages takes place to compensate for the loss of data during the transmission. In a reliable one-way request, the recipient acknowledges the receipt of a message sent. If the recipient fails to acknowledge the message, the message is sent again. In the reliable two-way request, the recipient as well as the initiator of the message acknowledges receipt of the message.

Wireless Transport Layer Security

WTLS is the security layer that provides privacy, server and client authentication, and data integrity. WTLS forms the *Security layer* of the WAP architecture. It is an optional layer that provides the main security elements to the WAP network. It is a wireless version of the industry standard *Transport Layer Security* (TLS), which is equivalent to *Secure Sockets Layer* (SSL).

In the Web architecture, financial and confidential information was not very secure without the implementation of SSL. Data could be easily read during the transmission. SSL solved this problem by delivering data in an encrypted form and, therefore, made data available only to entrusted users. Since WTLS is based on SSL, all the functionalities of SSL are incorporated in the Security layer of the WAP architecture. WTLS also minimizes the overhead of establishing a secure connection between a client and a server. In addition to this, it reduces the transaction time and provides client-server authentication, thus implementing data integrity.

Wireless Datagram Protocol

WDP is the transport layer that specifies how bearer services, such as SMS, CSD, CDPD, and GPRS, should be used to provide consistent service to the upper layers. Bearer services help to establish connections between wireless devices and the WAP gateway. WDP forms the *Transport layer* of the WAP architecture. This layer is the lowest layer in the protocol stack. It isolates the higher layers from the bearer-specific network details and, therefore, provides transparent communication between applications and bearer services.

Bearer Services

Wireless devices need to establish a connection with the WAP gateway to send data to a Web server and receive data from a Web server. A *bearer service*, therefore, acts as the communication path between a WAP device and a WAP gateway. Some examples of bearer services are GSM and CDPD. In GSM networks, you can either use *Short Message Service* (SMS) or *Circuit-Switched Data* (CSD) to connect a WAP device to the WAP gateway. GSM stands for Global System for Mobile communication. A digital mobile telephone system is used to digitize and compress data that is transferred over the network.

WAP is independent of all the available bearer services. The WAP architecture is an optimal design that caters to different bearer services. Although each bearer service offers a different level of quality with respect to the output, delays, and error rates, the layers of the WAP protocol stack remain the same, regardless of the type of bearer service that is used.

Following are some of the bearer services with a brief description of their functionality:

- **Short Message Service (SMS).** This is a text message service that sends and receives short messages of 106 to 140 characters on a mobile device.
- **Circuit-Switched Data (CSD).** This is a communication technology that provides the data speed of 9600 bps.
- **General Packet Radio Switching (GPRS).** This is a wireless communication service that provides continuous connection to the Internet for mobile phones and computer users. It operates at a speed that ranges from 56 to 114 kbps. For a GPRS connection, the subscriber charges are based on the volume of data transferred rather than the duration of a connection.
- **Time Division Multiple Access (TDMA).** This is a communication technology that transmits digital wireless signals by allocating unique time slots to each user on each channel.
- **Code Division Multiple Access (CDMA).** This is a wireless transmission technology that is used for services such as digital wireless personal communications and secure military calls.

Other Services and Applications

The WAP architecture facilitates other services and applications to use the components of the WAP architecture. These services and applications are the services that were available on a mobile phone before the advent of WAP. This implies that WAP is independent in itself. When operating, it does not interfere with any other application or service that is available on the mobile phone.

WAP Gateway

A WAP gateway forms a bridge between the wireless environment and the Internet. Information in the Internet scenario is stored on Web servers. Web servers understand the HTTP protocol, which is not included in the WAP protocol suite. The WAP client (i.e. the micro-browser) uses a protocol called WSP to retrieve information from the server. This prevents the WAP client from downloading information from a Web server.

As a result, the WAP gateway plays the role of translating the WSP request into an HTTP request and sending it to the appropriate Web server. The functions of the WAP gateway are

◆ **WSP to HTTP protocol conversion.** The request from a WAP device to a WAP gateway travels using the WSP protocol. The WAP gateway converts this protocol request into an HTTP request that is understood by Web servers.

◆ **CODEC functionality.** The coder/decoder (CODEC) functionality is a feature of WAP gateway that converts the WML and WMLScript content into a compact bytecode form that is optimized for low-bandwidth devices. During this process of conversion, the gateway also checks the WML contents for errors. The conversion of the data takes place in the memory of the gateway and not on the secondary storage medium, such as hard disk, which ensures that no data is accessible to others on the gateway. Therefore, security of data is maintained.

◆ **Security.** A WAP gateway provides security with the help of WTLS protocol. WTLS encrypts data and makes it available to entrusted users only. However, the raw form of data in the gateway memory is a major security gap for unauthorized access.

Summary

The importance of an organized structure to define the protocol stack provides a base for explaining the otherwise complicated working of wireless devices. Taking the cue from this fact, this chapter discussed the foundational supporting technology of Spread Spectrum, which defines the frequency manipulations in the noisy ISM band.

A major part of this chapter briefly discussed the overall structure and working of the Bluetooth protocol stack. You learned of concepts such as duplexing, which facilitates the two-way transfer of heterogeneous frequency traffic. As a first step towards understanding the concept of protocols, you learned about the various layers of the OSI Reference Model that define the architecture of any network system. Thereafter, you learned about the various layers of the Bluetooth protocol stack and the relationship between each of them. In the final sections of the chapter, you learned about the architecture of WAP, which is yet another mode of wireless communications using protocol layers for network communication.

This is just the beginning of the journey that'll take you deep into the intricacies of Bluetooth devices and their functioning. Rest assured, the next few chapters talk in depth about each of the different protocol layers of the protocol groups.

Check Your Understanding

Multiple Choice Questions

1. Which of the following operational modes of SS technology generate a redundant bit pattern or a chip code?
    a. DSSS
    b. FHSS
    c. THSS

2. Which of the following are the lower layers of the transport protocol group?
    a. HCI
    b. L2CAP
    c. LM
    d. LC
    e. Radio
    f. Baseband

3. Which of the following are the layers of the WAP protocol stack?
    a. WAP Gateway
    b. Bearer services
    c. WAE
    d. WSP
    e. WTP
    d. WDP

Short Questions

1. What are the characteristics of the SS technology?
2. What are the advantages of using circuit-switched networks?
3. What does a data packet contain?
4. Write short notes on the characteristics of the following technologies:
    a. Time Division Duplexing
    b. The layers of the OSI Reference model
    c. RFCOMM

Answers

Multiple Choice Answers

1. a.   DSSS.
2. c, d, e, and f. LM, LC, radio, and baseband.
3. c, d, e, f, and g. WAE, WSP, WTLS, WTP, and WDP.

Short Answers

1. The characteristics of SS technology are:
    ◆ The noise-like SS signals use a wide-band for transmission and are, therefore, hard to detect. The band of transmission is intentionally made wider than the information to induce the noise-like feature in the signal.
    ◆ SS signals are harder to jam due to *Low Probability of Intercept* (LPI) and *Anti-Jam* (AJ).
    ◆ PN codes generated by the SS signals are faster than the information bandwidth or data rate.
    ◆ The transmit power level of SS transmitters is similar to that of narrow-band transmitters. Wider SS signals, however, transmit at a lower density than narrow-band transmitters. As a result, both Spread and narrow-band signals occupy the same band creating little or no interference for each other.

2. The advantages of using circuit-switched networks are:
    ◆ Transmission of large amounts of data
    ◆ Guaranteed transmission capacity
    ◆ Separate control signaling and transfer of payload data
    ◆ Execution of control information processing and control signaling (routing) mainly at circuit setup and termination

3. A data packet consists of:
    ◆ The address of the destination
    ◆ The size of the packets
    ◆ The sequence of the packets
    ◆ Error-checking information
    ◆ Payload data

4. a. **Time Division Duplexing.** The simultaneous two-way communication pro-
        vided by duplexing can also be performed in time. This technique that trans-
        mits data by the orthogonal division of time, with different time slots
        assigned to different users, is called Time Division Duplexing. The transmit-
        ting and receiving of data in this technique operates on the same frequency
        channel but at different times at fixed intervals. The switch between the two
        functions is fast enough to preserve the simultaneous, two-way communica-
        tion.

    b. **The layers of the OSI Reference Model.** The OSI Reference Model earned
        acclaim as being a structured and practical introduction to easily explain the
        otherwise complicated concept of computer networking. The seven layers of
        the OSI Reference Model include:

    ◆ **Layer 7 (L7), or the Application layer.** This layer makes up the user inter-
      face for providing various application services.

    ◆ **Layer 6 (L6), or the Presentation layer.** This layer provides conversion
      alternatives to eliminate differences in data representation.

    ◆ **Lsayer 5 (L5), or the Session layer.** This layer structures and organizes
      non-communication issues between application processes.

    ◆ **Layer 4 (L4), or the Transport layer.** This layer controls the transfer of
      data between systems by providing an end-to-end information exchange.

    ◆ **Layer 3 (L3), or the Network layer.** This layer relays and routes data
      between the users in a network.

    ◆ **Layer 2 (L2), or the Data Link layer.** This layer corrects transmission
      errors between adjacent nodes.

    ◆ **Layer 1 (L1), or the Physical layer.** This layer functions as the procedural
      mode for data transfer between network entities.

PART II

Bluetooth—
A Technical Insight

Chapter 4

Baseband

As mentioned in the preceding chapter, the Bluetooth protocol stack is categorized as the transport protocol group, the middleware protocol group, and the application group. From this chapter on, the book delves deeper into the concepts related to the individual layers of the transport protocol group. The lowest layer of the transport protocol group is the radio layer (covered in Chapter 2, "Introduction to Radio," and more specifically in the context of Bluetooth in Chapter 3, "Architecture of Bluetooth"). Therefore, this chapter moves straight to the second lowest protocol layer—the baseband layer.

The baseband layer and the radio layer can be functionally correlated to the Physical layer of the OSI Reference Model. From the brief discussion on baseband in the previous chapter, you can visualize this layer as an intermediary channel between the radio layer and the upper layers of the transport protocol group. The various functions of the baseband, such as authentication and encryption, along with those provided for the hop sequences, such as channel coding and decoding, low-level timing control, and link management, are covered in detail in this chapter.

Defining the Placement of the Baseband

Based on the placement of the various layers of the Bluetooth protocol stack, the layers of the transport protocol group can be classified as:

◆ The lower protocols, which consist of the radio, the baseband, the Link Controller, and the Link Manager

◆ The upper protocols, which consist of the L2CAP and other application-specific higher protocols

In addition, you can actually separate the low-level functions of the Bluetooth hardware module from the input/output functioning of the Bluetooth host based on this classification. The hardware, popularly referred to as the Bluetooth module, consists of the radio and the Link Controller (along with the baseband).

Figure 4-1 illustrates the functional categorization of the lower protocols of the transport protocol group.

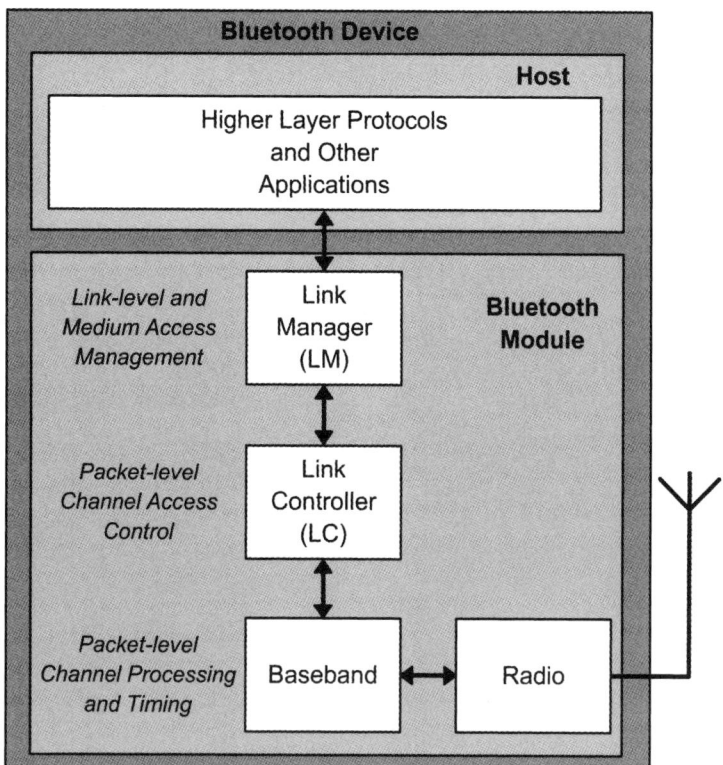

FIGURE 4-1 *The lower protocols of the transport protocol group*

The task of sending and receiving data is performed by the radio by using the medium of the air interface. The Link Controller uses the underlying services of the baseband to determine the type of transmitted data, the type of data to be received, the carrier frequency, and the transmit power. The baseband services are also used for controlling various device and piconet functions such as link creation, hop sequence, timing selection, and other operational functions that will be clear as you proceed through the chapter. Before moving any further, take a look at a diagrammatic representation of the functions of the baseband, shown in Figure 4-2.

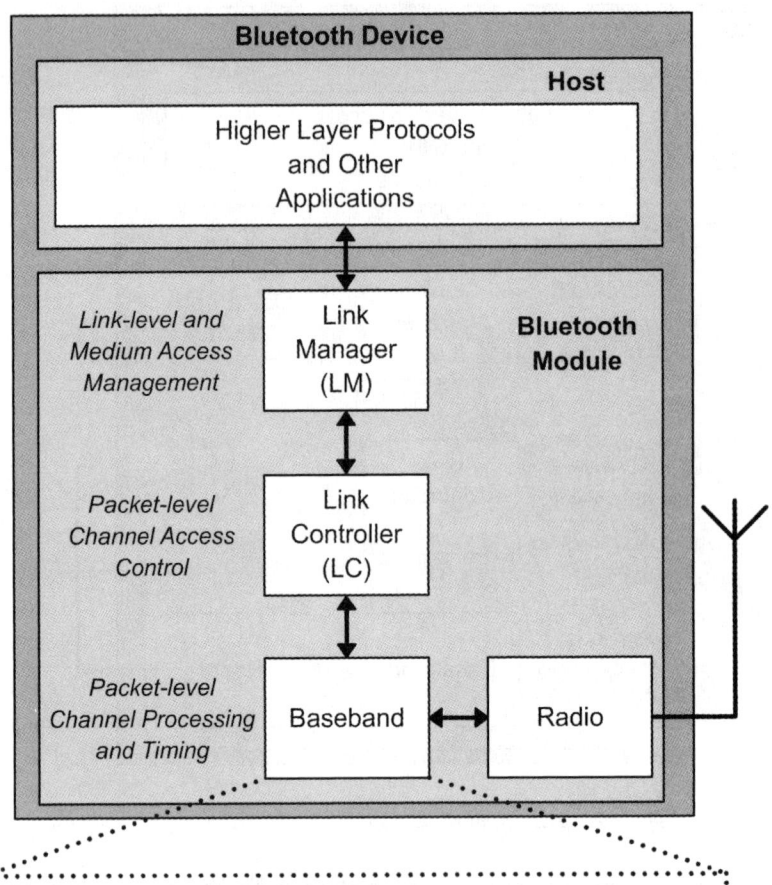

FIGURE 4-2 *Functions of the baseband*

The entire sequence of device connection, link management, and packet-based data transmission takes place on the network that is created by the piconet. As you already know, a piconet includes the master and its slaves, which are created when a link is established between two or more devices. It is, therefore, very easy to define a master and a slave in a network. A master is a device that holds the reigns of the network, and a slave is a device that takes commands from a master.

The next section discusses the two important components, or roles, of a Bluetooth piconet.

The Piconet Roles

As you know, a PAN network, or a piconet, is established by linking Bluetooth devices. As a result, each Bluetooth device in a piconet is either a *master* or a *slave*.

At a given time, a piconet consists of a single master and up to seven active slave units. The synchronized channel timings and hop sequences between these units form the foundation for exchange of information between the devices. This is interesting isn't it? The operational FHSS space used by Bluetooth radios actually consists of a series of a well-defined frequency hops over a randomly selected set of frequencies that operate at a rate of 1600 hops per second.

This information has been brought across quite often through the preceding chapters. If you look at the earlier concepts, you'll realize that the member devices in a piconet follow almost the same pattern of hops as long as they are communicating. The baseband functions define the frequency-hopping sequence of a piconet, the do's and don'ts for a particular device before joining a piconet, and the coordinated transmission and reception of data packets between the devices in a piconet.

The links between the devices in a piconet change constantly and depend solely on the need for two devices to communicate with each other. As a result, such links are often described as dynamic or ad hoc. In addition, the establishment of a connection between the two devices is also independent of any support entity such as an intermediary base station, a corporate WLAN, and a domestic WLAN. It is the baseband protocol that decides and defines the rules for communication between the devices of a piconet.

An important point to remember is that the role of a master or a slave is not held simultaneously. Although a Bluetooth device can play the roles of both a master and a slave, the master is the controlling unit that determines the type of data and the time of data transmission. The slave units, on the other hand, simply listen and wait for receipt of packets and respond to it accordingly. As you'll recall, a scatternet is a link between the masters and slaves of different piconets. Chapter 1, "Introduction to Bluetooth," defined the scatternet as an overlap of piconets. It is therefore evident that the formation of scatternets widens the expanse of communication between devices in multiple piconets.

You can seat the children of a playgroup class in a circle, square, or rectangle, which in technical language defines the topology of the seating arrangement. Similarly, the structure or topology of a network, as you are well aware, can be described by the terms ring, bus, or star. Similarly, in a piconet, the structure of the link between a master and its slave devices can be categorized as the following topologies:

◆ **A point-to-point link.** A point-to-point topology, as the name suggests, forms a link between a master unit and a single slave unit. Figure 4-3 shows a point-to-point link between a master and a slave unit in a piconet.

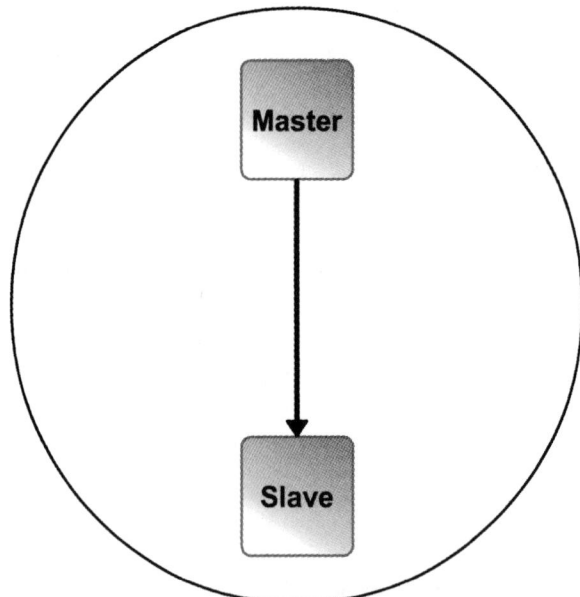

FIGURE 4-3 *A point-to-point link between a master and a slave unit*

◆ **A point-to-multipoint link.** A point-to-multipoint link is a link between a single master unit and several slave units. The maximum number of associated slave units in such a link is seven. Figure 4-4 shows a point-to-multipoint link between a master and a slave unit in a piconet.

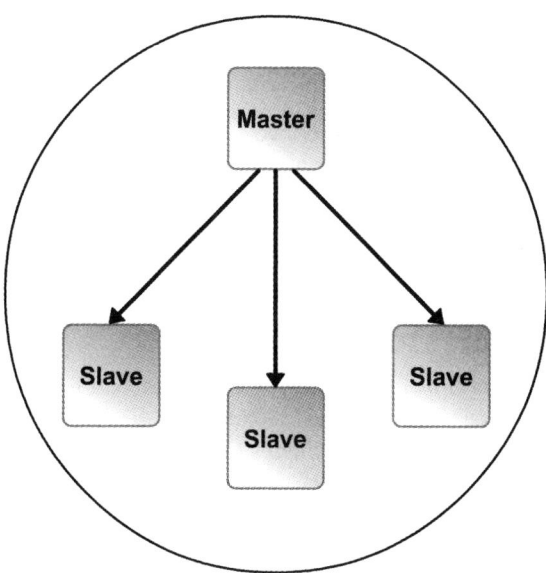

FIGURE 4-4 *A point-to-multipoint link between a master and a slave unit*

The topology of the link between the devices in a scatternet is entirely different from the links in a piconet. Figure 4-5 illustrates the topology of a scatternet.

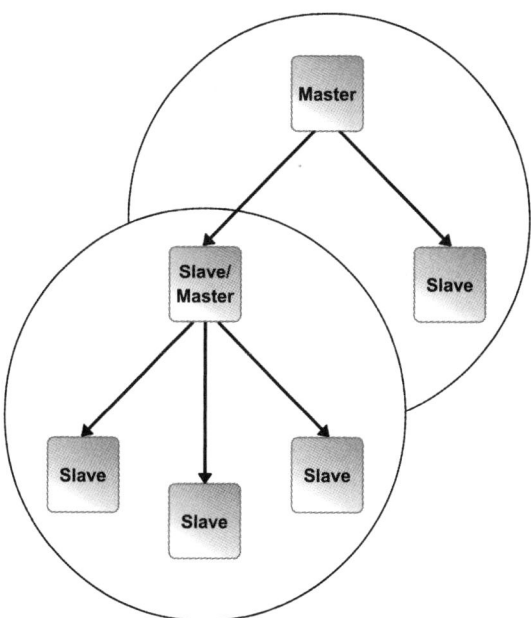

FIGURE 4-5 *The topology of a scatternet*

Notice that the diagram illustrates a piconet with a point-to-multipoint topology between a master and its slaves. The master of the piconet, in turn, is a slave to the master of another piconet. That's exactly how scatternets are formed.

The link between the devices in a piconet can be described as a physical channel for information exchange. The physical link is actually the center of action that primarily ensures that devices are in sync with each other so that they can freely exchange information without any interruptions. The following section discusses the events that occur on the Bluetooth physical channel.

The Physical Channel in Bluetooth

For any two digital devices to communicate, it is necessary for them to connect through a radio link. The radio link, or the physical channel, in Bluetooth is defined by the pseudo-random frequency-hopping sequence that is used to interchange data between devices The physical channel is, therefore, the very basis of any wireless communication.

However, before moving on to discussing the components used for the computation of the hopping sequence of a Bluetooth device, the next section delves a bit into time slots.

Time Slots

The physical channel is made up of time slots that are used to exchange data between the master and the slave devices. According to the flow of information, time slots can be categorized as one of the following types:

- ◆ **Master-to-slave time slots.** The time slots that are used by the master to transmit data to the slave are called *master-to-slave* time slots.

- ◆ **Slave-to-master time slots.** The time slots that are used by the slave to transmit data to the master are called *slave-to-master* time slots.

Each time slot is 625 microseconds in length and corresponds to a single RF hop frequency. The hop rate through the RF channels, as you are well aware, is 1600 hops/sec. The initiation of data transmission is always aligned to the beginning of a time slot. Figure 4-6 shows the master-to-slave and slave-to-master slots for single-slot packets.

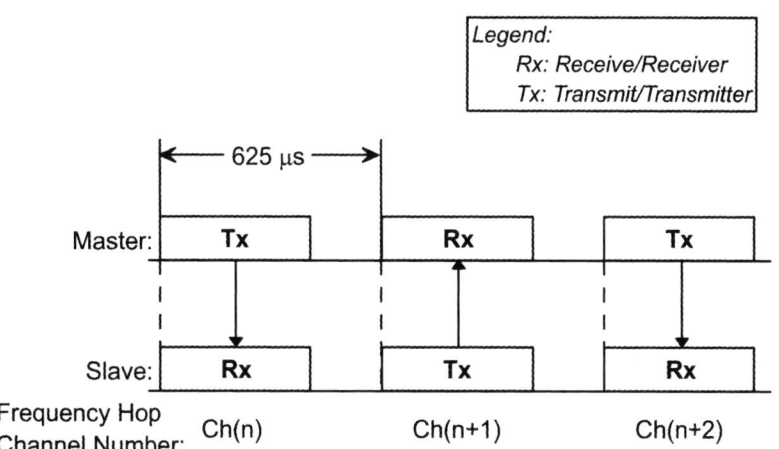

FIGURE 4-6 *The slot timings for single-slot packets*

A TDD scheme is used to define the transmission between a master and a slave device. The packets that are transferred during information exchange can extend up to five time slots. Of these, the Bluetooth specification defines only the one, three, and five time slots for data transmission. The RF hop frequency for a single slot packet is derived from the current clock value. On the other hand, the RF hop frequency for a multiple slot packet is derived from the clock value of the first packet. At the end of the transmission of a multiple packet, the current clock value is used to determine the next packet's RF hop frequency.

Time slots correspond to RF hop frequencies. The two factors that are used to compute the hopping sequence of a Bluetooth device are the device address (BD_ADDR) and the clock value.

The Bluetooth Device Address

The *Bluetooth device address* (BD_ADDR) is a 48-bit IEEE MAC address that is electronically engraved on each Bluetooth device. The IEEE functions as a number authority. It assigns a unique bit address to each Bluetooth device that is comparable to the Medium Access Control (MAC) address of other 802.xx LAN devices.

Each MAC address consists of the following parts:

◆ **Lower Address Part (LAP).** The 24 bits of LAP are used for the generation of the sync word for piconet identification and frequency hopping. The lower parts of the BD_ADDR signify the unique portion of the Bluetooth device address. The lower bits of the BD_ADDR help to maintain a large base of unique identifiers and also reduce the amount of data that is passed within the Bluetooth module.

◆ **Upper Address Part (UAP).** The 8 bits of UAP are used to initialize the Cyclic Redundancy Checksum (CRC) and Header Error Check (HEC) calculations for packet header error checking and for frequency hopping.

NOTE

The CRC and HEC calculations are discussed in subsequent chapters.

◆ **Non-significant Address Part (NAP).** As is evident from its name, this part of the BD_ADDR is not of much use for any computations. The 16 bits of NAP, however, can sometimes be used to initialize the encryption engine stream for authentication and encryption key generation.

Figure 4-7 shows the structure of the 48-bit Bluetooth device address.

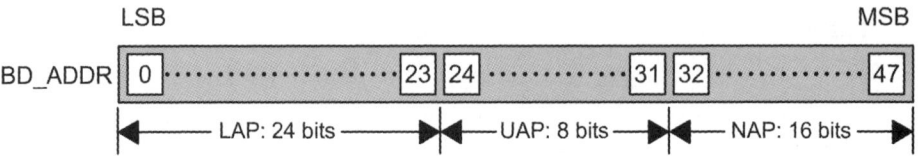

FIGURE 4-7 *The 48-bit Bluetooth device address*

NAP and UAP form the *Organization Unique Identifier* (OUI) part of the device address that is assigned by the numbering authority to various organizations. LAP, on the other hand, is assigned internally by different organizations. That's one component used in the computation of the frequency-hopping sequence.

The Bluetooth Clock Value

The Bluetooth clock in a Bluetooth device can be compared to the clocks that we use in everyday life. The Bluetooth clock is a 28-bit native clock that ticks 3200 times per second. The ticks of the Bluetooth clock can also be measured in terms of μseconds. As a result, you can say that a Bluetooth clock ticks once in every 312.5 μsec representing a clock rate of 3.2 KHz. Can you relate the clock ticks to the frequency-hopping rate of a Bluetooth device? The clock tick of 3200 times per second in a Bluetooth device is actually twice the frequency-hopping rate of 1600 hops per second.

However, the Bluetooth clock is also different from time clocks. Consider the following example. You do come across situations where your time clock is either running fast or slow as compared to the current time. What do you do in such situations? What do you do when you use a time clock as a wake-up alarm? In both these situations, you either adjust or turn off the time clock. Well, a Bluetooth clock is a free-running clock that does not need to be adjusted or turned off.

The Bluetooth clock decides when a device is ready to transmit data or listen for the incoming data. The four types of clocks on a Bluetooth system are as follows:

◆ **The native clock (CLKN).** The native clock functions as a reference to all other clocks and is actually the hardware oscillator value in the Bluetooth device.

◆ **The estimated clock (CLKE).** The estimated clock value helps to speed up the process of establishing a connection between devices during paging. The offset derived from the clock value during an inquiry is added to the CLK to obtain the value of the estimated clock. In other words, CLKE is the estimated clock value of a paging device made to the native clock of the receiving device.

◆ **The master clock (CLK).** The devices in a piconet hop in unison by using the same channel timings and hop sequences. The value of the master clock is obtained by adding an offset to the native clock. The offset is zero for the master because the CLK is identical to the master's CLKN. The derived value of the master clock is communicated to the slave units of a piconet. Based on the value of the master clock, the slave units add an offset to their native clock. In doing so, the slave units synchronize their channel timings and hop sequences to that of the master unit. The offset is updated at regular intervals to ensure that the master clock value does not drift away from the native clock value. All the devices of a piconet use the value of the master clock to schedule the transmission and reception of data between the devices. The four critical periods of the master clock value fall at 312.5 ms, 625 ms, 1.25 ms, and 1.28 ms and correspond to the CLK 0, CLK 1, CLK 2, and CLK 12 timer bits, respectively. The master-to-slave transmission begins at the even-numbered slots when CLK 0 and CLK 1 are at zero. Figure 4-8 shows the critical periods of the Bluetooth clock.

◆ **The Bluetooth clock.** The Bluetooth clock defines the channel timing and the hop sequence of the radio transreceiver in the Bluetooth device. The value of the Bluetooth clock is obtained by adding an offset to the value of the native clock. The value of the offset is defined by the native clock of the master and is used to keep all devices in a piconet synchronized. A slave device uses the value of the master's Bluetooth clock during a piconet communication.

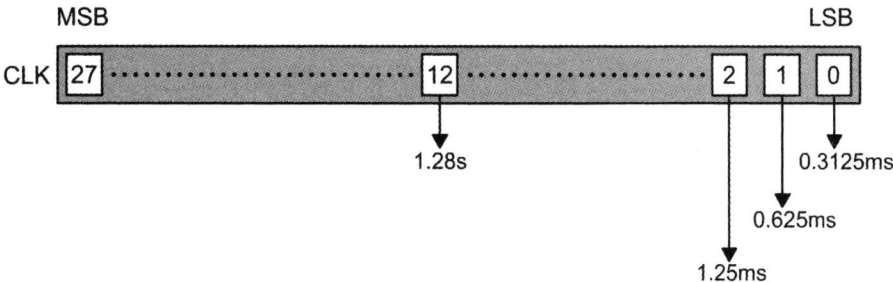

FIGURE 4-8 *The critical periods of the Bluetooth clock*

NOTE

LSB: Least-Significant Bit (LSB) defines the lowest value of a bit in a binary representation.

MSB: Most Significant Bit (MSB) defines the highest value of a bit in a binary representation.

The conceptual representation in Figure 4-9 will help you to understand the relationship between the various types of Bluetooth clocks and the offset.

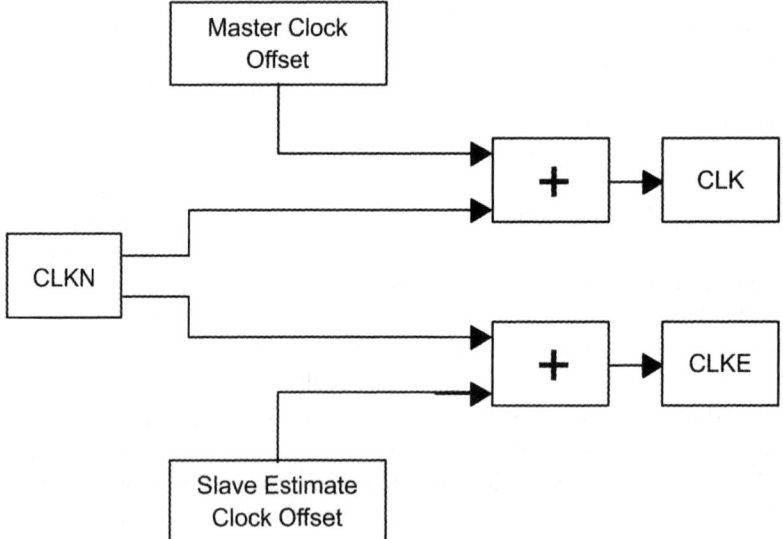

FIGURE 4-9 *A conceptual representation of the relationship between the Bluetooth clock and the offset*

The preceding section discussed the topology of links formed between a master and a slave unit in a piconet. The link between the devices is a physical link that is used for the exchange of data packets. It is a type of link that determines the type of data packet to be transferred during the data exchange. The next section looks at the two types of links that can be created between a master and slave units of a piconet.

The Link Between Master and Slaves in a Piconet

The baseband supports the following two types of physical links between the devices of a piconet:

◆ *Synchronous Connection-Oriented* (SCO) link

◆ *Asynchronous Connection-Less* (ACL) link

SCO Links

An SCO link can be described as symmetric, point-to-point links between a master and a slave in a piconet. The following example helps to explain the functioning of a SCO link. How do you ensure the availability of seats for your favorite opera to avoid any last-minute disappointments? You book the seats in advance, don't you? The connection-oriented SCO links also do just that. They establish a session in advance to ensure that the data arrives in the same order as it is sent. The session booking reserves a channel bandwidth with reserved time slots for regular exchange of data packets. The SCO link mostly carries voice data.

A master can support a maximum of three simultaneous SCO links to the same or different slave units. A slave can also support three SCO links, but to the same master. An SCO link provides a circuit-switched type of network for a time-bound and regular exchange of data. When a link is established between a master and a slave(s), the master sends data packets in the reserved *master-to-slave* slots at regular intervals. The intervals that are counted in slots and defined by the parameter T_{SCO} are called SCO intervals. Because SCO intervals are time-bound, there is no retransmission of the data packets. After receiving data packets, the slave responds with a data packet in the *slave-to-master* slot. The response is withheld only if the slave discovers a different destination address in the packet header. However, a slave may also respond in situations where it incorrectly decodes the slave address in the packet header.

To set up an SCO link, the master uses the LM protocol to send an SCO setup message containing the timing parameters by using the LM protocol. The timing parameters are used to specify the limits for the reserved slots in terms of the SCO interval, T_{SCO}, and the starting offset (D_{SCO}). The initial flag that indicates the initialization procedure of 1 or 2 is set up to avoid introduction of offsets by clock wraparounds.

ACL Links

An ACL link can be described as an asymmetric, point-to-multipoint link between a master and a slave in a piconet. Unlike SCO links, ACL links do not initiate a session before the transmission of the data packets. As a result, there is no reservation of time slots and the order of arrival of the data packets is often different from the order in which they were sent.

A master can support a number of ACL links to multiple slave units. However, at any given time, only one ACL link can exist between two devices. In addition, the data from the master to the slave units is transmitted on a per-slot basis and does not necessarily follow a sequential pattern. The ACL links provide packet-switched connections between the master and active slaves that use the unreserved and available time slots for a data exchange. The data transmission is, therefore, sporadic and based on the availability of data from the upper layers of the protocol stack.

A slave uses the next master-to-slave slot to respond to an ACL packet received from a master. However, this response from a slave is permitted only if the data packet received from the master is addressed in the preceding master-to-slave slot. If the slave fails to decode the slave address in the packet header, it is unable to ascertain the destination address of the packet. The response from the slave is, therefore, withheld. As a result, ACL packets are best used for generic broadcast transmissions that are not addressed to any specific slave.

The type of links between the master and the slave also determines the type of data packet transmitted. However, you'll recall that most of the discussions related to data packets in the preceding chapters often referred to the terms packet header and payload. The following section explains the concepts related to the structure of a data packet that is used for data transmission between the master and the slaves of a piconet.

The Structure of a Data Packet

How is data transmitted between devices across a piconet channel? The answer to this question is "by the use of data packets." That's correct! Have you wondered about the structure and composition of this essential element of data transmission? Before discussing the parts of a data packet, here's a recap of some concepts related to the packet-based data transmission in wireless devices.

The preceding chapter, which covered protocol layers, discussed the role of the L2CAP layer in the segmentation and reassembly of the data packets between the upper- and lower-level protocol layers. Each upper-level data packet is segmented into smaller *Protocol Data Units* (PDUs) for transmission to the lower-level protocol layers. The baseband orders the sequence of the PDUs by using retransmit and timeout notifications.

Each data packet can be broken into the following three parts:

- ◆ **The access code.** The access code is used to identify the presence of a packet and address the packet to the specified device.
- ◆ **The header.** The header contains the control information that includes the details of the packets and the link.
- ◆ **The payload.** The payload contains the actual message information or the data based on whether the transmission is a high-level protocol transmission or whether the data is simply being passed down the protocol stack.

Figure 4-10 shows the structure of a Bluetooth data packet.

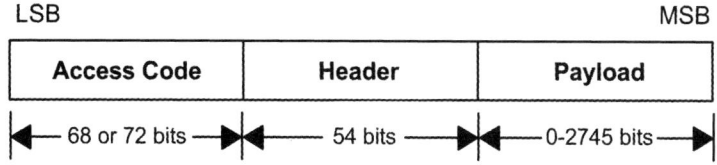

FIGURE 4-10 *The structure of a Bluetooth data packet*

The Access Code

The access code is derived from the master's Bluetooth device address. In an activated link between devices, the access code identifies the status of a packet to determine if it is transmitted to or from the master unit. The access code is a 72-bit field of the following three types:

◆ *Channel Access Code* (CAC)

◆ *Device Access Code* (DAC)

◆ *Inquiry Access Code* (IAC)

Channel Access Code

The CAC identifies a piconet and is, therefore, used by all its devices during transmission over a live connection. The CAC is a part of all data packets that are transmitted over a particular piconet. The CAC includes three parts. Figure 4-11 shows the format the access code consisting of the preamble, sync word, and trailer.

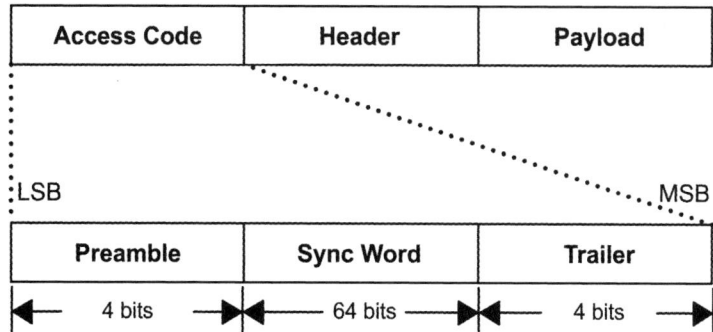

FIGURE 4-11 *The format of the access code*

◆ **Preamble.** The 4-bit preamble consists of a fixed and alternate pattern of ones and zeros. The sequence of either 1010 or 0101 is used for DC offset compensation. The pattern of the ones and the zeros in the preamble depends on the value of the *Least Significant Bit* (LSB) of the sync word. If the LSB of the sync word is binary one, the 1010 pattern is used. Similarly, if the LSB of the sync word is binary zero, the 0101 pattern is used. Figure 4-12 shows the correlation between the access code and the LSB of the sync word.

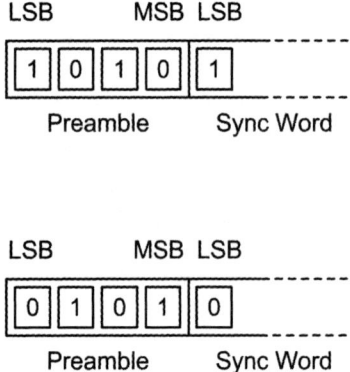

FIGURE 4-12 *The correlation between the preamble of the access code and the LSB of the sync word*

◆ **Synchronization information or sync word.** The 64 bits of synchronization information or the sync word are derived from the 24-bit Lower Address Part (LAP) of the Bluetooth device address by using the algorithm definition in the Bluetooth Specification document. The use of LAP ensures a larger hamming distance between the sync words. This aids in the detection and correction of errors generated during the creation of the sync word.

◆ **Trailer.** The 4-bit trailer consists of a fixed and alternate pattern of ones and zeros. You'll surely spot a lot of similarity in the structure of the preamble and the trailer. Both the preamble and the header are 4-bit patterns with a structure that is either a 1010 pattern or a 0101 pattern. However, the difference lies in the fact that whereas the choice of bit patterns in the preamble depends on the LSB of the sync word, the pattern in the trailer depends on the Most Significant Bit (MSB) of the sync word. In addition, the choice of patterns is the opposite of the binary value of the MSB. As a result, if the MSB of the sync word is a binary one, the 0101 pattern is used. Similarly, if the MSB of the sync word is a binary zero, the 1010 pattern is used. Figure 4-13 shows the correlation between the access code and the MSB of the sync word.

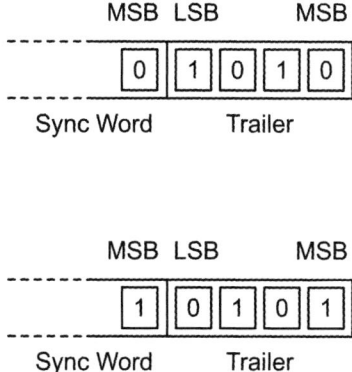

MSB LSB   MSB

| 0 | 1 | 0 | 1 | 0 |

Sync Word   Trailer

MSB LSB   MSB

| 1 | 0 | 1 | 0 | 1 |

Sync Word   Trailer

FIGURE 4-13 *The correlation between the trailer of the access code and the MSB of the sync word*

Device Access Code

The DAC is used during signaling when the devices page signals or respond to signals before the data transmission. The DAC code is, therefore, derived from the Bluetooth address of a specific device. The paging signal is a message that is sent to initiate the process of data transmission between two devices. As a result, the DAC does not include the header and payload information. In addition, the size of the access code is further reduced to 68 bits by the exclusion of the 4-bit trailer.

Inquiry Access Code

True to its name, the IAC is used during an inquiry. The inquiry process in Bluetooth devices is discussed later in the chapter. All the same, you can easily relate to the sequence of events in this process. The following are the two types of IACs:

◆ **General Inquiry Access Code (GIAC).** During the inquiry process, all devices use GIAC for the detection of other Bluetooth devices. The Bluetooth specification has fixed GIAC as 0x9E8B33.

◆ **Dedicated Inquiry Access Code (DIAC).** DIAC, unlike the GIAC, is reserved by the Bluetooth specification and used to detect specific types of devices such as cellular handsets or printers during the inquiry process. For example, to establish a link with a device for printing services, instead of sending a GIAC to all devices, you can send DIAC as a part of an inquiry to specific devices that provide printing services. The generated access code determines the type of LAP to be used for a particular device. For example, in the case of CAC, the LAP of the master device is used. In the case of DAC, the LAP of the slave device is used, and in the case of IAC codes, a reserved LAP (0x9E8B33) is used. DIACs use LAPs ranging from 0x98E8B00 to 0x9E8B3F. Currently, the only DIAC definition for the various classes of devices is based on the LAP 0x9E8B00.

The next part of a data packet is the header, which contains all the control information about a packet.

The Header

The header, including the Header Error Check (HEC) consists of 18-bits of information. The $1/3$ scheme of the *Forward Error Correction* (FEC) code is used for the encoding of the 18-bits of information in the packet header. The resultant header of 54 µs is obtained by replicating the data three times to occupy three µs or 3-bit periods on air. The format of a packet header includes the following fields:

◆ **The Active Member Address (AM_ADDR).** The AM_ADDR is a 3-bit address assigned by the master to each slave unit that joins a piconet. As a result, AM_ADDR serves as a connection handle to direct the data exchange between the master and the slave units. In addition, AM_ADDR also helps the master to uniquely identify the responses from multiple (seven) slaves of a piconet. AM_ADDR stays as a part of the header as long as the slave is a part of the piconet. When the slave disconnects or temporarily moves to the parked state, it gives up AM_ADDR and is assigned a new AM_ADDR on reconnection. An AM_ADDR of zero is used for a broadcast packet that is sent to all the slave units of a piconet. However, the FHS packet is an exception to this rule and carries a zero AM_ADDR. This is because the FHS packet has no AM_ADDR assigned to it during its first transmission.

◆ **The Packet Type or the Type Code (TYPE).** The TYPE code is the 4-bit information that specifies the type of data carried by a particular data packet, the number of time slots occupied, and the type of error correction used for the payload. The non-addressed devices ignore a channel for the amount of time that is specified for the time slots in the TYPE code. The values assigned to the TYPE code are SCO, ACL, NULL, and POLL. The type of packet used in data transmission is an important concept that will be discussed in detail in later sections.

◆ **The Flow Control (FLOW).** The FLOW field is a 1-bit flag that controls the flow of ACL packets over ACL links. A device uses the STOP command of the FLOW flag to affirm its inability to receive data due to an overloaded buffer. As a result, the FLOW bit is set to zero and the flow of packets is stopped. After emptying the buffer, the GO command is returned to set the FLOW flag to one and reinitiate the flow of data packets.

◆ **The Acknowledgement Indication (ARQN).** The 1-bit ARQN flag informs the sender of the successful reception of a data packet after the CRC validation. The CRC validation is generated by a polynomial and is used to verify the data integrity of each data packet. A binary one or an *Ac*knowledge (ACK) indicates the successful reception of a data packet while a binary zero or a *Negative-Ac*knowledge (NAK) indicates a failure in the reception of a data packet. NAK is the default value of the ARQN field and is assumed on non-receipt of a message from the sender.

◆ **The Sequence Number (SEQN).** The SEQN flag is used to estimate the order of the data packets. The SEQN flag is toggled each time a new data packet is sent. As a result, a duplicate packet with the same SEQN flag can be easily identified and discarded.

◆ **The Header Error Check (HEC).** The HEC is an 8-bit field that represents the octal notation of the CRC function performed on a packet header. The recipient device ignores the remainder of a data packet following a failure of the HEC.

Figure 4-14 shows the structure of a packet header with all the header fields.

LSB			MSB
L_CH	FLOW	LENGTH	UNDEFINED
2	1	9	4

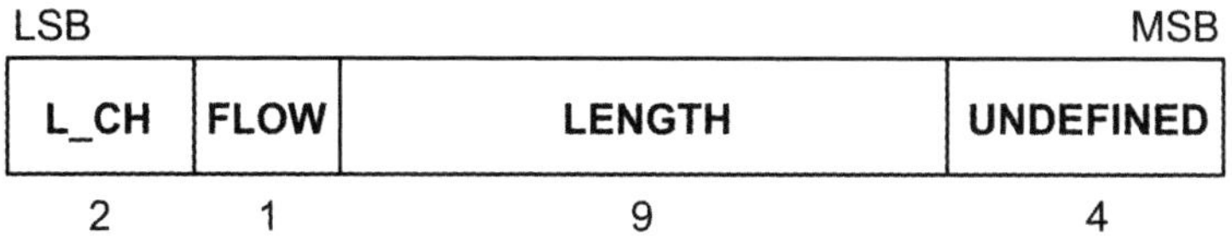

FIGURE 4-14 *The structure of a packet header with all the header fields*

The Payload

The payload is either a real-time audio or data. You'll recall that ACL links support data transmission while SCO links support both voice and data transmission. Voice fields are 240 bits in length as compared to the 80-bit length of a Data Voice (DV) packet. A Bluetooth data packet carrying data and voice traffic over an SCO link is called a Data Voice packet. In addition to carrying voice and data, the payload includes a 16-bit CRC for detection and correction of errors generated in the payload. An SCO packet does not include the CRC. The payload of all ACL packets can be split in the following three parts:

◆ **Payload header.** The size of the payload header present only in the data fields, is directly proportional to the size of the data packet. The payload header field consists of the following fields:

 ◆ **The logical channel (L_CH).** An L2CAP message can last for many ACL packets. In addition, an LMP message is carried through a single slot ACL packet. As a result, the status of a particular ACL payload needs to be clarified. The logical channel specifies that the payload is a start or fragment of an L2CAP packet or an LMP message. The value of the L_CH binary code determines the type of packet. For example, an L_CH binary code of 01 indicates that the packet is a continuation of multiple fragmented packets. Similarly, a binary value of 10 indicates reception of a single packet and the first fragment of a multiple fragmented packet. An LMP packet has the L_CH binary code value of 11.

◆ **The flow flag.** The flow flag controls the flow of data at the L2CAP level. The data flow over a channel is continued if the bit is a binary bit. In contrast, if the bit is a binary zero, then the data flow is stopped. An important point to note is that if the value of L_CH indicates reception of an LMP message with a binary code of 11, the flow bit is set to zero and ignored.

◆ **The length field.** The 8-bit length field specifies the length of the payload data in bytes.

Figure 4-15 shows the structure of a payload header with all the fields.

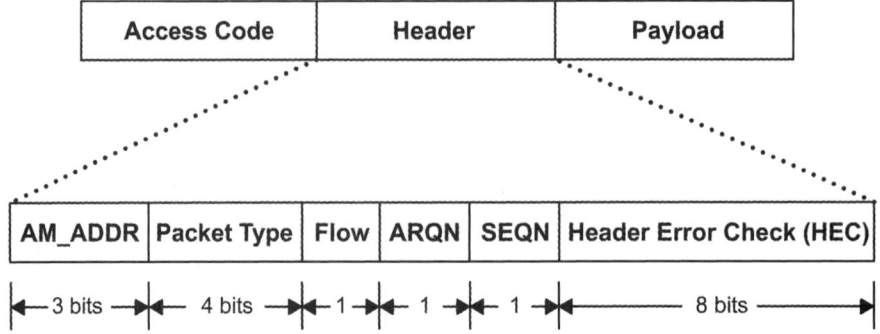

FIGURE 4-15 *The structure of a payload header with all the fields*

◆ **Payload body.** The payload body contains the user data whose length is specified by the length field of the payload header.

◆ **Cyclic Redundancy Checksum (CRC).** The CRC bits are used to check the integrity of the payload data after the destination device receives it. CRC bits are appended to the payload and calculated over the entire payload data.

The discussion in the preceding section pertains to the structure of both ACL and SCO packets. However, there are a few structural differences between an SCO packet and an ACL packet. An SCO packet, like an ACL packet, consists of an access code, a header, and a payload. However, as SCO links are synchronized, they do not require flow control and data retransmission. Therefore, the flow, ARQ, and SEQN fields of the header and the CRC field are redundant. In addition, depending on the FEC rate selected by the packet ($1/_3$, $2/_3$, or none), the payload size is fixed at 30 bytes with a source data of 10, 20, or 30 bytes.

Packet Types

The transmitted data packet can also be a DV packet, which is a mix of both ACL and SCO packets. A DV packet contains a 10-byte long voice field that is an HV1-style, non-FEC protected data and is transmitted at regular intervals. The data field, however, is protected with a $2/_3$ FEC coding and contains a CRC field, the flow field, and the ARQ and SEQN flags. Although the voice fields are not retransmitted, the retransmission of the data field occurs along with the ongoing transmission of the SCO voice field.

Figure 4-16 shows the structure of a DV packet.

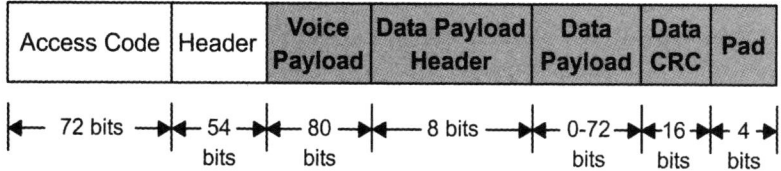

FIGURE 4-16 *The structure of a DV packet*

In addition to the ACL and SCO packets, data packets can also be categorized as

♦ **The ID packet.** An ID packet is used during the pre-connection operation, where the link between the devices is yet to be established and the timings between the devices are dissimilar. An ID packet includes only the access code with information about the source and destination of the transmitted data. Therefore, ID packets are used by strong signaling mechanisms that use the access code (DAC or IAC) for device detection.

♦ **The NULL packet.** A NULL packet is used during a one-way link, where the recipient of the data does not return any response packet. Although an acknowledgement for a NULL packet is not required, an acknowledgement of receipt of the sent packet is always sent. A NULL packet includes the access code and the packet header.

♦ **The POLL packet.** A POLL packet is structurally similar to a NULL packet. However, unlike NULL packets, POLL packets always send back an acknowledgement irrespective of whether the recipient sends back data or not.

♦ **The FHS packet.** An FHS packet is sent by an inquirer during the inquiry process, by a master to a slave during the paging process, or by a device during the role-switching process when the master and slave switch roles.

♦ **The Data Voice (DV) packet.** data DV packet contains combined data made up of data and voice. The payload is segmented into 80 bits of voice fields and 150 bits of data field. The voice field is not protected by FEC while the data field is encoded with a rate $^2/_3$ FEC.

♦ **The Header Value 1 (HV1)packet.** An HV1 packet is an SCO packet that is used for the transmission of voice and transparent synchronous data. Voice packets need CRC and are never retransmitted. The payload length of a HV1 packet is fixed at 240 bits.

♦ **The HV2 packet.** An HV2 packet is an SCO packet that has a fixed payload length of 240 bits and does not contain CRC or any payload header.

♦ **The HV3 packet.** An HV3 packet is also an SCO packet with a fixed payload length of 240 bits and does not contain CRC or a payload header.

◆ **The Data Medium rate 1 (DM1) packet.** A DM1 packet is an ACL packet that contains only data information. The payload header of a DM1 packet is 1 byte long with a length indicator that specifies the number of user bytes, not including the payload header and the CRC code.

◆ **The Data High rate 1 (DH1) packet.** A DH1 packet is an ACL packet that is similar to a DM1 packet. The only difference between the two packets is that the information in a DH1 packet is not FEC encoded.

◆ **The DM3 packet.** A DM3 packet is an ACL packet that contains an extended payload. The payload header is 2 bytes long. The length indicator of the payload header specifies the number of user bytes, not including the payload header and the CRC code.

◆ **The DH3 packet.** A DH3 packet is similar to a DM3 packet except that the payload information is not FEC coded. During the transmission of a DH3 packet, the hop frequency does not change for the duration of three time slots.

◆ **The DM5 packet.** A DM5 packet is an ACL packet that contains an extended payload. The payload header is 2 bytes long. The length indicator of the payload header specifies the number of user bytes, not including the payload header and the CRC code. During the transmission of a DM5 packet, the hop frequency does not change for the duration of five time slots.

◆ **The DH5 packet.** A DH5 packet is similar to a DM5 packet except that the payload information is not FEC coded. During the transmission of a DH5 packet, the hop frequency does not change for the duration of five time slots.

◆ **The AUX1 packet.** An AUX1 packet is similar to a DH1 packet except that it has no CRC code.

The next section discusses another categorization of the different packet types.

The Type Field of Bluetooth Packets

The 4-bit TYPE field of the packet header defines 16 different types of packets for the ACL and SCO links. The 16 packets are further segmented into the following control packets:

◆ Segment one consists of four types of single-slot data

◆ Segment two consists of six or more types of single-slot data

◆ Segment three consists of four types of three-slot data

◆ Segment four consists of two types of five-slot data

Table 4-1 lists the various Type fields of a data packet.

Table 4-1 The Type Fields of a Data Packet

Segment	TYPE	Name	Details
1	Common	ID	Includes the DAC or the IAC code and occupies only one time slot.
1	Common	NULL	Used to obtain link information and link control. Has no payload and occupies one time slot. Receipt of this packet is not acknowledged.
1	Common	POLL	Used by the master to ascertain if the slaves are up. Has no payload and occupies one time slot. Receipt of this packet is acknowledged.
1	Common	FHS	Used for obtaining the **BD_ADDR** and clock value of the sender during the page master response, inquiry response, and frequency hop synchronization. $2/3$ FEC coded, and occupies one time slot.
2	Common	DM1	Used to support control messages in a link and also carry regular user data. Occupies one time slot.
2	SCO	HV1	Carries 10 information bytes and is used for voice transmission, is $1/3$ FEC coded, and occupies one time slot.
2	SCO	HV2	Carries 20 information bytes and is used for voice transmission. $2/3$ FEC coded and occupies one time slot.
2	SCO	HV3	Carries 30 information bytes and is used for voice transmission. Is not FEC coded and occupies one time slot.
2	SCO	DV	Carries both data and voice packets. The data fields are $2/3$ FEC coded while the voice fields are not coded. Occupies one time slot.
2	ACL	DM1	Carries 18 information bytes, is $2/3$ FEC coded, and occupies one time slot.
3	ACL	DH1	Carries 28 information bytes, is not FEC coded, and occupies one time slot.
3	ACL	DM3	Carries 123 information bytes, is $2/3$ FEC coded, and occupies three time slots.
3	ACL	DH3	Carries 185 information bytes, is not FEC coded, and occupies three time slots.

(continued on next page)

Table 4-1 The Type Fields of a Data Packet (continued)

Segment	TYPE	Name	Details
3	ACL	DM5	Carries 226 information bytes, is $2/_3$ FEC coded, and occupies five time slots.
4	ACL	DH5	Carries 341 information bytes, is not FEC coded, and occupies five time slots.
4	ACL	AUX1	Carries 30 information bytes, is similar to DH1 but has no CRC code, and occupies one time slot.

Now that you know the types of links between devices and the types, structure, and features of Bluetooth packets, the following section moves on to the most interesting part of the wireless communication—the process of inquiry and paging in Bluetooth devices.

Link Connection in Bluetooth Devices

Before data is transmitted between devices, it is essential that the devices discover each other and link up. How do two devices discover each other? How does one device know that it will receive information in the form of data from another device? How does one device tell another device that it is ready to receive data?

The link control layer is responsible for configuring and controlling the links and the packet-centric baseband. Before discussing discovery and linking of devices, answer these questions: At a traffic signal, how do you know when to stop or move? Or better still, as a student, how do you know if you are ready for an exam? Well, you study the circumstance and estimate the status of the situation or the person. In the case of the traffic signal, if the light is red, you stop and if it is green, you move. In the case of your exams, you estimate the status of your preparation and take the exam if you are well prepared. Consider another example. All of us at some time or the other is referred to as a child, a kid, a teenager, a young man, and so on. How would you define the terms child, kid, and teenager? Well, they are the states of human life.

Similarly, a device maintains various states that determine that the device is ready for linking. The major states of the Bluetooth device, which are also termed as the states of the Bluetooth Link Controller, are:

- The connection state
- The inquiry state
- The inquiry scan state
- The inquiry response state
- The page state

◆ The page scan state

◆ The page response state

◆ The standby state

The Connection State

The connection state indicates a support for active connection by devices. The connection state can be further divided into active, hold, sniff, and park states. During the active connection state, the master and slaves of a piconet actively participate in receiving and transmitting data. The slave adds the relevant offset to its CLKN and so switches to the master's CLK. The channel timings and the frequency hops between the devices are thus synchronized.

In the hold mode, a device temporarily stops supporting the ACL traffic so that the channel is available for other scanning, paging, and inquiry operations. The Active Member Address (AM_ADDR) is withheld and at the end of the hold time, the device synchronizes to the CAC to listen for incoming traffic.

In the sniff mode, a slave is assigned a specific slot number (D_{sniff}), slot time (T_{sniff}) and time period (N_{sniff}) to listen for traffic. During this time a slave listens for packets till all the packets with its AM_ADDR stop and the time out period ceases. After that, the slave waits for the next sniff period. A slave saves power by sleeping in the free slots that come in between the sniff slots.

In the park state, a slave remains synchronized to the channel but does not actively participate in any of the piconet communications. On the contrary, a slave surrenders its AM_ADDR and is given a DM_ADDR. During this time, the slave stays in the Low Power Sleep mode listening out for traffic only occasionally.

The Inquiry State

True to its name, a unit is said to be in the inquiry state when it attempts to discover other devices in its piconet. An inquiry is used for fresh connections where the connecting devices do not have each other's Bluetooth device addresses. An inquiry is skipped in cases of previous connections. The master transmits inquiry requests at two different frequencies within the same transmit time slot. As a result, the frequency hop rate is doubled to 3200 hops per second. During an inquiry, FHS packets are forwarded to the inquirer and connection-related data, such as CLKN, BD_ADDR, and BCH parity word are collated at the inquirer's end.

The Inquiry Scan State

The inquiry state is followed by the inquiry scan state, signifying that a device is ready to establish a link with new units. In this state, the device listens to a combination or GIAC and one or more DIAC. On the other hand, the receiving unit listens to IAC at one frequency hop that is long enough to overlap 16 frequency hops. Although optional, most devices at some time or the other enter into the inquiry scan state to show their availability to other inquiring devices. Because the inquiring device doesn't know about the channel timings and frequency hop sequences of other devices, it uses the GIAC and DIAC codes to listen for traffic in an extended period. After receiving of a valid inquiry, the devices move to the inquiry response substate and respond by using FHS packets.

The Inquiry Response State

Only slave units send the inquiry response messages. This state is initiated when the slave receives an inquiry and decides to respond. The response message is an FHS packet that includes the slave's Bluetooth device address and the native clock information.

The Page State

If a potential master has access to the Bluetooth address of the slave unit, it uses the paging process to connect to the specific slave unit. To do this, the master repeatedly transmits the DAC of the target device. The access code and timing information from previous connections is used to transmit a paging message to the intended slave unit.

To establish a connection with a device, in the page state, the master device continuously transmits the Bluetooth device address of the target device. Because the slave unit is not yet synchronized to the channel timings and hop sequences of the master, the target BD_ADRR is used to estimate the page-hopping sequence of the slave. Remember that the master has access to BD_ADDR due to the retention of this information after a previous connection or by the initiation of an inquiry process. There are equal chances of an incorrect page-hopping sequence estimation made by the master. As a result, the master and slave are unable to discover each other, and therefore, will not connect. How does Bluetooth address such an obvious problem? Well, the master transmits the target device's BD_ADDR in the same transmit time slot but at two different hop frequencies. As a result, the master's hop frequencies increase to 3200 hops per second, which is double the normal hopping rate of 1600 hops per second. Due to this increase in hopping sequence the probability of catching with the slave's hop sequence is increased.

Page Scan

A device periodically enters the page scan state to allow other devices to connect with it. After receiving of a paging packet, the device enters the slave response state, acknowledges the receipt of the packet, and waits for the FHS packet. After accepting the FHS packet, a slave updates its CLK timing and sync word reference before moving into the connection state.

After the master and the slave transmit and receive the paging message, they both estimate and synchronize their hopping frequencies. The two devices that are now in the response state exchange information to initiate the connection setup. The information exchanged during this time includes the channel access code, the channel hopping sequence, and the master's CLK value that the slave uses to match its clock with the master's native clock. As a consequence, a piconet is formed and procedures required for the formation of a usable connection between the devices are initiated.

Figure 4-17 shows the various states of Bluetooth Link Controller.

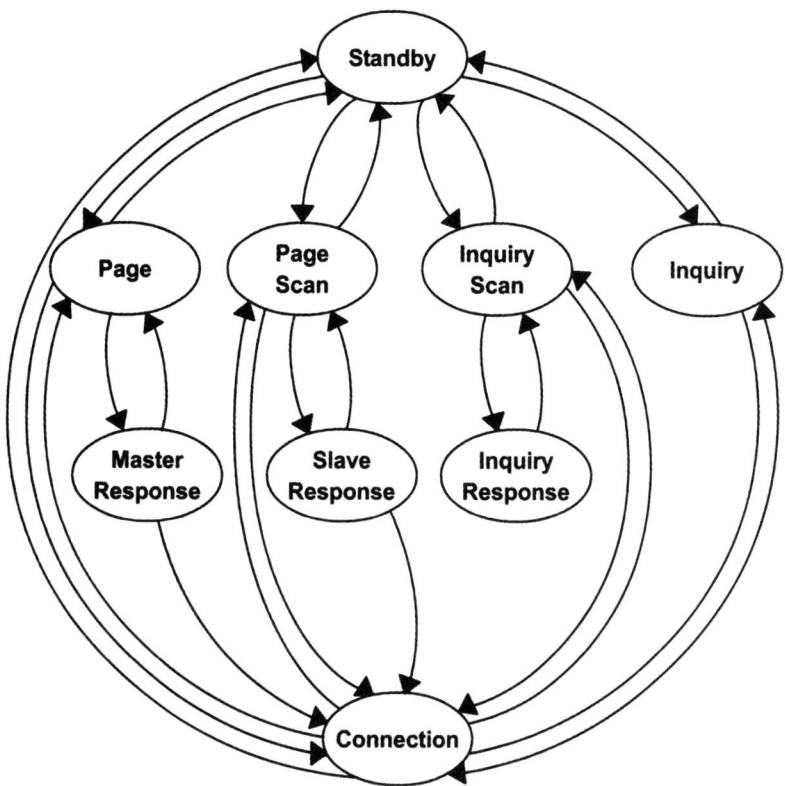

FIGURE 4-17   *The various states of Bluetooth Link Controller*

The Page Response State

The piconet formation takes place during the page response state. On receipt of a page message from the master, the channel timings and the frequency-hopping sequences are synchronized. As a result, both the master and the slave enter into response state and exchange information to initiate a connection.

The Standby State

The standby state defines an inactive state where the Bluetooth radio is shut off and there is no transmission of data between devices. As a result, devices are unable to identify any access codes. This state enables a low power operation of a device.

Once the states of a device are clear, you'll be able to understand the entire process of device discovery, inquiry, and paging between the devices. The next section discusses the process that leads to the formation of a piconet.

Device Discovery and Inquiry

The connection between wireless devices is sporadic and ad hoc with phases where devices are in and out of connections. For two devices to communicate, the first and foremost requirement is that they should be in the range of each other. The LC uses the process of inquiry to initiate the entire process of device discovery.

The process of device discovery begins with the inquiry process, which is nothing but the transmission of a simple message equivalent to "Hello, is anybody there?" This is the state of an inquiry device or the inquirer. The scanning device at the other end constantly listens for inquiries that it can respond to.

The inquiry device uses the GIAC to transmit ID packets containing the *Inquiry Access Code* (IAC). Some devices also use the current DIAC specification called the *Limited Inquiry Access Code* (LIAC) for the inquiry process. However, LIAC is used only by devices that "know" each other through a previous connection as a method for connectivity that is quicker and for a shorter period of time.

When the slave receives an inquiry in the form of the ID packet, it generates a random number (N^{Rand}) that ranges from 0 and 1023. The current position of the inquiry hop sequence is frozen. During the N^{Rand} time slots, the slave is not in the inquiry response substate but in either the page state or in page response substate. After N^{Rand} time slots, the slave moves to the inquiry response state and sends back a response in the form of an FHS packet.

Figure 4-18 shows the various steps that form a part of the inquiry process.

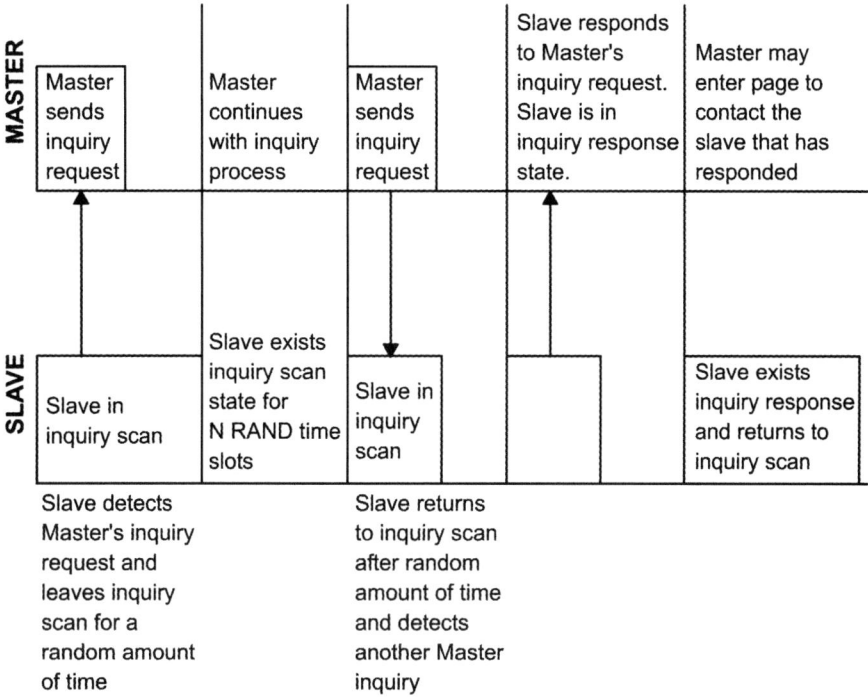

FIGURE 4-18 *The inquiry process between two devices*

The inquiry process is followed by connection establishment and paging.

Establishing Connection and Paging

After the master receives a response to its "Is anyone there" message, the next question asked is "Will you connect with me?" The outcome of the question in Bluetooth technology initiates the paging process. To create a connection, a device moves to the page state and sends out a number of paging packets. Paging packets are nothing but ID packets that are based on the device address of the paged device.

Initially, the inquirer is in the page state while the other device is in the page scan state. The paging device sends two page messages on two different hop frequencies to estimate the page frequency of the scanning device. The scanning device listens to the inquiry, identifies its DAC, and sends back a slave response message with its DAC in an FHS packet. The paging device at this time is listening to two different frequencies, expecting a response from the slave. The response packet from the scanning device is sent exactly one time slot later at the same hopping frequency received earlier. During the response state, the value of the received clock timing and the frequency-hopping sequence is frozen to ensure that both the time and the frequency are aligned to that of the paging unit. The scanning slave device uses the values of CLK and BD_ADDR to calculate the hop sequence of the paging device. When the scanning device moves from the estimated hop sequence to the calculated hop sequence, both devices move to the connection state. The paging device becomes the master, and the scanning device becomes the slave of the piconet.

Figure 4-19 shows the various steps that form a part of the paging process.

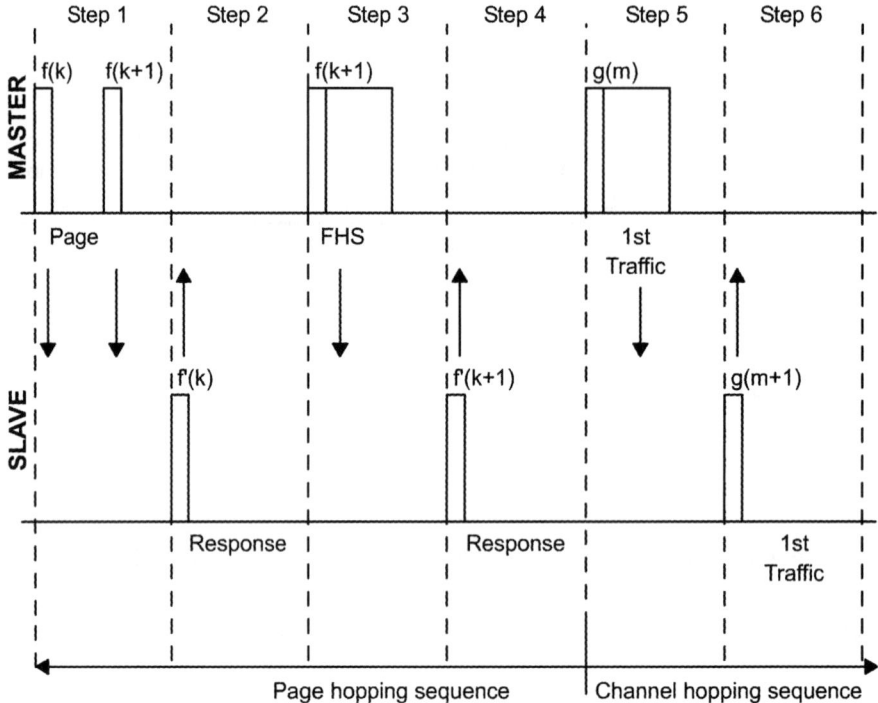

FIGURE 4-19 *The paging process between a master and a slave*

Summary

The primary functions of the baseband include channel coding and decoding, the control of low-level link timing, and link management. All these functions are performed during the transfer of a single data packet. Communicating devices in a piconet exist in the two operational modes of either a master or a slave. Linked devices exchange information in the form of data packets that are sent over SCO and ACL links.

In this chapter, you learned about the process of device identification and connection. The value of the Bluetooth clock and the Bluetooth device address (`BD_ADDR`) play the most important role in this process. The address uniquely identifies each device while the clock time is used for the synchronization of the master and slave channel timings and frequency hops. You also learned about the baseband supported SCO and AXL links that determine the structure of the data packets exchanged between connected devices. Before linking and connecting with each other, the master and slave devices continuously perform inquiry and paging procedures to allow device link-ups. You learned about the various states of the Link Controller, which configures and controls the links of the packet-oriented baseband.

Having highlighted the importance of synchronized channel timings and frequency hops between the master and slave of a piconet, you now need to understand the functions of the Link Manager Protocol. The LMP is responsible for negotiating the properties of the air interface between Bluetooth devices. As a result, LMP performs activities such as bandwidth allocation for the L2CAP data traffic and bandwidth reservation for support of the incoming audio traffic. The LMP is discussed in detail in the next chapter.

Check Your Understanding

Multiple Choice Questions

1. The Bluetooth device address consists of ?
   a. MAC
   b. LAP
   c. AM_ADDR
   d. LAP
   e. UAP

2. Which of the following statements is true?
   a. An SCO link is a symmetric point-to-point link that carries only voice data.
   b. An ACL link is an asymmetric point-to-point link that carries both voice and data

3. Which of the following are parts of the packet header?
   a. BD_ADDR
   b. FLOW
   c. TYPE
   d. AM_ADDR
   e. ARQN
   f. HEC
   g. SEQN

Short Questions

1. Describe the four types of clocks on a Bluetooth system.
2. What are the three parts of a data packet?
3. Explain the two types of Inquiry Access Codes in Bluetooth?
4. Which are the eight states of a Bluetooth device?

Answers

Multiple Choice Answers

1. b, d, e. LAP, NAP, and UAP.
2. a. An SCO link is a symmetric point-to-point link that carries only voice data.
3. b, c, d, e, f, and g. FLOW, TYPE, AM_ADDR, ARQN, HEC, and SEQN.

Short Answers

1. The four types of clocks on a Bluetooth system are as follows:
    -   **The native clock (CLKN).** The native clock functions as a reference to all other clocks and is actually the hardware oscillator value in the Bluetooth device.
    -   **The estimated clock (CLKE).** The estimated clock value helps to speed up the process of establishing a connection between devices during paging.
    -   **The master clock (CLK).** The devices in a piconet hop in unison by using the same channel timings and hop sequences. The value of the master clock is obtained by adding an offset to the native clock.
    -   **The Bluetooth clock.** The Bluetooth clock defines the channel timing and the hop sequence of the radio transreceiver in the Bluetooth device. The value of the Bluetooth clock is obtained by adding an offset to the value of the native clock.

2. Each data packet can be broken into the following three parts:
    -   **The access code.** The access code is used to identify the presence of a packet and address the packet to the specified device.
    -   **The header.** The header contains the control information that includes the details of the packets and the link.
    -   **The payload.** The payload contains the actual message information or the data based on whether the transmission is a high-level protocol transmission or whether the data is simply being passed down the protocol stack.

3. The two types of IACs are:
    -   **General Inquiry Access Code (GIAC).** During the inquiry process, all devices use GIAC for the detection of other Bluetooth devices. The Bluetooth specification has fixed GIAC as 0x9E8B33.
    -   **Dedicated Inquiry Access Code (DIAC).** DIAC, unlike the GIAC, is reserved by the Bluetooth specification and used to detect specific types of devices such as cellular handsets or printers during the inquiry process.

4. The eight states of a Bluetooth device are:
   ◆ The connection state
   ◆ The inquiry state
   ◆ The inquiry scan state
   ◆ The inquiry response state
   ◆ The page state
   ◆ The page scan state
   ◆ The page response state
   ◆ The standby state

Chapter 5

*Link Manager
Protocol*

The concepts discussed so far highlight the use of the protocol layers in network management and data transmission between devices. By now, you know that the network protocol provides various services to ensure the transmission of data between devices. However, an equally important role of the protocol is to use mechanisms to deliver the protocol services. In fact, the *Link Manager Protocol* (LMP) does just that.

The previous chapter discussed the role of the Link Manager (LM) as a controller of the baseband functions. The Link Manager is actually a firmware provided with the link control hardware that is responsible for link set up, link security, and control of the link between communicating devices. As a result, all the link-based tasks of the devices are controlled by their LMs. But, how are the operations between the LMs coordinated? How do the LMs communicate? Well, the LMs use the Link Manager Protocol to communicate with each other. The LMP, in turn, uses the underlying services of the baseband to manage the links and the data packets that are crucial for inter-device communication.

The Bluetooth specification defines the role of the LMP in terms of the messages exchanged between the LMs. The specification, however, does not detail the exact operation of the LMP instructions. This chapter discusses the content of the messages of the LMP during piconet management, security management, and link management. The LMP functions over the logical channel that facilitates the exchange of data between devices. Therefore, this chapter begins by discussing the logical channels in Bluetooth.

The Bluetooth Logical Channels

The previous chapter discussed the importance of the physical channel for data exchange between devices. The Bluetooth framework also includes logical channels that are control channels used to carry link-related control data between a master and a slave of a piconet. This data carried between the master and the slave helps to maintain and control the link between the devices. You know that data transmission takes place in the form of data packets. During data exchange between devices, the control data is matched to various parts of the data packets. This mapping of the control data helps in controlling the links at the hardware and firmware levels.

The following are the five logical channels in Bluetooth that help to transfer data of various types between devices.

◆ **Link Controller (LC) channel.** The LC channel is used at the Link controller level. The control data of the LC channel is carried in all the data packet headers except the non-header ID packet. This channel carries low-level control data such as the flow control information and data defining the characteristics of the payload. This channel is considered to be at the hardware level because the Link Controller is a hardware component of a Bluetooth device.

◆ **Link Manager (LM) channel.** The LM channel is used at the LM level, which is just above the LC layer. The control data of the LM channel is carried between the LMs of a master and slave devices in the payload either over an active Synchronous Connection-Oriented (SCO) or an Asynchronous Connectionless (ACL) link. This channel uses the protected Data Medium (DM) rate packets indicated by L_CH code 11 in the payload header. This channel is considered to be at the firmware level closer to the firmware, unlike the LC layer, which is closer to the hardware.

◆ **User Asynchronous (UA) channel.** The UA channel is used to carry asynchronous user data in the payload of a data packet. The data of this channel is also carried in the DV packets over an SCO link and sometimes in one or more baseband packets. This channel can be fragmented across more than one baseband data packets that use L_CH code 10 for UA start packet and L_CH code 01 for continuation packets. L_CH code 10 is used in non-fragmented packets or for the first fragment of a multi-part packet transmission. All other packets use the LCH_code 01 for UA indication.

◆ **User Isochronous (UI) channel.** A UI channel is similar to a UA channel except that it carries isochronous user data.

◆ **User Synchronous (US) channel.** A US channel carries synchronous user data in the payload of a data packet. The control data is carried over an SCO link that can be interrupted for the transmission of high priority data on another LM, UA, or UI channel.

Of these five channels, this chapter focuses on the data transmitted on the LM channel. As discussed earlier, the logical field of the packet header is set to 11 to identify the use of the LM channel for the transmission of control data.

The communication between the LMs of various devices is maintained by the LMP. The LMP operates over the LC protocol, which takes care of sequenced and reliable information transmission, retransmission when necessary, and error detection and correction of transmission between devices. The function of the LMP, therefore, does not include operations related to information delivery. The following section looks at the functions of the LMP.

Link Manager Protocol

Bluetooth devices communicate with each other by using LMs, which exchange messages to control and maintain the links between devices. The LMP functions as a command-response, packet-oriented communication protocol facilitating the exchange of messages between the LMs of various devices. The LMP carries control data that determines the type of service to be rendered. The control data passed from the higher protocols is, therefore, used to either communicate with the LMs of different devices or send control signals to its own baseband and radio layers.

The LM, as you know, takes care of functions such as link setup, link configuration, and authentication. Before moving any further, look at the illustration shown in Figure 5-1 representing the functions of the Link Manager.

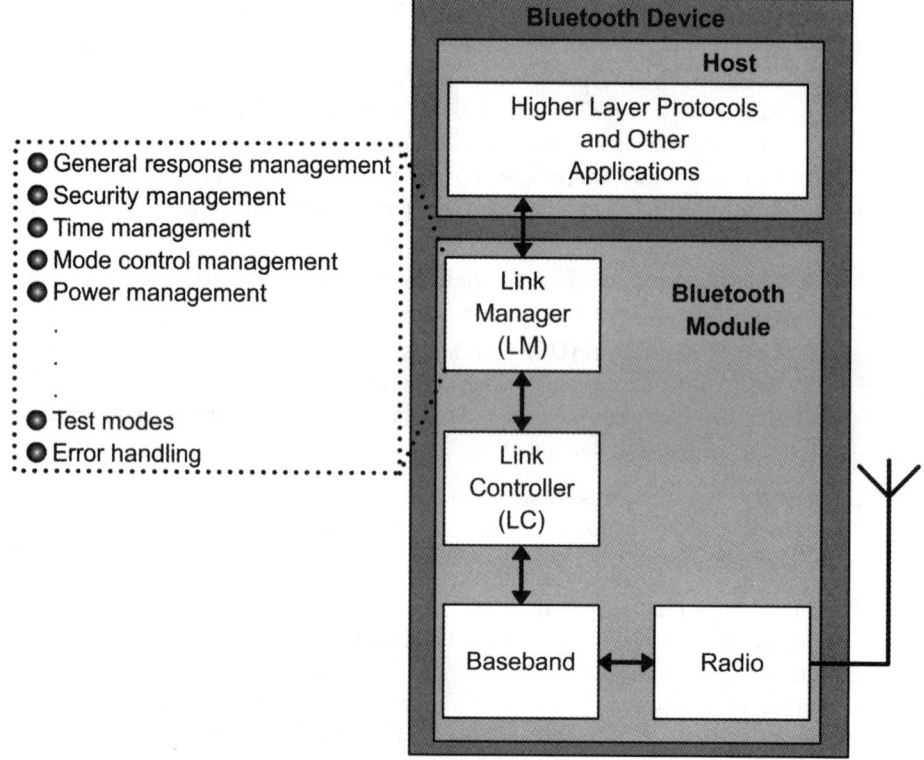

FIGURE 5-1 *The functions of the Link Manager*

The control data that flows between communicating devices is in the form of messages that are known as *LMP Protocol Data Units* (LMP_PDUs). LMP_PDUs are transported through the time-oriented baseband link protocol. As a result, these messages are single-slot DM or DV packets that are carried in the payload of ACL packets with the header L_CH value of 11. Each LMP_PDU consists of the following three fields.

- ◆ **The transactionID field.** The 1-bit transactionID field contains the unique transaction identifier (TID). The TID identifies the LM transaction that is initiated by either a master or a slave device. The value of the TID is zero (0) if a master initiates the transaction and one (1) if a slave initiates the transaction.

- ◆ **The OpCode field.** The 7-bit OpCode field is used to identify the sequence and the type of the LMP_PDU.

- ◆ **The content field.** The 0 to 17 bytes of the content field carry application-specific information in the form of message parameters. The parameters occupy an integral number of bytes. For example, a DV Base Band PDU (DV BB_PDU), when supported, is often used instead of an LMP_PDU of nine bytes. In addition, a DM1 Base Band PDU (DM1 BB_PDU) can be used instead of an LMP_PDU. This is because an LMP_PDU easily fits into a DM1 Base Band PDU (DM1 BB_PDU).

Figure 5-2 illustrates the payload body of an LMP PDU, containing the TID, the OpCode, and the content field.

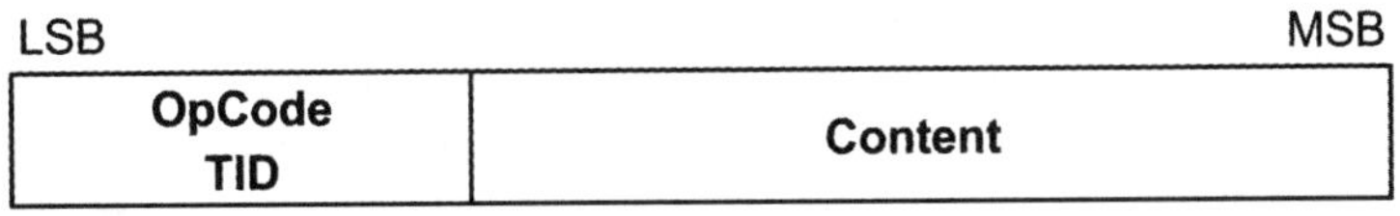

LSB   MSB

OpCode TID	Content

FIGURE 5-2 *The payload body of an LMP PDU*

The following sections discuss the various LMP_PDUs that are exchanged between the LMs of communicating devices. Based on the services offered, the LMP_PDUs can be classified into the following groups. The services offered are

- ◆ General response management
- ◆ Security management
- ◆ Time management
- ◆ Mode control management
- ◆ Power management
- ◆ Information transfer management
- ◆ Connection and link management

The initiation of a link setup between two devices requires for the exchange of general response PDUs. The next section discusses the function of these PDUs during the general request/response transaction between two devices.

General Response Management

As discussed earlier, the logical channel field or the L_CH field is used to identify an LMP_PDU. You may recall that the value of the flow control field in the packet header is used to stop the transmission of L2CAP packets. As a result, the flow bit field value of the LMP_PDU is set to zero by the transmitting device.

The baseband links between Bluetooth devices are maintained and managed by the LM. The LM controls the working of the baseband by using the ACL links. Once the ACL links are set, the LMP packets are then used to set up SCO links over an ACL connection.

During the link-up between devices, the LM in one device initiates an LMP_PDU transaction with the LM of another device. The receiving LM, in turn, responds by using the next transaction sequence to send back an LMP_PDU. The response of the receiving device includes an `LMP_accepted` PDU or an `LMP_not_accepted` PDU. As is evident, these PDUs signify the acceptance or non-acceptance of the LM request from the transaction initiator. Therefore, the outcome of the LM response results in the following two types of LMP_PDU transactions.

♦ The LM of the two communicating devices initiates a PDU transaction by sending a request. The receiving LM either accepts or rejects the request. Accordingly, the LM response includes an `LMP_accepted` PDU or an `LMP_not_accepted` PDU, in addition to the requested information in case of an accepted request. Alternatively, the LM rejecting a request can send a corresponding request LMP_PDU to open negotiations for the original request. Figure 5-3 illustrates a general LMP_PDU response containing the request/response transaction and the negotiation phases.

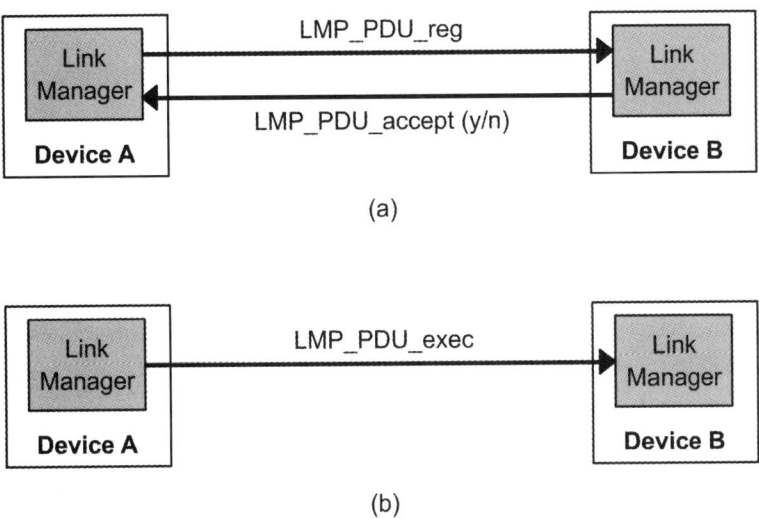

FIGURE 5-3 *A general request/response LMP_PDU transaction*

◆ Another transaction arising from a request by a communication initiator is a compulsory request acceptance by a slave in response to a request sent by a master's LM. The command request initiated by the master results in a response from the slave without any scope for rejection or negotiation.

NOTE

Each PDU is either mandatory or optional, as is indicated in the M/O (Mandatory/Optional) column of the tables in the subsequent sections of this chapter. It is obvious that an LM does not need to transmit an optional PDU. However, it needs to identify all the optional PDUs that it receives and send valid responses when required. An LMP does not send a response if the optional PDU received does not require a response. When an optional PDU necessitates a response, the reason code used to indicate this is *unsupported LMP feature*.

Security Management

Security services are important because they ensure the confidentiality and integrity of the data in the data packets. The encryption services are used to maintain the confidentiality of the data while authentication provides access control methods to ensure that the transmitted data is not manipulated.

The baseband layer contains an engine for encrypting and ciphering the data. The engine defines algorithms to generate the encryption key and procedures to authenticate devices. The engine is configured and controlled by the higher-layer protocols and is synchronized at both ends of a link. The LMP provides the services necessary for the negotiation of the encryption codes at both ends of a Bluetooth link. The authentication of Bluetooth devices is a mandatory function, whereas the encryption of Bluetooth link is optional. As a result, the security services provided by the LMP include the following:

◆ Device authentication

◆ Link encryption

The following sections define the various PDUs that are used for device authentication and link encryption in Bluetooth devices.

Device Authentication

The authentication of a Bluetooth device follows a challenge-response transaction. The transaction defines the roles of a verifier and a claimant. The intent of this procedure is to authenticate the identity of each participating device to identify the masquerading intruders and the legitimate users.

Device authentication is initiated by using a random starting point. The verifier uses an LMP_au_rand PDU to send a 16-byte random number challenging the authenticity of the claimant. The claimant uses the random number, the claimant's BD_ADDR, and a secret key to calculate the response that is sent back to the verifier in an LMP_sres PDU. A correct response from the claimant results in successful authentication. An incorrect response from the claimant results in unsuccessful authentication. Unsuccessful authentication leads to a termination of the connection using an LMP_detach PDU containing the reason code *authentication failure*. Table 5-1 lists the two PDUs that are used for device authentication, as specified in the Bluetooth specification 1.0 B.

Table 5-1 The LMP PDUs Used for Device Authentication

PDU	Contains	Mandatory (M)/Optional (O)
LMP_au_rand	random number	M
LMP_sres	authentication response	M

LMP_au_rand and LMP_sres PDUs are exchanged between devices with a common link key. The common link key is used along with the random number to calculate the claimant's response. A device can choose to use identical or separate link keys for the authentication of other devices. Figure 5-4 illustrates a device authentication transaction in the presence of the link key.

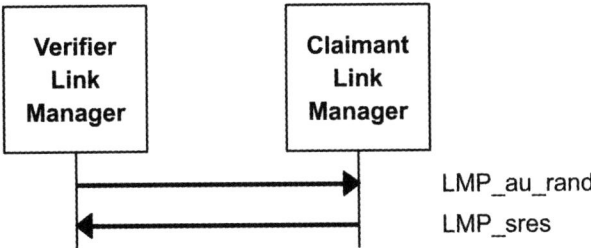

FIGURE 5-4 *An authentication transaction between devices with a link key*

If a link key is absent in a device, the claimant response has an `LMP_not_accepted` PDU containing the reason code *missing key*. Figure 5-5 illustrates a device authentication transaction in the absence of the link key.

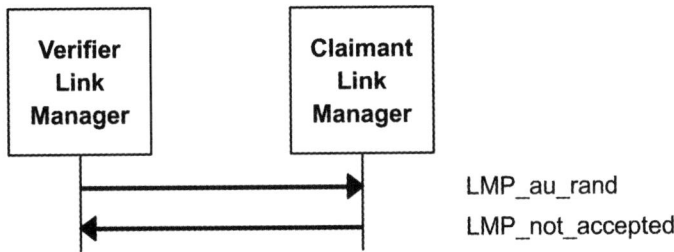

FIGURE 5-5 *An authentication transaction between devices without a link key*

In the absence of a common link key, the devices are paired to create an initialization key. Pairing can be defined as a security procedure that uses LMP_PDUs to automatically establish a link key between mutually authenticated users. Both the devices calculate the initialization key by using the random number and a 48-bit Personal Identification Number (PIN). The initialization key (K_{init}) thus created is used by both the devices for preliminary authentication prior to the generation of a permanent link key.

K_{init} is created when the master sends an `LMP_in_rand` PDU to the slave. The generation of the authentication response is based on the initialization key instead of the link key. A link key is created only at the end of successful authentication.

The two types of link keys created are *unit* keys and *combination* keys. A unit key is derived from the input parameters of a single device. A combination key, on the other hand, is derived from the input parameters of both the devices. The combination key is preferred because it provides a stronger bond between the devices.

Different PDUs are used for the authentication with the K_{init} and authentication with a link key. The initiation of authentication with the K_{init} uses an LMP_in_rand PDU while that with a link key uses an LMP_au_rand PDU.

NOTE

To understand the K_{init} calculation, you can refer to Section 14.5.3 of the Bluetooth specification.

Table 5-2 lists the PDUs that are used in the pairing procedure for authenticating the identity of the participating devices, as specified in the Bluetooth specification 1.0 B.

Table 5-2 The LMP PDUs Used for Device Pairing

PDU	Contains	M/O
LMP_au_rand	random number	M
LMP_in_rand	random number	M
LMP_sres	authentication response	M
LMP_comb_key	random number	M
LMP_unit_key	key	M

The following three situations arise as a consequence to the pairing procedure.

◆ The claimant accepts the pairing and replies to the verifier's LMP_in_rand PDU with an LMP_accepted PDU. Both the devices then calculate the K_{init} and authentication is done. The verifier creates the link key if the authentication response is correct; else it ends the connection using an LMP_detach PDU with a reason code as *authentication failure*. Figure 5-6 represents a situation in which a claimant accepts pairing.

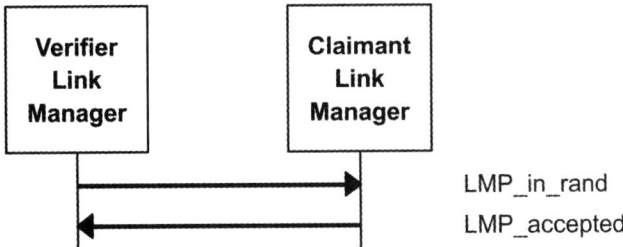

FIGURE 5-6 *The pairing procedure when the claimant accepts pairing*

◆ In devices with a fixed PIN, a claimant requests for a switch to the role of a verifier role. In such a case, a new random number is sent back in an `LMP_in_rand` PDU. The other device with a variable PIN accepts the random number and generates the response with an `LMP_accepted` PDU. The roles are switched, and authentication proceeds after pairing, as described in the preceding sections. However, if the role switch is requested for a device with a variable PIN, the other device with a fixed PIN rejects the pairing using an `LMP_not_accepted` PDU with the reason code as *pairing not allowed.* Figure 5-7 represents a situation in which the claimant requests for a role switch.

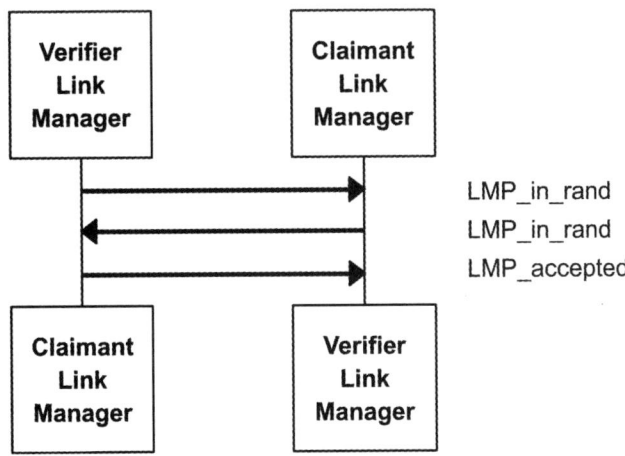

FIGURE 5-7 *The pairing procedure when the claimant accepts pairing and requests to become the verifier*

◆ The claimant receives an `LMP_in_rand` PDU from the verifier and rejects the pairing using an `LMP_not_accepted` PDU with the reason code as *pairing not allowed*. Figure 5-8 represents the situation in which a claimant rejects pairing.

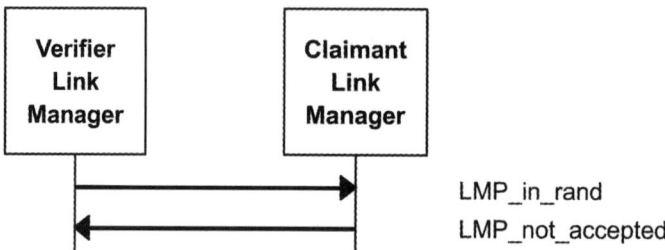

FIGURE 5-8 *The pairing procedure when the claimant rejects pairing*

During pairing, the devices can select a different key within a piconet. If the link key is derived from the combination keys, the link key can be changed. However, if the link key is derived from the unit key, the devices go through the pairing procedure to change the link key. Once a new link key is created, the old key is discarded. Figure 5-9 illustrates the completion of authentication with the change of the link key.

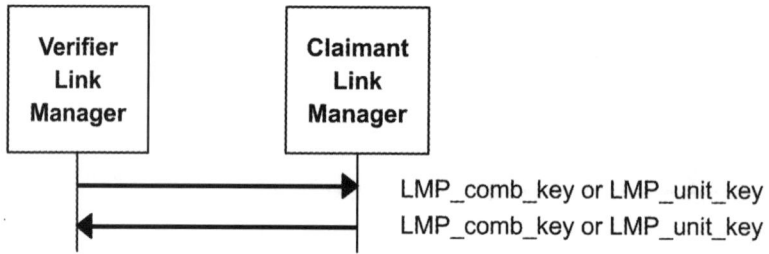

FIGURE 5-9 *Successful change of the link key*

Table 5-3 lists the PDUs that are used in the procedure for changing the link key of paired devices, as specified in the Bluetooth specification 1.0 B.

Table 5-3 The LMP PDUs Used for Changing the Link Key in Paired Devices

PDU	Contains	M/O
LMP_comb_key	random number	M
LMP_unit_key	key	M

The current link key can also be changed. However, this change is temporary and is used for a finite number of connections. The new link key is stored in the non-volatile memory and used for all further connections until it is changed again. The current link can either be a temporary key or a semi-permanent key. It is important to remember that although the change in the key is temporary, the change is valid only for a single session. Devices usually opt for a temporary change in the current link key to support encrypted broadcasts. Figure 5-10 illustrates the successful change of the current link key to a temporary key.

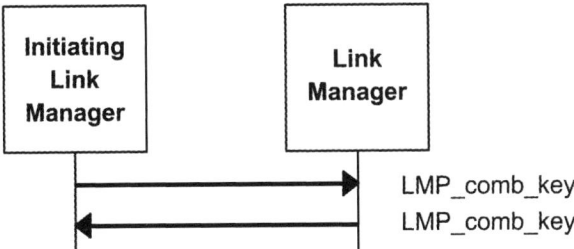

FIGURE 5-10 *Successful change of the current link key to a temporary key*

Figure 5-11 illustrates the creation of the semi-permanent link key.

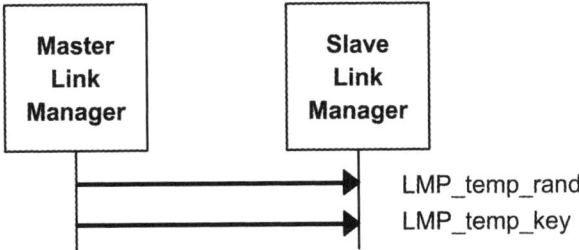

FIGURE 5-11 *Change of the current link key to a semi-permanent key*

Table 5-4 lists the PDUs that are used in the procedure for changing the current link key of paired devices, as specified in the Bluetooth specification 1.0 B.

Table 5-4 The LMP PDUs Used for Changing the Current Link Key in Paired Devices

PDU	Contains	M/O
LMP_temp_rand	random number	M
LMP_temp_key	key	M
LMP_use_semi_permanent_key	Nil	M

Link Encryption

The Bluetooth link is encrypted to ensure the confidentiality of the data transmitted over it. Bluetooth wireless technology uses the 1-bit stream cipher-based technique to encrypt its links.

The devices in a piconet can use encryption to protect the confidentiality of the data only after they have authenticated themselves at least once. The master generates a temporary master key (K_{master}) to ensure that all the slaves in a piconet use the same encryption parameters. All the slaves use the K_{master} as the current link key before the encryption begins.

The LMP does not actually perform link encryption but provides services to manage the process of encryption. The process of encryption involves the following steps:

The master and the slave first need to decide whether or not to use encryption. In addition, they need to decide whether to use encryption for point-to-point packets or broadcast packets.

The master sends an `LMP_encryption_key_size_req` PDU with an approximate or suggested size of the key, $L_{sug, m}$, to determine the size of the encryption key. The slave responds with an `LMP_accepted` PDU if the suggested size of the encryption key is acceptable to the slave. If not, the slave sends the master an `LMP_encryption_key_size_req` PDU with a value for the suggested encryption key size. The values are evaluated and sent/resent till both the master and the slave agree upon the size of the encryption key. Figure 5-12 illustrates the negotiations between the master and the slave to determine the size of the encryption key.

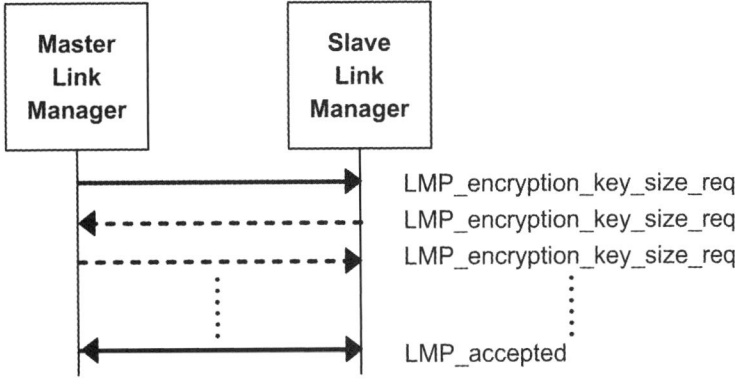

FIGURE 5-12 *The negotiations to set the size of the encryption key*

The master sends an `LMP_start_encryption_req` PDU to initiate the encryption procedure. During encryption, the master is first configured to transmit unencrypted packets and receive encrypted packets. The slave transmits and receives encrypted packets. In the last stage of encryption, the master is configured to transmit and receive encrypted packets.

To end the encryption procedure, the master sends an `LMP_stop_encryption_req` PDU, which reverses the process undertaken after sending an `LMP_start_encryption_req` PDU. To terminate the encryption procedure, the master is first configured to transmit encrypted packets and receive unencrypted packets. The slave transmits and receives unencrypted packets. In the last stage, the master is configured to transmit and receive unencrypted packets.

Table 5-5 lists the LMP PDUs that are used in the encryption procedure, as specified in the Bluetooth specification 1.0 B.

Table 5-5 The LMP PDUs Used for Managing Link Encryption

PDU	Contains	M/O
LMP_encryption_mode_req	encryption mode	O
LMP_encryption_key_size_req	key size	O
LMP_start_encryption_req	random number	O
LMP_stop_encryption_req	Nil	O

Time Management

The synchronization of the clock timings between the master and the slaves in a piconet is an important aspect of the Bluetooth wireless communication. The LMP services are used to request other devices for updated clock information. The following are the different services offered with respect to device clock timings.

◆ Clock offset request
◆ Slot offset request
◆ Timing accuracy information request

Clock Offset Request

The payload header of the synchronizing FHS packet that a slave receives contains the clock difference between the slave clock and the master clock (clock offset). The clock offset is updated after the receipt of packets from the master. After a slave leaves the piconet, the master can use the slave's clock offset to estimate the channel at which the slave will wake up to a page scan. For this estimate, the master sends an LMP_clock_offset_req PDU to request for the slave's current offset. Figure 5-13 illustrates the clock-offset procedure that is used by a master to access a slave's clock offset.

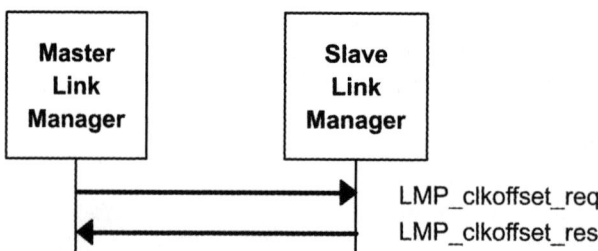

FIGURE 5-13 *The clock offset request*

Table 5-6 lists the LMP PDUs that are used for the clock offset information, as specified in the Bluetooth specification 1.0 B.

Table 5-6 The LMP PDUs Used for Managing Clock-offset Information

PDU	Contains	M/O
LMP_clkoffset_req	nil	M
LMP_clkoffset_res	clock offset	M

Slot Offset Request

The slot timings of different piconets vary. Consider a situation in which a slave in a particular piconet wants to switch over and take up the role of a master in an adjacent piconet. In such a situation, the slave needs to have access to information regarding the slot timing differences between the two piconets. The slot offset request is a unidirectional request used to obtain information regarding the slot timing differences between two adjacent piconets. The device wanting the role switch initiates the procedure that is reciprocated by an `LMP_slot_offset` PDU sent from the other device. An `LMP_slot_offset` PDU is sent before an `LMP_accepted` PDU. The `LMP_slot_offset` PDU carries the slot offset and the `BD_ADDR` parameters. The slot offset is calculated in µs and is the time between the start of the master's TX slot in the piconet and the start of the masters TX slot in the piconet where the `BD_ADDR` device is the master

The slot offset information is useful during inter-piconet communications. Figure 5-14 illustrates the slot offset procedure that is used to calculate the slot time difference between two adjacent piconets.

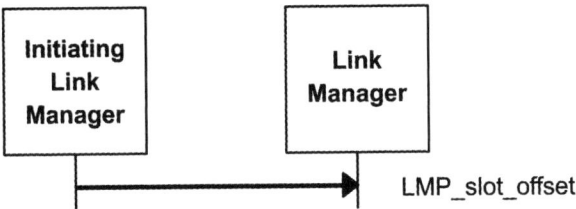

FIGURE 5-14 *The slot offset request*

Table 5-7 lists the LMP PDU that is used for the slot offset information, as specified in the Bluetooth specification 1.0 B.

Table 5-7 The LMP PDU Used for Managing Slot Offset Information

PDU	Contains	M/O
LMP_slot_offset	slot offset and the BD_ADDR	M

Timing Accuracy Information Request

The timing accuracy information services are important in Bluetooth because they are used to maintain clock synchronization during link communication. This information is used for a device in a piconet to optimize its wake-up time after a long duration of inactivity.

The timing accuracy parameters include the long-term drift and the long-term jitter of the receiving device's clock. The long-term drift is measured in parts per million (ppm) and the long-term jitter is measured in μs. These parameters are used during the sniff, hold, and park modes that are discussed in the subsequent sections. Not all devices support this LMP service. Therefore, on receipt of a timing accuracy information request, an LMP_not_accepted PDU intimates non-support for this service with the reason code of *unsupported LMP feature*. Figure 5-15 illustrates the timing accuracy information request procedure.

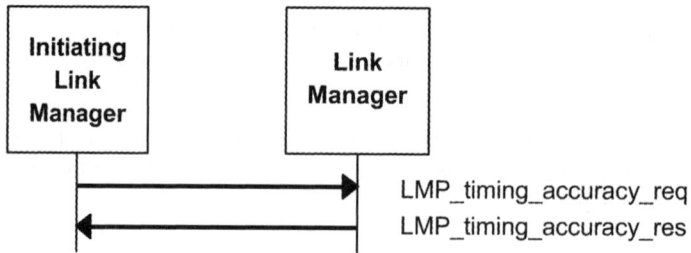

FIGURE 5-15 *The timing accuracy information request*

Table 5-8 lists the LMP PDUs that are used for timing accuracy information, as specified in the Bluetooth specification 1.0 B.

Table 5-8 The LMP PDUs Used for Timing Accuracy Information Request

PDU	Contains	M/O
LMP_timing_accuracy_req	nil	O
LMP_timing_accuracy_res	long-term drift and long-term jitter	O

Mode Control and Management

In course of their association with a piconet, devices use methods or modes to reduce the power utilization. As a result, a Bluetooth device exists in a number of modes and states. The LMP provides services to manage and control the states and modes of devices to ensure smooth operation. The services provided by the LMP for the control and management of device states and modes can be classified into according to the following three modes of a device:

◆ The hold mode
◆ The sniff mode
◆ The park mode

In addition to these modes, the LMP services are also used during a switch of roles between a master and a slave in a piconet. Therefore, this section begins by discussing the LMP services used for a role switch between a master and a slave.

Switch of Master/Slave Roles

A paging device assumes the role of a master in a piconet. However, a situation such as the implementation of the LAN access profile using PPP requires a switch between the roles of a master and a slave. The LMP switch of master/slave role service allows a slave in a piconet to take up the role of a master.

Figure 5-16 illustrates the master/slave roles before and after a switch.

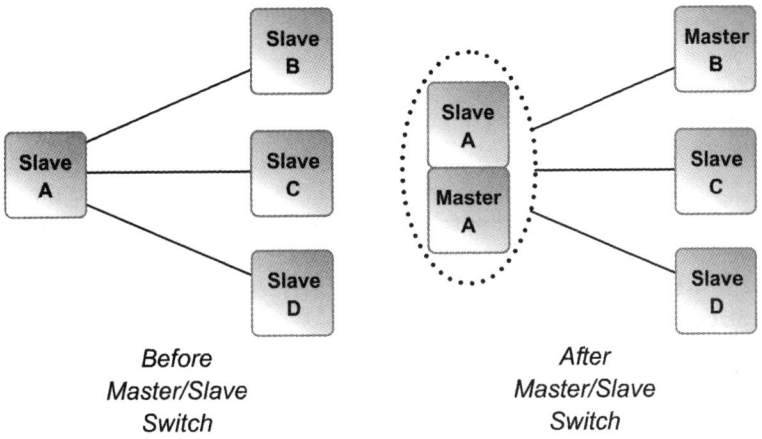

Before Master/Slave Switch   *After Master/Slave Switch*

FIGURE 5-16 *A change of roles during the master/slave switch*

A slave device wanting a switch in the roles initiates the switch by finalizing the transmission of the current L2CAP packet before sending an LMP_switch_req PDU. If the other device accepts the role switch, it returns a response with an LMP_accepted PDU. Similarly, if the other device rejects the role switch, it returns a response with an LMP_not_accepted PDU. If a request for the role switch is accepted, the slave assumes the role of the master and the master becomes the slave. Figure 5-17 illustrates the procedure of a master/slave role switch within a piconet.

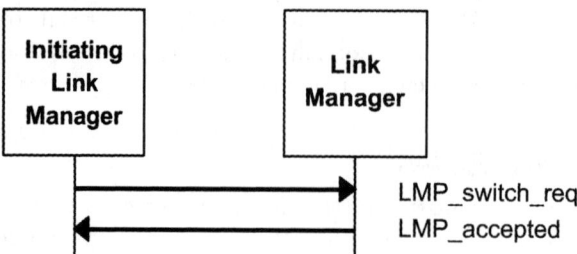

FIGURE 5-17 *A successful master/slave role switch*

The next section explains the PDUs that are exchanged during the hold, sniff, and park modes of a device.

Hold Mode

A slave is said to be in the *hold* mode when the ACL connections are suspended in installments for a time period that is called the *hold time*. When a slave is in the hold mode, the ACL transmissions from a master are held back for the specified time period but the SCO transmissions continue as scheduled. The hold mode is used as a power-saving technique when there is no need to send data for a long time. During this time, the transreceiver is switched off to save power. A device can move into the hold mode in the following situations:

◆ A master may force a slave device to move into the hold mode if a previous request to move a slave into the hold mode has been accepted. In such a case, the current hold time cannot exceed the hold time in the previously accepted hold mode.

◆ A slave may force a master device to move into the hold mode if a previous request to move a master into the hold mode has been accepted. In such a case, the current hold time cannot exceed the hold time in a previously accepted hold mode.

◆ Either a master or a slave can request to move into the hold mode. Once a device agrees to move into the hold mode, it responds to an `LMP_hold_req` PDU with an `LMP_accepted` PDU. Conversely, if a device rejects the request, the response contains an `LMP_not_accepted` PDU with the reason code as *unsupported parameter value*.

Table 5-9 lists the LMP PDUs that are used for the hold mode service, as specified in the Bluetooth specification 1.0 B.

Table 5-9 The LMP PDUs Used for Hold Mode

PDU	Contains	M/O
LMP_hold	hold time	O
LMP_hold_req	hold time	O

Sniff Mode

A slave device usually listens to each even-numbered slot to ascertain if the master is transmitting data. However, in the *sniff* mode, a slave can refrain from listening to the slots for an ACL link. This is because the master transmits at a reduced duty cycle at every T_{sniff} slave listening opportunity. As a result, communication in the sniff mode is reduced to periodic sniff slots.

Before moving into the sniff mode, a master and a slave negotiate the timing for the sniff slots using a sniff interval (T_{sniff}) and a sniff offset (D_{sniff}). The offset defines the time for the first sniff slot, after which the slots follow periodically separated by an interval of T_{sniff}. For transmission over a link that is in the sniff mode, the master initiates the transmission in the sniff slot. The transmission is controlled by the sniff attempt parameter and the sniff timeout parameter. The former determines the number of sniffing slots for the slave, while the latter determines the number of additional slots that the slave needs to listen in to in order to continue receiving packets at its Active Member address (AM_ADDR). A device can move into the sniff mode in the following situations:

◆ A master may force a slave device to move into the sniff mode with an LMP_sniff PDU. The LMP parameters include the timing parameters that define the operation of the slave in the sniff mode.

◆ A master or a slave may request to move into the sniff mode with an LMP_sniff_req PDU. The master and the slave negotiate the timing parameters after which the receiving device agrees to move into the sniff mode. The success of the agreement is indicated with an LMP_accepted PDU and the ACL link moves into the sniff mode. Conversely, if a device rejects the request, the response contains an LMP_not_accepted PDU, with the reason code as *unsupported parameter value*. In such a case, the negotiation is terminated and there is no change in the mode.

◆ Another situation is that a slave moves from the sniff mode to the active mode. The end of the sniff mode is indicated by sending an LMP_unsniff_req PDU and is reciprocated with an LMP_accepted PDU. If the requesting device is a slave, it moves into the active mode after receiving an LMP_accepted PDU. On the other hand, if the requesting device is a master, then the slave moves into the active mode after receiving an LMP_unsniff_req PDU.

Table 5-10 lists the LMP PDUs that are used for the sniff mode service, as specified in the Bluetooth specification 1.0 B.

Table 5-10 The LMP PDUs Used for Sniff Mode

PDU	Contains	M/O
LMP_sniff	timing control flags, D_{sniff}, T_{sniff}, sniff attempt, and sniff timeout	O
LMP_sniff_req	timing control flags, D_{sniff}, T_{sniff}, sniff attempt, and sniff timeout	O
LMP_unsniff_req	nil	O

Park Mode

When a slave is in the hold or sniff mode, it is still a member of the piconet, and there-fore, retains its AM_ADDR. In addition, though both the hold and sniff modes affect ACL transmissions, but the SCO transmissions are not interrupted.

However, there may be situations when during a period of device inactivity, a slave con-tinues to burn power merely because it is still a member of the piconet. In such situations, power consumption can be reduced if the slave moves into the *park* mode. A slave that is in the park mode is dissociated from the piconet. In this mode, the device gives up its AM_ADDR but maintains the timing synchronization of the piconet. As a result, if required, the slave can avoid redoing the inquiry and paging procedures and quickly change its mode to rejoin the piconet.

A slave in the parked mode gives up its BD_ADDR and is assigned two new but temporary 8-bit addresses—the all-zero parked member address (PM_ADDR) and the access request address (AR_ADDR). The master uses this PM_ADDR to unpark the slave device.

The readmission of parked devices into the piconet is facilitated by the use of the master-defined lower bandwidth *beacon* channel. The beacon channel is used for the periodic transmission of broadcast packets containing LMP_PDUs. The PDUs, such as LMP_set_broadcast_scan_window, LMP_unpark_BD_addr_req, and LMP_unpark_PM_addr_req that are sent by the master to the parked slaves are not sent individually but are broadcast.

The device can move into the park mode in the following situations:

◆ A master may force a slave device to move into the park mode. To do so, the master completes the transmission of the current L2CAP message and sends an LMP_park PDU. The slave receives the PDU, completes the transmission of the current L2CAP message, and sends back an acceptance response with an LMP_accepted PDU.

◆ A master may request to move a slave into the park mode. To do so, the master completes the transmission of the current L2CAP message and sends an `LMP_park_req` PDU. If the slave accepts to move into the park mode, it completes the transmission of the current L2CAP message, and sends the response with an `LMP_accepted` PDU. The master device then sends an `LMP_park` PDU. Conversely, if a slave rejects the request, the response contains an `LMP_not_accepted` PDU.

◆ In addition to a master's request to move a slave into the park mode, a slave can also request to be placed in the park mode. To do so, the slave completes the transmission of the current L2CAP message and sends an `LMP_park_req` PDU. If the master accepts the request, it completes the transmission of the current L2CAP message, and sends the response with an `LMP_park` PDU. Conversely, if the master rejects the request, the response contains an `LMP_not_accepted` PDU.

◆ The master can also choose to unpark one or many of its slaves. The master uses a broadcast LMP message containing the `PM_ADDR` or the `BD_ADDR` of the slaves that it wants to unpark. The broadcast message also includes an `AM_ADDR`, which is assigned to the slaves by the master. The slaves are always unparked at the beacon slots. To check for the success of the unpark request, the master polls each unparked slave. The slave responds to the POLL packets with the response containing an `LMP_accepted` PDU.

Table 5-11 lists the LMP PDUs that are used for the park mode service, as specified in the Bluetooth specification 1.0 B.

Table 5-11 The LMP PDUs Used for Park Mode

PDU	Contains	M/O
LMP_park_req	nil	O
LMP_sniff	timing control flags, $D_B, T_B, N_B,$ PM_ADDR, AR_ADDR, D_{Bsleep}, $N_{Bsleep}, D_{access}, T_{access}, N_{acc\text{-}slots}, N_{poll}$, M_{access} and access scheme	O
LMP_set_broadcast_scan_window	timing control flags, broadcast scan window, and D_B (optional)	O
LMP_modify_beacon	timing control flags, D_B (optional) $T_B, N_B, D_{access}, T_{access}, N_{acc\text{-}slots}, N_{poll}, M_{access},$ and access scheme	O

(continued on next page)

Table 5-11 The LMP PDUs Used for Park Mode (continued)

PDU	Contains	M/O
LMP_unpark_PM_ADDR_req	timing control flags, D_B (optional), AM_ADDR, PM_ADDR, AM_ADDR (optional), PM_ADDR(optional) that is a total of 1-7 pairs of AM_ADDR, PM_ADDR	O
LMP_unpark_BD_ADDR_req	timing control flags, D_B (optional), AM_ADDR, BD_ADDR, AM_ADDR (optional), and BD_ADDR(optional)	O

 NOTE

The definitions of some parameters used in Table 5-11 are given below:
D_B: The timing of the first beacon slot
T_B: The intervals between beacon trains
N_B: The number of beacon slots in a single beacon train
D_{access}: The time from the first beacon instance to the first access slot
T_{access}: The width of the access window used by the parked slaves to request for unparking
M_{access}: The number of access window repetitions
$N_{acc-slots}$: The number of slave-to-master access slots
N_{poll}: The number of slots after the access window used by the slave to listen on after requesting for an unpark

During mode management, especially in the park mode, the PDUs are used to negotiate a change in a device mode to conserve power during the period of inactivity. The following section discusses the other PDUs that are used in power management to ensure proper power utilization.

Power Management

A Bluetooth device can regulate its power by increasing or decreasing the output power. An LMP_incr_power_req PDU is sent to request for an increase in power. If the receiving device is already transmitting at maximum power, it returns a response with an LMP_max_power PDU. It is important to note that a request for an increase in power is accepted for a second time only if a prior request for a decrease in power has been accepted. Similarly, an LMP_decr_power_req PDU is sent to request for a decrease in power. If the receiving device is already transmitting at minimum power, it sends back a response with an LMP_min_power PDU. An LMP_incr/decr_power_req PDU includes a 1-byte reserved space containing referential parameters for future use. Table 5-12 lists the LMP PDUs that are used for the power management service, as specified in the Bluetooth specification 1.0 B.

Table 5-12 The LMP PDUs Used for Power Management

PDU	Contains	M/O
LMP_incr_power_req	one byte for future use	O
LMP_decr_power_req	one byte for future use	O
LMP_max_power	nil	O
LMP_min_power	nil	O

The next section looks at the PDUs that are used to exchange vital information regarding the LMP.

Information Exchange Management

As you know, the LMs of two devices exchange information to coordinate data transfer between the devices. Although this functionality of the LM has been reiterated time and again, this chapter has not yet elaborated on the content that is exchanged between the LMs of communicating devices. The information exchange services of the LMP facilitate the transfer of crucial information between LMs. The following are the different features offered during the exchange of information between the LMs of two devices:

◆ The LMP version
◆ A name request
◆ LMP features

LMP Version

An LMP_version_req PDU is used to include information about the LMP version supported by the device sending the PDU. The receiving device sends its own LMP version in an LMP_version_res PDU. The version number includes the following three parameters:

◆ **Version number (VersNr).** The version number specifies the version of the LMP supported by the particular device.

◆ **Company ID (CompId).** The company ID is used to track the problems with the lower protocol layers. Each company that creates a unique implementation of the LM uses a unique CompId. The same company is also responsible for assigning and maintaining the sub-version number.

◆ **Sub-version number (SubVersNr).** The sub-version number is a unique number that specifies the RF/BB/LM implementations.

Table 5-13 lists the LMP PDUs that are used for the management of information exchange between LMs, as specified in the Bluetooth specification 1.0 B.

Table 5-13 The LMP PDUs Used for Information Exchange Management

PDU	Contains	M/O
LMP_version_req	VersNr, CompId, and SubVersNr	M
LMP_ version_res	VersNr, CompId, and SubVersNr	M

Figure 5-18 illustrates the request/response procedure that takes place between two LMs for an LMP_version PDU.

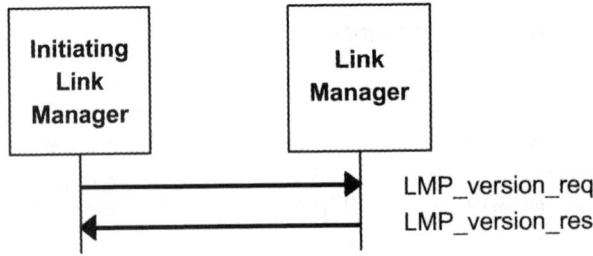

FIGURE 5-18 *The LMP_version request/response transaction*

Name Request

Each Bluetooth device is associated with a user-friendly name that consists of 248 bytes coded according to UTF-8 standards. The device name is longer than a single DM1 packet and is, therefore, fragmented over one or more DM1 packets.

The LMP name request service can be used to request for the name of another Bluetooth device. An `LMP_name_req` PDU is sent containing a name offset that identifies the expected fragment. The addressed device responds by sending an `LMP_name_res` containing the desired name offset, the name length, and the name fragment. The name length in an `LMP_name_res` PDU contains the total number of bytes in the name of the Bluetooth device. Table 5-14 lists the LMP PDUs that are used for the name request service.

Table 5-14 The LMP PDUs Used for Name Request

PDU	Contains	M/O
LMP_name_req	name offset	M
LMP_name_res	name offset, name length, and name fragment	M

Supported Features

The supported features service includes information regarding optional features that are supported by the baseband, the radio, and the LM. Often, the Bluetooth radio and the LC support only a few of the features that are specified for the BB and the radio in the Bluetooth specification 1.0 B. However, a device needs information regarding the supported features of the BB, the LM, or the radio prior to sending packets other than the ID, FHS, POLL, DM1, or DH1 packets. As a result, the supported features service is used to exchange information regarding the optional features supported by the specified layers. The optional features are:

◆ Channel-quality-driven data rate changes

◆ Low-power modes that include the Hold, Park, and Sniff modes

◆ Multi-slot packets that include 3- and 5-slot packets

◆ Master or Slave switch and slot offset messages needed during the role switch

◆ Timing accuracy messages

◆ Optional paging schemes

◆ Power control for low-power radios which is otherwise mandatory for radios over 0 dBm

◆ Voice coding schemes

◆ Encryption

◆ SCO supported links specially HV2 and HV3 packets

◆ Receive Signal Strength Indication (RSSI) used by the higher protocol layers

The request for this service is initiated with an LMP_features_req PDU that is responded to with an LMP_features_res PDU. During this exchange of PDUs, the LMs access information about the optional features supported by each other's BB/LM/radio. Table 5-15 lists the LMP PDUs that are used to exchange information about the supported features.

Table 5-15 The LMP PDUs Used for Supported Features

PDU	Contains	M/O
LMP_features_req	features	M
LMP_features_res	features	M

Figure 5-19 illustrates the request/response procedure that takes place between two LMs for exchange of information regarding optional features that are supported by the baseband, the radio, and the LM.

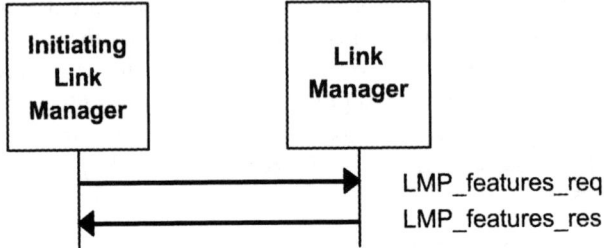

FIGURE 5-19 *The LMP_features request/response transaction*

Communication between devices is initiated only after the two devices are connected. He next section discusses the PDUs that are exchanged between the LMs to indicate the establishment and termination of a connection.

Connection Management

The LMP functions as a transport protocol that facilitates the exchange of control information between the LMs in devices. The PDUs exchanged during this information transfer does not include the PDUs of the higher-level protocols such as the L2CAP protocol or the host. As a result, when a host application needs to communicate with a host in another device, it sends an LMP connection service PDU to initiate the connection. The following are the different services offered during the exchange of information between the LMs of two devices:

♦ Connection establishment

♦ Connection termination

Connection Establishment

A connection between the host applications in two devices is established when one of the devices sends an `LMP_host_connection_req` PDU. After the receiving device agrees to the connection, the LMs of the two devices negotiate the various parameters for link establishment, authentication, and quality of service. On completion of the negotiations, each of the LMs sends an `LMP_setup_complete` PDU to the other LM. Table 5-16 lists the LMP PDUs that are used to establish a connection between two devices.

Table 5-16 The LMP PDUs Used for Connection Establishment

PDU	Contains	M/O
LMP_host_connection_req	nil	M
LMP_setup_complete	nil	M

Connection Termination

A connection between the master and slave devices can be terminated by using the LMP detach service. The response to an `LMP_detach` PDU contains the reason code stating the reason for the termination of the connection. An `LMP_detach` PDU does not entertain any negotiations for resuming connections but immediately terminates the link between the devices.

In addition to all the preceding services that help to manage the links between devices, the LM also provides certain additional services. These services, discussed next, include the following:

◆ Channel quality-driven change
◆ Quality of services
◆ SCO links
◆ Control of multi-slot packets
◆ Paging scheme
◆ Link supervision
◆ Test mode
◆ Error handling

Channel Quality-Driven Change

The channel quality-driven change service facilitates evaluation of the Forward Error Correction (FEC) that is to be used during the transmission of the data packets. Most Bluetooth devices transmit either DM or DH packets. The payload in a DM packet is protected with a $^2/_3$ FEC code while that of a DH packet isn't protected with any FEC code. However, a device is configured to use DM packets or DH packets or to automatically adjust the packet type according to the channel quality. To facilitate an automatic adjustment of the packet type, a device sends an `LMP_auto_rate` PDU to the other device. The receiving device measures the quality in LC and sends back a response with an `LMP_preferred_rate` PDU containing the data rate. Table 5-17 lists the LMP PDUs that are used to choose the FEC code.

Table 5-17 The LMP PDUs Used for Choosing the FEC Code

PDU	Contains	M/O
LMP_auto_rate	nil	O
LMP_preferred_rate	data rate	O

Quality of Service (QoS)

The QoS service as the name suggests, is used to define the parameters for the poll interval. The poll interval is the maximum time between subsequent transmissions from a master to a slave. The poll interval is used to support bandwidth allocation, latency control, and also negotiate the number of repetitions of the broadcast packets between a master and a slave.

If a master notifies the slave of the quality of service, it sends an `LMP_quality_of_service` that includes the new poll interval and the N_{BC}. The slave in this case, is left with no choice but to accept the notification. On the other hand, if either the master or the slave request for the new poll interval and the N_{BC}, the notification is sent with an `LMP_quality_of_service_req` and can be accepted or rejected. As a result, a request such as this is always negotiated dynamically. In addition, if the request is from the slave, the N_{BC}, which is always sent from the master to the slave, holds no relevance and is, therefore, ignored by the master. The response from the master or the slave is either an `LMP__accepted` or `LMP_not_accepted` PDU, which is based on the acceptance or the rejection of the notification. Table 5-18 lists the LMP PDUs that are used to choose the quality of service.

Table 5-18 The LMP PDUs Used for Choosing the QoS

PDU	Contains	M/O
LMP_quality_of_service	Poll interval and N_{BC}	O
LMP_quality_of_service	Poll interval and N_{BC}	O

SCO Links

The connection between two Bluetooth devices is over an ACL link. Once an ACL link is established, the SCO link service can be used to establish one or more SCO links. An SCO link mainly carries voice data and is never retransmitted. The master supports three simultaneous SCO links while the slave supports only two or three SCO links. An SCO link reserves slots that are separated by an SCO interval (T_{SCO}) and an SCO delay (D_{SCO}). After these parameters are set, the subsequent slots follow periodically after each T_{SCO} interval. Table 5-19 lists the LMP PDUs that are used to manage the SCO links.

Table 5-19 The LMP PDUs Used for Managing the SCO Links

PDU	Contains	M/O
LMP_SCO_link_req	SCO handle, timing control flags, D_{SCO}, T_{SCO}, and air mode	O
LMP_remove_SCO_link_req	SCO handle and reason code	O

Control of Multi-Slot Packets

The number of slots in the return packets of the slave can be restricted by the master with an LMP_max_slot PDU. This message includes the max slots parameter that allows the slave to use only a maximal number of slots. The slave, in turn, can request to use a maximal number of slots by sending an LMP_max_slot_req with the max slots parameter. The default value for max slots is one slot. Two PDUs are used to control multi-slot packets. Table 5-20 lists the LMP PDUs that are used to control multi-slot packets.

Table 5-20 The LMP PDUs Used for Controlling Multi-Slot Packets

PDU	Contains	M/O
LMP_max_slot	max_slots	M
LMP_max_slot_req	max_slots	M

Paging Scheme

The paging scheme is used to control the mode and the type of scheme to be used during the paging between the devices in a piconet. A Bluetooth system defines an optional paging scheme in addition to the mandatory paging scheme. The construction of the paging train defines the type of paging scheme.

The negotiation for a page mode or a page scan mode is initiated by device A, which negotiates the paging scheme to be used when it pages the second device B. Device B can accept or reject the scheme forwarded by device A. However, if device B rejects the paging scheme, the old settings are not rejected. On the other hand, a switch back to the mandatory scheme can be rejected. Table 5-21 lists the LMP PDUs that are used to control the paging scheme between the devices in a piconet.

Table 5-21 The LMP PDUs Used for Controlling the Paging Scheme

PDU	Contains	M/O
LMP_page_mode_req	paging scheme and paging scheme setting	O
LMP_page_scan_mode_req	paging scheme and paging scheme setting	O

Link Supervision

The link supervision service is used to control the maximum wait time or the value of the supervision timeout for a station before it declares a link failure. Each Bluetooth link has a timer that is used to identify the link loss when a device moves out of range, a device's power is down, or there is any other such failure. Table 5-22 lists the LMP PDU that is used to control the value of the supervision timeout for a station.

Table 5-22 The LMP PDU Used for Link Supervision

PDU	Contains	M/O
LMP_supervision_timeout	supervision timeout	O

Test Mode

The LMP PDUs support different Bluetooth test modes that define the certification and compliance testing of the radio and the baseband. The end users of the devices do not recognize these functions. An LMP_test_activate PDU initiates the test mode under the test (DUT) where DUT is always a slave. The slave or DUT responds with an LMP_accepted PDU if it enters the test mode locally. On the other hand, if DUT remains in normal operation it sends an LMP_not_accepted PDU with the reason code as '*PDU not allowed.*'

Error Handling

An error can be raised due to various reasons and LMP message are no exception to this phenomenon. Errors can arise in LMP messages due to an unrecognized OpCode or invalid parameters. On receiving an invalid OpCode, the LM responds with an `LMP_not_accepted` PDU with the reason code as *unknown LMP PDU*. The OpCode parameter that is sent back is the unrecognized OpCode. On the other hand, if the LM receives a PDU with invalid parameters, it responds with an `LMP_not_accepted` PDU with the reason code as *invalid LMP parameters*.

The other errors detected are those of link loss or of a response time that exceeds the maximum response time. In both these cases, the code contains the reason code as *procedure is terminated*. The LM monitors the number of erroneous messages and disconnects if the number exceeds a fixed threshold value.

Summary

Connected and communicating devices exchange vital information with each other that is far removed from the actual data transferred between the devices. This vital information or the control data that is exchanged between the link managers of communicating devices helps to control and manage the connection. However, the LMs do not directly exchange the control data but use the underlying services of the LMP.

In this chapter, you learned how the PDUs play an important role in transferring information between the LMs of communicating devices. According to the scope and functionality of the rendered service, the PDUs can be classified for services such as security management, time management, mode management, and power management.

What has been discussed so far pertains to the lower-level protocol layer that defines the operational features of Bluetooth technology. The next chapter moves on to the upper-level protocols, beginning with the Host Controller interface, which is a firmware used to separate the upper- and lower-level protocols.

Check Your Understanding

Multiple Choice Questions

1. Two devices need to be authenticated. If the devices are paired before authentication, which of the following combinations is used to create the initialization key?

   The K_{init} and PIN

   The K_{init} and the random number

   The Unit key and the combination key

   The PIN and the random number

2. A master and a slave have decided to use encryption for point-to-point packets. Which of the following parameters will be included in the request/response PDUs for link encryption?

   The PIN, the random number, and the key size

   The encryption key, the mode, and the key size

   The Encryption mode, the key size, and the random number

   The Random number, the key size, the encryption mode

3. Which of the following parameters are included in the version number?

   The Version number, the sub-version number, and the company Id

   The Version number, the LMP feature supported, and the company Id

   The Company name, the company Id, and the version number

   The LMP version, the sub-version, and the device Id

4. A Bluetooth radio in a device supports only a few of the features that are specified for the radio in the Bluetooth specification 1.0 B. Which of the following PDUs can be used to include information regarding optional features that are supported by the radio?

   `LMP_version_req`

   `LMP_quality_of_service_req`

   `LMP_features_req`

   `LMP_modify_beacon`

5. How many SCO links can a slave device support?

   Four or five

   Two or three

   One or two

   Three or four

Short Questions

1. Of the three LMP services given below, elaborate on two along with a full description and flow of the PDU that governs the respective services.

   Power control

   Error handling

   Clock offset request

2. Consider two devices, A and B, that need to be authenticated. However, the two devices do not have a common link key. How can these devices be authenticated in the absence of a common link key? Specify and explain the authentication procedure in this case in brief.

3. State three purposes of using LMP messages.

4. What information exchange is facilitated by the link supervision service?

5. Describe the fields of an LMP PDU in brief.

6. A piconet consists of eight devices each named sequentially as Device A, Device B, Device C, and so on. Device A is the master while the other seven devices are the slaves. The master device (Device A) needs to estimate the channel at which Device E will wake up to a page scan. The problem is that Device E has left the piconet. In such a situation, how will Device A estimate the channel Device E will wake up to?

7. Consider a situation in which a device, a slave in a piconet, is currently inactive. However, as a member of the piconet it continues to burn power. How can the master reduce the power consumption of the slave during its period of inactivity?

Answers

Multiple Choice Answers

1. d. The PIN and the random number
2. b. The Encryption key, the mode, and the key size
3. a. The Version number, the sub-version number, and the company Id
4. c. `LMP_features_req`
5. b. Two or three

Short Answers

1. a. A Bluetooth device can regulate its power by increasing or decreasing the output power. An `LMP_incr_power_req` PDU is sent to request for an increase in power. If the receiving device is already transmitting at maximum power, it returns a response with an `LMP_max_power` PDU. Similarly, an `LMP_decr_power_req` PDU is sent to request for a decrease in power. If the receiving device is already transmitting at minimum power, it sends back a response with an `LMP_min_power` PDU. An `LMP_incr/decr_power_req` PDU includes a 1-byte reserved space containing referential parameters for future use.

   b. Errors can arise in LMP messages due to an unrecognized OpCode or invalid parameters. On receiving an invalid OpCode, the LM responds with an `LMP_not_accepted` PDU with the reason code as *'unknown LMP PDU'*. On the other hand, if the LM receives a PDU with invalid parameters, it responds with an `LMP_not_accepted` PDU with the reason code as *'invalid LMP parameters.'*

   c. The payload header of the synchronizing FHS packet that a slave receives contains the clock difference between the slave clock and the master clock (clock offset). The clock offset is updated after the receipt of packets from the master. After a slave leaves the piconet, the master can use the slave's clock offset to estimate the channel at which the slave will wake up to a page scan. For this estimate, the master sends an `LMP_clock_offset_req` PDU to request for the slave's current offset.

2. In the absence of a common link key, the devices A and B will need to perform pairing to complete the procedure of authentication. Pairing can be defined as a security procedure that uses LMP_PDUs to automatically establish a link key between mutually authenticated users. Both the devices calculate the initialization key by using the random number and a 48-bit Personal Identification Number (PIN). The initialization key (K_{init}) thus created is used by both the devices for preliminary authentication prior to the generation of a permanent link key.

3. Bluetooth devices communicate with each other by using LMs, which exchange messages to control and maintain the links between devices. The LMP functions as a command response, packet-oriented communication protocol facilitating the exchange of messages between the LMs of various devices. The LMP carries control data that determines the type of service to be rendered. The control data passed from the higher protocols is, therefore, used to either communicate with the LMs of different devices or send control signals to its own baseband and radio layers. The LM, thus, takes care of functions such as link setup, link configuration, and authentication.

4. The link supervision service is used to control the maximum wait time or the value of the supervision timeout for a station before it declares a link failure. Each Bluetooth link has a timer that is used to identify link loss when a device moves out of range, a device's power is down, or there is any other such failure.

5. Each LMP_PDU consists of the following three fields.

   The transactionID field: The -bit transactionID field contains the unique transaction identifier (TID). The TID identifies the LM transaction that is initiated by either a master or a slave device. The value of the TID is zero (0) if a master initiates the transaction and one (1) if a slave initiates the transaction.

   The OpCode field: The 7-bit OpCode field is used to identify the sequence and the type of the LMP_PDU.

   The content field: The 0 to 17 bytes of the content field carry application-specific information in the form of message parameters. The parameters occupy an integral number of bytes.

6. To estimate the channel at which Device E will wake up to a page scan, the master Device A sends an `LMP_clock_offset_req` PDU to request for the slave's current offset. The slave updates this clock offset after the receipt of packets from the master. As a result, even after a slave leaves the piconet, the master can use the slave's clock offset to estimate the channel at which the slave will wake up to a page scan.

7. The master can force the slave device to move into the park mode. In the park mode, the power consumption of the slave can be reduced because it is dissociated from the piconet. To do so, the master completes the transmission of the current L2CAP message and sends an `LMP_park` PDU. The slave receives the PDU, completes the transmission of the current L2CAP message, and sends back an acceptance response with an `LMP_accepted` PDU. At the end of this transaction the slave moves into the park mode.

Chapter 6

Software Protocols

In the preceding chapters, we defined the roles of the radio, baseband, and the Link Manager (LM). The radio layer ensures that the receiving and transmitting devices are matched, to enable data transfer. The instantiation of the air interface separating the devices is facilitated by the baseband. Various operational functions such as device discovery, definition of the frequency hopping sequence, and definition of master and slave roles, are carried out before a connection between two devices is finally set up. The Link Manager, as its name implies, manages and supervises the link between two devices. The LM ensures proper bandwidth allocations, device authentication, pairing, and data encryption. All these functions are initiated and negotiated by the exchange of the Protocol Data Unit (PDU).

In a Bluetooth system, the radio, baseband, and Link Manager are packaged together and implemented either in the form of an independent module attached to the host or as an integrated unit placed in the host containing other applications that run using the transport protocols. The host, in this context, is the Bluetooth device that implements the Bluetooth higher layers. For example, a PC can be converted to a Bluetooth-enabled PC by simply inserting an add-on card containing the radio, baseband, and the Link Manager. In this case, the PC is called the host and the Bluetooth card is the module.

The structure of the host and module can also be mapped to laptops, PDAs, and mobile phones. As a result, the host can implement the radio, baseband, and LM separately by using add-on cards or plug-in cards as external accessories. This means that the module takes care of the operational functions of connectivity and link management by using the radio, baseband, and LM. Recall that the host contains the transport layer of L2CAP and the middleware protocol layer group consisting of RFCOMM, Service Discovery Protocol (SDP), Object Exchange (OBEX) protocol, and Telephony Control (TCS) protocol that are now separated from the module. How is the continuity of information exchange maintained if the layers are placed separately in two different physical units? It is evident that to provide interoperability between these two non-integrated units, the transport layers of the host have to be connected in some way to the module. The SIG has defined the Host Controller Interface (HCI), a standard interface, to provide a link between the host and the module. The HCI helps to interpret the information between the host and the module; information received from the host is directed to the module and the information collected from the device is passed on to the module.

This chapter discusses the standard interface of the HCI that most devices use to separate the upper and lower protocol layers of the host and the module. The immediate upper layer that the HCI interfaces with is the L2CAP layer. The HCI accepts data packets from the L2CAP layer and sends it to the lower protocol layers. This chapter, therefore, also discusses the upper L2CAP layer and the basic functioning of the middleware protocol layers of RFCOMM, SDP, OBEX, and TCS.

The Host Controller Interface

The HCI by virtue of its placement between the upper protocols and the module ensures that a Bluetooth application actually defines the power and capability of Bluetooth technology. The HCI primarily defines functions for the Bluetooth module that the host and its applications use to interact with the radio, baseband, and LM layers. The higher protocol layers can, therefore, have access to information regarding the result of an inquiry process, read the strength of an incoming signal, or read the audio settings of the baseband. The sole purpose behind the standardization of the HCI is to enable interoperability between the host and the module. The standardization also provides a platform for the use of HCI drivers to bring together the different modules manufactured by different vendors.

The Bluetooth module first implements the radio layer, after which the data is sent to the baseband and LMP over a physical bus. The driver for the physical bus used for the implementation of these layers is placed on the host, while the HCI is placed on the module to accept data over the bus. This is how the upper layers consisting of the L2CAP and the middleware protocol group are a part of the software framework of the Bluetooth system while lower layers are a part of the hardware framework. Figure 6-1 illustrates the placement of the HCI such that the Bluetooth system is separated into software and hardware frameworks.

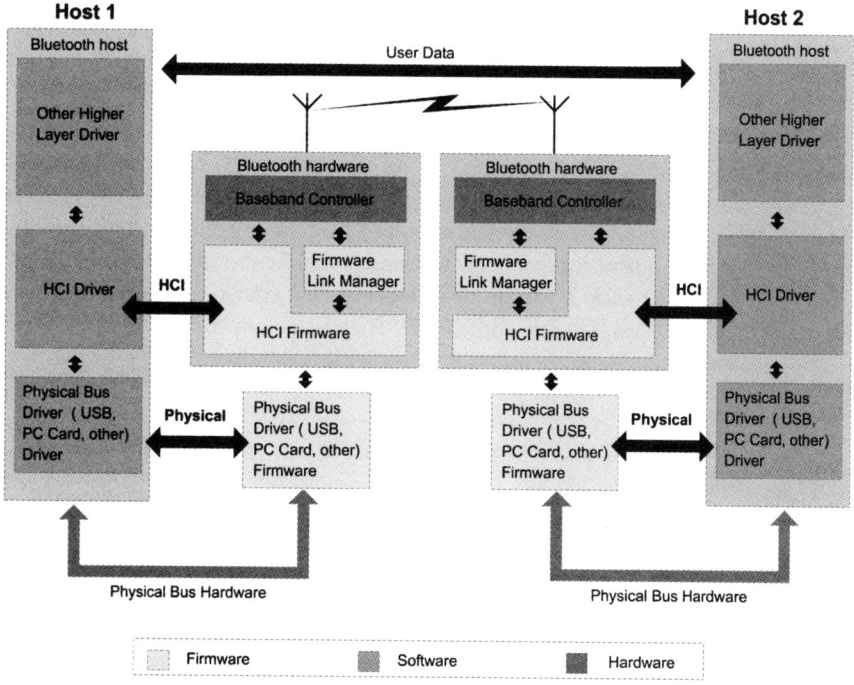

FIGURE 6-1 *The placement of the Host Controller Interface (HCI) in a Bluetooth system*

The earlier sections repeatedly referred to the basic structure of the Bluetooth system being made up of the host and the module. However, the possibility of having a Bluetooth system with the radio, baseband, and LM integrated along with the higher protocols in the host itself is also possible. Therefore, it's obvious that you may now wonder why the integrated structure takes a back seat as compared to the independent host-module structure. As you are aware, the slot timings of a Bluetooth device in an integrated structure demand faster response, often in microseconds, to the interrupts from the Bluetooth radio. Of course, the host does have the backup of spare Mega-Instructions Per Second (MIPS), but there's no guarantee of the availability of the processor when needed. The independent structure of the Bluetooth system, on the other hand, separates the upper and lower layers with separate processors. This, in turn, facilitates separate placement of layers with critical time limits (lower layers) so that the response from the host (upper layers) is faster.

The HCI system exists across the following three segments:

◆ **The HCI firmware.** In the module, the HCI firmware is located on the Host Controller (the hardware in an HCI-enabled Bluetooth device). The HCI firmware uses HCI commands to access the baseband commands, Link Manager commands, hardware status registers, control registers, and event registers.

◆ **The HCI driver.** In the host (containing the software entities), the HCI driver is the driver for the Host Controller that is placed above the physical bus. The HCI driver helps to format the data that is accepted from the Host Controller. The host receives asynchronous notifications relating to the HCI events. HCI events are nothing but happenings or occurrences, as simple as device discoveries or link establishment that take place in the module. After the host is made aware of the events, it parses the received event packet to evaluate and estimate the type of event.

◆ **The Host Controller Transport layer.** In the intermediate layers between the HCI driver on the host and the HCI firmware on the module, the Host Controller Transport layer helps to transfer data without any knowledge of its contents. The various kinds of Host Controller Transport layer used in Bluetooth include USB, UART, and RS232. It is important to note that the host receives asynchronous notifications regarding HCI events regardless of the transport layer used.

 NOTE

The Bluetooth hardware consists of an analog part and a digital part. The analog part is the radio and the digital part is called the Host Controller. The Host Controller is the digital signal processing part of the hardware that is made up of the Link Controller (LC) and a CPU core. The LC performs functions such as baseband processing, FEC coding, and ARQ protocol coding. The CPU core handles inquiries, filters page requests without the knowledge of the host, and often authenticates remote links.

Figure 6-2 illustrates the two parts of the Bluetooth system created by the separate placement of the higher and lower protocol layers.

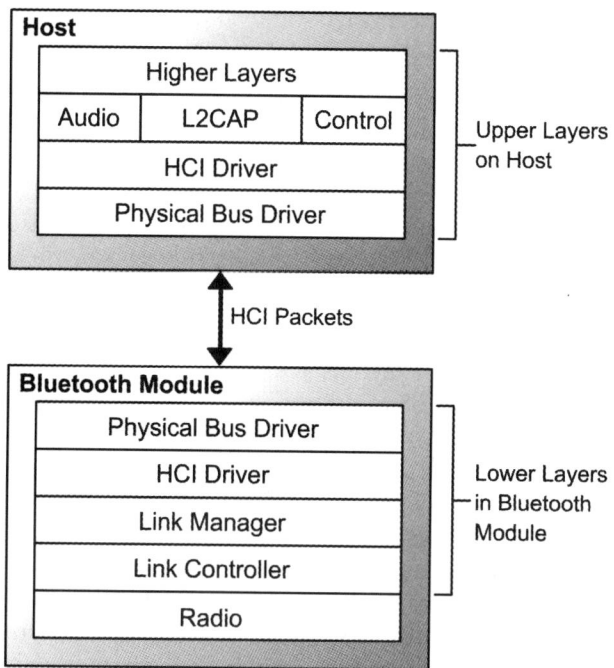

FIGURE 6-2 *The host and the module in the Bluetooth system*

The exchange of information between the HCI layer in the host and the module takes
place by using the HCI command and event packets. In addition to this, other packets
containing HCI error codes and the flow control parameters are also exchanged between
the HCI driver and firmware.

HCI Commands

The command packets carry control and management information from the HCI driver
(in the host) to the Host Controller (in the module). The host of the Bluetooth system
uses the HCI commands to control and monitor the status of the Bluetooth module. In
this way, the HCI commands are used to access the hardware capabilities of the module.
The HCI commands involve the Link Manager during the exchange of the LMP commands with remote Bluetooth devices.

The HCI policy commands provide the host with methods for managing the piconets and are used to control the behavior of a local or remote LM. In addition, HCI commands such as the Host Controller commands, baseband commands, information commands, and status commands are used to access the registers of the Host Controller.

The purpose of the Host Controller Transport layer is to provide a medium for the exchange of information that is specific to the HCI. The Transport layer facilitates transfer of ACL data, SCO data, and HCI commands from the host to the Host Controller (in the module). The time taken in the exchange of the HCI commands differs. Therefore, events are used to report back the results of the commands to the host. The HCI-specific information exchanged using the Host Controller Transport layer is specified by using various formats of the HCI packets. The formats of the HCI packets can be of the following types:

- ◆ **Host Controller and baseband commands.** The Host Controller and baseband commands allow the host to access the capabilities of the baseband, Host Controller, and Link Manager of the Bluetooth hardware. The host is, therefore, able to access and configure the hardware registers containing operational parameters of the Bluetooth device. The commands also enable control of Bluetooth devices. The host uses the Host Controller and baseband commands to modify the behavior of a local device.

- ◆ **Informational parameters.** The manufacturer of the Bluetooth device fixes the informational parameters of a device that provide referential information about the hardware and the firmware of the device. These commands are electronically engraved on the device during manufacture. As a result, these commands are pre-fixed or static, and cannot be modified by the host. The informational commands also contain information about the capabilities of the baseband, Host Controller, and Link Manager.

- ◆ **Status parameters.** The status commands contain information about the current state of the baseband, Host Controller, and Link Manager. The status parameters can be modified by the Host Controller but not by the host. The host can only reset the values of specific status parameters.

- ◆ **Link control commands.** The link control commands help the Host Controller control the connections to other Bluetooth devices. The Link Manager performs the underlying functions of controlling and maintaining the piconets and the scatternets formed as a result of successful connections. The Link control commands help the LM perform inquiries and create and modify link layer connections with other remote Bluetooth devices.

- ◆ **Link policy commands.** The link policy commands are used to modify the behavior of the LM resulting in the change of link layer connections with remote Bluetooth devices. These commands allow the LM to create and maintain piconets that are based on the adjustable policy parameters enforced. The link policy commands, therefore, provide the host with indirect methods to influence the piconet management capability of the LM.

◆ **Testing commands.** The testing commands provide the conditions for testing the functionalities of the Bluetooth hardware.

HCI Events

The command packets carry control and management information from the Host Controller (in the module) to the HCI driver (in the host). The exchange of information between the HCI layers triggers events that are associated with methods. Each event method, in turn, is associated with the event data and its return parameters. The HCI specification consists of a list of various HCI events that range from *Inquiry Complete Event* to *Page Scan Repetition Mode Change Event*.

HCI Flow Control

The HCI transport interfaces transmit data at a rate that is higher than that of the radio and air interfaces. As a result, the speed of data transmission from the host to the module is faster than that from the module to the host. In the case of some Bluetooth modules, data can be buffered till it is ready for transmission. This prevents bottling of data traffic flowing to and from the HCI layers. However, in some Bluetooth modules such as Bluetooth PC cards, the memory of the host is larger than that of the module. As a result, the module is unable to transmit data fast enough and is also not able to store the data due to space shortage. How then is traffic overloading between the HCI layers handled? Flow control of the HCI provides the mechanism to slow down the data transportation across the HCI layers in the host and the module in case of overloading.

Flow control prevents the clogging of the Host Controller data buffers with ACL data that is intended for a remote and non-responding device. The problem of overloading is a rare occurrence because the host accepts data with a speed that is equal to its transmission from the module. The host manages the data buffers of the Host Controller.

HCI Error Codes

The error codes, as the name suggests, are defined to indicate the reason for the failure in the execution of a command in the HCI. A total of 35 error codes have been defined for the HCI that are listed in the HCI specification. Some examples of HCI error codes are *Unknown HCI Command* and *LMP PDU Not Allowed*.

Now that you understand the mode used for the exchange of information between the HCI layers of the host and the module, the next section discusses the medium or the HCI Transport layer that is used to exchange this information.

The HCI Transport Layers

As mentioned earlier, the Host Controller Transport layer present between the HCI firmware in the Bluetooth module and the HCI driver in the host facilitates transfer of HCI packets between the host and the module. The Transport layer ensures transparency between the host and the module so that the HCI driver functions regardless of the Transport layer used during the exchange of the data packets. Similarly, the Transport layer functions without any knowledge about the type of data transmitted from the host to the module. Such a structure ensures that the host or the HCI is upgraded without affecting the Transport layer. The following are the three Bluetooth-defined transport layers:

- ◆ Universal Asynchronous Receiver Transmitter (UART) Transport layer
- ◆ RS-232 Transport layer
- ◆ Universal Serial Bus (USB) Transport layer

UART Transport Layer

The UART Transport layer uses the Bluetooth HCI over a serial interface between two UARTs on the same PCB. The assumption made by the HCI UART is that the UART communication used is free from errors. In addition, the layer does not decode the event and data packets flowing through it.

RS-232 Transport Layer

The RS-232, unlike the UART Transport layer, is a serial interface with error correction. The HCI RS-232 Transport layer uses the Bluetooth HCI over a single physical RS-232 interface between the host and the Host Controller. The layer does not decode the event and data packets flowing through it.

USB Transport Layer

The USB Transport layer provides USB hardware for the Bluetooth hardware embodied either as a USB dongle, or integrated on the motherboard of a notebook PC. A USB Bluetooth device-specific class code is used to load an appropriate driver stack irrespective of the vendor that manufactured the device. In the process the HCI commands are differentiated from the USB commands across the control endpoints.

 NOTE

The description of the USB Transport layer is sourced from the specification of the Bluetooth SIG and other references in the Bluetooth specification.

The HCI is placed below the L2CAP layer and is an essential part of the specification. The purpose of providing the HCI layer is to facilitate interoperability between the host and the module that are developed by different vendors. In a tightly embedded system, the HCI layer may not exist at all. In the absence of an HCI layer, the L2CAP passes data packets directly to the LM. It is evident from the previous statement that irrespective of the presence or absence of the HCI, the *Logical Link Control and Adaptation Protocol* (L2CAP) transfers the data from the higher layers of the Bluetooth stack and the applications to the lower layers of the Bluetooth protocol stack. The traffic from the applications is directed to the L2CAP layer first. As a result, this layer acts like a screen between the higher protocol layers (and the applications) and the lower protocol layers. Intrigued? Has this generated some interest in knowing more about this higher layer of the Bluetooth protocol stack? The next section discusses the L2CAP layer in detail.

The Logical Link Control and Adaptation Protocol

Before discussing hard-core L2CAP-related content, let's understand how the L2CAP layer came to be a part of the Bluetooth specification. The lower layers of the protocol stack, supported by low power consumption, security strictures, regulatory issues, and TDD selection, are equipped to handle the RF transmission medium in the 2.4 GHz ISM band. However, the efficiency of these layers is challenged when the packet size of the transmitted data is large as is the case with the Internet traffic.

These considerations called for the inclusion of an adaptation layer to maintain consistency in the larger upper-layer PDUs and the smaller lower-layer PDUs. The adaptation layer thus formed was initially called the Level-2 Medium Access Control (MAC-2) layer. In the summer of 1998, the SIG decided to change the name MAC-2 to a more descriptive and phonetically pleasing name, that is, Logical (level 2) Link Control and Adaptation Protocol (L2CAP).

The placement of the L2CAP between the device applications and the lower protocol layers shields the functions of the higher and lower protocol layers from each other. Therefore, the higher layers are oblivious of the lower layer functions of frequency hopping at the radio and baseband layers or of the packet formats used to transmit data between two devices. The L2CAP layer is specifically concerned with functions such as protocol multiplexing, sharing of the air interface between multiple protocols and applications, segmentation and reassembly of data packets, and negotiations regarding an acceptable level of service. Figure 6-3 illustrates the placement of the L2CAP layer within the other protocol layers.

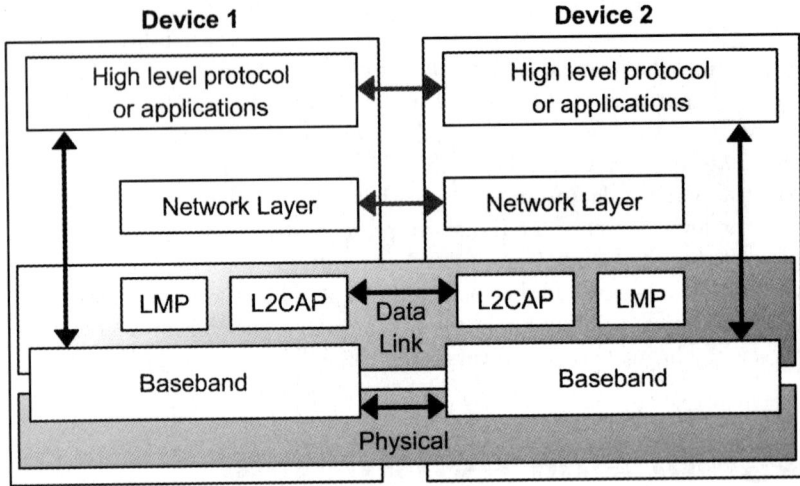

FIGURE 6-3 *The placement of the L2CAP layer*

The baseband supports both Asynchronous Connectionless (ACL) and Synchronous Connection-Oriented (SCO) links. ACL links facilitate transfer of best effort traffic while the SCO links support transmission of real-time voice traffic in a reserved bandwidth. The L2CAP layer is concerned with the transmission of ACL packets only.

Assumptions

The L2CAP is based on certain assumptions that are listed below:

◆ The Link Manager Protocol is used to set up the ACL link between two devices. The baseband is responsible for the orderly transfer of data packets. The chances of packet corruption and duplication during transmission are not ruled out. At most one ACL link exists between any two devices.

◆ The baseband provides the impression of full-duplex communication channels at all times. This does not mean that all L2CAP communications are bi-directional. Unidirectional communication and multicasts, however, do not need duplex channels.

◆ The baseband always performs data integrity checks when requested. After these checks, the baseband sends back the data till it is acknowledged or till a timeout occurs. Timeouts occur due to loss of the acknowledgment, even after the successful transmission of data. The baseband layer uses a 1-bit sequence number to counter duplication. L2CAP provides a secure channel that uses the mechanisms available at the baseband level.

NOTE

The use of baseband packets is prohibited if reliability is required. This is because all broadcasts start the first segment of an L2CAP packet with the same sequence bit.

Functional Requirements of the L2CAP

The L2CAP demands a simple and cost-effective protocol to support that transfer of data between two devices. Economic use of power and high bandwidth efficiency at the L2CAP level increases the power efficiency of the radio. The functional requirements of the L2CAP are as follows:

◆ **Protocol Multiplexing.** This is the most important functional requirement supported by the L2CAP. The L2CAP allows the simultaneous use of multiple links between two devices. The baseband does not support a "type" field identifying the higher protocol layer that is being multiplexed. As a result, L2CAP needs to take on this function by supporting protocol multiplexing. The L2CAP is therefore able to differentiate between higher protocol layers of Service Discovery Protocol (SDP), RFCOMM, and Telephony Control.

◆ **Segmentation and Reassembly.** The Segmentation and Reassembly (SAR) functionality of the L2CAP supports protocols that use packets larger than those supported by the baseband. The size of the packets received from the upper protocol layers is larger than the size of packets accepted at the baseband layer. The L2CAP, therefore, segments the packets into smaller chunks so that they are accepted at the baseband layer. Similarly, the packet chunks are reassembled at the baseband level into larger L2CAP packets, after an integrity check.

◆ **Quality of Service (QoS).** Most of the protocols support the concept of group addresses. The baseband supports piconet, which links a group of devices hopping together using the same clock. Similarly, the L2CAP groups abstraction. As a result, the process of connection establishment of the L2CAP allows exchange of information based on the QoS agreement between two Bluetooth devices.

NOTE

Multiplexing in the L2CAP enables multiple applications to simultaneously use a link between two devices. This feature, therefore, also allows multiple higher layers to pass over a single ACL connection. The lower baseband layer does not support a type field that is basically used to identify the higher field that is multiplexed. The L2CAP layer, however, needs to be aware of the different upper layer protocols (SDP, RFCOMM, and TCS). This is also one of the reasons why multiplexing is needed in the L2CAP layer.

The data packets are labeled by using channel numbers so that they are routed to the correct destination. The channel number consists of a 2-byte channel identifier (Destination_CID) that follows the length field of the packet header. Special channel numbers are reserved for signaling channel.

The functional requirements of the L2CAP fulfill the expectations from a high-level protocol layer interfacing between the application and the lower-level protocol. However, some features are outside the scope of the L2CAP.

The Scope of the L2CAP

The following are the features that are outside the scope of L2CAP implementations:

◆ L2CAP does not transport audio designated for SCO links.

◆ L2CAP does not ensure data integrity or enforce a reliable channel.

◆ L2CAP does not perform retransmissions or checksum calculations.

◆ L2CAP does not support a reliable multicast channel.

◆ L2CAP does not support the concept of a global group name.

The following section discusses the medium used for the transfer of data between two L2CAP layers.

The L2CAP Channels and the Channel Identifier

The L2CAP layer provides a duplex communication channel for the orderly transmission of the L2CAP data packets. However, the L2CAP layer does not implement any mechanism to ensure reliable transmission of the data packets. The retransmission process of the baseband is used to provide reliable data transmission.

Logical links or channels are used to transfer data during inter-device communications. The L2CAP channels can be of the following three types:

◆ **Connection-oriented (CO) channels.** These are persistent channels that are used for bi-directional communication. A connection-oriented channel is established only after a signaling connection exchange.

◆ **Connectionless (CL) channels.** These are short-lived unidirectional channels that are used for broadcast transmissions within a group of Bluetooth devices. Being a unidirectional channel, a device wanting to respond to these transmissions needs to use other channels for the response transmission.

◆ **Signaling channels.** These channels are used to exchange control information before establishing or configuring connection-oriented channels. Signaling channels derive features from both CO and CL channels. As a result, they are persistent and bi-directional like CO channels and also do not need explicit connections before beginning any communication, which is the feature of CL channels.

Figure 6-4 illustrates the different channels used for the transfer of L2CAP packets.

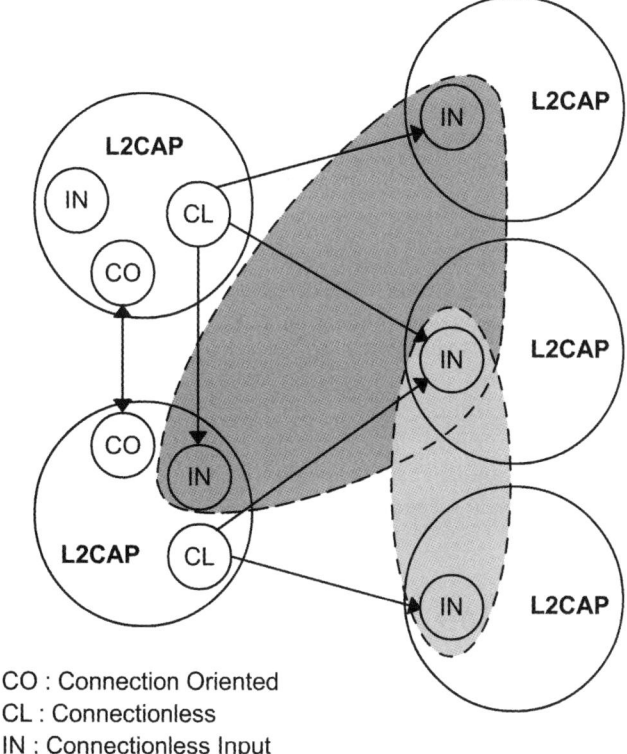

CO : Connection Oriented
CL : Connectionless
IN : Connectionless Input

⬭ : Group

FIGURE 6-4 *The L2CAP channels*

A channel in each device has endpoints that define the start and end of the traffic flow. The endpoint of a channel is assigned a locally generated 16-bit unique Channel Identifier (CID). A different CID, therefore, identifies each channel endpoint. The global and well-defined channels have reserved CIDs, whereas the other channels are allotted dynamically generated CIDs as and when needed. Two L2CAP entities need bi-directional channels to initiate a communication between them. Therefore, two L2CAP entities can have many CO and CL channels between them, but only a single signaling channel. As a result, every L2CAP entity will have one signaling channel with a reserved CID of 0x0001 that is used by all other signal channels between the L2CAP entity and other remote devices. Table 6-1 lists definitions for some CIDs sourced from the Bluetooth specification 1.0B.

Table 6-1 The Definitions of Some CIDs

CID	Assigned for...
0x0000	Null identifier
0x0001	Endpoints of a L2CAP signaling channel
0x0002	Destination point of an L2CAP-CL channel
0x0003-0x003F	Reserved CIDs
0x0040-0xFFF	Dynamically allocated CIDs for either L2CAP-CL or CO channels

The CIDs of a channel can also be categorized as connection-oriented CIDs, connectionless CIDs, and signaling CIDs. The CID of the connection-oriented channel identifies the endpoints that are used during the connection between two devices. The flow of data in a connectionless channel is unidirectional. These channels, used primarily for broadcast messages, therefore support a group of channels where the CID actually represents more than one remote device. The signaling channel uses reserved CIDs. All L2CAP channels support signaling channels.

Operation between Devices

The CO channel represents a connection between two devices, where a CID identifies the endpoints of the channel. The data in the CL channel flows in a single direction and supports a channel group. In such a case, the CID of the source represents one or more remote devices. There are some CIDs, like that of a signaling channel, that are reserved for special purposes. A signaling channel is used to negotiate the changes in the characteristics of a channel and also helps to create and establish CO channels. Table 6-2 lists the various types of channel identifiers.

Table 6-2 The Types of Channel Identifiers

Type	Local CID	Remote CID
Connection-oriented CID	Dynamically generated	Dynamically generated
Connection-less CID	Dynamically generated	Fixed at 0x0002
Signaling CIDs	Fixed at 0x0001	Fixed at 0x0001

Operation between Layers

The architecture of the L2CAP implementation during inter-layer operations is as follows:

◆ The L2CAP implementation should transfer data between higher-layer protocols and lower-layer protocols.

◆ Each L2CAP implementation should support a set of signaling commands for use between L2CAP implementations.

◆ L2CAP implementations should be prepared to accept certain events from the lower layers and generate events to the higher layers. The process of event generation between the layers is implementation-dependant.

Figure 6-5 illustrates the L2CAP implementation during inter-layer operations.

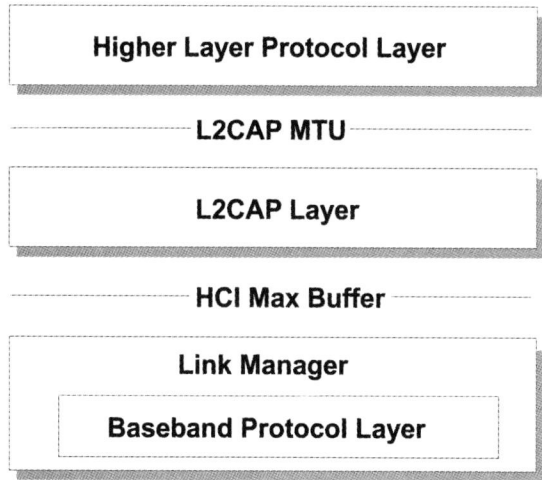

FIGURE 6-5 *The L2CAP operation between layers*

Segmentation and Reassembly

Segmentation and Reassembly (SAR) operations support a maximum transmission unit size (MTU) that is larger than even the largest baseband packet. This mechanism, therefore, improves efficiency and reduces overhead by transmitting the larger higher-layer protocol packets over smaller lower-layer baseband packets. The packets received by the L2CAP are up to 64 Kb in size. On the other hand, the maximum size of data packet accepted by the baseband is 2745 bits. The MTU of the largest baseband payload for a DH5 packet is 341 bytes. It is obvious that the L2CAP packets are larger in size than baseband packets. As a result, the L2CAP packets are segmented into multiple baseband packets so that they are small enough to be passed over the baseband layer. The segmentation process is reversed in the baseband layer, where the packets are reassembled into single large L2CAP packets.

The SAR implementation ensures that at the transmitting end, the outgoing MTU and the L2CAP packets are segmented into smaller chunks so that they are passed to the LM through the HCI. Similarly, at the receiving end, the small chunks are reassembled into large L2CAP packets by using the control information from the HCI and the information from the packet header.

The integrity of the transmitted data is maintained by using the length field of the L2CAP packet header as a consistency check. L2CAP packets with mismatched length fields fail the integrity check and are discarded. The process of discarding packets is silent in the case of transmissions through unreliable channels. Reliable transmissions, however, need to inform the upper layers that a particular channel has become unreliable. Figure 6-6 illustrates the SAR variables used during the segmentation and reassembly of L2CAP packets.

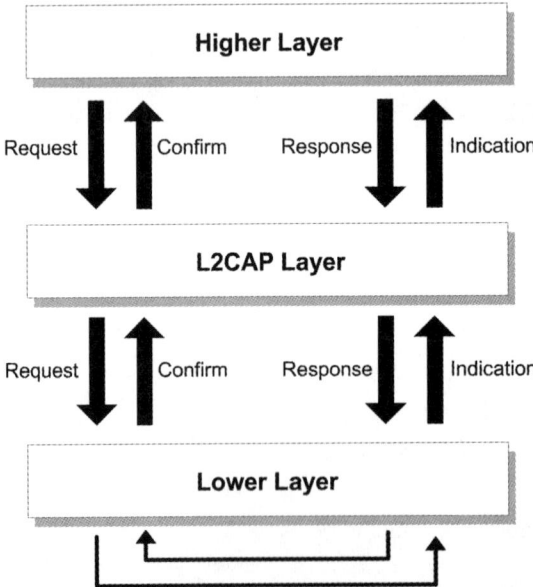

FIGURE 6-6 *The segmentation and reassembly of L2CAP packets*

The L2CAP entity exists in various states marked by numerous events and actions. Events cause the state of an L2CAP machine or entity to change. Actions are performed in response to events. The next section discusses the states of a L2CAP machine, and the events and actions that cause a transition in the states.

The next section describes the structure of a L2CAP packet. The L2CAP packets are called L2CAP_PDUs.

The L2CAP Data Packet

Each L2CAP data packet or PDU like any other data packet has two parts, the header and the payload. Depending on the type of channel used, L2CAP data packets can be of the following two types:

- ◆ Connection-oriented L2CAP data packets (CO L2CAP) PDUs
- ◆ Connectionless L2CAP data packets (CL L2CAP) PDUs

The Connection-oriented L2CAP Data Packets

The header field of the L2CAP_PDU_CO, like all other header fields, uses a little-endian byte order where the least significant byte is transmitted first. Table 6-3 lists the fields of the connection-oriented L2CAP data packets.

Table 6-3 The Structure of the Connection-oriented L2CAP Data Packets

Field	Size	Description
The L2CAP_PDU_CO header		
Length	2 bytes	Excludes the length of the L2CAP header.
Destination_CID	2 bytes	Specifies the CID of the destination endpoint of the L2CAP channel used.
The L2CAP_PDU_CO payload		
Payload	Length of the L2CAP_PDU_CO header in bytes	Contains the L2CAP_PDU_CO payload. Maximum size of 65,535 bytes.

The Connectionless L2CAP Data Packets

The header field of the L2CAP_PDU_CL uses a little-endian byte order. The other fields of the PDU header follow the little-endian mode of transmission. The Protocol/Service Multiplexor (PSM) field of the header is used to identify the higher layer slated to receive the payload of the Connectionless L2CAP PDU. Table 6-4 lists the fields of the connection-less L2CAP data packets.

Table 6-4 The Structure of the Connectionless L2CAP Data Packets

Field	Size	Description
The L2CAP_PDU_CL header		
Length	2 bytes	Excludes the length of the L2CAP header and the CID field
Destination_CID	2 bytes	Specifies the CID of the destination endpoint of the L2CAP channel. Has a fixed value of 0x0002
PSM	>= 2 bytes	Specifies the protocol and service Multiplexor
The L2CAP_PDU_CL payload		
Payload	Length-field size of PSM in bytes	Contains the L2CAP_PDU_CL payload. Maximum size of 65,535 bytes-size of PSM that is typically 2 bytes.

Figure 6-7 illustrates the structures of the CO and CL data packets as compared to a baseband data packet.

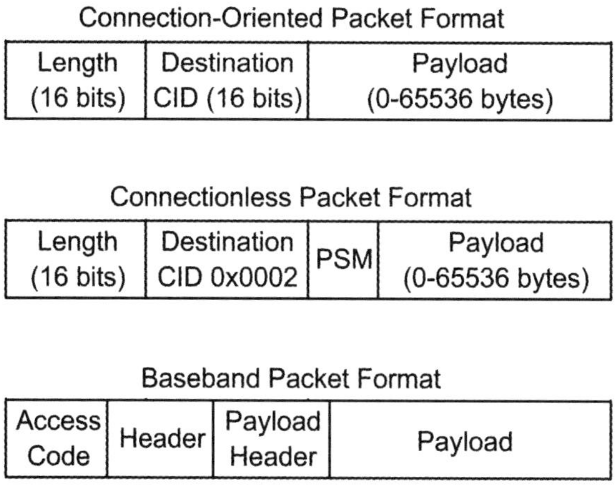

Connection-Oriented Packet Format

Length (16 bits)	Destination CID (16 bits)	Payload (0-65536 bytes)

Connectionless Packet Format

Length (16 bits)	Destination CID 0x0002	PSM	Payload (0-65536 bytes)

Baseband Packet Format

Access Code	Header	Payload Header	Payload

FIGURE 6-7 *The structure of CO, CL, and baseband data packets*

Channel management in L2CAP facilitates multiplexing and signaling, both of which are important functions of the L2CAP.

Signaling

Signaling commands are passed between L2CAP layers to exchange control information about the various states of the L2CAP connections. The states defined for the L2CAP entities are connecting, configuring, and disconnecting.

The signaling data packet, like all data packets, contains a header that includes the length fields and destination_CID fields. The CID of the destination device is reserved and has the value of 0x0001. The signaling commands of the payload are used to initiate connections, terminate connections, or initiate activities over a link. Signaling commands contain the following three parts:

◆ The command code, which is a unique identifier used to match the requests with the corresponding responses

◆ The data length

◆ Zero or more bytes of data

The signaling commands are represented in the form of request or responses. Each request has a corresponding response that is identified by command code. Table 6-5 lists the command codes of the signaling commands as sourced from the Bluetooth specification 1.0B.

Table 6-5 The Code Definitions for the Signaling Commands

Code	Defines
0x00	Reserved
0x01	Command reject
0x02	Connection request
0x03	Connection response
0x04	Configure request
0x05	Configure response
0x06	Disconnection request
0x07	Disconnection response
0x08	Echo request
0x09	Echo response
0x0A	Information request
0x0B	Information response

Figure 6-8 illustrates the structure of a signaling command packet.

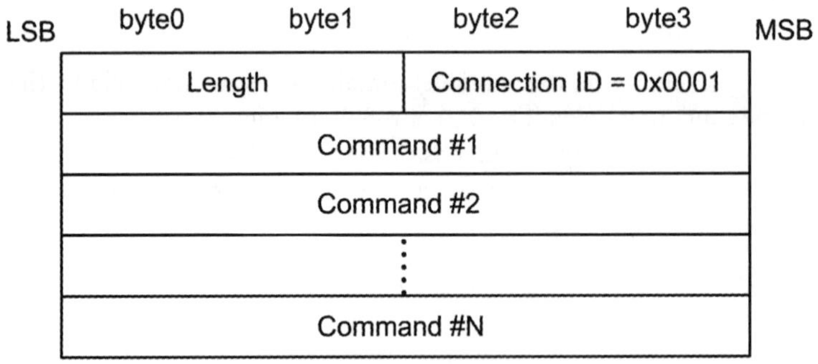

FIGURE 6-8 *The structure of a signaling packet*

The L2CAP State Machine

The L2CAP has a state machine that is driven by the signals from the upper layers and the L2CAP signals carried across the lower layers. The states of a L2CAP entity represent only the bi-directional CO and CL channels and not the unidirectional signaling channels. The L2CAP machine exists in the following three operational states:

◆ CLOSED

◆ CONFIG

◆ OPEN

The states of the L2CAP entity also determine the stages of connection, configuration, and disconnection during which the L2CAP entity moves into the CONFIG, OPEN, and CLOSED states. In the beginning, before connecting, the endpoint is CLOSED signifying that the channel is not associated with the CID. This is the state that the link defaults to after disconnection. The baseband is not required because no data transmission takes place at this time.

Connection

Before opening a channel, the channel endpoint needs to be connected and configured. For establishing a connection, the local L2CAP entity requests a connection with another remote device. In this case, the request generates from the higher-level protocols and is passed to the remote device. As a result, the local entity enters the W4_L2CAP_Connect_RSP state and waits for a response from the remote device.

Similarly, when a local device receives an indication from a remote device requesting a connection, the indication is recognized as a request and passed to the upper-level layers. As a consequence, in this case too, the local entity enters the W4_L2CAP_Connect_RSP state and waits for a response from the remote device.

After the local entity acquires theW4_L2CAP_Connect_RSP state, in both cases, it enters the CONFIG state after receipt of the response from the remote device.

The Configuration

A CO channel needs to be configured before transmission of data. The process of configuration includes inter-device negotiations till both the sides agree upon the same options. The *Configuration Request* and *Configuration Response* commands are used during the negotiations.

The options negotiated include the MTU, flush timeout, and Quality of Service (QoS). The value of the MTU determines the size of the largest L2CAP packet that can be handled by the local device. The flush timeout defines the time taken for the Link Controller to transmit a L2CAP segment before it is flushed out. The QoS is used to negotiate the flow specifications for transmission in a single direction. The flow specifications negotiated include options such as the token rate, token bucket size, latency, delay variation, and peak bandwidth. Although the flow specifications are negotiated for a single directional transfer, the entire process is repeated for transfers in the opposite direction. Figure 6-9 illustrates the structure of a Configuration Request packet.

LSB   byte0   byte1   byte2   byte3   MSB

Code=0x04	Identifier	Length
Destination CID		Flags
Options		

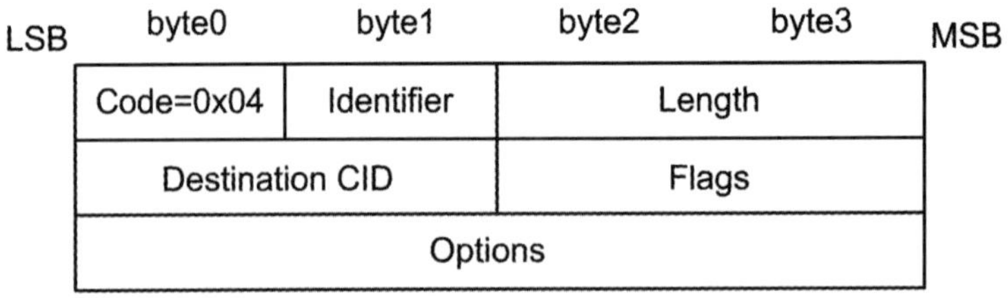

FIGURE 6-9 *The Configuration Request packet*

The negotiations end after finalization of the configuration parameters. The L2CAP entities enter the OPEN state that demarcates the beginning of data transfer. When negotiations between the local and remote entity fail, the entity does not move into the OPEN state. In such a case, the command packets return the reason code specifying the reason for the failure in attaining the state. Table 6-6 lists the reason codes that signify the reason for the failure in the change of state from CONFIG to OPEN, as sourced from the Bluetooth specification 1.0B.

Table 6-6 The Reason Codes

Reason Value	Description
0x0000	Command not understood
0x0001	Signaling MTU exceeded
0x0002	Invalid CID in request
Others	Reserved

The Disconnection

A channel is closed prior to disconnection. Before disconnecting a local entity sends a request to the other entity requesting a disconnection. A disconnect request from the upper layers is passed to the remote device, after which the local entity enters the W4_L2CAP_Disconnect_RSP state and waits for a response from the remote device. If the local device receives an indication from the remote device requesting disconnection, it sends the disconnection request to the upper layers, enters the `W4_L2CAP_Discon-nect_RSP` state, and then waits for an appropriate response. On receipt of the expected response the local device enters the CLOSED state. Figure 6-10 illustrates the structure of a Disconnection Request packet.

LSB	byte0	byte1	byte2	byte3	MSB

Code=0x07	Identifier	Length	
Destination CID		Source CID	

FIGURE 6-10 *The Disconnection Request packet*

The cycle of CLOSED-CONFIG-OPEN-CLOSED states continues and is synonymous with the continuation and discontinuation of data transmission between two devices. Figure 6-11 illustrates the various states of the L2CAP.

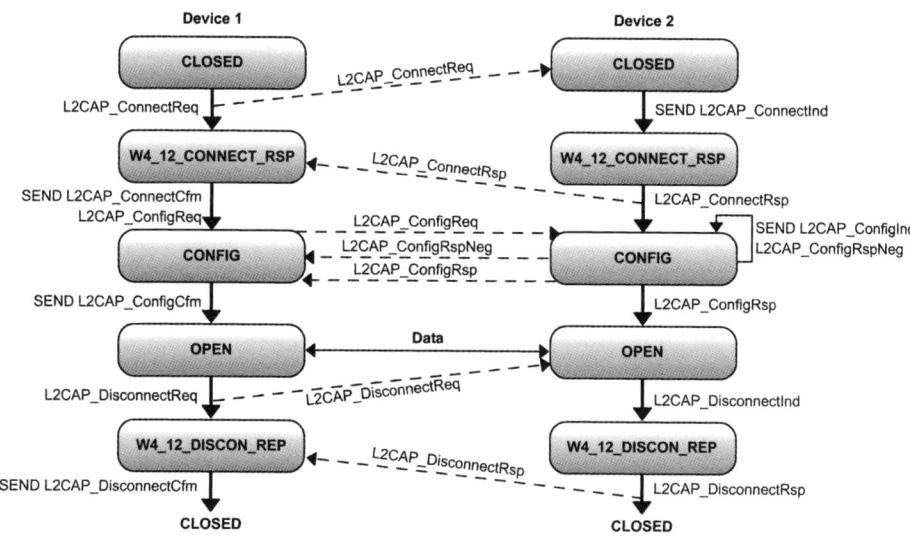

FIGURE 6-11 *The L2CAP state machine*

The exchange of requests and responses between the local and remote device triggers events, which in turn generate actions that are specific to the L2CAP layer. Before discussing the various types of events occurring in the L2CAP, the following list describes the naming conventions followed for the request/ response packets during the L2CAP interactions:

♦ The prefix of the lower layer offering the service to the higher layer is used as the interface (vertical interface) between the two layers. For example, L2CA.

♦ The interface between the two entities residing in the same layer (horizontal interface) uses the prefix of the protocol. This is done by adding a "P" to the value of the layer identification derived earlier. Thus, L2CA becomes L2CAP.

♦ Events starting above are called Requests (Req) and their replies are called Confirms (Cfm).

♦ Events starting below are called Indications (Ind) and their replies are called Responses (Res).

♦ Responses requiring processing are called Pending (Pnd). Confirms and Responses assume positive replies. Negative Confirms and Responses are denoted by adding the "Neg" suffix. For example, L2CAP_ConnectCfm_Neg.

Figure 6-12 illustrates the use of the naming conventions for the L2CAP layer interactions.

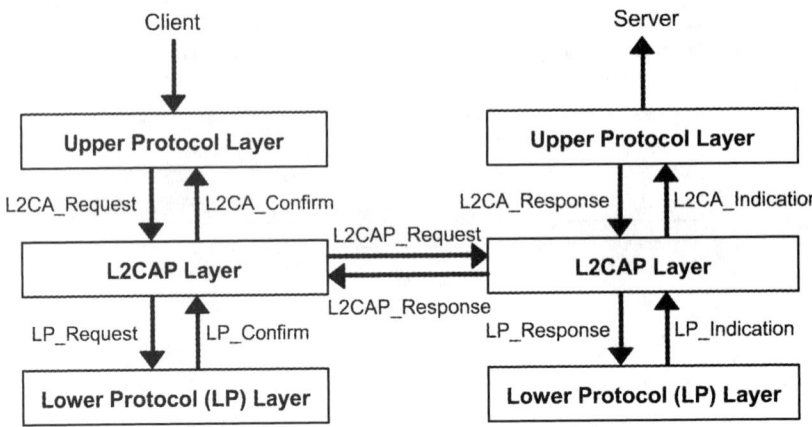

FIGURE 6-12 *The L2CAP layer interactions*

The L2CAP state machine also defines the events and actions that are generated between the protocol layers.

L2CAP Events

Events are incoming messages to the L2CAP layer. Based on the source of origin, events can be categorized as:

- ◆ Lower layer to L2CAP events that include indications and confirms from lower layers.
- ◆ Upper layers to L2CAP events that include requests and responses from higher layers.
- ◆ L2CAP to L2CAP signaling events that include data received from peers, request and response signals from peers, and events caused due to timer expirations.
- ◆ L2CAP to L2CAP events that accept data packets.
- ◆ Timer events that occur due to timeouts.

Lower Layer to L2CAP Events

The messages (events) exchanged between the lower layers (baseband) and the L2CAP when establishing a connection are:

- ◆ **LP_ConnectCfm.** This event confirms a request for establishing a lower-layer (baseband) connection. The message includes the authentication challenge in situations that require authentication for the establishment of the physical link.
- ◆ **LP_ConnectCfmNeg.** This event confirms the failure of a request for establishing a lower-layer (baseband) connection. This event is generated due to reasons such as a refused request, failure of LMP authentication challenge, or simply because the device is non-contactable.
- ◆ **LP_ConnectInd.** This event indicates success in the establishing a lower-layer connection.
- ◆ **LP_DisconnectInd.** This event indicates an LMP-directed shutdown of the lower-layer protocol or the occurrence of a timeout event.
- ◆ **LP_QoSCfm.** This event confirms a request received for a particular QoS.
- ◆ **LP_QoSCfmNeg.** This event confirms the failure for a request received for a particular QoS.
- ◆ **LP_QoSViolationInd.** This event indicates a violation of the QoS agreement detected by the lower-layer protocol.

Upper Layers to L2CAP Events

The messages (events) exchanged between the upper layers and the L2CAP are:

- ◆ **L2CA_ConnectReq.** This event signifies the receipt of a request from the upper layer for establishing a channel to a remote device.

◆ **L2CA_ConnectRsp.** This event signifies the generation of a response from the upper layer to the indication of a request for connection from a remote device.

◆ **L2CA_ConnectRspNeg.** This event signifies a rejection or negative response from the upper layer to the indication of a request for connection from a remote device.

◆ **L2CA_ConfigReq.** This event signifies the receipt of a request from the upper layer for configuring or reconfiguring the channel.

◆ **L2CA_ConfigRsp.** This event signifies the generation of a response from the upper layer to the indication of a request for configuring or reconfiguring the channel.

◆ **L2CA_ConfigRspNeg.** This event signifies a rejection or negative response from the upper layer to the indication of a request for configuring or reconfiguring the channel.

◆ **L2CA_DisconnectReq.** This event signifies the receipt of a request from the upper layer for immediate disconnection of the channel.

◆ **L2CA_DisconnectRsp.** This event signifies the generation of a response from the upper layer to the indication of a request for disconnection of the channel.

◆ **L2CA_DataRead.** This event signifies the receipt of a request from the upper layer for the transfer of received data from the L2CAP entity to the upper layer.

◆ **L2CA_DataWrite.** This event signifies the receipt of a request from the upper layer for the transfer of data from the upper layer to the L2CAP entity for further transmission over an open channel.

L2CAP to L2CAP Signaling Events

The messages (events) exchanged between the upper layers and the L2CAP are:

◆ **L2CAP_ConnectReq.** This event signifies the receipt of a Connection Request packet.

◆ **L2CAP_ConnectRsp.** This event signifies the receipt of a Connection Response packet with a positive result indicating that a connection has been established.

◆ **L2CAP_ConnectRspPnd.** This event signifies the receipt of a Connection Response packet indicating that the request received at the remote endpoint is being processed.

◆ **L2CAP_ConnectRspNeg.** This event signifies the receipt of a Connection Response packet indicating that a connection could not be established.

◆ **L2CAP_ConfigReq.** This event signifies the receipt of a Configuration Request packet indicating that the remote endpoint wants to negotiate channel parameters.

◆ **L2CAP_ConfigRsp.** This event signifies the receipt of a Configuration Response packet indicating that the remote endpoint agrees with all the channel parameters being negotiated.

◆ **L2CAP_ConfigRspNeg.** This event signifies the receipt of a Configuration Response packet indicating that the remote endpoint does not agree with all the channel parameters being negotiated.

◆ **L2CA_DisconnectReq.** This event signifies the receipt of a Disconnection Request packet indicating that the channel should initiate the process of disconnection.

◆ **L2CAP_DisconnectRsp.** This event signifies the receipt of a Disconnection Response packet.

L2CAP to L2CAP Events

The event in the L2CAP to L2CAP layer includes the L2CAP_Data event that signifies receipt of a data packet.

Timer Events

Timer events occur after timeouts and can use be of the following two types of timers:

◆ Response Timeout Expired (RTX) timer

◆ Extended Response Timeout Expired (ERTX) timer

Response Timeout Expired Timer

The Response Timeout Expired (RTX) timer is used to terminate the channel when the remote endpoint stops responding to signaling requests. The timer starts with the transmission of the signaling request to the remote device and is disabled after receiving a response from the device. Often the process of request and response packet exchange exceeds the initial timer. As a result, the timer expires and the request message is either resent in the form of a duplicate request or the channel identified in the request is disconnected. During the transmission of the duplicate request, the timer is reset to a value that is at least double the original value.

Although the value of the timer is independent of the mechanism used for its implementation, the standard value of the initial and maximum value of the timer is taken as 1 second and 60 seconds, respectively. The timer disappears on receipt of a response corresponding to a request, that is, after the final expiration of the channel. The maximum time lapse between the start of the timer and the initiation of the channel disconnection (in the absence of a response) is 60 seconds. Each outstanding signaling request including an Echo Request should be associated with one RTX timer.

Extended Response Timeout Expired Timer

The ERTX timer is used instead of the RTX timer in cases where the remote endpoint is in the middle of processing a request signal. The timer starts when the remote endpoint sends a response indicating that the processing for a request is pending. Such a situation is encountered on receipt of the L2CAP_ConnectRspPnd event. The running timer is disabled after receipt of a formal response or after the loss of a physical link. After the expiration of the initial timer, a duplicate request is sent or the channel is disconnected. After transmitting the duplicate message, the initial ERTX timer disappears only to be replaced by a new RTX timer. The disappearance of the ERTX timer and the start of the RTX timer is followed by the repetition of the entire procedure of the RTX timer.

As in the case of the RTX timer, the ERTX timer is also independent of the mechanism used for its implementation. However, the minimum initial value of the ERTX timer is 60 seconds and the maximum value is 300 seconds. The maximum time lapse between the start of the ERTX timer and the initiation of the channel disconnection (in the absence of a response) is 300 seconds. Each outstanding request received for a pending response should be associated with one ERTX timer. In addition to this, an outstanding request should always be associated with a RTX or ERTX timer.

L2CAP Actions

Actions in the L2CAP layer are the outcome of L2CAP events resulting in the formation of outgoing messages. Based on the source of origin and the type of message, L2CAP actions can be categorized as follows:

◆ L2CAP to lower-layer actions that include the requests and responses from the lower layers.

◆ L2CAP to upper-layer actions that include indications and confirms from the higher layers.

◆ L2CAP to L2CAP signaling actions that are almost similar to L2CAP to L2CAP signaling events.

◆ L2CAP to L2CAP actions that like L2CAP to L2CAP events accept data packets.

◆ Timer events that occur due to timeouts.

L2CAP to Lower Layer Actions

The messages (actions) exchanged between the L2CAP and the lower layers (baseband) are:

◆ **LP_ConnectReq.** This action signifies the receipt of a request from the L2CAP asking the lower layer to create a connection. In the absence of a physical link to the remote device, the action message is sent to the lower protocols so that a physical connection is created.

The lower layers return the following actions at the end of processing the above request:

- ◆ **LP_ConnectCfm.** This action confirms satisfactory processing of a request.
- ◆ **LP_ConnectCfmNeg.** This action confirms an unsatisfactory processing of a request.

The following actions are used by the L2CAP to request the lower protocols to accommodate a particular QoS parameter:

- ◆ **LP_QoSCfm.** This action confirms that the request received for accommodating a particular QoS has been satisfactorily processed.
- ◆ **LP_QoSCfmNeg.** This action confirms that the request received for accommodating a particular QoS has not been processed satisfactorily.

The following actions are used by the L2CAP to signify the status of the responses:

- ◆ **LP_ConnectRsp.** This action generates a positive response accepting the indication for a previous connection request.
- ◆ **LP_ConnectRspNeg.** This action generates a negative response denying the indication for a previous connection req.

L2CAP to Upper Layer Actions

The messages (actions) exchanged between the L2CAP and the upper layers are:

- ◆ **L2CA_ConnectInd.** This action indicates the receipt of a Connection request from a remote device.
- ◆ **L2CA_ConnectCfm.** This action confirms acceptance of a Connection request after the receipt of a Connection message from a remote device.
- ◆ **L2CA_ConnectCfmNeg.** This action signifies the failure of a Connection request. The expiration of an RTX timer for an outstanding Connection request as a substitute for a negative Connection response could result in this action.
- ◆ **L2CA_ConnectPnd.** This action confirms receipt of a pending Connection response from a remote device.
- ◆ **L2CA_ConfigInd.** This action indicates receipt of a Configuration request from a remote device
- ◆ **L2CA_ConfigCfm.** This action confirms receipt of a Configuration request following the receipt of a Configuration response from a remote device.
- ◆ **L2CA_ConfigCfmNeg.** This action confirms the failure of a Configuration request. The expiration of an RTX timer for an outstanding Connection request as a substitute for a negative Connection response could result in this action.
- ◆ **L2CA_DisconnectInd.** This action indicates receipt of a Disconnection request from a remote device. It also indicates disconnection of the remote device because of a failed response to a signaling request.

◆ **L2CA_DisconnectCfm.** This action confirms the processing of a Disconnect request following the receipt of a Disconnection response from a remote device.

◆ **L2CA_TimeOutInd.** This action indicates expiration of the RTX and ERTX timers. This indication occurs an implementation-dependent number of times till the L2CAP sends an L2CA_DisconnectInd.

◆ **L2CA_DataWrite.** This action signifies the receipt of a request from the upper layer for the transfer of data from the upper layer to the L2CAP entity for further transmission over an open channel.

◆ **L2CA_QoSViolationInd.** This action indicates a violation of the QoS agreement.

L2CAP to L2CAP Signaling and Data Actions

The L2CAP signaling and data actions are similar to the L2CAP signaling and data events. The only difference lies in the fact that the signaling actions are used to specify transmission of messages while the signaling events specify their receipt or reception.

Before establishment of a connection, the two devices negotiate and agree upon various configuration parameters. The implementation of these parameters takes place by the use of options. The next section discusses the configuration parameter options.

The Configuration Parameter Options

Options are mechanism used to increase the ability of the L2CAP during negotiations of the connection parameters. Options are transmitted in the form of information elements and include an option type, length, and one or more data fields. Figure 6-13 illustrates the structure of the configuration parameter option.

LSB	byte0	byte1	byte2	byte3	MSB
	Type	Length	Option data		

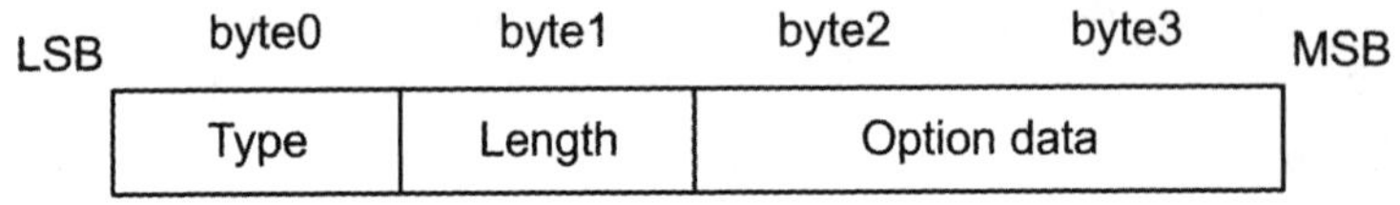

FIGURE 6-13 *The structure of the configuration parameter option*

The configuration parameter options can be of the following three types:

◆ Maximum Transmission Unit (MTU)

◆ Flush timeout

◆ Quality of Service (QoS)

Maximum Transmission Unit Option

The *Maximum Transmission Unit* (MTU) option is used to specify the maximum size of the payload that the sender is capable of accepting. The MTU is of type 0x01 and its length is 16 bytes that carries an informational element of two-octet MTU size. The MTU field defines the size of the largest L2CAP packet (in bytes) accepted by the originator of the request in the particular channel. The default MTU size is 672 bytes. All L2CAP implementations, however, should support a minimum MTU size of 48 bytes. Figure 6-14 illustrates the structure of the MTU configuration parameter option.

```
0                                                    31
 ┌──────────────┬──────────────┬──────────────────────┐
 │  Type=0x01   │  Length=2    │        MTU           │
 └──────────────┴──────────────┴──────────────────────┘
```

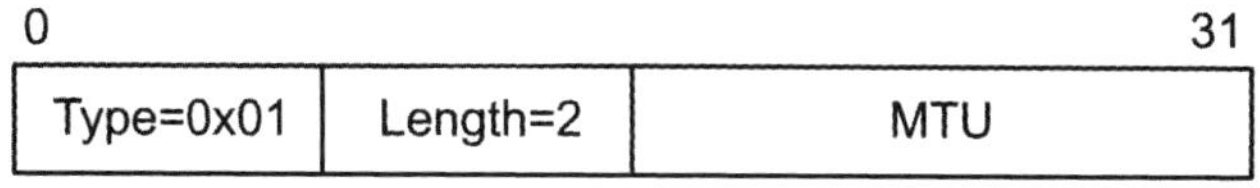

FIGURE 6-14 *The structure of the MTU option*

Flush Timeout Option

The flush timeout option is used to specify the amount of time taken by the originator's LC or LM to transmit an L2CAP segment successfully before it is flushed out. The flush timeout option is of type 0x02 with a payload size of 16 bits. The flush timeout value is defined as a unit of time and measured in milliseconds.

The flush timeout of the signaling link is used to determine the maximum number of request retransmissions at the L2CAP level before the disconnection of the channel. This is because long flush timeouts allow more request retransmissions at the Physical layer with better reliability as compared to short flush timeouts. Better reliability of transmissions eliminates the need for retransmissions at the L2CAP level.

Figure 6-15 illustrates the structure of the flush timeout configuration parameter option.

```
0                                                    31
 ┌──────────────┬──────────────┬──────────────────────┐
 │  Type=0x02   │  Length=2    │    Flush Timeout     │
 └──────────────┴──────────────┴──────────────────────┘
```

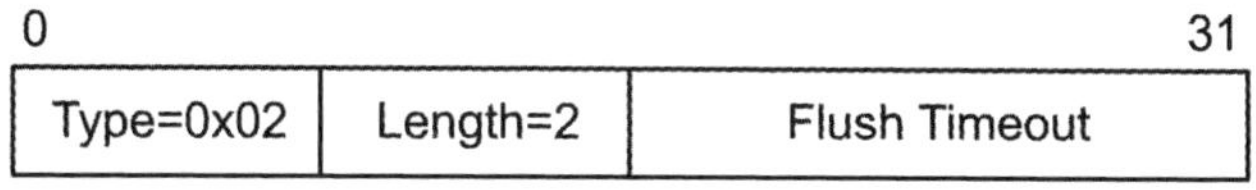

FIGURE 6-15 *The structure of the flush timeout option*

Quality of Service

The Quality of Service option is used to specify the flow of data between the layers of the protocol stack as they traverse the L2CAP layer. The QoS option is of type 0x03. The definitions of the QoS option differ according to their inclusion in the request/response messages:

◆ In the configuration request, the QoS option defines the flow agreement of the outgoing traffic from the device transmitting the request to the device receiving the request.

◆ In the positive Configuration response, the QoS option defines the flow agreement of the incoming traffic from the device sending the response.

◆ In the negative Configuration response, the QoS option defines the preferred preference for the incoming traffic from the perspective of the device sending the response.

The L2CAP also provides certain service primitives that are required for testing, as discussed in the next section.

Service Primitives

The services primitives and their parameters can be of the following types:

◆ **Connection.** Setup, configure, and disconnect

◆ **Data.** Read and write

◆ **Group.** Create, close, add member, remove member, and get membership

◆ **Information.** Ping, get info, and request a callback when an event occurs

◆ **Connectionless traffic.** Enable and disable

The layers above the L2CAP are the layers of the middleware protocol group that function as an interface between the underlying transport protocols and the application layers. The interface of the middleware group defines standard protocols that lets the application group use the higher protocol layers without any direct communication with the lower layers of the protocol stack. The middleware group consists of the following:

◆ The RFCOMM that is a serial port abstraction.

◆ The IrDA protocol or the Object Exchange (OBEX) that is used to enhance interoperability between devices.

◆ The Telephony Control Protocol (TCS) that facilitates control of telephone calls used for audio or data.

◆ The Service Discovery Protocol (SDP) that, true to its name, facilitates discovery of the available and needed services.

The next section discusses each of the protocols of the middleware group in detail.

RFCOMM

An important aspect of Bluetooth technology is its ability to transmit data without using physical wires to connect the devices, which is the technology of wireless communication. RFCOMM resides over the L2CAP and is a cable replacement protocol developed for use with Bluetooth wireless communication. RFCOMM borrows its standards from the 07.10 specification of the European Telecommunication Standard Institute (ETSI). Figure 6-16 illustrates the placement of the RFCOMM layer in the Bluetooth protocol stack.

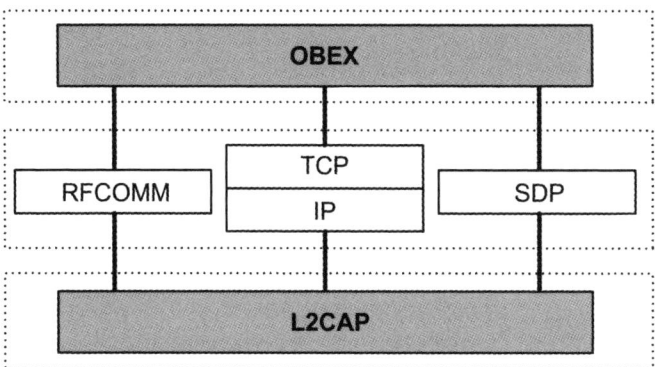

FIGURE 6-16 *The placement of the RFCOMM protocol layer*

The name RFCOMM is derived from RF and COMM. The serial interfaces of PCs are called COM ports. RFCOMM, therefore, stands for the layer of the protocol stack that defines a wireless instance (RF) of a virtual COM port.

As an effective mode for replacing cables, RFCOMM provides the protocol stack with the support of serial communication that is similar to the serial communication in cable technology. RFCOMM protocol provides a Protocol Data Unit (PDU) structure to emulate the RS-232 control and data signals over the baseband layer. The upper-level services such as OBEX are thereby provided with capabilities to transport both control and data signals by using the serial line transmissions. RFCOMM supports approximately 60 simultaneous connections between two Bluetooth devices. The RFCOMM provides the following services:

◆ Control signals
◆ Null Modem emulations
◆ Multiple emulated serial ports

Control Signals

The control signals emulated by RFCOMM are in the form of the nine circuits of an RS-232 interface. Table 6-7 lists the pins and circuit names of the nine circuits of an RS-232 interface.

Table 6-7 The Pins and Circuit Names of the Nine Circuits of an RS-232 Interface

Code	Defines
102	Signal Common
103	Transmit Data (TD)
104	Received Data (RD)
105	Request to Send (RTS)
106	Clear to Send (CTS)
107	Data Set Ready (DSR)
108	Data Terminal Ready (DTR)
109	Data Carrier Detect (DCD)
125	Ring Indicator (RI)

Null Modem Emulation

As stated earlier, RFCOMM is based on the 07.10 specification of the ETSI. However, during the transfer of states in non-data circuits, the specification for TS 07.10 does not distinguish between Data Terminal Equipment (DTE) and Data Circuit-Terminating Equipment (DCE) in serial communications. DTE is a device, such as a computer or a terminal, placed at the endpoint of a communication path. DCE, on the other hand, is a device, such as a modem, that is placed between the endpoints of a communication path. The function of a DCE is to facilitate the communication process.

The RS-232 control signals are sent in the form of a number of DTE or DCE independent signals. The process used for the transfer of RS-232 control signals between two connected devices of the same type creates an implicit null modem. Although none of the currently available single null modem cable wiring schemes seem to have been successful, it is expected that the RFCOMM null modem scheme will work in most cases.

Multiple Emulated Serial Ports

Two Bluetooth devices using an RFCOMM communication may open up to 60 multiple emulated serial ports that are specific to their usage. The Data Link Connection Identifier (DLCI) is used to identify an ongoing communication between a client and a server application. The DLCI is unique for a single RFCOMM session between two devices. It is represented by 16 bits, but has a usable value range of 2.....61. Figure 6-17 illustrates the structure of the multiple emulated serial ports.

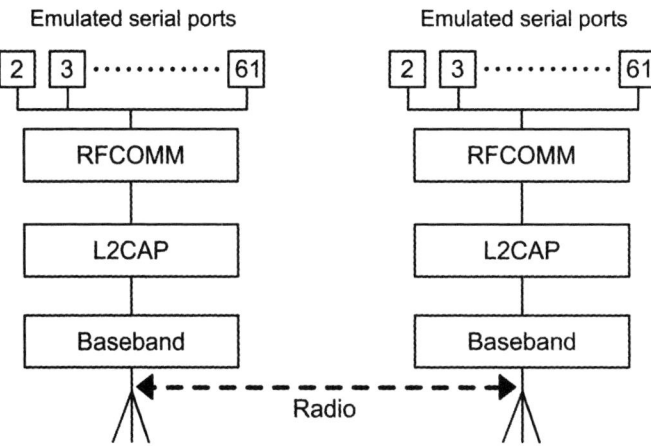

FIGURE 6-17 *Multiple emulated serial ports*

In a client-server environment, both the client and the server applications may be placed on the two sides of an RFCOMM session. It is possible that the clients on either side of the session makes connections that are independent of each other. As a result, the concept of server channels is used to divide the DLCI value space between the two communicating devices.

An RFCOMM entity runs multiple TS 07.10 multiplexer session when a Bluetooth device supporting multiple emulated serial ports has its connection endpoints in different devices. Each multiplexer session, in such a case, uses its own L2CAP CID. Figure 6-18 illustrates the multiple emulated serial ports between two Bluetooth devices.

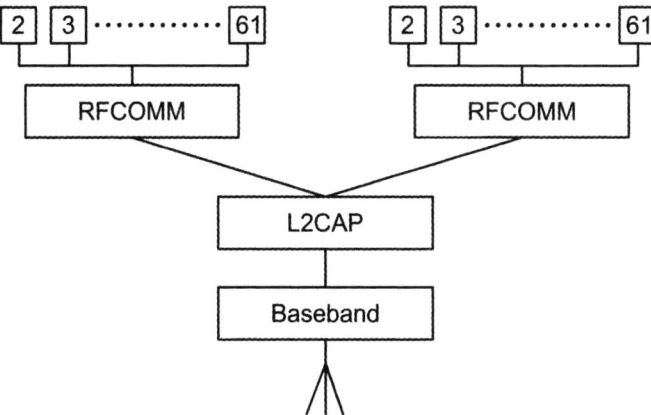

FIGURE 6-18 *The emulated serial ports coming from two Bluetooth devices.*

NOTE

Multiplexing is a mechanism that combines a number of signals for transmission on a shared medium such as a telephone. A multiplexor is used to combine the signals at the transmitter end while a demultiplexor is used to split the signals at the receiver end. A communication channel can be shared between independent signals by using multiplexing techniques such as time division, frequency division, and code division.

Communication between the L2CAP layer and the RFCOMM layer takes place through RFCOMM channels or the Data Link Connection (DLC) that use the IrOBEX protocol to exchange files based on the Bluetooth-specific profiles. To do so, a communication path is set up between the two applications running on two different Bluetooth devices. The communication path has two communication endpoints and a communication segment between the running applications. Figure 6-19 illustrates the RFCOMM communication segment created between the running applications of two devices.

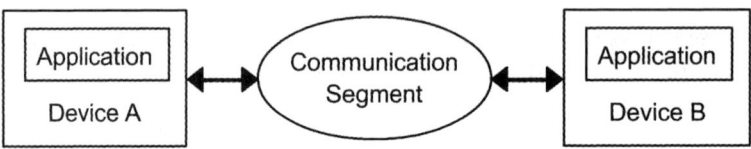

FIGURE 6-19 *The RFCOMM communication segment*

The devices supported by RFCOMM can be of the following two types:

♦ **Type 1 Devices.** These are the devices that form the communication endpoints, as in the case of Bluetooth-enabled computers and printers Figure 6-20 illustrates RFCOMM communication in Type 1 devices.

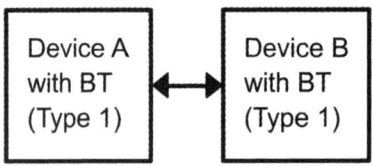

FIGURE 6-20 *RFCOMM communication in Type 1 devices*

♦ **Type 2 Devices.** These are the devices that form the communication segment, as in the case of connecting LAN networks at one end and a Bluetooth-enabled device at the other end. Figure 6-21 illustrates an RFCOMM communication in Type 2 devices.

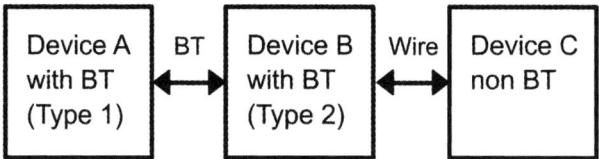

FIGURE 6-21 *RFCOMM communication in Type 2 devices*

The fact that RFCOMM is based on the TS 07.10 specification has been recapitulated quite often in the preceding sections. The next section discusses the various TS 07.10 adaptation s for RFCOMM.

The TS 07.10 Adaptations for RFCOMM

The following are the TS 07.10 adaptations for RFCOMM:

◆ Media adaptation
◆ The TS 07.10 multiplexer startup and closure procedures
◆ The DLCI allocation in RFCOMM server channels
◆ Multiplexer control commands
◆ The flow control methods

Media Adaptation

The RFCOMM specification does not use the open and closing flags of the TS 07.10 basic option frame. In its place, only the fields contained between the flags are exchanged between the L2CAP and RFCOMM layers.

The TS 07.10 Multiplexer Startup and Closure Procedures

RFCOMM does not support the startup and closure procedures of the TS 07.10 (section 5.7) specification. Instead, the RFCOMM specification states that at any time, at least one RFCOMM session must exist between a pair of Bluetooth devices. An RFCOMM session is identified by the Bluetooth address (BD_ADDR) of the two devices.

Before setting up a new DLC, a check for existing RFCOMM sessions is carried out by the initiating entity. Thereafter, a previously existing RFCOMM session is used to establish the new DLC instead of creating a new RFCOMM session. The startup, closedown, and link loss handling procedures of RFCOMM are described here:

◆ **The startup procedure.** The device that opens the first emulated serial port connection establishes the multiplexer control channel. To do so, the following steps are involved:

The L2CAP service primitives are used to establish the L2CAP channel to the peer RFCOMM entity.

The RFCOMM multiplexer is started by sending Set Asynchronous UnBalanced Mode (SABM) command on DLCI 0 and the User Asynchronous (UA) response from the peer entity is then awaited. The SABM command is a low-level command packet used by the RFCOMM to start a link between two devices.

The DLC for the user data traffic is established.

◆ **The closedown procedure.** The device that closes the last connection (DLC) on a particular RFCOMM session closes the multiplexer. The multiplexer is closed by closing the corresponding L2CAP channel. The multiplexer can be closed by sending a DISConnect (DISC) command frame on DLCI. A DISC command is a low-level RFCOMM command frame that is used to terminate an RFCOMM connection. Although this procedure is optional, it is mandatory to send a correct UA response to a DISC.

◆ **Link loss handling.** On receipt of a link loss notification, the local RFCOMM entity is responsible for sending a connection loss notification to the pro emulation (proxy) for each of the active DLCs. As a result, all resources that are associated with the RFCOMM are freed.

The DLCI Allocation in RFCOMM Server Channels

I have already discussed the reason for the division of the DLCI value space between the two communicating devices. The concept of server channels and a direction bit is used for this division. The RFCOMM server channel is a subset of the bits in the address field of the TS 07.10 frame.

A server channel registering with an RFCOMM interface is assigned a Server Channel number that ranges between 1 and 30. The initiating device in an RFCOMM session is given the direction bit (D) of 1 while the other devices have D=0. During the process of establishing a new DLC on an existing RFCOMM session, the direction bit is used with the server channel to determine the DLCI to be used for connection to a specific application. The value of the DLCI is derived by combining the server channel of the application on the other device with the inverse value of the direction bit. The DLCI is, thereafter, used for the bi-directional transmission of all packets between the endpoints.

Multiplexer Control Commands

Some multiplexer commands of the TS 07.10 specification are exchanged on the control channel (DLCI 0) before the establishment of a DLC. Table 6-8 lists the multiplexer commands used in RFCOMM sessions.

Table 6-8 The Multiplexer Commands of the RFCOMM

Command	Description
Remote Port Negotiation (RPN) command	Can be used before opening a new DLC to change the port settings
Remote Line Status (RLS) command	Used to indicate the status of the remote port line
DLC Parameter Negotiation (PN) command	Used before opening a new DLC

The Flow Control Methods

Wired ports use flow control such as Ready To Send (RTS) Clear To Send (CTS) on RS-232 and UART links to control communications. The flow control between the RFCOMM and L2CAP layers depends on the service interface supported by a particular implementation. The different flow control mechanisms supported by RFCOMM are:

◆ **L2CAP flow control.** The flow control mechanism used in the L2CAP is provided by the LM layer in the baseband. The flow control mechanism between the L2CAP and RFCOMM layers is implementation-specific.

◆ **Wired serial port flow control.** The wired serial port flow control is of two types. The software flow control uses characters such as XON and XOFF, while the hardware flow control uses characters such as RTS, CTS, DTR, and DSR.

◆ **RFCOMM flow control.** The RFCOMM flow control is of two types. The RFCOMM protocol flow control commands operate on the aggregate data flow between two RFCOMM entities. This mechanism, therefore, affects all DLCIs. The modem status command operates on individual DLCIs.

◆ **Serial flow control using the port emulation entity.** The Type 1 devices require some port drivers to provide flow control services specified by the API they are emulating. An application may request for flow mechanisms such as XON/XOFF or RTS/CTS expecting the port driver to handle the flow control. In Type 2 devices the port driver performs flow control on the non-RFCOMM part of the communication path using the control parameters sent by the peer RFCOMM entity (represented by a Type 1 device). As a result, the port driver does not perform flow control.

Lower-Level Interactions

The lower-level interactions of the RFCOMM can be described in terms of reliability and low power modes.

Reliability

RFCOMM uses the services of the L2CAP to create L2CAP channels to RFCOMM entities on other devices. Frame commands such as SABM and DISC that are sent on DLCI 0 require response from the remote entity. These frames are, therefore, acknowledged on RFCOMM level but not retransmitted when acknowledgement is absent. Data frames such as Unnumbered Information with Header error check (UIH) do not require any response and are unacknowledged. It is evident that the RFCOMM needs the L2CAP channels with maximum reliability so that the frames are delivered in order, without duplication. Unreliable transmission of frames by the L2CAPis handled by the RFCOMM by using link loss notifications.

Low Power Modes

The L2CAP channels toward a device may be idle or in a state of inactivity. In such a case, the device is put into a low power mode (park, hold, or sniff) without interference from the RFCOMM. The RFCOMM affirms its latency requirements to the L2CAP. The L2CAP uses this latency requirement parameter to decide on the low power mode to be used.

The low power modes do not induce any latency delays in the RFCOMM protocol. Latency sensitivity is inherently dependent on the application. Therefore, an RFCOMM service implementation may also state the latency requirements that are aggregated and conveyed to the L2CAP.

The next section discusses the Object Exchange (OBEX) layer of the middleware protocol group.

OBEX

Object Exchange (OBEX) is the session protocol layer (originally called IrOBEX) developed by the Infrared Data Association (IrDA), which helps in the spontaneous exchange of objects. In the specification, OBEX is termed as "IrDA interoperable" not implying direct communication with IrDA devices, but providing Bluetooth devices with common applications to use in either forms of wireless communication. OBEX in Bluetooth, to some extent, can be functionally considered similar to the HTTP protocol. Like HTTP, OBEX uses a client-server model for exchange of objects that is independent of the transport API.

The folder-listing object in OBEX can be used to browse through the contents of the folder on a remote device. Bluetooth uses connection-oriented OBEX in the following ways:

◆ The connection-oriented protocols of the Bluetooth architecture are mapped to OBEX.

◆ Application profiles using OBEX and Bluetooth use the connection-oriented OBEX to provide the functionality specific to a particular profile.

◆ The use of both connection-oriented and connectionless OBEX raises interoperability issues and is, therefore, not desirable.

◆ Within a Bluetooth system, the OBEX protocol simply enables exchange of data objects.

Figure 6-22 illustrates the placement of OBEX in the Bluetooth protocol stack.

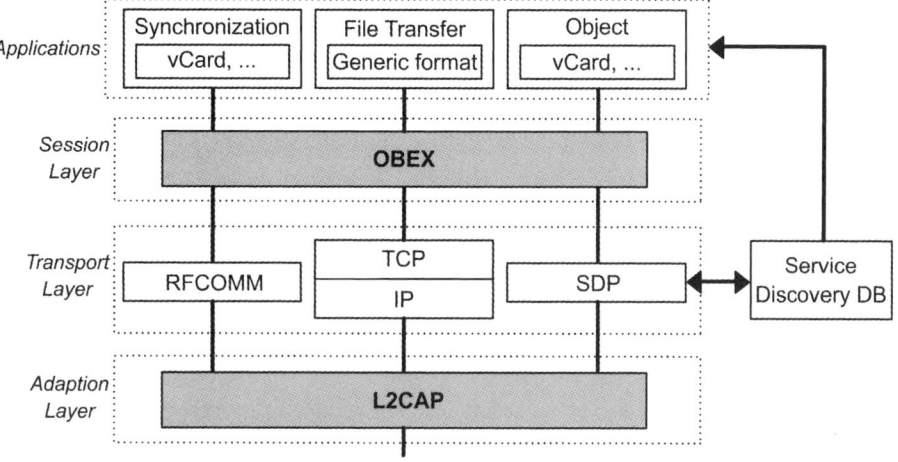

FIGURE 6-22 *The placement of OBEX*

A typical use of OBEX can be explained with the example of business card transfer to other devices or file transfers that are used by many applications. The implementation of OBEX over RFCOMM supports serial cable emulation and is based on the transport protocol that is embedded on ETSI 07.10. In order to support Bluetooth devices, OBEX needs to fulfill the following requirements:

◆ The device supporting OBEX should function as a client, server, or both.

◆ Servers running simultaneously on a device should use separate RFCOMM server channels.

◆ Service or server applications using OBEX should register appropriate information into the service discovery database. This feature of OBEX is detailed in the Bluetooth specification.

Defining OBEX Objects and Protocol

OBEX objects, like all other objects, contain headers made up of the header ID and the header value. The header ID provides information about the contents and formats used, while the value header consisting of one or more bytes is specified in the format detailed in the header ID. The specified headers include Count, Name, Length, Type, Description, Time, HTTP body, End body, Connection ID, Who, Application parameters, Authenticate challenge, Authenticate response, Object class, and other user-specified headers.

The transfer of objects in OBEX follows the request-response cycle. The requests from the client are answered by responses from the server. This does seem very similar to the HTTP mode of object transfer, doesn't it? A new request from the client is issued only after receipt of a response for the previous request. The request packet contains a one-byte opcode, a two-byte length indicator, and the required or optional data. The content of the optional data depends on the operation used during the transfer or exchange of the object. Some of these operations include connect operation, disconnect operation, get, push, set path, and abort.

How Does OBEX Work?

When a client initiates a request, the server prepares to receive the request. However, before entering into the listening mode the server needs to do the following:

◆ Open an RFCOMM server channel
◆ Register the server capability into the service discovery database

After this, the server is able to listen to the client request. OBEX detects data packets in the byte stream by the opcode or response codes depending on whether the packet is a request or a response packet. Although OBEX packets do not have end flags, indicating the end of a packet, the two bytes after the op or response code are taken as the length of the code. As a result, the whole length of the packet can be estimated and its boundaries can, therefore, be determined.

An OBEX client starts with the start of an OBEX connection. The session is initiated with a Connect request. The format of the request packet is as follows:

◆ Byte 0 contains the 0x80 opcode.
◆ Bytes 1 and 2 contain the `Connect Request` packet length.
◆ Byte 3 contains the OBEX version number.
◆ Byte 4 contains the flags.
◆ Bytes 5 and 6 contain the maximum length of the OBEX packet.
◆ Byte 7 to n contains the optional headers.

On receipt of the `Connect Request`, the server accepts the connection by sending back a successful response. After the connection is established, it remains functional, disconnected only by corresponding request/response or by failures. The format of the response packet is as follows:

- ◆ Byte 0 contains the response code.
- ◆ Bytes 1 and 2 contain the `Connect Request` packet length.
- ◆ Byte 3 contains the OBEX version number.
- ◆ Byte 4 contains the flags.
- ◆ Bytes 5 and 6 contain the maximum length of the OBEX packet.
- ◆ Byte 7 to n contains the optional headers.

A `Disconnect Request` is sent to change the host or close a connection to a particular OBEX application. The format of the `Disconnect Request` packet is as follows:

- ◆ Byte 0 contains the 0x80 opcode.
- ◆ Bytes 1 and 2 contain the `Disconnect Request` packet length.
- ◆ Byte 3 contains the optional headers.

The format of the packet after the client pushes the OBEX object to the server is:

- ◆ Byte 0 contains the 0x02 (0x82 in the case of a final bit set).
- ◆ Bytes 1 and 2 contain the packet length.
- ◆ Byte 3 contains the sequence of the headers.

The format of the packet after the client pulls the OBEX object from the server using the GET operation is:

- ◆ Byte 0 contains the 0x03 (0x83 in the case of a final bit set).
- ◆ Bytes 1 and 2 contain the packet length.
- ◆ Byte 3 contains the sequence of the headers beginning with Name.

Every request packet is answered by a response packet with the following format:

- ◆ Byte 0 contains the response code.
- ◆ Bytes 1 and 2 contain the Response packet length.
- ◆ Byte 3 contains the optional response headers.

The next layer of the middleware protocol group is the Telephony Control Protocol (TCS). The core specification of TCS deals with the protocol layer providing telephony communication.

Telephony Control Protocol

The Telephony Control Protocol is personified by the Telephony Control protocol specification–BINary (TCS-BIN) or TCS layer that is based on the existing ITU-T Q.931 protocol. TCS is a binary, packet-based encoding for telephony control that resides over the L2CAP. Simply put, TCS defines how telephone calls should be sent over Bluetooth links. The guidelines provided include specifications for point-to-point and point-to-multipoint signaling. Although TCS-BIN is well equipped to handle the version 1.0 telephony profiles, it also uses the AT commands over RFCOMM.

TCS-BIN

TCS-BIN is a bit-oriented protocol that defines call controlling signals for speech- and data-based calls between Bluetooth devices. All call controlling functions, such as establishing and terminating calls are supervised by TCS-BIN. It also defines the mobility management procedures used for handling groups of Bluetooth TCS devices, called *wireless user groups*. These procedures include group membership management, sharing telephony services among member devices, and methods to implement faster connections between two members.

AT Commands

TCS-AT is not defined as a named and separate protocol in the specification. AT commands provide commands for modem control especially for legacy applications. AT commands also provide commands for mobile phones. The AT commands are based on the ITU-T Recommendation V.20 and ETS 300 916 (GSM 07.07). The use of these commands for fax services is specified in 3.1.1.3.3 Palm OS telephony Control support.

The transport protocol group also includes the Service Discovery Protocol (SDP) that provides devices with services to locate each other in a network.

Service Discovery Protocol

Service Discovery Protocol is a simple protocol that allows devices to locate each other and gather information about the services of other devices. In a LAN environment of fixed networks, the process of configuring and managing the services is a static procedure, handled by the system administrator. However, the temporary and ad hoc networks in Bluetooth keep changing and, therefore, require a dynamic and flexible solution for service configuration and management.

SDP provides protocols for self-configuration in the peer-to-peer and ad hoc usage scenarios of Bluetooth. SDP functions over reliable packet transmissions use a one request Protocol Data Unit (PDU)–one response PDU model for transactions. SDP provides locating services for end user applications and should, therefore, be placed between the Transport layer and the Application layer of the OSI Reference Model. SDP, however, cannot be mapped to the Session layer of the OSI Reference Model because the Session layer is responsible for dialog control between users. A dialog can be defined as a formal conversation between users where they agree to exchange data.

SDP Services

To determine the available Bluetooth services, a device may act as an SDP client querying for the available services, as an SDP server providing information about the available services, or both. A Bluetooth device can have only one SDP server but may act as a client to many other remote devices. The SDP protocols are concerned with providing information about available services. The utilization of these services is facilitated by other Bluetooth or third-party protocols. SDP does not provide notification mechanisms to identify the availability or non-availability of an SDP server or any specific service. The client may, however, use polling as an effective mechanism to detect the availability or non-availability of services. SDP services can be of the following types:

◆ Service records
◆ Service classes

Service Records

An SDP service provides information, performs an action, or controls resources, and is implemented as software, hardware, or both. The SDP server, or the service provider, as it is otherwise called, maintains a list of service records describing the various services it provides. This list of service records is called the *service registry*. A service record consists of a list of service attributes with information about the service class (for example printing, faxing, information services, or audio services), information about the interacting protocol layers, and descriptive information about the service. Each service corresponds to a service record with a service record handle. A service record handle is unique within a particular server and is allocated dynamically. A special service record describing the services of the server and its supported protocols is provided with a service record handle of 0x00000000.

The service attributes of a service record define the supported services, which include the service type, service ID, supported protocols, service name, and service description. The service attributes consist of a 16-bit attribute ID and a variable length value. Each entry of the service record is a (attribute, value) pair. The attribute values consist of a header and a data field. The header field, in turn, includes the data type and the data size of the attribute header. The data types of the header field can be null, unsigned integer, signed twos-complement integer, Universally Unique Identifier (UUID), text string, Boolean, data element sequence (a set), data element alternative (select one), and URL.

Service Classes

Each SDP service is an instance of a service class. A service belongs to a service class that defines its attributes by ID, the intended use, and the format of the attribute value. Service records include both service-specific attributes and universal service attributes.

A service class is allotted a unique identifier called a UUID. The concept of UUID is adopted from the International Organization for Standardization (ISO). A UUID is a 128-bit value created algorithmically and is unique across space and time. As a result, UUIDs are created for every new service and do not require the back up of a central registry containing a list of the identifiers. The SIG, however, does maintain a registry of well-known UUIDs that are used for services associated with published profiles. The technique of maintaining a registry of popular UUIDs ensures that UUIDs are available by simply specifying the service in a search request.

A service class acts as a super class when more specific attributes are defined in the sub-class of another service. The sub-class inherits the attributes of the super class. The ServiceClassIDList, an attribute of the service record, contains a list of all the class IDs for a particular service class. Figure 6-23 illustrates the relation between the super class and the sub-class of an SDP service class.

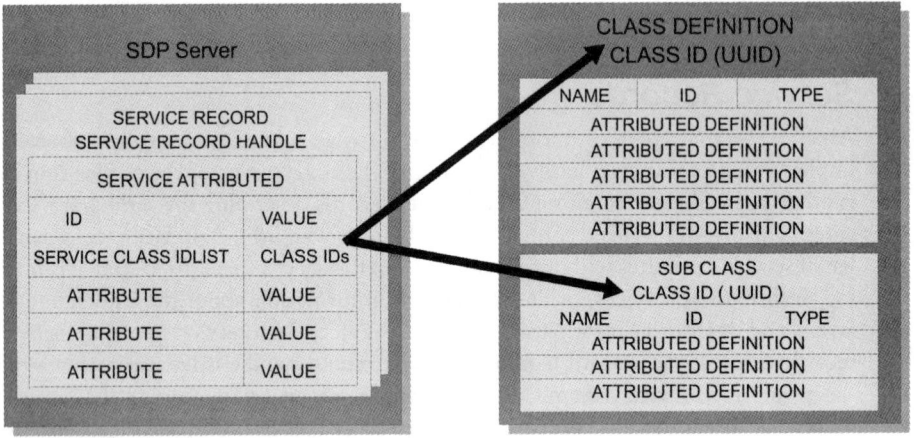

FIGURE 6-23 *The relation between the super class and the sub-class*

How SDP Services Are Discovered

The SDP is used to discover services and not access them. The processes that support service discovery are *searching* and *browsing*. Searching is based on the UUIDs and is used when the client is looking for a specific service The value of the UUID specified in the search criteria is matched with the all the service record attribute values and the matching service record is returned at the end of the search.

Browsing is used when a client needs to identify a particular service on a remote device. This technique discovers a particular service by adding a special service attribute called the BrowseGroupList (supported by all service classes) to the search criteria. The BrowseGroupList contains a list of UUIDs of browse groups arranged hierarchically. When the search criteria is based at the top level of the browse hierarchy; that is, at the PublicBrowserRoot, the UUID returns all the service records browsed at both the top level and at the lower level (BrowserGroupDescriptor) of the browse hierarchy. The BrowserGroupDescriptor consists of a GroupID attribute containing the UUIDs for the describing browser group. When the services of the group are browsed, the client reads the `GroupID` attribute of the `BrowserGroupDescriptor` and then searches on this `GroupID`.

The Plug and Play Mechanism

Bluetooth *Plug and Play* (PnP) is used to override the need for custom drivers for the third-party hardware drives. The third-party hardware drives use custom drives to use the features of their hardware. The Bluetooth PnP provides a means for identifying the right driver to be loaded in response to a discovered service.

Error Handling

An SDP transaction consists of a request-response PDU, where each request PDU is answered with corresponding response PDU. On receiving a request in improper format, the server does not send a response PDU, but generates an error PDU (`SDP_ErrorResponse`).

Summary

A Bluetooth device typically consists of the host and the module. The module consists of the radio that enables the device use the Bluetooth technology. The host implements the upper or higher protocol layers (L2CAP and above) while the module implements the lower protocol layers of the radio, LM, and the baseband. The upper layers of the protocol layer are oblivious of the functions and happenings in the lower layer. The layer responsible for segregating the upper and lower protocol layers is the Host Controller Interface (HCI). The HCI can be viewed as a transport layer placed inside the device. The other transport layer or the L2CAP is an over-the-air protocol that the upper protocols communicates across a Bluetooth link. The L2CAP resides between the HCI and the protocol layers of the middleware group. These layers of the middleware group define standard protocols that allow applications to use higher-level protocols without any direct communication with the lower layers.

In this chapter, you learned about the standard interface, or the HCI, that facilitates access to the services and capabilities of the lower protocol layers. In the context of the L2CAP, you learned about the primary functions of the L2CAP that include multiplexing, signaling, and segmentation-reassembly of packets. You also learned about the RFCOMM, OBEX, TCS, and SDP protocols of the middleware group.

Having discussed all the layers of the protocol stack, the next chapter moves on to an interesting part of the Bluetooth specification that defines the various profiles and usage models for Bluetooth. The profiles form an important part of the specification because they enable interoperability between devices. Each profile described in the specification defines the principles that are used to connect two devices.

Check Your Understanding

Multiple Choice Questions

1. State whether the following statements are true or false.
   a. The HCI is placed in the Bluetooth module.
   b. RTS, CTS, and XON are the timer events of L2CAP.
   c. RFCOMM is a cable replacement protocol.
   d. OBEX is based on the IrDA technology.
   c. SDP services include service records, service classes, error handling, and PnP.

2. Which of the following are the protocols of the middleware transport group?
   a. L2CAP
   b. OBEX
   c. RFCOMM
   d. HCI
   e. TCS
   f. SDP

3. Which of the following are HCI transport layers?
   a. USB
   b. SDP
   c. TCS-BIN
   d. UART
   e. TCS-AT
   f. RS-232

4. Which of the following statements is true?
   a. Signaling enables simultaneous use of links by multiple applications.
   b. Signaling is used to exchange control information about the states of an L2CAPconnection.

Short Questions

1. Describe the HCI system.
2. What is HCI flow control?
3. Describe the different types of L2CAP channels.
4. What is a CID?
5. What is a UUID?
6. Define the L2CAP events and actions.

Answers

Multiple Choice Answers

1. a. False
    b. False
    c. True
    d. True
    e. False

2. b, c, e, and f. OBEX, RFCOMM, TCS, and SDP.
3. a, d, and f. USB, UART, and RS-232.
4. b. Signaling is used to exchange control information about the states of an L2CAPconnection.

Short Answers

1. The HCI system exists across the following three segments:

   ◆ **The HCI firmware.** In the module, the HCI firmware is located on the Host Controller (the hardware in an HCI-enabled Bluetooth device). The HCI firmware uses HCI commands to access the baseband commands, Link Manager commands, hardware status registers, control registers, and event registers.

   ◆ **The HCI driver.** In the host (containing the software entities), the HCI driver is the driver for the Host Controller that is placed above the physical bus. The HCI driver helps to format the data that is accepted from the Host Controller. The host receives asynchronous notifications relating to the HCI events. HCI events are happenings or occurrences, as simple as device discoveries or link establishment that take place in the module. After the host is made aware of the events, it parses the received event packet to evaluate and estimate the type of event.

   ◆ **The Host Controller Transport layer.** In the intermediate layers between the HCI driver on the host and the HCI firmware on the module, the Host Controller Transport layer helps to transfer data without any knowledge of its contents. The various kinds of Host Controller Transport layer used in Bluetooth include USB, UART, and RS232. It is important to note that the host receives asynchronous notifications regarding HCI events regardless of the transport layer used.

2. The HCI transport interfaces transmit data at a rate that is higher than that of the radio and air interfaces. As a result, the speed of data transmission from the host to the module is faster than that from the module to the host. In the case of some Bluetooth modules data can be buffered till it is ready for transmission. This prevents bottling of data traffic flowing to and from the HCI layers. However, in some Bluetooth modules such as Bluetooth PC cards, the memory of the host is larger than that of the module. As a result, the module is unable to transmit data fast enough and is also not able to store the data due to space shortage. How then is traffic overloading between the HCI layers handled? Flow control of the HCI provides the mechanism to slow down the data transportation across the HCI layers in the host and the module in case of overloading.

3. Logical links or channels are used to transfer data during inter device communications. The L2CAP channels can be of the following three types:

   ◆ **Connection-oriented (CO) channels.** These are persistent channels that are used for bi-directional communication. A connection-oriented channel is established only after a signaling connection exchange.

   ◆ **Connectionless (CL) channels.** These are short-lived unidirectional channels that are used for broadcast transmissions within a group of Bluetooth devices. Being a unidirectional channel, a device wanting to respond to these transmissions needs to use other channels for the response transmission.

   ◆ **Signaling channels.** These channels are used to exchange control information before establishing or configuring connection-oriented channels. Signaling channels derive features from both CO and CL channels. As a result, they are persistent and bi-directional like CO channels and also do not need explicit connections before beginning any communication, which is the feature of CL channels.

4. An L2CAP channel in each device has endpoints that define the start and end of the traffic flow. The endpoint of a channel is assigned a locally generated 16-bit unique Channel Identifier (CID). A different CID, therefore, identifies each channel endpoint. The global and well-defined channels have reserved CIDs, while the other channels are allotted dynamically generated CIDs as and when needed.

5. Each SDP service is an instance of a service class. A service belongs to a service class that defines its attributes by ID, the intended use, and the format of the attribute value. Service records include both service-specific attributes and universal service attributes. A service class is allotted a unique identifier called a UUID. The concept of UUID is adopted from the International Organization for Standardization (ISO). A UUID is a 128-bit value created algorithmically and is unique across space and time. As a result, UUIDs are created for every new service and do not require the back up of a central registry containing a list of the identifiers.

6. Events are incoming messages to the L2CAP layer. Actions in the L2CAP layer are the outcome of L2CAP events resulting in the formation of outgoing messages.

Chapter 7

You learned the fundamentals and the operational structure of Bluetooth in Chapter 5, "Link Manager Protocol." The discussions so far have examined the various aspects of the Bluetooth core specification. By now you are familiar with the structure of the protocol stack that facilitates the transfer of information (data) from one Bluetooth device to another. But that's not the end of the story of how Bluetooth came into being and revolutionized the concept of wireless communication. What remains to be examined is the use of this technology. Not in everyday life, but the idea here is to understand how the different parts of the specification are used to ensure the functioning of a Bluetooth device.

Several companies are presently manufacturing Bluetooth devices. Although the specification provides guidelines to ensure that the manufacturers adhere to universal product standards, the interoperability between the devices is addressed differently. The interoperability between devices manufactured by different vendors depends upon the services that are provided for specific usage. The specific services and their usage are defined by profiles. Bluetooth profiles, therefore, define various configurations and operational modes that can be used to create usage scenarios.

The importance of profiles is evident from the fact that a part of the Bluetooth specification has been devoted exclusively for describing the implementations of the usage scenarios. The concept of profiles enables minimizing the risk of interoperability between products from different vendors. The Bluetooth specification 1.0 actually consists of two parts. The first part or the core specification, as you know, defines the layers of the Bluetooth protocol stack. The second part is devoted to profiles, defining the common operations, capabilities, settings, and the data, as a standard for the vendors.

This chapter is an overview of the profiles, their rationale, and operational modes that provide a standardized base for slotting the Bluetooth technology into various groups of devices and applications.

Introduction to Bluetooth Profiles

The purpose behind profile definitions is to provide interoperability between devices manufactured by different vendors. If you reflect on this concept, you'll appreciate that the implementation of the profiles ensures that all manufacturers deploy the same communication standards to make the devices interoperable. Interesting, isn't it? How the concept of profiles took form is another story, not directly related to Bluetooth. The concept of profiles actually originated from the *International Organization for Standardization* (ISO), which defined profiles to ease the implementation of a technology in the following ways:

◆ Reducing the implementation options so that applications could share the same features.

◆ Defining parameters so that different applications could function in the same way.

◆ Defining standard mechanisms for combining different standards.

◆ Defining guidelines for the user interface.

Taking a cue from these observations, the Bluetooth SIG, in the Bluetooth specification volume 2, defines the following parameters that are universal to all Bluetooth profiles:

◆ The user models describe a number of user scenarios that can be implemented during any Bluetooth radio transmission.

◆ The profiles define parameter ranges for each protocol.

◆ The profiles define options in each protocol that are mandatory.

Profiles can, therefore, be looked at as definitions describing the general behavior of Bluetooth devices so that they can communicate with other devices. The behavior of a profile is defined in terms of features that are characteristic to a particular profile but interoperable so that they work in all devices regardless of the manufacturer. The features of a profile can be mandatory, optional, conditional, or excluded. What is important to remember is that these profiles are process-mandatory. This means that the implementation of the profile is restricted in the sense the features have to be implemented in the specified manner. The Bluetooth specification (profile section) defines a total of 13 profiles that can be broadly categorized into two groups. The first group represented by the fundamental building blocks is frequently used by the other profiles. The second group, on the other hand, consists of the concrete usage cases that implement the profiles in real-life device models. For example, the File Transfer Profile is a usage profile based on the Generic Object Exchange Profile.

The four fundamental profiles are as follows:

◆ Generic Access Profile (GAP)

◆ Service Discovery Application Profile (SDAP)

◆ Serial Port Profile (SPP)

◆ Generic Object Exchange Profile (GOEP)

The nine usage profiles are:

◆ Cordless Telephony Profile

◆ Intercom Profile

◆ Headset Profile

◆ Fax Profile

◆ Dial-up Networking Profile

◆ LAN Access Profile
◆ Object Push Profile
◆ Synchronization Profile
◆ File Transfer Profile

Bluetooth-enabled, SIG conforming devices belong to at least one of the preceding 13 profiles. In addition, the four fundamental profiles of the first group also form the foundation for defining the future profiles and usage models. Figure 7-1 illustrates the Bluetooth version 1.0 profile families categorization based on the protocol stack relationships as sourced form the Bluetooth specification 1.0B.

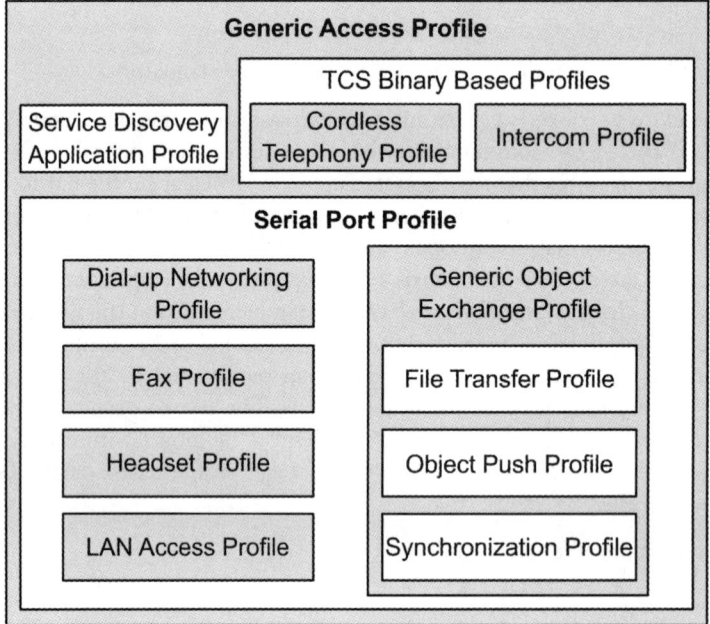

FIGURE 7-1 *The Bluetooth version 1.0 profile family*

The Bluetooth version 1.0 profiles can also be categorized into three groups based on the logical services that they provide. These three groups are:

◆ **The generic profiles.** This group of profiles consists of the GAP profile, which is the core profile for all other profiles and the Service Discovery Profile, which maps the Application layer to the SDP layer of the Bluetooth protocol stack.

◆ **The telephony profiles.** This group of profiles consists of the Cordless Telephony, Headset, and Intercom profiles that use the TCS-BIN layer to control telephony functions.

◆ **The serial profiles**. This group of profiles consists of the Serial Port, GOEP, File Transfer, Object Push, and Synchronization profiles. This group can be further sub-divided into two groups. The first group, which is a direct derivative of the Serial Port Profile, consists of the Fax, Headset, Dial-up Networking, and LAN Access profiles. The second group, which is the parent for object exchange group profiles, consists of the File Transfer, Object Push, and Synchronization profiles.

 NOTE

In this chapter, I'll follow the former classification of fundamental and usage profiles. I'll discuss the four fundamental profiles in this chapter and the nine usage profiles in Chapter 8, "Bluetooth Usage Models."

The Bluetooth user should be able to connect a Bluetooth device to another Bluetooth device. In cases where two devices do not share a common application, the user should be in a position to evaluate the basic Bluetooth capabilities of the devices and connect them thereafter.

The Generic Access Profile

The *Generic Access Profile* (GAP) forms a common foundation for all other profiles. A Bluetooth device complying with GAP has to fulfill all the mandatory capabilities of the profile, as described in the Bluetooth specification. GAP relates to device discovery and connection establishment between two unconnected Bluetooth units. As a result, this profile defines the use of the *Link Controller* (LC) and the *Link Manager Protocol* (LMP) of the lower layers of the Bluetooth protocol stack. Figure 7-2 illustrates the distribution of the Bluetooth protocol layers for GAP as sourced form the Bluetooth specification 1.0B.

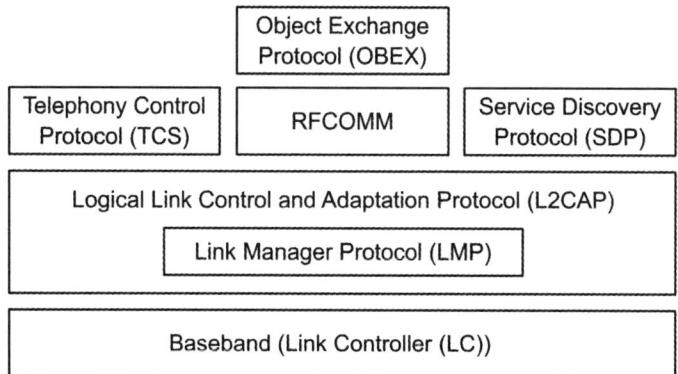

FIGURE 7-2 *The distribution of the Bluetooth protocol stack for the GAP profile*

GAP, true to its name, describes common and non-specific profiles that can be used by other profiles and also by devices implementing several profiles. Other than device discovery and connectivity between devices, GAP also defines procedures related to security that use the higher-level protocol layers of L2CAP, RFCOMM, and OBEX.

GAP facilitates interoperability and information exchange between devices regardless of the manufacturer and the implemented application. In addition, GAP, being a generic profile, is implemented in all those devices that do not conform to any other Bluetooth profile, to ensure interoperability between the devices.

GAP is described in terms of its fundamental features, establishment procedures, security aspects, and the idle mode procedures.

Fundamental Features

The features of GAP are as follows:

◆ It specifies the requirement specifications on names, values, and coding schemes for the names of the parameters and procedures used at the user interface level.

◆ It defines the modes of operation that are generic and not service- or profile-specific.

◆ It defines general procedures that are used to discover the identities, names, and capabilities of other Bluetooth devices, when they are in a discoverable mode. The specification includes only those procedures that do not use channels or connection establishment.

◆ It defines general procedures for bonding between Bluetooth devices. Bonding in Bluetooth is a high-level security procedure that establishes a trust relationship between devices. After bonding, devices can exchange information over an encrypted link.

◆ It defines general procedures that can be used for connecting with other Bluetooth devices.

Each Bluetooth profile describes the roles of two devices and GAP is no exception to this specification. The two role devices in this profile take the generic names of *Device A* or *A-party* and *Device B* or *B-party*. The A-party device is the paging device during the process of establishment of a link between devices or is the initiator when another procedure is initiated on an established link. The B-party device, on the other hand, is the paged device or the acceptor.

The parameters that a Bluetooth device needs to support for the implementation of interoperability at the generic procedure levels are as follows:

◆ **Device Address (BD_ADDR).** The BD_ADDR, as you know, is the unique address of a Bluetooth device received from a remote device during the process of device discovery. At the user interface level, the device address is known as the Bluetooth Device Address, while at the baseband level, the device address is represented as a 48-bit address.

◆ **Names.** A device conforming to GAP specification accepts names that are 248 bytes long. However, some devices such as cell phones, limited by small display capabilities, use names that are only 20 characters long.

◆ **Personal Identification Number (PIN).** The PIN is a unique identification number of a device. The PIN is either a manually entered number or an internally stored number, used during the process of authentication or bonding and helps in recognizing a particular Bluetooth device. A manually entered PIN goes through the process of bonding before the device is validated. Similarly, if the PIN is requested by a device and made available from the device memory, the devices perform authentication to validate their legitimacy.

◆ **Class of the device.** The class of a device is a parameter exchanged between devices when they are in the discovery mode. As a result of this request, the remote device states its device type and supported services that are used by the initiator for establishing a connection.

◆ **Discovery modes.** The two types of discovery modes that a device can exist in are the limited discovery mode and general discovery mode. In the limited discovery mode, the device is available for only a short period of time or during a specific event. During this time, the device moves into the *Scan* state and checks for the *Limited Inquiry Access Code* (LIAC). However, in the general discovery mode, the device is constantly available to respond to the inquiries (General Inquiry Access Code, or GIAC) from other devices. A Bluetooth device that does not respond to incoming inquiries is prohibited from doing so by baseband activities. During this time the device is said to be in undiscoverable mode and never enters the INQUIRY_RESPONSE state.

◆ **Connectivity modes.** A Bluetooth device is in connectivity mode during its *Page Scan* state. In this state, the device transmits a chain of messages or pages, as they are called, to other Bluetooth devices that lie within its coverage area. A device that is in non-discoverable state does not receive these messages and, therefore, does not respond to them.

◆ **Pairing modes.** Pairing occurs after the establishment of a communication link between two devices. You'll recall from the discussions in Chapter 5 that pairing is necessary between devices connecting for the first time. During pairing the Bluetooth devices make use of the security code or PIN to create a common link key that is subsequently used for linking. The two types of pairing modes in which a device can exist are the non-pairable mode and the pairable mode. A Bluetooth device is said to be in a pairable mode when it accepts pairing and bond creation, a process initiated by the remote device, whereas in the non-pairable mode, a Bluetooth device does not accept pairing. The PDUs accepted during pairing are also different for the two modes. In the pairable mode, the device receives an initial authentication request in an `LMP_in_rand` PDU that is followed by an `LMP_au_rand` PDU. The device responds to these request PDUs with an `LMP_accepted` PDU. However, in the case of the non-pairable mode, the Bluetooth device receives an `LMP_in_rand` PDU and responds to it with an `LMP_not_accepted` PDU containing the reason code, *pairing not allowed*.

Establishment Procedures

The initiator, before starting the establishment procedure, needs to have access to certain information in the inquiry response or the name request response FHS packets. The information that needs to be made available to the initiator devices includes the `BD_ADDR`, clock, class of device, and page scan mode. The establishment procedures can be of the following two types:

◆ Link establishment
◆ Channel establishment

Link Establishment

The link establishment procedure is implemented to create a physical ACL link between two devices by using the paging procedure of the Bluetooth IrDA interoperability specification and the *Generic Object Exchange Profile* (GOEP). The parameters used for establishing a physical link between two devices include the access code and the page mode (received during the previous inquiry). At the end of this procedure, a physical link is created between the devices and the master-slave roles are established. Devices connected by a physical link use the LMP procedures without interacting with the host on the remote device.

The host on the remote device is contacted only if the paging device needs to implement other procedures that are beyond the phase of the physical link. To do so, the paging device sends a host connection request to the remote device during the process of link establishment, but before establishing the channel. A device that is in the security mode 3 authenticates other devices after sending the host connection request. Encryption is performed at the end of authentication, and on completion of the entire procedure, a message is exchanged between the two devices.

Channel Establishment

At the end of the link establishment phase, a message is exchanged between the two devices. After the exchange of the message, a channel or logical link is set up a by using the file transfer profile of the Bluetooth specification. Security procedures are implemented at the end of the channel establishment.

 NOTE

The GOEP profile is discussed in the later sections of this chapter. The file transfer profile, however, is discussed in the next chapter.

Security Aspects

Security is the ultimate test for ensuring the confidentiality and integrity of transmitted data. Chapter 9, "Bluetooth Security," discusses the processes of authentication and encryption that ensure secure transmission of data through the air interface, without any alterations or modifications. GAP defines security implementations by two methods— authentication and security mode. The process of authentication is covered in detail in Chapter 9. This section discusses the various levels of security implementation defined in the Bluetooth specification to promote usage protection and information confidentiality. In GAP, the following three levels or modes implement security on communicating devices:

◆ **Security mode 1: non secure.** A device in security mode 1 does not initiate any security and is, therefore, in a non-secure mode. As a result, a device in security mode 1 never sends `LMP_au_rand`, `LMP_in_rand`, or `LMP_encryption_mode_request` PDUs. Here the devices are in the discovery mode where connections are initiated.

◆ **Security mode 2: service level enforced security.** A device in security mode 2 initiates security procedures at higher layers after the channel is established. The application of this security mode takes place at the L2CAP layer and includes procedures for setting the security policies application layers running parallel with the lower protocols. The security procedures are implemented only after the receipt of the `LMP_Connection_Request` PDU.

◆ **Security mode 3: link level enforced security.** Security mode 2 initiates security procedures at lower layers (Link Manager) before the channel is established. As a result, authentication in this security mode occurs before the transmission and receipt of the `LMP_setup_complete` PDU.

A device at a given time can only be in one of these security modes. Consequently, a device in security mode 3 cannot opt for a selective authentication of other devices, but will authenticate all devices that try to establish a link with it.

Idle Modes Procedures

The connectivity and security modes are implemented by Bluetooth devices in response to incoming stimuli in the form of pages, inquiries, or connection requests. The idle mode, on the other hand, enlists the procedures that are implemented by the device that sends the stimuli. The idle mode procedures, therefore, include limited and general inquiry, device and name discovery, and bonding.

Inquiry Procedures

The inquiry procedures are initiated to discover devices in limited or general discoverable modes. The idle procedures for inquiry are, therefore, of two types, limited inquiry and general inquiry.

The Limited Inquiry Procedure

The limited inquiry procedure provides the initiator device with information regarding the limited discoverable devices, in the form of their BD_ADDR, clock, class of device, and page scan mode. This type of inquiry procedure is implemented by devices that need to discover other devices made discoverable only for a short period of time. The device in limited discoverable mode may or may not scan for the LIAC. Therefore, the initiator may decide to use either the limited or general inquiry procedure. In addition, the remote device that is within the coverage area of the initiator has to be made discoverable so that it can receive the inquiry response.

The General Inquiry Procedure

The general inquiry procedure provides the initiator device with information regarding the general discoverable devices, in the form of their BD_ADDR, clock, class of device, and page scan mode. A device in the general discoverable mode is within the range of the initiator and is set to scan for the inquiry page by using the GIAC. The general inquiry procedure can also be used to discover devices that are in limited discovery mode. Either way, the general inquiry idle mode is used by devices to discover other devices that are continuously available or available for a specific condition. In addition, the remote device that is within the coverage area of the initiator has to be made discoverable so that it can receive the inquiry response.

Name Discovery Procedures

The name discovery mode provides the initiator device with the BD_ADDR of connected devices, more specifically those devices that are within its coverage area and respond to the paging message. The name discovery procedures are of two types, name request and device discovery.

The Name Request Procedure

The name request procedure is used to recover the Bluetooth device name of a connected device. The process for retrieving the device name does not require completing the entire procedure to create a link between the two devices.

The Device Discovery Procedure

The device discovery procedure provides the initiator with information regarding the discoverable devices, in the form of their BD_ADDR, clock, class of device, page scan mode, and the Bluetooth device name. As a result, this procedure is performed on devices that are discoverable and connectable.

Bonding Procedures

Bonding is performed as a part of the pairing procedure to create and exchange a common link key between two devices. The link key created is also stored for future use. Bonding, therefore, creates a relationship between two devices. The bonding procedure can either be general or dedicated. In general bonding, the device performs the bonding procedure along with other communications such as accessing the higher protocol layers. On the other hand, dedicated bonding is a procedure performed solely for creating a bond between two devices without any upper layer transactions.

The Serial Port Profile

The *Serial Port Profile* (SPP) is a transport protocol profile that describes the basic operations required to create RFCOMM-based communications between two peer devices. The basic operations, therefore, define the features and procedures for setting up RS-232 emulated or a similar kind of serial cable connection between the devices. The scenarios for this profile describe the procedures implemented by legacy applications that use the Bluetooth cable replacement technology through virtual serial port abstractions. By using SPP, the legacy applications are able to replace a wired serial interface with a wireless one. Figure 7-3 illustrates the distribution of the Bluetooth protocol layers for SPP as sourced form the Bluetooth specification 1.0B.

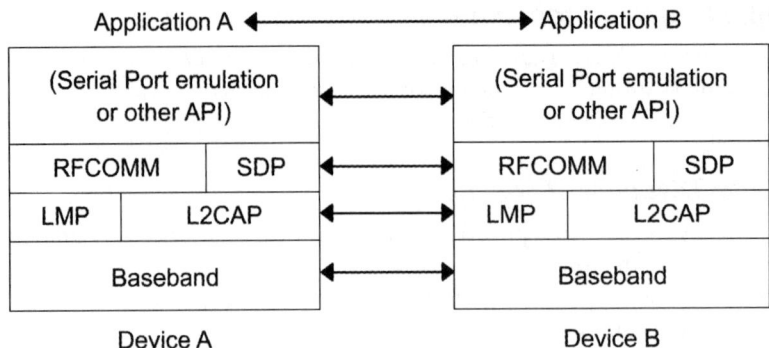

FIGURE 7-3 *The distribution of the Bluetooth protocol stack for the SPP profile*

SPP is built on GAP and, therefore, all mandatory and optional requirements of GAP are mandatory and optional for this profile too. This profile supports the PPP networking in the following implementations:

◆ LAN access for a single Bluetooth device

◆ LAN access for multiple Bluetooth devices

◆ PC-to-PC accessibility using PPP networking over serial cable emulations

The SPP profile is described in terms of its fundamental features, procedures, security aspects, and interoperability requirements.

Fundamental Features

The fundamental features of SPP are as follows:

◆ Service discovery procedures are performed to set up emulated serial cable connections. Link establishment is initiated by Device A.

◆ The master and slave roles are not fixed.

◆ Bonding, in this profile, is not explicit. As a result, bonding is an optional procedure.

◆ RFCOMM is used to transfer the data, modem control signals, and configuration commands.

◆ Security procedures such as authorization, authentication, and encryption are implemented. Support for authentication and encryption are mandatory so that the device can participate in corresponding procedures when requested by the peer device. The devices are paired during the connection establishment phase to implement the security procedures.

◆ This profile supports only one-slot packets with data rates of up to 128 kbps. Support for higher data rates is optional.

◆ This profile supports point-to-point connections.

◆ Concurrency, in this profile, is not limited. As a result, a single device supports multiple and simultaneous executions of the profile.

◆ Virtual serial ports (or their equivalent) are set up on two devices that are then connected with Bluetooth to emulate a serial cable connection between the two devices. A legacy application can run on any one of the devices by using the virtual serial ports creating an impression of a real serial cable connection between the two devices (use of the RS-232 control signaling).

Procedures

The two role devices in this profile take the generic names of Device A and Device B. Device A is the device that takes initiative for the connection between the two devices. Device B, on the other hand, is the device that waits for another device to take initiative for the connection.

 NOTE

The order of the connection is in no way related to the order in which the legacy applications are executed on the two devices. As a result, it is not necessary that if the legacy application on Device B is executed first, the connection between the devices will initiate from Device B.

The following are the three application procedures required for a serial connection between two devices:

◆ Set up a virtual connection.

◆ Accept the link and establish a virtual serial connection.

◆ Register the service record in the local Service Discovery Protocol (SDP) database.

Set up a Virtual Connection

The following procedures are followed to set up an emulated serial port (or its equivalent port) in the remote device:

1. The SDP is used to submit a query and find out the channel number of the RFCOMM server in a particular application running on the remote device. The search for the channel number uses the browsing capability to enable the user select a port or service from a list of available ports or services in the peer device. If the required port or service is known in advance, the Service Class ID is used to search for the necessary parameters of the desired service.

2. Authentication and encryption of the remote device are optional procedures.

3. A new L2CAP channel to the RFCOMM entity is requested.

4. An RFCOMM session is initiated on the L2CAP channel.

5. A new data link connection is started on the RFCOMM session by using the acquired server channel number.

At the end of these procedures, a virtual serial port is readied for communication between the applications on the two devices.

Accept the Link and Establish a Virtual Serial Connection

The following procedures are followed to accept the link and establish a virtual serial connection:

1. A remote device requests for participating in the authentication procedure and later to turn on encryption.

2. A new L2CAP channel session establishment is accepted.

3. A new RFCOMM channel session establishment is accepted on the acquired L2CAP channel.

4. A new data link connection is started on the RFCOMM session. This generates a local request to authenticate and turn on encryption on the remote device.

Register the Service Record in the Local SDP Database

The implementation of this procedure registers a service record for the emulated serial port in the SDP database. This, in turn, facilitates the creation of a Service Database that can respond to the SDP queries.

All applications or services that are accessible by RFCOMM need to provide an SDP service record containing parameters that can be used to access a particular application or service. A device supporting legacy applications on serial ports needs to register the services, a process that is aided by a helper application so that the user is able set up the serial port.

In addition to the three procedures, SPP also supports power mode and link loss handling.

Power Mode and Link Loss Handling

The units that are active in SPP have different power requirements. As a result, the power modes are usually not used. However, a request from a unit to use a power save mode is not rejected or denied.

The RFCOMM data link connections and the L2CAP channels are not released when a particular unit moves into the park, sniff, or hold mode. The RFCOMM data connection is shut down only if the possibility of a link loss is detected. When the communication on higher levels is resumed later, the RFCOMM session is re-initialized by implementing the RFCOMM session procedure.

Interoperability Requirements

The SPP profile uses the Link Manager to establish a baseband link between the devices. The Link Controller is used for invoking the inquiry and paging processes. In addition to this, the SPP profile also uses the RFCOMM and L2CAP layers to develop L2CAP channels that can be used to create RFCOMM links with appropriate RFCOMM servers. The use of multiple layers necessitates interoperability between the layers so that they work in unison.

The interoperability requirements of the SPP profile is, therefore, defined for the L2CAP, RFCOMM, Link Controller, and Link Manager layers.

The L2CAP Interoperability Requirements

The L2CAP interoperability requirements of the SPP profile are mandatory and defined for the following:

◆ **Channel types.** SPP uses only connection-oriented channels. This means that broadcasts between the devices are not used in this profile. The value for the RFCOMM defined in the Assigned numbers document in the PSM field of the request packet is used to identify the RFCOMM entity before the establishment of the L2CAP channel.

◆ **Signaling.** The request for an L2CAP connection can be initiated by Device A only. This is the only requirement that needs to be fulfilled during the signaling process.

◆ **Configuration options.** The L2CAP requirements for the configuration options include specifications for the *Maximum Transmission Unit* (MTU), flush timeout, and *Quality of Service* (QoS). The SPP profile does not enforce any restrictions on the MTU size over the MTU requirements that are already stated in the L2CAP specification. The serial port data is carried over a reliable L2CAP channel. As a result, the specification for the flush timeout is set to the default value of 0xfff. The requirement for negotiating Quality of Service is optional in the SPP profile.

The RFCOMM Interoperability Requirements

The RFCOMM interoperability requirements of SPP are defined for the following:

◆ **RS-232 control signals.** As per the TS 07.10 specification, changes in the RS-232 control signals should be sent (in the form of information) to all devices along with the Modem Status Command. RFCOMM can also be used with an adaptation layer implementing any type of API (which is not a virtual serial port). The use of all RS-232 signals except for the flow control signal (which is the RTR signal in TS 07.10) is optional.

◆ **Remote line status indication.** Any changes in the RS-232 line status should be sent (in the form of information) to all devices along with the Remote Line Status Command. This is done in cases where a physical serial port (or its equivalent) is used by a local device to send the information regarding the change in the RS-232 line status resulting in overrun, parity, or framing errors.

◆ **Remote port negotiation.** Device A can inform Device B about the RS-232 port setting by using the Remote Port Negotiation Command even before DLC establishment. This is done when the API to the RFCOMM exposes the settings of the RS-232 port. Device B is allowed to send the Remote Port Negotiation Command.

◆ **SDP interoperability requirements.** Device A does not contain any service records related to SPP. To access a service record supporting SPP, the SDP client entity in Device A connects and interacts with the SDP client entity in Device B by using the SDP and L2CAP procedures for service discovery. As such, Device A plays the role of a local device while Device B plays the role of the remote device.

The Link Controller Interoperability Requirements

The Link Controller interoperability requirements of SPP are defined for the following:

◆ **Inquiry.** When Device A invokes an inquiry, the general inquiry procedure discussed in the GAP specification is implemented. Only Device A is allowed to inquire within the execution of SPP.

◆ **Inquiry scan.** The GIAC is used for the inquiry scan based on the discoverable modes that have already been discussed in the GAP profile specification. Therefore, SPP uses only the limited discoverable mode that is appropriate for the application located in Device B. The generalized serial port service for legacy applications defined by SPP does not correspond to any of the major service class bits in the Class of device field. Therefore, the Class of device field in the INQUIRY_RESPONSE message of Device B does not contain information about whether Device B is in the execution of the SPP profile.

◆ **Error behavior.** The LC level features of the profiles are triggered by the LMP procedures. Therefore, most of the errors are caught at the LMP layer. Some LC procedures such as inquiry or paging, however, are independent of the LMP layer. The errors generated by these procedures are, therefore, not only difficult but also impossible to detect.

◆ **Paging**. during execution of the SPP profile, only Device A can initiate paging. However, if there already is a baseband connection between Device A and Device B, then at the beginning of the execution of this profile, the paging process is skipped in Device A. The connection in such a state is set up using the results of the previous paging by Device B. The Link Manager Interoperability Requirements

The Link Manager interoperability requirements of SPP are defined for the following:

◆ **LM configuration options.** The SPP profile requires extra support for encryption in Device A and Device B. This support is in addition to the other procedures of the Link Manager specification that were discussed in Chapter 5.

◆ **LM error behavior.** When a device tries to use a mandatory feature not supported by its counter device, the initiator sends an `LMP_detach` PDU with a response code of *unsupported LMP feature*. This way, a device of the SPP profile is always able to handle request rejections for optional features.

◆ **Link policy.** The SPP profile does not support fixed master and slave roles. In addition, the requirement for the use of power modes is also not specified. The Link Manager of the device is, therefore, responsible for deciding the power mode depending on the latency requirements.

Service Discovery Application Profile

With the basic knowledge about Bluetooth devices, you'll readily agree that service discovery is a significant component of most Bluetooth applications. Almost all the profiles of the specification include an element representing service discovery. The procedure implemented for service discovery in *Service Discovery Application Profile* (SDAP) is very similar to that of GAP.

SDAP actually defines a service discovery application model and abstractions of service primitives that are very similar to application programming interfaces (APIs). The profile uses the SDP middleware protocol layer to locate services on other Bluetooth devices. It is interesting to note that SDAP does not directly specify the method implemented for the service discovery, but relies on the SDP to do so. In other words, SDAP defines the creation and behavior specifications for an application that will use the SDP for service discovery. The abstractions of the service primitives describe the functional characteristics of the application. The service discovery application of SDAP is a user-initiated application. The service discovery interactions between the two SDP entities of the Bluetooth devices enable a specific transport service such as the RFCOMM or a usage scenario such as cordless telephony over the two devices.

SDAP describes the use of the LC and the LMP, security alternatives, and also the use of higher protocol layers of L2CAP, RFCOMM, and OBEX. The investigation for available services is initiated by searches for both known, specific services and general services. The Bluetooth unit contains the application that is used for locating services in other devices. Figure 7-4 illustrates the distribution of the Bluetooth protocol layers for the SDAP profile as sourced form the Bluetooth specification 1.0B.

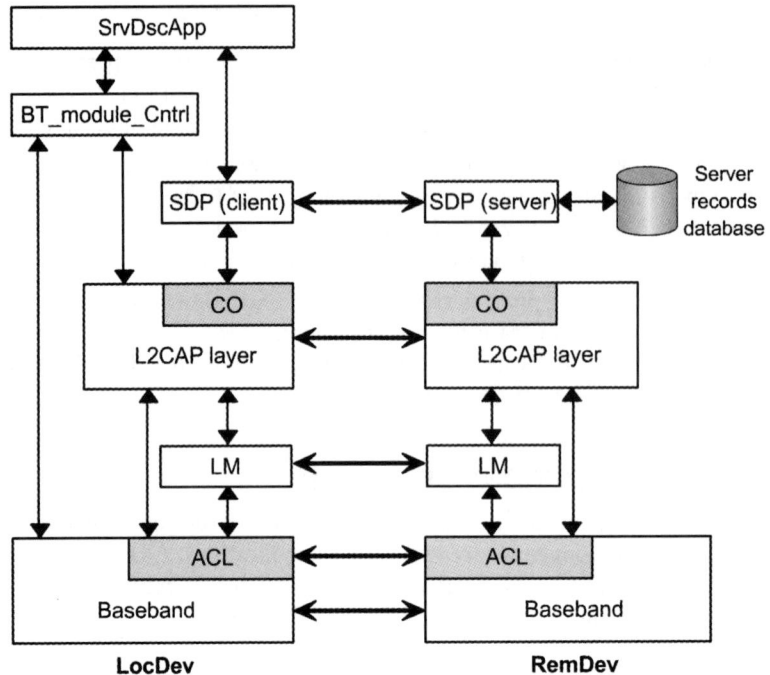

FIGURE 7-4 *The distribution of the Bluetooth protocol stack for the SDAP profile*

An SDP transaction takes place between the service discovery application of a local device and the SDP server of a remote device. The service discovery application interfaces with the SDP client to generate service inquiries that are sent to the SDP server of a remote device. The SDP server receives the inquiries and sends appropriate responses to the SDP client.

The SDP uses the connection-oriented channels for transport services in the L2CAP. The L2CAP, in turn, uses asynchronous connectionless ACL links to transfer the SDP PDUs. The process of service discovery is provided by the inquiries and pages that require the service discovery application to interface with the baseband through the BT_module_Cntrl entity. The BT_module_Cntrl entity controls the instructions that decide the various search modes of the service discovery procedures.

The role devices in this profile take the generic names of *Local Device (LocDev)* and *Remote Device (RemDev)*. A local device is the initiator of the service discovery procedure. It should contain at least the client part of the Bluetooth SDP architecture. The service discovery application or the SrvDscApp, in a LocDev, is used to initiate the service discoveries and display the corresponding results. The remote device, on the other hand, is the responder that replies to the service inquiries generated by a LocDev. A RemDev should contain at least the server part of the Bluetooth SDP architecture. A RemDev contains a database of the service records, which it consults when creating the response messages for a LocDev inquiry.

A LocDev can have both the client and server installed in the same device and a RemDev can have both the SrvDscApp and the server installed in the same device. The role of a LocDev and a RemDev in a particular device depends on the SDP transaction and the initiator of the transaction. A device can perform the role of a LocDev in one SDP transaction and that of a RemDev in another. The roles of a LocDev and a RemDev are, therefore, neither permanent nor exclusive.

SDAP is described in terms of its fundamental features, user requirements, user interface aspects, Application layer, message sequence charts, service discovery, configuration options, Link Manager, and link control.

Fundamental Features

The fundamental features of SDAP are as follows:

◆ The Bluetooth devices should be initialized and powered-on. During initialization the link key is created and used for subsequent procedures of authorization, authentication, and encryption.

◆ To create a link between the devices, the inquiry and paging processes are initiated to determine the `BD_ADDR` of the remote device.

◆ A LocDev need not serve as the Bluetooth master. Similarly, a RemDev need not serve as the Bluetooth slave. Both the master and slave that belong to the same piconet can initiate service discovery. However, a slave in a particular piconet can also initiate a service discovery in a new piconet. For this the slave needs to send a notification to the master of the original piconet stating that it will be unavailable for a specific period of time.

User Requirements

The Bluetooth user should be able to connect to two Bluetooth devices even if they do not share a common application. If the devices do not share a common application, the user should be able to identify it by using the basic Bluetooth capabilities. The user requirements for the SDAP include:

◆ Search for known and specific services by their service class

◆ Search for known and specific services by their service attributes

◆ Service browsing for general services to determine the available services

> **NOTE**
>
> As with all other profiles, a claim for *conformance* to this profile means that all capabilities specified as mandatory shall be supported in the specified manner. Similarly, optional and conditional capabilities should be supported according to the specification.

User Interface Aspects

The requirements for the user interface are implemented in the following procedures:

- **Pairing.** SDAP does not impose any restrictions on pairing. As a result, the process of pairing between devices may or may not be performed. The SrvDscApp supervises the process of pairing between a LocDev and an unconnected RemDev(s). A LocDev initiates a service discovery after which it is the responsibility of the SrvDscApp to allow pairing before connection or bypass the procedure altogether. A LocDev initiates the process of service discovery only after the establishment of a legitimate and functional baseband link with a RemDev(s).

- **Mode selection.** SDAP assumes that a LocDev shall be able to initiate inquiries and/or page states under the supervision of the SrvDscApp. A parallel assumption is also made stating that a RemDev shall enter the inquiry scan and/or page scan mode to make its services (such as fax, printing, and PSTN gateway) available to other devices. The SrvDscApp can also initiate inquiries for previously connected RemDevs. The roles of master and slave are, therefore, in no way related to a LocDev and RemDev. Therefore, a LocDev is not always the master and a RemDev is not always the slave.

Application Layer

The Application layer of SDAP includes the service discovery application and the abstraction primitives.

The Service Discovery Application

The service discovery application describes the framework of the SrvDscApp. The three alternatives for the SrvDscApp are as follows:

- **Alternative A: SrvDscApp_A.** The SrvDscApp located on a LocDev sends an inquiry to its user asking for information about the desired service search. The SrvDscApp searches for the devices using a Bluetooth inquiry procedure. A LocDev connects to each device that is found and performs procedures to set up a link. After this, an inquiry is generated for the desired services.

- **Alternative B: SrvDscApp_B.** The inquiry for devices is performed before collecting the user input for the service search.

NOTE

The process of paging, link creation, and service discovery in the case of SrvD-scApp_A and SrvDscApp_A is performed sequentially for each RemDev. Therefore, a LocDev does not have to page to a new RemDev before completing the service search with a previous RemDev and disconnecting from it.

◆ **Alternative C: SrvDscApp_C.** A LocDev directed by the SrvDscApp first pages all the RemDevs, creates links with all of these devices (seven in all), and then generates an inquiry for the service search.

Figure 7-5 illustrates the operational framework of the alternative SrvDscAPPs as sourced form the Bluetooth specification 1.0B.

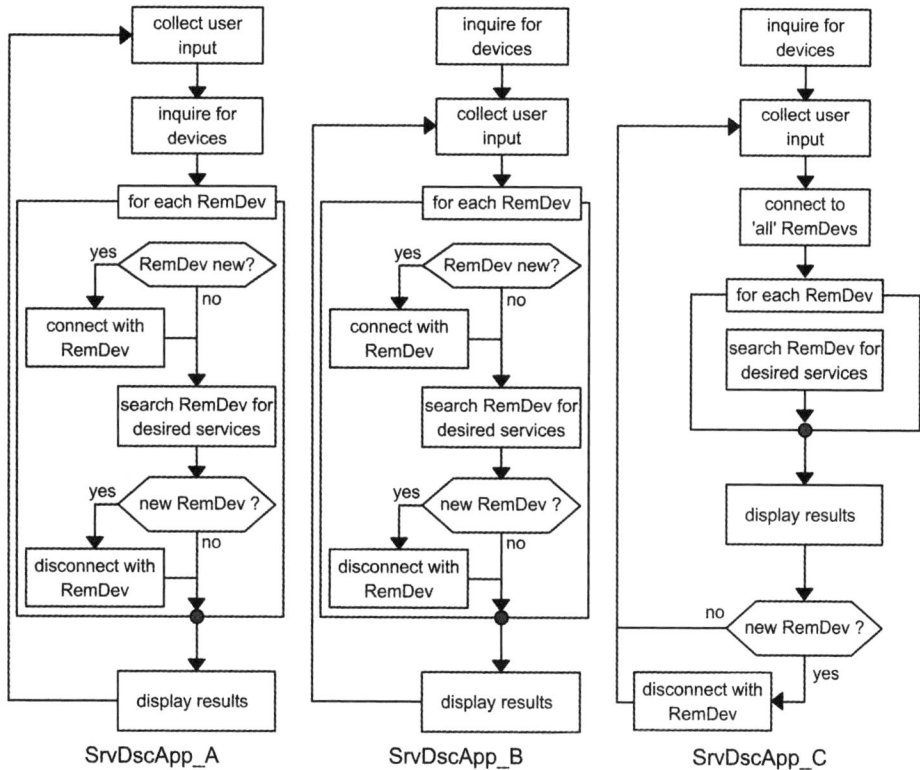

FIGURE 7-5 *The alternative SrvDscAPPs*

The service search initiated by a LocDev is for the following three types of RemDevs:

♦ **Trusted devices.** These are the RemDevs that do not have current connections with a LocDev but have already established a trust relation with the LocDev.

♦ **Connected device.** These are RemDevs that are already connected to a LocDev.

♦ **Unknown or new devices.** These are RemDevs that do not have any current connections or trust relations with a LocDev.

The SrvDscApp activates the inquiry and/or paging processes to discover trusted and unknown devices (RemDevs). However, to discover a connected device, the SrvDscApp needs to access the BD_ADDR of all the devices within the coverage of the LocDev. The BT_module_Cntrl in a LocDev maintains a list of the devices in the vicinity of the LocDev that is made available to the SrvDscApp.

The Abstraction Primitives

The functionality of the abstraction primitives provides a functional framework describing the user expectations from the SrvDscApp. It is the responsibility of the Bluetooth protocol to directly or indirectly meet the expectations of the service primitives. The syntax and semantics of the service primitives may be platform dependent as in the case of operating systems, and hardware platforms such as a mobile phone, a PDA, or a notebook. Table 7-1 lists the minimum set of enabling service primitives that need to support the SrvDscApp.

Table 7-1 The Minimum Set of Enabling Service Primitives

Service Primitive	Description
serviceBrowse	Initiates a search for services that belong to the browseGroup services of the RemDev (list). This search can be qualified further by using a list of RemDevRelation parameters.
serviceSearch	Initiates a search for the devices listed in the list of the RemDevs support services that are mapped to the requested list of services. Each service in the list has a service pattern that is a superset of the searchPattern. The values and attributes of each service contained in the attributeList are also retrieved.
enumerateRemDev	Initiates a search for a RemDev that is in the vicinity of a LocDev.
terminatePrimitive	Terminates the actions that are performed due to the invocation of the service primitives identified by the primitiveHandle.

Message Sequence Charts

Message sequence charts represent the various phases encountered during the exchange of messages in SDAP. The message sequence charts are supported by the following three procedures of SDAP:

- ◆ Device discovery
- ◆ Device name discovery
- ◆ Service discovery

Figure 7-6 illustrates the message exchange phases performed during the execution of SDAP.

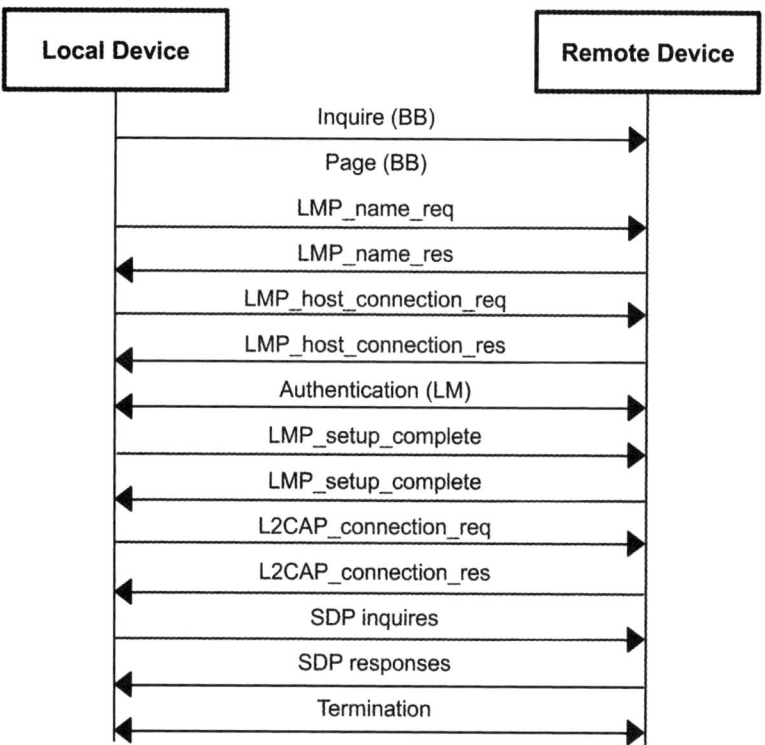

FIGURE 7-6 *The message sequence chart in SDAP.*

Service Discovery

The SrvDscApp uses the SDP as a mechanism for informing the LocDev user about the available services in a RemDev. The following procedures are used to retrieve information for accessing a desires service in a RemDev:

◆ **Exchange of the SDP PDU.** A number of SDP PDUs are exchanged during the process of inquiry and retrieval of information about a particular Bluetooth profile. The SDP PDUs are exchanged in the following sequence:

1. The LocDev first sends an `SDP_serviceSearchReq` PDU containing a service search pattern. The service search pattern contains the *Universally Unique Identifier* (`UUID`) that is associated with the particular profile (`profile_XYZ_UUID`).

2. The SDP server returns a response PDU containing one or more 32-bit service record handles that correspond to a service record containing the specified `profile_XYZ_UUID` (Hndl in Figure 7-7).

3. The LocDEv enters the Hndl in an SDP_serviceAttribute PDU along with one or more attribute Ids (protocolDescriptorList in Figure 7-7).

4. The SDP server responds to this by returning the requested list of protocols.

5. If a service record corresponding to the desired search pattern is not found in the SDP server, the `serviceRecordHandleList` and totalServiceRecord-Count parameters of the `SDP_serviceSearchReq` are set to their minimal value.

6. If the service attribute does not exist in the SDP server, the `SDP_serviceAttributeReq` PDU contains an empty `attributeList` and the `attributeListByteCount` is set to its minimal value.

7. If the desired service attributes are retrieved from the SDP server, the LocDev sends an `SDP_serviceSearchAttributeReq` PDU containing the desired profile (`profile_XYZ_UUID`) and the attributes. The response from the SDP server includes the requested attributes from the service records matching the service search pattern.

Figure 7-7 illustrates an example of SDP PDU exchanges that take place during the inquiry and retrieval of information (the attribute protocolDescriptorList) from devices supporting a specific Bluetooth profile .

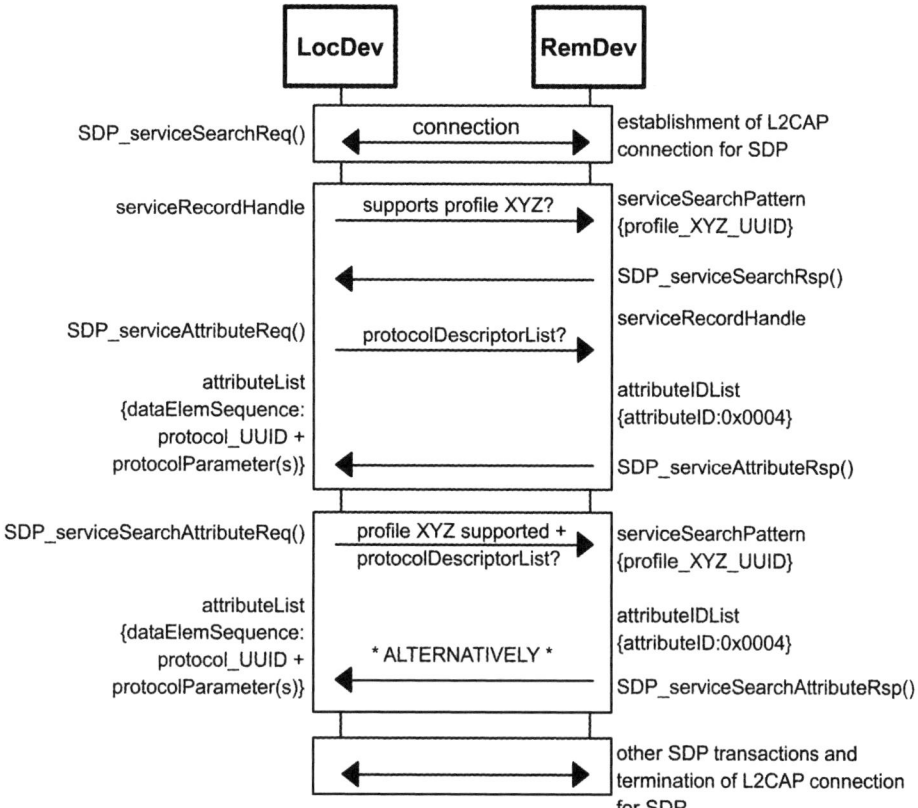

FIGURE 7-7 *The SDP PDU exchange between two Bluetooth devices.*

◆ **Channel types.** SADP uses only connection-oriented channels that do not allow L2CAP broadcasts.

◆ **Signaling.** Only the LocDev can initiate an L2CAP connection request for retrieving SDP-related information, which is performed by issuing a L2CAP connection request PDU.

Configuration Options

SDAP requirements for the configuration options include specifications for the Maximum Transmission Unit (MTU), flush timeout, and Quality of Service (QoS):

◆ **MTU.** It is advantageous to select a large MTU to ensure efficient use of the communication resources. However, the MTU selection should consider the physical restraints imposed by the involved devices and continue to honor the

QoS agreement with other devices or applications. It is assumed that during the lifetime of an L2CAP connection created for SDP transactions, one of the devices may connect to another device. If the new connection created has non-default QoS requirements, then the MTU for the previous SDP session is re-negotiated to accommodate the QoS constraints imposed by the new connection.

◆ **Flush timeout.** The SDP transactions are carried over a reliable L2CAP channel. Therefore, the specification for the flush timeout is set to the default value of 0xfff.

◆ **QoS.** The requirement for negotiating Quality of Service is optional in SDAP. The SDP traffic is treated as the best-effort service traffic and all QoS negotiations use the respective default settings.

Link Manager

The parameters that a Bluetooth device needs to support for the implementation of inter-operability at the LMP level include LMP capabilities, error behavior, and link policy.

LM Capabilities

The capabilities of the Link Manager with respect to SDAP are expressed in terms of mandatory, optional, and excluded features. The excluded features are those that degrade the operation of a device and are, therefore, never activated by a working Bluetooth device. Table 7-2 lists the mandatory (M), optional (O), conditional (C), and excluded (X) features of the LM for the SDAP as sourced from the Bluetooth specification 1.0B.

Table 7-2 The Mandatory, Optional, Conditional, and Excluded Features of the LMP

LM feature	Support in LMP	Support in LocDev	Support in RemDev
Authentication	M	C	C
Pairing	M	-	-
Changing the link key	M	-	-
Changing the current link key	M	-	-
Encryption	O	C	C
Clock offset Request	M	-	-
Timing accuracy Information request	O	-	-
LMP version	M	-	-

LM feature	Support in LMP	Support in LocDev	Support in RemDev
Supported features	M	-	-
Switch of master and slave roles	M	-	-
Name request	M	-	-
Detach	M	-	-
Hold mode	M	-	-
Sniff mode	O	-	-
Park mode	O	-	-
Power control	O	-	-
Channel quality driven DM/DH	O	-	-
Quality of Service	M	-	-
SCO link	O	X	X
Control of multiple slots packets	M	-	-
Concluding parameter negotiation	M	-	-
Host connection	M	-	-

Error Behavior

When a device tries to use a mandatory feature not supported by its counter device, the initiator sends an `LMP_detach` PDU with a response code of *unsupported LMP feature*. As a result, a device of SDAP is always able to handle request rejections for optional features.

Link Policy

SPP does not support fixed master and slave roles. In addition, the requirement for the use of power modes is also not specified. The Link Manager of the device is, therefore, responsible for deciding the power mode depending on the latency requirements.

Link Controller

The parameters that a Bluetooth device needs to support for the implementation of inter-operability at the Link Controller (LC) level include LC capabilities, inquiry, inquiry scan, paging, page scan, and error behavior.

LC Capabilities

Table 7-3 lists the mandatory (M), optional (O), conditional (C), and excluded (X) features of the LC for SDAP as sourced from the Bluetooth specification 1.0B.

Table 7-3 The Mandatory, Optional, Conditional, and Excluded Features of the LC

LM feature	Support in LMP	Support in LocDev	Support in RemDev
Inquiry	M	C	-
Inquiry scan	M	-	C
Paging	M	C	-
Page scan			
Type R0	M	-	C
Type R1	M	-	C
Type R2	M	-	C
Packet types			
ID packet	M	-	-
Null packet	M	-	-
Poll packet	M	-	-
FHS packet	M	-	-
DM1 packet	M	-	-
DH1 packet	M	-	-
DM3 packet	M	-	-
DM3 packet	O	--	
DH3 packet	O	-	-
DM5 packet	O	-	-
DH5 packet	O	-	-
AUX packet	M	X	X
HV1 packet	M	X	X

LM feature	Support in LMP	Support in LocDev	Support in RemDev
HV2 packet	O	X	X
HV3 packet	O	X	X
DV packet	M	X	X
Inter-piconet capabilities	O	-	-
Voice codec	-	-	-
PCM (A-law)	O	X	X
PCM (M-law	O	X	X
CVSD	O	X	X

Inquiry

The LocDev advises the baseband to enter into the inquiry state as instructed by the SrvDscApp. The change in the state, however, may not be immediate and depends on the QoS requirements of the existing and ongoing connections. An inquiry that is invoked by a LocDev uses the GIAC for the general inquiry procedure. The user of the SrvDscApp is able to set the duration of the inquiry where the actual residence time in the inquiry state complies with the suggestion specified in the 10.7.3 of the Bluetooth Baseband specification.

Inquiry Scan

Inquiry scans are device-dependent, extensive policies. A device in discoverable mode can be exposed by the inquiries sent by other devices. A RemDev enters into an inquiry scan by using the GIAC so that it is discovered by an inquiry from an SrvDscApp action.

Paging

The LocDev advises the baseband to enter into the paging mode whenever the SrvDscApp needs to connect to a RemDev in order to inquire about its service records. The change in the state, however, may not be immediate and depends on the QoS requirements of the existing and ongoing connections. An inquiry that is invoked by a LocDev uses the GIAC for the general inquiry procedure. The LocDev pages according to the paging class (R0, R1, or R3) that is specified by a RemDev.

Page Scan

Like inquiry scans, page scans are device-dependent, extensive policies. Devices in connectable mode can establish links with other devices by using the pages sent by the other devices. A LocDev sends a page resulting from a SrvDscApp action by using the 48-bit BD_ADDR of a RemDev.

Error Behavior

The LC level features of the profiles are triggered by the LMP procedures. Therefore, most of the errors are caught at the LMP layer. Some LC procedures such as inquiry or paging, however, are independent of the LMP layer. The errors generated by these procedures are, therefore, almost impossible to detect.

Generic Object Exchange Profile

The *Generic Object Exchange Profile* (GOEP), like SPP, provides a base for building the concrete usage profiles of File Transfer, Object Push Profile, and Synchronization Profile. GOEP uses OBEX capabilities to provide interoperability between applications. As discussed in Chapter 6, "Software Protocols," OBEX is very similar to HTTP that is used for exchange of objects on the *World Wide Web* (WWW). The exchange of objects in OBEX is based on the *push* and *pull* technology that is implemented among portable devices functioning within a dynamic environment. The push technology is based on a model in which the data is automatically delivered to users. In the pull technology, the client pulls the information from the server. The information is constantly present on the network but the client is able to view the information only after a voluntarily requests for it.

GOEP defines the primitives for exchange of objects based on the object push and object pull technology. It also defines procedures to establish and terminate OBEX connections. GOEP, like SPP, is not directly used by applications. In fact, it uses a set of IrDA protocols that provide interoperability at the Application layer to utilize both the IrDA and Bluetooth transports. The exchange of objects between devices stretches for long durations and, therefore, GOEP, like OBEX, maintains sessions.

The profile stack in GOEP consists of the baseband, LMP, and L2CAP layers. RFCOMM is used to provide a transport protocol by emulating a serial port connection between the devices. Figure 7-8 illustrates the distribution of the Bluetooth protocol layers for GOEP as sourced form the Bluetooth specification 1.0B.

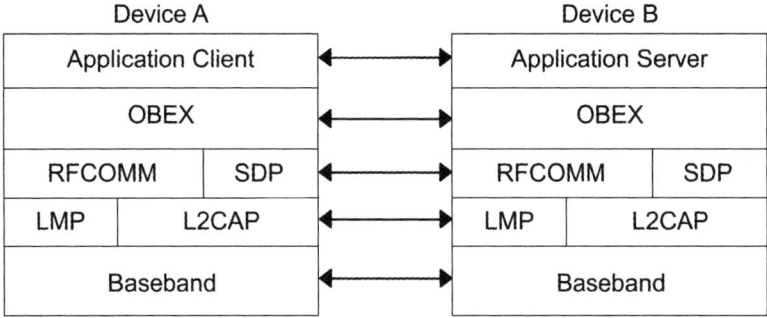

FIGURE 7-8 *The distribution of the Bluetooth protocol stack for GOEP.*

Like all other profiles, GOEP also defines two role devices that take the specific names of a *client* and a *server*. The role of the client and server cannot be mapped to those of a master and slave. The client device is that which pushes or pulls objects to and from a server. The server device is the device that provides the exchange service so that objects can be pushed to or pulled from it. During the exchange of objects, it is possible that at times both sides could be pushing and pulling objects. As a result, the role of a client and server becomes ambiguous. This scenario of ambiguous client-server roles does not apply to GOEP. The distinction between a client and a server in the OBEX model is not based on their ability to push or pull objects, but on the fact that the client is the device that initiates the operation and locates the server by using specific exchange services. To help a client locate a server, it is natural to expect a server to be in a connectable and discoverable mode. Therefore, the client performs all the procedures related to inquiry and link establishment.

Bonding is performed even before a client uses the services of a server. An OBEX initialization procedure is performed for a link level bonding that is implemented the first time. During bonding, the user manually enters the Bluetooth PIN code on both the client and server devices. Bonding is followed by pairing and, therefore, devices need to support this feature. Bonding is dependent on the application profiles. The GOEP application profiles support bonding to provide security at the time of connection by sending the authentication parameters and encrypting user data at the link level.

Fundamental Features

The fundamental features of GOEP are expressed in terms of the following:

◆ **Establishing an OBEX session.** This feature is used to establish a session between the client and the server to facilitate exchange of payload data.

◆ **Pushing a data object.** This feature is used during the transfer of data from the client to the server. The data is pushed to the server in OBEX packets by using the Put operation of the OBEX protocol.

◆ **Pulling a data object.** This feature is used during the transfer of data from the server to the client. The data is pushed to the client in OBEX packets by using the Get operation of the OBEX protocol.

OBEX Operation

The OBEX operations performed in GOEP are specified by the OBEX protocol. These operations include Connect, Disconnect, Put, Get, Set Path, and Abort. The supports for each of these operations are specified in the application profiles using GOEP. Although the IrOBEX specification does not specify the wait time for a client expecting a response from the server before termination of the operation, an optimum time of 30 seconds more is specified in the Bluetooth specification.

Initialization of OBEX

The initialization of OBEX is a process that requires user intervention from both the client and the server devices. This process is initiated after authentication by the server, but before the establishment of the first OBEX connection. Authentication is performed on a password that is entered by the client and server devices and stored, thereafter, for future use. A OBEX password is similar to the Bluetooth PIN code.

Session Establishment in OBEX

The Connect operation is used to establish an OBEX session. An OBEX session can also be established by overriding the authentication procedure. For this, it is important that all the application profiles using GOEP should support an OBEX session without requiring any authentication. OBEX sessions can also be established after OBEX authentication. Although the OBEX authentication procedure is based on HTTP, it does not support all the features of HTTP in GOEP.

Summary

This chapter looked at how the Bluetooth specification is implemented in applications. The implementations ensure interoperability between devices from different manufacturers. Profiles present technologies with implementation techniques that can be used in different devices and applications. The Bluetooth profiles are no exceptions, because they too ensure standardized implementations of Bluetooth to increase the workability of this robust and revolutionary technology.

In this chapter, you learned about the different profiles that are implemented by the Bluetooth version 1.0. This chapter dealt with the profiles of the fundamental group. The chapter also discussed the requirement parameters that devices need to support for the implementation of the profiles.

The future of Bluetooth seems bright, more so because of the common appearance and ambiance provided by the profiles. The familiar and easily recognizable profiles should be able to break the market barriers and provide a powerful entry point for Bluetooth devices.

Check Your Understanding

Multiple Choice Questions

1. State whether the following statements are true or false.

    a. The intent behind the creation of Bluetooth profiles was to increase interoperability between devices from different manufactures.

    b. The Bluetooth profile specification defines ten profiles in all.

    c. In Serial Port Profile (SPP), the RFCOMM is used to transfer data, modem control signals, and commands.

    d. The role devices in SDAP are SrvDscAPP, LocDev, and RemDev.

2. Which of the following are the fundamental profiles defined in the Bluetooth specification?

    a. Cordless Telephony Profile

    b. Generic Access Profile

    c. Headset Profile

    d. Service Discovery Application Profile

    e. File Transfer Profile

    f. Serial Port Profile

    g. Generic Object Exchange Profile

3. Which of the following are the three types of RemDevs in SDAP?

    a. Trusted device

    b. Untrusted device

    c. Connected device

    d. Unknown device

4. Which of the following parameters are included in the configuration options for SPP?

    a. Signaling

    b. Maximum Transmission unit

    c. Remote Port Negotiation

    d. Quality of Service

    e. Flush timeout

Short Questions

1. Describe the categorization of the Bluetooth profiles based on their logical services.

2. List the various parameters needed to support device interoperability in GAP.

3. Describe the three security levels implemented in GAP.

4. What is bonding?

5. Discuss the L2CAP interoperability requirements in SPP.

6. Discuss the user interface requirements of pairing and mode selection in SDAP.

7. Discuss the push and pull technology application in a GOEP client and server.

Answers

Multiple Choice Answers

1. a. True

    b. False

    c. True

    d. False

2. a, c, f, and g. Generic Access Profile, Service Discovery Application Profile, Serial Port Profile, Generic Object Exchange Profile.

3. a, c, and d. Trusted device, connected device, and unknown device.

4. b, d, and f. Maximum Transmission Unit, Quality of Service, and flush timeout.

Short Answers

1. The Bluetooth profiles can also be categorized into the following three groups based on the logical services that they provide:

    ◆ **The generic profiles.** This group of profiles consists of the GAP profile, which is the core profile for all other profiles and the Service Discovery Profile, which maps the Application layer to the SDP layer of the Bluetooth protocol stack.

    ◆ **The telephony profiles.** This group of profiles consists of the Cordless Telephony, Headset, and Intercom profiles that use the TCS-BIN layer to control telephony functions.

    ◆ **The serial profiles.** This group of profiles consists of the Serial Port, GOEP, File Transfer, Object Push, and Synchronization profiles. This group can be further sub-divided into two groups. The first group, which is a direct derivative of the Serial Port Profile, consists of the Fax, Headset, Dial-up Networking, and LAN Access profiles. The second group, which is the parent for object exchange group profiles, consists of the File Transfer, Object Push, and Synchronization profiles.

2. The various parameters needed to support device interoperability in GAP are:

    ◆ BD_ADDR

    ◆ Names

    ◆ PIN

    ◆ Class of device

    ◆ Discovery modes

    ◆ Connectivity modes

    ◆ Pairing modes

3. The following three security levels or modes are implemented on communicating devices in GAP:

    ◆ **Security mode 1: non secure.** A device in security mode 1 does not initiate any security and is, therefore, in a non-secure mode. As a result, a device in security mode 1 never sends `LMP_au_rand`, `LMP_in_rand`, or `LMP_encryption_mode_request` PDUs. Here the devices are in the discovery mode where connections are initiated.

    ◆ **Security mode 2: service level enforced security.** A device in security mode 2 initiates security procedures at higher layers after the channel is established. The application of this security mode takes place at the L2CAP layer and includes procedures for setting the security policies Application layers running parallel with the lower protocols. The security procedures are implemented only after the receipt of the `LMP_Connection_Request` PDU.

    ◆ **Security mode 3: link level enforced security.** Security mode 2 initiates security procedures at lower layers (Link Manager) before the channel is established. As a result, authentication, in this security mode, occurs before the transmission and receipt of the `LMP_setup_complete` PDU.

4. Bonding is performed as a part of the pairing procedure to create and exchange a common link key between two devices. The link key created is also stored for future use. Bonding, therefore, creates a relationship between two devices. The bonding procedure can either be general or dedicated. In general bonding, the device performs the bonding procedure along with other communications such as accessing the higher protocol layers. On the other hand, dedicated bonding is a procedure performed solely for creating a bond between two devices without any upper layer transactions.

5. The L2CAP interoperability requirements of the SPP profile are mandatory and defined for the following:

    ◆ **Channels.** SPP uses only connection-oriented channels. This means that broadcasts between the devices are not used in this profile. The value for the RFCOMM defined in the Assigned numbers document in the PSM field of the request packet is used to identify the RFCOMM entity before the establishment of the L2CAP channel.

    ◆ **Signaling.** The request for an L2CAP connection can be initiated by Device A only. This is the only requirement that needs to be fulfilled during the signaling process.

    ◆ **Configuration options.** The L2CAP requirements for the configuration options include specifications for the Maximum Transmission Unit (MTU), flush timeout, and Quality of Service (QoS). The SPP profile does not enforce any restrictions on the MTU size over the MTU requirements that are already stated in the L2CAP specification. The serial port data is carried over a reliable L2CAP channel. As a result, the specification for the flush timeout is set to the default value of 0xfff. The requirement for negotiating Quality of Service is optional in the SPP profile.

6. The requirements for the user interface are implemented in the following procedures:

   ◆ **Pairing.** SDAP does not impose any restrictions on pairing. As a result, the process of pairing between devices may or may not be performed. The SrvDscApp supervises the process of pairing between a LocDev and an unconnected RemDev(s). A LocDev initiates a service discovery after which it is the responsibility of the SrvDscApp to allow pairing before connection or bypass the procedure all together. A LocDev initiates the process of service discovery only after the establishment of a legitimate and functional baseband link with a RemDev(s).

   ◆ **Mode selection.** SDAP assumes that a LocDev shall be able to initiate inquiries and/or page states under the supervision of the SrvDscApp. A parallel assumption is also made stating that a RemDev shall enter the inquiry scan and/or page scan mode to make its services (such as fax, printing, and PSTN gateway) available to other devices. The SrvDscApp can also initiate inquiries for previously connected RemDevs.

7. The client device is that which pushes or pulls objects to and from a server. The server device is the device that provides the exchange service so that objects can be pushed to or pulled from it. During the exchange of objects, it is possible that at times both sides could be pushing and pulling objects. As a result, the role of a client and server becomes ambiguous. This scenario of ambiguous client-server roles does not apply to GOEP. The distinction between a client and a server in the OBEX model is not based on their ability to push or pull objects, but on the fact that the client is the device that initiates the operation and locates the server by using specific exchange services.

Chapter 8

The Bluetooth profiles, as discussed in the previous chapter, provide interoperability between devices from different manufacturers. This is an important feature that needs to be understood because Bluetooth product manufacturers, unlike other wireless device manufacturers, develop products that fit into one side of the link in the wireless bi-directional mode of communication. As a result, mobile manufacturers develop only mobile phones and not Personal Data Assistants (PDAs). Interoperability between devices gives the Bluetooth devices a commercial edge over other devices by providing universal standards for a wide range of products. Other manufacturers can use Bluetooth devices to develop products of their own that will work with other products. The standardization also enables manufacturers to concentrate more on manufacturing, which is their core activity, rather than try system integration to enable interoperability between devices.

The 13 profiles listed in the previous chapter can be portrayed as a vertical view through the protocol layer that do not specify the use of the application but mandate the options used by the protocol stack for a two-way communication between Bluetooth devices. In addition, the fundamental profiles and their features also define protocols that support different usage-oriented models. For example, the Headset Profile, which is a GAP- and SPP-compliant usage profile, supports off hook and variable volume transmissions between devices. Similarly, the Dial-up Networking Profile, which is also a GAP- and SPP-compliant usage profile, supports specific number dialing options. This chapter is a continuation of the discussion on Bluetooth profiles, more precisely on the nine usage profiles, their fundamental features and procedural requirements.

Introduction to Bluetooth Usage Models

You'll be surprised to know that even before the official formulation of the Bluetooth specification, the Bluetooth Web site described the various usage models that would be implementing the Bluetooth wireless technology. The specification was drawn up to standardize Bluetooth products by promoting interoperability between various devices. The usage profiles, also referred to as usage scenarios or usage models, described the general implementation of the Bluetooth technology with emphasis on the end user's view of the scenarios and their benefits. Although the usage scenarios defined in the Bluetooth specification constitute the initial set of scenarios, there have been many more additions to the usage profiles, as discussed in Chapter 11, "Future of Bluetooth."

The nine usage profiles discussed in this chapter are:

◆ Cordless Telephony Profile

◆ Intercom Profile

◆ Headset Profile

◆ Fax Profile

◆ Dial-up Networking Profile

◆ LAN Access Profile

◆ Object Push Profile

◆ Synchronization Profile

◆ File Transfer Profile

The Cordless Telephony Profile

The importance of telephones as a verbal mode of communication need not be restated. All of us use multiple telephones today. Multiple telephones are used at home (cordless or wired), in the office, in the form of a mobile phone while traveling, and of course sometimes the public telephone service. Wouldn't it be wonderful if you could use a single phone instead of these multiple phones? Bluetooth communication makes it possible to have a three-in-one telephone of the Cordless Telephony Profile that can function as a mobile phone, a cordless phone connected to a cordless phone base station, and also as an intercom. The use of a multiple voice access point strengthens the Bluetooth wireless dream of using a single personal telephone in multiple environments of the home, office, and public areas. This usage scenario does not only make accessibility easier but also reduces the need for maintaining separate telephone instruments and numbers for each usage. In other words, what this means is that a single telephone number suffices for all the usage areas.

The Cordless Telephony Profile is based upon telephony functions and defines the procedures for the three-in-one phone usage scenario. In addition to its general use as a wireless (cordless) telephony service within homes or small offices, the three-in-one phone can also be used as an extended and additional mode of communication by using the Bluetooth cellular phone as a short-range bearer to access-fixed telephony services through various base stations. For example, within your home, a handset could be connected to a wall mounted telephone, which in turn could connect to the PSTN. Similarly, the same handset could be connected to the internal telephone network of your office and also connect to your mobile phone while you're traveling. Figure 8-1 illustrates the distribution of the various protocol layers for the Cordless Telephony Profile.

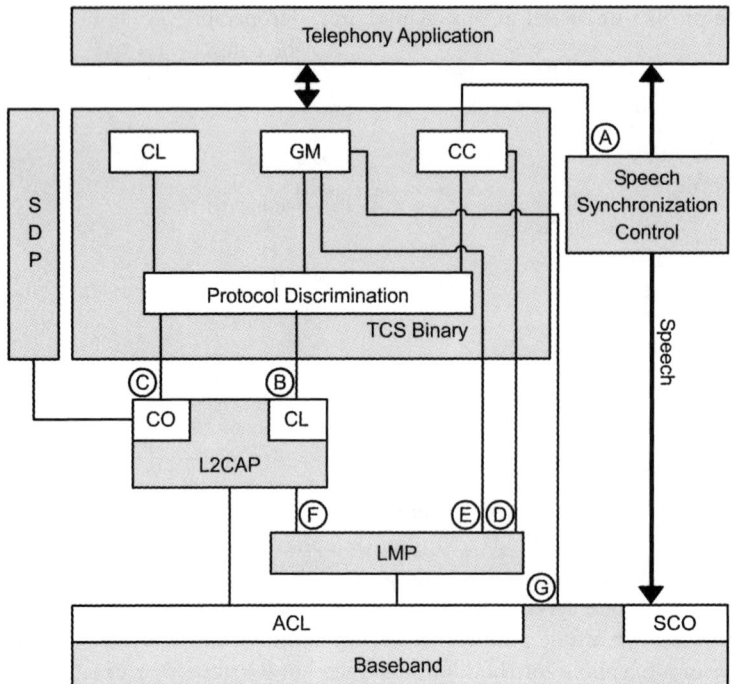

FIGURE 8-1 *The distribution of the protocol stack for the Cordless Telephony Profile*

Like all the fundamental profiles, the Cordless Telephony Profile also defines the following two device roles:

◆ **Gateway (GW).** The gateway is the device that connects to the external network and receives all incoming calls. The gateway is responsible for handling all call setup requests originating to and from the external network. In a way, the terminal can be looked at as the master of a piconet that can connect to at least seven other piconets. However, restrictions on the SCO capacity limit the number of simultaneous active voice links to three. A home-based *Public Switched Telephony Network* (PSTN) or *Integrated Services Digital Network* (ISDN) base station, a *Global System for Mobile Communications* (GSM) gateway, and a satellite gateway are examples of the gateway devices in the Cordless Telephony Profile setup.

◆ **Terminal (TL).** The terminal device is the wireless user terminal receiving calls from the gateway and providing corresponding speech and/or data links to the user. A cordless phone, a dual-mode cellular phone, and a PC are examples of the terminal device in the Cordless Telephony Profile setup.

Before examining the fundamental features and the interoperability requirements of the Cordless Telephony Profile, the next section discusses the common terminologies associated with this profile.

Terminologies

The following are a few terminologies that are associated with the Cordless Telephony Profile:

- ◆ **Call Line Identification Presentation (CLIP).** This defines the ability of the profile to make the number of the calling party available to the called party before accepting a call.

- ◆ **Call Information.** This defines the ability of the profile to provide supplementary information during the active phase of a call.

- ◆ **Connection Management.** This defines the ability of the profile to accept and request connections for the TCS-BIN procedures. The request for connections is accepted from terminals only.

- ◆ **Dual Tone Multiple Frequency (DTMF) signaling.** This defines the ability of the profile to send external calls in the form of DTMF signals to the other party over an external network.

- ◆ **Incoming external call.** This call initiates from an external network that is connected to the gateway.

- ◆ **Initialization.** This is the process that is infrequent and provides the terminal with access rights to a specific gateway.

- ◆ **Intercom call.** This call originates from one terminal and is destined to another terminal.

- ◆ **Multi-terminal support.** This defines the ability of the gateway to handle multiple active terminals being registered at the same time.

- ◆ **On hook.** This is a term associated with the terminal that defines the action of call termination often referred to as going on-hook. A call that is on-hook releases all radio resources associated with it.

- ◆ **Outgoing external call.** This is the call that initiates from a terminal and extends toward an external network that is connected to the gateway.

- ◆ **Post-dialing.** This defines the ability of the terminal to send dialing information after the outgoing call request setup message is sent.

- ◆ **Register recall or hook flash.** This defines the ability of the terminal to request for a register recall and the ability of the gateway to transmit the request to the local network. In layman's words, after the acceptance of a register recall request, the register with the dial tone is seized to facilitate input of additional digits or actions.

Fundamental Features

The calls within a telephony infrastructure originate either from the user end or from the terminal. In the former case, the gateway passes the calls to the terminals while in the latter case the calls from the terminals are routed to their destination through the gateway. The terminals that are outside the coverage of the gateway send periodic pages to the gateway requesting for a connection. The gateways, on their part, page scan frequently so that the roving devices can discover and connect to them. After being connected, the gateway and the terminal switch to the master-slave mode so that the master device can efficiently allocate a bandwidth for information transmission and exchange. A connection-oriented L2 and, if required, a connectionless L2CAP channel is established that is used for TCS signaling during a telephony session.

After discovering and connecting to the gateway, the terminal moves into the park mode to save power. During this time, the terminal can be contacted through broadcasts that use beacon slots. The beacon slots must be spaced so that on receiving incoming calls, the terminals have enough time to unpark themselves. The gateway uses broadcasts for distributing configuration information between parked devices in beacon slots.

On receiving an incoming call or during an outgoing call, the terminal moves into the active mode and uses the already established L2CAP channels to transport voice over SCO links by using the TCS control signals.

The steps initiated during the establishment of a call from one terminal to another define the fundamental features of the Cordless Telephony Profile, which are as follows:

- ◆ Incoming calls are connected to the gateway and then routed to the destination terminal. Outgoing calls are also initiated from the terminals and connected to the gateway in the same manner.
- ◆ Calls are made from the terminal to a user on the network that has a gateway connected to the network.
- ◆ Calls are received from the network to which a gateway is connected.
- ◆ Direct calls can be made between terminals.
- ◆ Supplementary services used are provided by DTMF signaling and register recall of the external network.

The Cordless Telephony Profile implements security by facilitating the authentication of all the devices within a voice piconet. Therefore, a known device can be granted access to a particular GW, but if an unknown device is allowed to connect to a particular GW, it can misuse the capabilities of the GW by making telephone calls through it. As a result, the Cordless Telephony Profile allows only trusted devices to connect to the GW. In addition, encryption of the traffic within the piconet strengthens the security implementations negating the chances of data manipulations.

TCS-BIN

TCS-BIN as defined in Chapter 6, "Software Protocols," provides group management facilities that are used to locate devices and discover their services. The TCS-BIN procedures also provide information about the handling of the lower protocol layers. The TCS-BIN procedures defined for the Cordless Telephony Profile are as follows:

◆ Connection management

◆ Call control procedures

◆ Group management procedures

◆ Supplementary services

◆ Link loss detection by the Gateway

Connection Management

The connection management procedures of TCS-BIN are defined for both the gateway and the terminal. After a successful connection between the TL and the GW, a connection-oriented L2CAP connection for TCS signaling is set up and configured by trusted TLs only. On the other hand, in the case of an intercom call, the connection that is set up is between two TLs. As a result, the TL initiating the call establishes the L2CAP link and is responsible for its configuration thereafter.

A TL capable of participating in two piconets remains the member of the GW piconet and simultaneously takes part signaling toward the GW during an intercom call. On the other hand, a TL restricted to a single piconet detaches from the GW signaling, while the intercom call is active. The connection to the GW is established at the end of the intercom call.

Call Control Procedures

The call control procedures defined for the Cordless Telephony Profile are explained in detail in the TCS-Binary section of the Bluetooth specification. However, the procedures for call class, call connection, call confirmation, call clearing, and in-band tones and announcement are defined below:

◆ **Call class.** The call class is used to define the type of call in the SETUP messages. The two types of call class are external call and an intercom call. An external call is that which is initiated between a TL and a third party through an external network such as a PSDN, ISDN, or GSM. An intercom call, on the other hand, is initiated between two TLs and is set up by the GW only if the participating TLs are the members of the same Wireless User Group (WUG).

◆ **Call connection.** When the bearer capability of a call is "Synchronous Connection-Oriented," the SCO link establishment sub-procedure should be initiated before sending a CONNECT. Similarly, when the bearer capability of a call is "Asynchronous Connection-Oriented," the audio path of the call should be connected to a unit only after receipt of CONNECT, or CONNECT ACKNOWLEDGE.

◆ **Call Confirmation.** When an incoming external call delivers the SETUP message on a connection channel, the incoming unit accepting the call should acknowledge the message by executing the call confirmation procedure.

◆ **Call clearing.** The call clearing procedures facilitate the release of the SCO connection by the lower protocol layers. LMP sub-procedures are used to release the SCO links after receipt of a RELEASE message. The LMP sub-procedures are also used to release SCO links after receipt of the RELEASE COMPLETE message.

◆ **In-band tones and announcements.** The GW provides the in-band tones and announcements during calls. The SCO link establishment sub-procedure is initiated and the in-band tones and announcements are sent in the Progress Indicator information (element #8) containing the message "In-band information or appropriate pattern is now available."

Group Management Procedures

The following are the group management procedures defined for the Cordless Telephony Profile:

◆ **Obtain access rights.** This procedure is initiated by the TL, toward the GW, when it wants to become the member of a particular WUG. The GW may accept or reject the request from the TL depending on factors such as the configuration or presence of a physical access between the TL and the base. After accepting a request, the TL is granted access rights and is added to the WUG. This is followed by the initiation of the configuration distribution procedure.

◆ **Configuration Distribution procedure.** During this procedure, the link key information is exchanged between the TL and the GW. However, the TL does not always store the key to uphold the security implementations during this procedure. If the TL stores the key during the configuration distribution procedure, it does not overwrite the existing keys to the other WUG members. The key generated during the configuration distribution procedure is used in the absence of any previous link keys.

◆ **Fast-inter-member access.** This procedure is usually used during intercom calls, when two TLs of the same WUG need to establish their own piconet. The terminals can detach from the gateway after sending a LISTEN ACCEPT message to terminate the L2CAP channel to the gateway. The L2CAP channel is terminated by using the `LMP_detach` PDU.

Supplementary Services

Supplementary services include the internal services provided within the WUG or the external services provided by the network to which the GW is connected. Although the profile definition contains no mention of the specific external services, it does provide means to access these services. The supplementary services for the cordless telephony services include DTMF signaling and Call Line Identity. It is mandatory that the TL is enabled to request for DTMF signaling toward the gateway. Similarly, it is mandatory that the gateway be able to accept DTML signaling requests from the TLs. In addition, the gateway to an external network that provides call line identity should make the corresponding information available to all its users.

Link Loss Detection by the Gateway

If there is a loss of link before the receipt of the INFO ACCEPT message, the GW regards the WUG update as unsuccessfully terminated and the TL to be detached. In addition, if a unit in Call Control (CC) state (other than Null) detects a loss of link, it immediately moves to the Null state and does not perform any release procedures.Interoperability Requirements

The interoperability requirements for the Cordless Telephony Profile are defined for the L2CAP, Link Manager Protocol, and Link Controller layers.

L2CAP Interoperability Requirements

The L2CAP interoperability requirements defined for the Cordless Telephony Profile include specifications for the following:

◆ **Channel types.** The Cordless Telephony Profile supports both connection-oriented and connectionless channels. Connectionless channels are used by the gateway to broadcast information to the TLs. It is the TL that initiates the creation of a link by establishing connection-oriented channels to the GW. To do so, the TL uses the 0x0007 value (for TCS-BIN-CORDLESS) in the Protocol/Service Multiplexor (PSM) field of the Connection Request packet. The value used in the PSM field of the Connection Request packet for an intercom call is 0x0005, which is also the default value for TCS-BIN.

◆ **Configuration options.** The configuration options for the Cordless Telephony Profile includes specifications for the Maximum Transmission Unit (MTU), flush timeout, and Quality of Service (QoS). The minimum L2CAP implemented MTU used for this profile must support 171 octets. As a result, this profile supports a maximum of 7 TLs. The flush timeout used for the GW and the TL is the default value of 0Xffff, while the QoS negotiations between the GW and the TL are optional.

LMP Interoperability Requirements

The LMP interoperability requirements defined for the Cordless Telephony Profile include specifications for the following:

- **Link policy.** The GW implements the power saving modes in the TLs to conserve power during their inactive states. As a result, when the TL is not signaling, the GW puts the TL in the power saving park mode. The GW itself moves into the sniff mode to save power during a call.

- **Master-Slave switch.** The GW supporting the *Multiple-Terminal Support* (feature #7) functions like the master of the piconet. Therefore, when a TL requests for a connection to the GW, the GW in turn requests for a master-slave switch. If the TL rejects the request, it is detached. As a result, a TL that does not accept master-slave switch requests is not guaranteed service by all GWs.

LC Interoperability Requirements

The LC interoperability requirements defined for the Cordless Telephony Profile include specifications for the following:

- **Inter-piconet capabilities.** The inter-piconet capability is defined as the ability of the master in maintaining a synchronized piconet during the free slot page scans. The LC requirement for this profile also defines the ability of the master in terms of facilitating the entry of new members by allowing them to join the piconet. The inter-piconet capabilities are available to those GWs that conform to the *Multiple-Terminal Support* (feature #7). The TL however, is not bound by any conformance and possesses inter-piconet capabilities.

- **Inquiry scan.** A device that functions as the GW in the Cordless Telephony Profile is bounded by two specifications for the *Class of Device* field. The *Telephony* bit in the *Service Class* field should be set. In addition, the *Major Device* class indicated should be *Phone*.

The Intercom Profile

The Intercom Profile supports intercom functionalities that can be added to the three-in-one phone. This functionality represents the intercom or walkie-talkie operation that allows direct voice connection between two devices. The two devices use the TCS-BIN protocol for a direct, two-way communication through the Bluetooth air interface without involving any third-party carrier. The Intercom Profile operates best with the +20 dBm radios that function within a range of 50 to 100 meters. This profile, therefore, supports calls that are within the range of each other rather than the calls routed through PSTN or ISDN. Other audio devices such as special cordless handsets, advanced Cordless Telephony Profile–compliant headsets, and computers that support TCS-BIN can also use the Intercom Profile.

The use of TCS-BIN ensures that the intercom function works almost like a telephone call. The Intercom Profile provides signaling across ACL links from the L2CAP to the TCS stack. The data, like all other audio data, flows in SCO packets through the TCS-BIN. As a result, the TCS-BIN group management functions help to create the WUG environment that facilitates establishment of intercom calls. The intercom calls are a direct phone-to-phone connection between devices and, therefore, do not require a master device intervention. As a result, any device is able to directly page and set up an intercom call with another device. It is evident that during an intercom call, a device leaves its existing piconet temporarily to establish a new piconet. At the end of the call, the device rejoins the original piconet by using the WUG-based TCS-BIN group management functions. Figure 8-2 illustrates the distribution of the Bluetooth protocol layers for the Intercom Profile as sourced from the Bluetooth Profile specification 1.0:

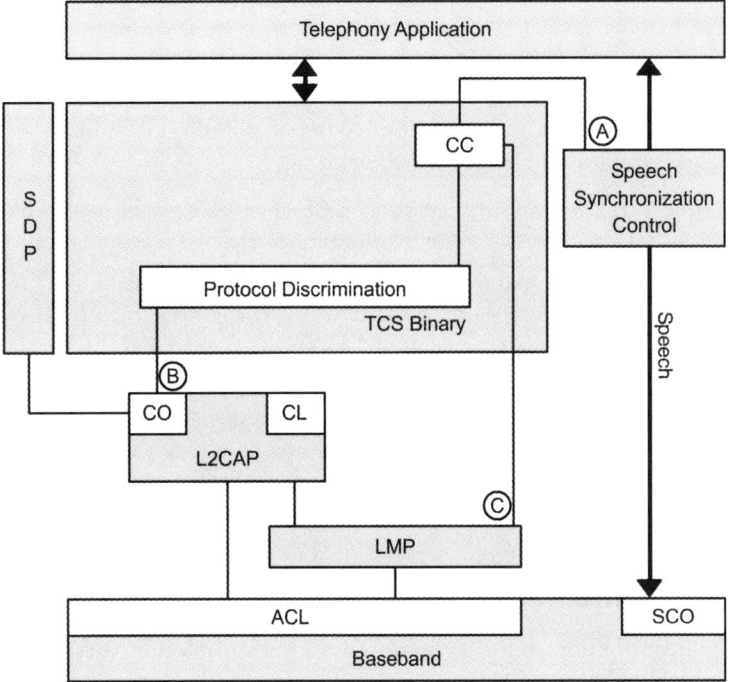

FIGURE 8-2 *The distribution of the Bluetooth protocol stack for the Intercom Profile*

Fundamental Features

The device roles in the Intercom Profile are defined by the device that makes the call (initiator) and the device that accepts the call (acceptor). The features of the Intercom Profile are defined by the following steps, which are initiated when a device intending to make an intercom call connects to another device:

◆ The initiator of the call has to have access to the Bluetooth address (BD_ADDR) of the acceptor. The device discovery procedure is used to obtain the BD_ADDR of the acceptor.

◆ The Intercom Profile does not implement a specific security mode. However, if the users, that is, the initiator and the acceptor of the call, decide to use a security mode, authentication needs to be performed to create a secure connection between the devices.

◆ The initiator is responsible for establishing the link and the channel for the communication. The security requirements enforced by either of the two devices determine the implementation of the authentication and encryption procedures.

◆ The intercom call is established after device authentication. At the end of the intercom call, the channel and link devoted to the call are released.

TCS-BIN

The call control procedures defined for the Intercom Profile are quite similar to those of the Cordless Telephony Profile that are explained in detail in the TCS-Binary section of the Bluetooth specification. These are defined below:

◆ **Call request.** A connection-oriented L2CAP channel is established between the devices before a request for an intercom call is made.

◆ **Call connection.** The mandatory SCO link establishment sub-procedure should be initiated before sending a CONNECT. The speech path between the units is connected only after receipt of CONNECT, or CONNECT ACKNOWLEDGE.

◆ **Call Confirmation.** When an incoming external call delivers the SETUP message on a connection channel, the incoming unit accepting the call should acknowledge the message by executing the call confirmation procedure.

◆ **Call clearing.** The call clearing procedures facilitate the release of the SCO connection by the lower protocol layers. LMP sub-procedures are used to release the SCO links after receipt of the last call-clearing message (RELEASE). The LMP sub-procedures are also used to terminate the L2CAP channel used for the TCS control signaling after receipt of the last call-clearing message.

In addition to the call control procedures, the loss of link is also described by using TCS-BIN procedures. When a unit in any Call Control (CC) state other than Null detects a loss of link, it immediately moves to the Null state. In such a case call clearing procedures are not implemented.

NOTE

The CC state of a device is a TCS state that allows the setting and clearing of voice and data calls between Bluetooth devices. The following are the five general states of TCS:

◆ **Null.** During this state there are no calls present.

◆ **Active.** During this state, calls are allocated to a specific device after setting up the channels.

◆ **Disconnect Request.** During this state, a request for disconnection is sent and its response is awaited.

◆ **Disconnect Indication.** During this state, the network on the outgoing side is disconnected. Therefore, the network on the incoming side is also asked to disconnect.

◆ **Release request.** During this state, a request for release of the channels is made.

Interoperability Requirements

The interoperability requirement for the Intercom Profile is defined for the L2CAP layer. The L2CAP interoperability requirements defined for the Intercom Profile include specifications for the following:

◆ **Channel types.** The Intercom Profile supports only connection-oriented channels. The value used in the PSM field of the Connection Request packet for an intercom call is 0x0005, which is also the default value for TCS-BIN.

◆ **Configuration options.** The configuration options for the Intercom Profile include specifications for the Maximum Transmission Unit (MTU), flush timeout, and Quality of Service (QoS). The minimum L2CAP implemented MTU used for this profile must support 3 octets. The flush timeout used for the GW and the TL is the default value of 0XFFFF, while the QoS negotiations between the GW and the TL are optional.

◆ **Signaling flows.** The signaling flow defined for the Intercom Profile includes specifications for the flow of signals during call establishment and call clearing.

◆ **Call establishment.** Figure 8-3 illustrates the flow of signals during the successful implementation of the call establishment procedure as sourced from the Bluetooth Profile specification 1.0.

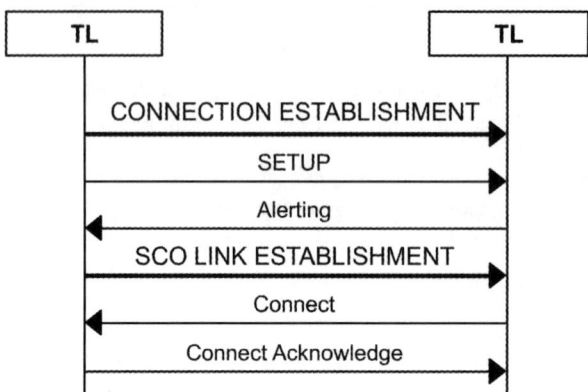

FIGURE 8-3 *The flow of signals during the implementation of the call establishment procedure*

◆ **Call clearing.** Figure 8-4 illustrates the flow of signals during the successful implementation of the call clearing as sourced from the Bluetooth Profile specification 1.0:

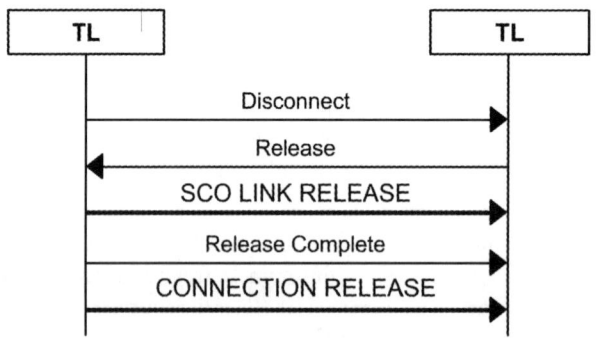

FIGURE 8-4 *The flow of signals during the implementation of the call clearing procedure*

The Dial-up Networking Profile

The Dial-up Networking Profile is an amalgamation of the computing and telephony services, which provide telephonic access to networks so that computing devices can access the network data. A dial-up data connection is used to connect a computer device to the telephone network through a telephone device. The connection between the two devices is either through the Remote Access Server (RAS) technology or through a cordless modem. For example, a laptop is able to connect to a PSTN through a modem and use the dial-up connection to access information on the Internet.

The connection between the computer and the telephone and that between the telephone and the PSTN of the typical wired environment has now been replaced by wireless technology. In this context, mobile technology has replaced the cabled connections between the telephone and the PSTN with the wireless Wide Area Network (WAN) connections. The remaining cables connecting the computer and the telephone device can easily be replaced by the newly developed Bluetooth technology. As a result, the implementation of the Dial-up Networking Profile provides a complete wireless solution between computing and telephony services. The two usage scenarios that are implemented in the Dial-up Networking Profile are:

◆ The use of a mobile phone or modem as a wireless device, to connect a computer to a dial-up Internet access server or to any other dial-up service

◆ The use of a mobile phone or modem to add call-receiving features to a computer

The process of connectivity between two devices is initiated by device discovery, inquiry, and inquiry scanning. This is followed by paging and the establishment of a baseband link. The LM configures the baseband link after which two L2CAP channels are set up. The first L2CAP channel is used for service discovery while the second is set up to access the service. The second L2CAP channel uses an RFCOMM connection to establish a dial-up connection. Figure 8-5 illustrates the distribution of the Bluetooth protocol layers for the Dial-up Networking Profile as sourced from the Bluetooth Profile specification 1.0:

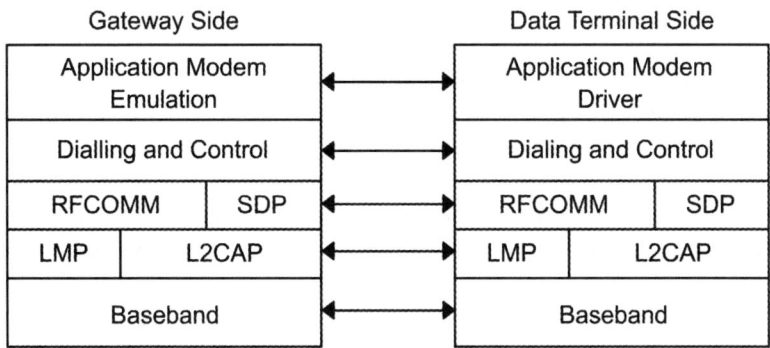

FIGURE 8-5 *The distribution of the Bluetooth protocol stack for the Dial-up Networking Profile*

The Dial-up Networking Profile defines the following two device roles:

◆ **Gateway (GW).** The gateway is the device that connects to a public network. Cellular phones and modems are examples of devices that operate like the gateway in the Dial-up Networking Profile setup.

◆ **Data Terminal (DT).** The data terminal is the device that uses the dial-up services of the gateway. Laptops and desktops are examples of devices that operate like data terminals in the Dial-up Networking Profile setup.

If the gateway-data terminal architecture is mapped to the conventional modem system architecture, you'll be able to relate to the gateway as the Data Circuit Endpoint (DCE) and the data terminal as the Data Terminal Endpoint (DTE).

The GW and DT provide serial port emulation by using Serial Port Profile (SPP) that transports the user data, AT commands, and modem control signals between the two devices. SCO links are used to transport audio.

Fundamental Features

The fundamental features of the Dial-up Networking Profile are:

◆ The DT uses the GW to connect to the Internet access server or to any other dial-up service.

◆ The DT uses the GW to receive data calls.

The Dial-up Networking Profile is also bounded by the following restrictions:

◆ This profile supports point-to-point configurations only.

◆ This profile supports single calls at a time.

◆ A modem support is not necessary for the identification of different incoming call types.

◆ This profile ensures data rates of up to 128 kbps. Therefore, the Dial-up Networking Profile supports single-slot packets. However, the requirement for higher data rates in this profile is optional.

◆ This profile does not define procedures to distinguish between two SCO links that originate form the same device. The differentiation of the SCO links originating from the same device is, therefore, a manufacturer-specific implementation.

◆ The initialization procedure is performed for the first-time connections between a cell phone or modem and a PC or laptop. The initialization procedure is manually initiated by entering the PIN code on the laptop or PC.

Security is implemented by the LMP and baseband procedures for authentication and encryption.

The Application Layer

The services supported by the Dial-up Networking Profile for the Application layer consists of the following:

◆ **Data calls.** The support for data calls by the DT and GW is mandatory. On the other hand, the support for audio feedback is optional. Therefore, both the DT and GW support *Data call without audio feedback,* a service feature that is mandatory for the Dial-up Networking Profile. The *Data call with audio feedback* feature for the DT and GW is, however, optional.

◆ **Fax services or voice calls.** The fax service is supported by the Fax Profile while voice calls are supported by the Cordless Telephony Profile. The Dial-up Networking Profile, therefore, does not support *Fax services with/without audio feedback* and *voice call* services.

Table 8-1 lists services that are supported by the Dial-up Networking Profile as sourced from the Bluetooth Profile specification 1.0.

Table 8-1 The Services Supported by the Dial-Up Networking Profile

Service	DT Support	GW Support
Data call without audio feedback	M	M
Data call with audio feedback	O	O
Fax service without audio feedback	N/A	N/A
Fax service with audio feedback	N/A	N/A
Voice call	N/A	N/A

Interoperability Requirements

The interoperability requirements for the Dial-up Networking Profile are defined for the AT commands used with the dialing and control procedures, and the call progress audio feedback.

AT Commands of the Dialing and Control Procedures

The GW has to provide support for command syntax, the fax class of service, and the fax service class selection procedures to ensure the basic functioning of the Dial-up Networking Profile. The specifications for these are as follows:

◆ **Command syntax, protocol, and result codes.** This profile specifies the command syntax, protocol, and result codes in the individual fax service class implementation document.

◆ **Fax class of service(s).** This profile supports Fax Class 1 that includes TIA-578-A and ITU T.31, Fax Class 2.0 that includes TIA-592-A and ITU T.32, and Fax Class 2 that includes non-industrial manufacturer-specific standards.

◆ **Fax service class selection procedures.** This profile does not support specific fax service classes. The two standard fax classes supported include Fax Class 1, Fax Class 2.0, and the non-industrial manufacturer-specific Fax Class 2.

The fax class supported by the GW is ascertained by checking the GW SDP or the implementation of the AT+FCLASS commands. Bluetooth devices that implement the Dial-up Networking Profile should support at least one of the fax service classes, but may also extend support for any or all of the specified fax service classes. Table 8-2 lists some of the commands used by the Dial-up Networking Profile as sourced from the Bluetooth Profile specification 1.0.

Table 8-2 The Commands used by the Dial-Up Networking Profile

Command	Description
&C	The received line signal detector behavior
&D	The data terminal ready behavior
&F	Set to configurations that are factory-defined
+GCAP	Request for a complete capability list
+GMI	Request for the identification of the manufacturer
+GMM	Request for the identification of the model
+GMR	Request for the identification of the revision
A	Answer
D	Dial
E	Command echo
H	Hook control
L	Loudness of the monitor speaker
M	Mode of the monitor speaker
O	Return to online data state
P	Select pulse dialing
Q	Result code suppression
S0	Automatic answer
S10	Automatic disconnect delay

Command	Description
S3	Command-line termination character
S4	Response for formatting character
S5	Command-line editing character
S6	Pause before blind dialing
S7	Connection completion timeout
S8	Comma dial modifier time
T	Select tone dialing
V	DCE response format
X	Result code selection and call progress-monitoring control
Z	Reset to default configuration

Call Progress Audio Feedback

The call progress audio feedback made available during the call establishment is optional for the Dial-up Networking Profile. When the GW provides audio feedback support for a call, it is also responsible for initiating an SCO link procedure to establish an audio link with an off-hook DCE. On the failure of the SCO link establishment, the call establishment procedure is implemented without any audio feedback.

The behavior and implementations for multiple SCO link establishments is not defined in the Dial-up Networking Profile. This is because the profile assumes that the DT in the Fax Profile is inactive in any other profile that uses SCO links.

Compliance with Fundamental Profiles

The Dial-up Networking Profile complies with both the General Access Profile (GAP) and Serial Port Profile (SPP). The compliance with GAP can be attributed to the support for modes, security, idle mode procedures, and bonding. Table 8-3 lists the GAP-compliant support for modes in the Dial-up Networking Profile as sourced from the Bluetooth Profile specification 1.0.

Table 8-3 The GAP Modes Supported by the Dial-Up Networking Profile

Service	DT Support	GW Support
Discovery modes		
Non-discoverable mode	N/A	M
Limited discoverable mode	N/A	O
General discoverable mode	N/A	M
Connection modes		
Non-connectable mode	N/A	X
Connectable mode	N/A	M
Pairing modes		
Non-pairable mode	M	M
Pairable mode	O	M

Table 8-4 lists the GAP-compliant support for security in the Dial-up Networking Profile as sourced from the Bluetooth Profile specification 1.0.

Table 8-4 The GAP Security Aspects Supported by the Dial-Up Networking Profile

Service	DT Support	GW Support
Discovery modes	M	M
Security modes		
Security mode 1	N/A	X
Security mode 2	C1	C1
Security mode 3	C1	C1

 NOTE

The C1 support specifies that the support for at least one of the security modes (2 and 3) is mandatory.

Table 8-5 lists the GAP-compliant support for idle mode and bonding procedures in the Dial-up Networking Profile as sourced from the Bluetooth Profile specification 1.0.

Table 8-5 The GAP Idle Mode and Bonding Procedures Supported by the Dial-Up Networking Profile

Service	DT Support	GW Support
General inquiry	M	N/A
Limited inquiry	O	N/A
Name discovery		O N/A
Device discovery	O	N/A
Bonding	M	M

 NOTE

The support for initiation of bonding is mandatory for the DT and the support for accepting bonding is mandatory for the GW.

In case of compliance with SPP, the mapping of the profiles designates the GW as the Device B and the DT as the Device A. The requirements for the L2CAP and RFCOMM remain the same as that of SPP. The SDP compliance is defined in terms of the service records. Table 8-6 lists the number of service records defined for the GW and DT as sourced from the Bluetooth Profile specification 1.0.

Table 8-6 The Service Record Definitions for the GW and DT

Service record	Value	Category
Service Class ID List	N/A	M
Service Class #0	Generic networking	M
Service Class #1	Dial-up networking	O
Protocol Descriptor List	N/A	M
Protocol Descriptor #0	L2CAP	M
Protocol Descriptor #1	RFCOMM	M

The Fax Profile

The Fax Profile defines procedures for sending and receiving faxes between devices supporting wireless connections. The Fax Profile is very similar to the Dial-up Networking Profile. You'll recall that the services for the application layer in the Dial-up Networking Profile defined specifications for the fax service class. Fax and data transmissions modulate and demodulate the transmitted data and commands between the endpoints of a telephone line. The protocol stack for the Fax Profile is similar to that of the Dial-up Networking Profile. The only difference between the two profiles lies in the implementation of security. Security implementation is mandatory for the Fax Profile, whereas it is optional for the Dial-up Networking Profile. In addition, the Dial-up Networking Profile transfers data calls between devices, while in the Fax Profile the information transferred over phone links is in the form of FAX. Figure 8-6 illustrates the distribution of the Bluetooth protocol layers for the Fax Profile as sourced from the Bluetooth Profile specification 1.0.

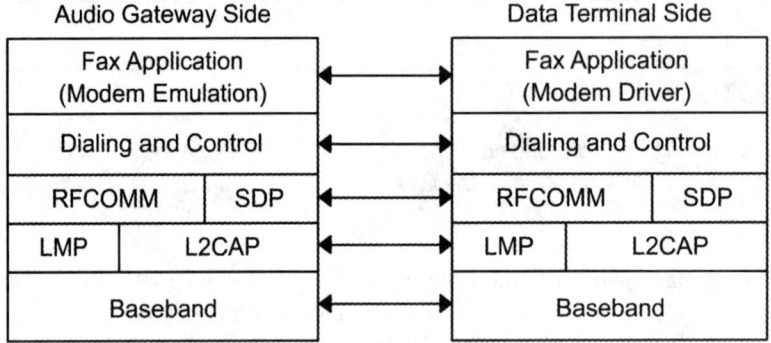

FIGURE 8-6 *The distribution of the Bluetooth protocol stack for the Fax Profile*

The Fax Profile defines the same role devices as that of the Dial-up Networking Profile. The two device roles of the Fax Profile are:

- **Gateway (GW).** The gateway provides the facsimile services. Cellular phones and modems are examples of devices that operate like the gateway in the Fax Profile setup.

- **Data Terminal (DT).** The data terminal uses the facsimile services of the gateway. Laptops and desktops are examples of devices that operate like data terminals in the Dial-up Networking Profile setup.

Fundamental Features

The fundamental features of the Fax Profile are:

◆ The DT has to have access to the Bluetooth address (BD_ADDR) of the GW. The device discovery procedure is used to obtain the BD_ADDR of the GW.

◆ The Fax Profile mandates implementation of security by using baseband and LMP mechanisms for the authentication of the devices and the encryption of user data.

◆ The DT initiates the process of link establishment.

◆ The master and slave roles in this profile are not fixed.

◆ A fax call is established. The Serial Port Profile provides serial port emulations that are used to transfer AT commands, user data, and modem control signals between the GW and the DT. The GW parses the AT commands and sends the responses to the DT.

◆ The fax audio feedback can be transported by an optional SCO link.

◆ At the end of the fax call all link and channels are released.

The Fax Profile is also bounded by the following restrictions:

◆ This profile supports point-to-point configurations only.

◆ This profile supports single calls at a time.

◆ The GW is not responsible for the identification of different incoming call types.

◆ This profile ensures data rates of up to 128 kbps. Therefore, the Dial-up Networking Profile supports single-slot packets. However, the requirement for higher data rates in this profile is optional.

◆ This profile does not define procedures to distinguish between two SCO links that originate form the same device. The differentiation of the SCO links originating from the same device is, therefore, a manufacturer-specific implementation.

◆ The Fax Profile does not support multiple instances of implementation in the same device.

The Application Layer

The support for fax services by the DT and GW is mandatory. On the other hand, the support for data and voice calls is not available. Therefore, both the DT and GW support *Fax services without audio feedback*, a service feature that is mandatory for the Fax Profile. The *Fax service with audio feedback* feature for the DT and GW is, however, optional. This profile mandates support for at least one of the following fax class services:

♦ Fax Class 1 that includes TIA-578-A and ITU T.31

♦ Fax Class 2.0 that includes TIA-592-A and ITU T.32

♦ Fax Class 2 that includes non-industrial manufacturer-specific standards

Table 8-7 lists services that are supported by the Fax Profile as sourced from the Bluetooth Profile specification 1.0.

Table 8-7 The Services Supported by the Fax Profile

Service	DT support	GW support
Data call without audio feedback	N/A	N/A
Data call with audio feedback	N/A	N/A
Fax service without audio feedback	M	M
Fax service with audio feedback	O	O
Voice call	N/A	N/A

Interoperability Requirements

The interoperability requirements for the Fax Profile are the same as those specified for the Dial-up Networking Profile. The requirements defined include specifications for the AT commands used with the dialing and control procedures and the call progress audio feedback.

AT Commands of the Dialing and Control Procedures

The GW has to provide support for command syntax, the fax class of service, and the fax service class selection procedures to ensure the basic functioning of the Fax Profile. The specifications for these are as follows:

♦ **Command syntax, protocol, and result codes.** This profile specifies the command syntax, protocol, and result codes in the individual fax service class implementation document.

♦ **Fax class of service(s).** This profile expects the GW device to support the command and responses of the following fax class of services:

 ♦ Fax Class 1 TIA-578-A and ITU T.31

 ♦ Fax Class 2.0 that includes TIA-592-A and ITU T.32

 ♦ Fax Class 2 that includes non-industrial manufacturer-specific standards.

♦ **Fax service class selection procedures.** This profile does not support specific fax service classes. The two standard fax classes supported include Fax Class 1, Fax Class 2.0, and the non-industrial manufacturer-specific Fax Class 2.

The fax class supported by the GW is ascertained by checking the GW SDP or the implementation of the AT+FCLASS commands. Bluetooth devices that implement the Dial-up Networking Profile should support at least one of the fax service classes, but may also extend support for any or all of the specified fax service classes.

The specification for the call progress audio feedback is the same as that for the Dial-up Networking Profile.

Compliance with Fundamental Profiles

The Fax Profile complies with the Generic Access Profile (GAP) and the Serial Port Profile (SPP). The compliance parameters for GAP remain the same as that for the Dial-up Networking Profile. However, in the case of SPP, the mapping of the profiles designates the GW as the Device B and the DT as the Device A. the requirements for the L2CAP and RFCOMM remain the same as that of SPP. The Fax Profile mandates support for SCO links in the GW and the DT. In cases where audio feedback is provided, the support for SCO links is optional.

The Headset Profile

The Headset Profile describes the usage scenario for making and receiving calls from a headset that is attached to a mobile phone. The Headset Profile provides for a hands-free mode of communication. A headset unit consists of a microphone and a pair of earphones. It can be used with computers, mobile phones, MP3 players, and other devices. Although headset models use buttons to drive the commands, an innovative implementation of hands-free communication is provided by voice-activated command and control of the headset. The Headset Profile is the only profile that uses the original modem control AT commands. The Bluetooth protocol layer for the Headset Profile includes the baseband, LMP, and L2CAP layers. The RFCOMM layer is the Bluetooth adaptation of the GSP 07.10 standard. The AT command-based headset control signaling functions are performed by the headset entity. Figure 8-7 illustrates the distribution of the Bluetooth protocol layers for the Headset Profile as sourced from the Bluetooth Profile specification 1.0.

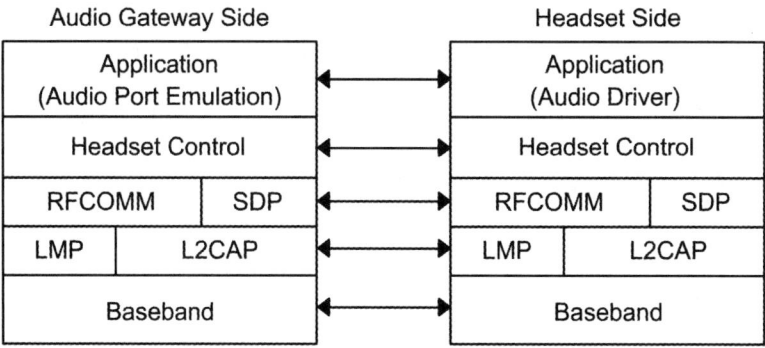

FIGURE 8-7 *The distribution of the Bluetooth protocol stack for the Headset Profile*

The Headset Profile defines the following two role devices:

- **Audio Gateway (AW).** The audio gateway is the device that functions like a gateway for audio input and output. Cellular phones and PCs are examples of devices that operate like the audio gateway in the Headset Profile setup.
- **Headset (HS).** The headset is the device that functions like the remote audio input output mechanism of the audio gateway.

Fundamental Features

The fundamental features of the Headset Profile are:

- The only active case between the two devices is assumed to be the ultimate headset for this profile.
- The Headset Profile mandates the use of Continuous Variable Slope Delta (CVSD) modulation for audio transmissions. CVSD is a monophonic voice codec with good error handling mechanisms that does not degrade under normal circumstances.
- The headset and the audio gateway support only a single audio connection at a time.
- The AW controls the establishment of the SCO link and its release after the termination of the call. The headset connects to the internal audio stream during the link establishment, and on disconnection releases the link. After a link is established, a bi-directional valid speech transfers between the devices on the SCO link.
- The Headset Profile supports basic interoperability that does not include functions such as the handling of multiple calls at the AW.

The AW can be used by the headset without the support of a secure connection. The security implementations of authentication and encryption are implemented by the end user. The GAP authentication procedure is initiated by entering the PIN code and the subsequent formation of the link keys creates a secure connection between two devices of the Headset Profile.

The link between the devices is created after the initiation or receipt of a call. During this time, the other device sends pages to the initiator or the acceptor, which is in the unpark state. The RFCOMM between the AW and the HS is used to emulate a serial port that facilitates the transfer of the user data along with the modem control signals and AT commands. The AT commands are parsed and sent back to the headset in the form of responses.

Interoperability Requirements

The interoperability requirements for the Headset Profile include specifications for the following features:

◆ **Incoming audio connection.** The AG initiates a connection between the devices after an internal or external user-generated event. This is followed by an unsolicited code RING that is used to alert the user. The RING is repeated until the establishment of the connection (SCO link). The connection is acknowledged by the user through the headset buttons. The HS then sends the AT+CKPD command to the AG.

◆ **Outgoing audio connection.** After sending the AT+CKPD command, the SCO link is established. The AG then initiates internal actions to establish or route an audio stream to the HS.

◆ **Audio connection release.** The buttons of the headset or the internal actions of the AG terminate a call. The AG then releases the link associated with the terminated call.

◆ **Audio connection transfer.** The transfer of the audio connection depends upon the device that initiates the transfer. The audio transfer from the AG to HS is initiated by a user action from the HS and is followed by the sending of the AT+CKPD command. The audio transfer from the HS to AG is initiated by a user action from the AG.

◆ **Remote audio volume control.** The AG sends unsolicited result codes of +VGM and +VGS to gain control over the microphone and speaker of the HS. The Headset Profile does not limit the number and order of the result codes that are sent to the HS as long the devices have an active and ongoing audio connection. The +VGM and +VGS commands are absolute values that are represented on a scale from 0 to 15. The HS can store the VGS and VGM settings after the release of the connection for control of volume levels in the next connection.

◆ **AT commands and result codes.** The format, syntax, and procedures of V.250 are used during the exchange of the command and result codes. Only a single command or a single unsolicited result code is expected for each command line.

◆ **Lower layer handling.** The layers below the headset entity are used to establish and release the connections between the AG and HS. Connection handling in the Headset Profile does not support devices that are in park mode. As a result, the mode of the devices is checked during the lower layer connection handling procedure. The HS and AG initiate connections between devices that are not in the park mode. In the absence of an RFCOMM session between the devices, a new RFCOMM session is initiated. At the end of the audio connection, the AG also releases the connection between the two devices. A connection between devices that are in the park mode is initiated only once. After the first request for a connection, the device moves into the unparked state. The initiation for the connection originates from both the AG and HS, the devices then move to the park state after the initial connection.

Compliance with Fundamental Profiles

The Headset Profile complies with both the General Access Profile (GAP) and Serial Port Profile (SPP). The compliance with GAP can be attributed to the support for modes, idle mode procedures, and bonding. Table 8-8 lists the GAP-compliant support for modes in the Headset Profile as sourced from the Bluetooth Profile specification 1.0.

Table 8-8 The GAP Modes Supported by the Headset Profile

Service	DT Support	GW Support
Discovery modes		
Non-discoverable mode	M	N/A
Limited discoverable mode	O	N/A
General discoverable mode	M	N/A
Connection modes		
Non-connectable mode	N/A	N/A
Connectable mode	M	M
Pairing modes		
Non-pairable mode	O	O
Pairable mode	O	O

Table 8-9 lists the GAP-compliant support for idle mode and bonding procedures in the Headset Profile as sourced from the Bluetooth specification 1.0.

Table 8-9 The GAP Idle Mode and Bonding Procedures Supported by the Headset Profile

Service	DT Support	GW Support
General inquiry	N/A	M
Limited inquiry	N/A	O
Name discovery	N/A	O
Device discovery	N/A	O
Bonding	M	M

In case of compliance with SPP, the mapping of the profiles designates the GW as the Device B and the DT as the Device A. The requirements for the L2CAP and RFCOMM remain the same as that of SPP. The SDP compliance is defined in terms of the service records for the AG and HS.

The LAN Access Profile

The LAN Access Profile instantiates the Internet bridge scenario and allows a Bluetooth device to access a fixed network. The access to the fixed network is made possible through a Bluetooth link that connects to a LAN access point. The functioning of this profile can be segmented into two parts. The first part defines the implementations required for connecting a Bluetooth device to a LAN by using Point-to-Point Protocol (PPP). The second part describes the PPP mechanisms that are used to form a network between the two Bluetooth devices. The LAN Access Profile can be used in the form of PANs, shared access points in meeting rooms, or public access points in the information kiosks. The LAN Access Profiles defines a PPP network in the following scenarios:

◆ LAN access for a single Bluetooth device

◆ LAN access for multiple Bluetooth devices

◆ PC-to-PC connectivity using PPP networking over emulated serial cables.

The PPP networks of the LAN Access Profile carry IP packets over RFCOMM and link the Internet Protocol (IP) stack to the Bluetooth protocol stack. The lower protocol layers of this profile include the baseband, LMP, and L2CAP. The RFCOMM layer is the adapted from GSM TS 07.10. Figure 8-8 illustrates the distribution of the Bluetooth protocol layers for the LAN Access Profile as sourced from the Bluetooth Profile specification 1.0.

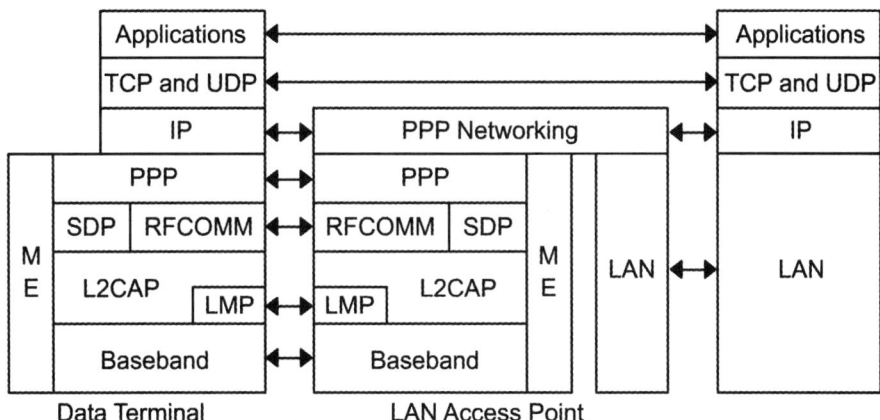

FIGURE 8-8 *The distribution of the Bluetooth protocol stack for the LAN Access Profile*

The LAN Access Profile defines the following device roles:

◆ **LAN access point (LAP).** The Bluetooth devices gain access to LAN by using the LAP. The LAP functions like a PPP server allowing access to LANs such as Ethernet, Cable Modem, USB, Firewire, and Home networking. The PPP connection transports PPP packets over RFCOMM and also controls the flow of the PPP data stream.

◆ **Data Terminal (DT).** The data terminal uses the services of the LAP. Laptops, desktops, notebooks, and PDAs are examples of devices that operate like data terminals in the LAN Access Profile setup.

Fundamental Features

The fundamental features of the LAN describe the characteristics for the following three PPP network scenarios:

◆ **LAN access by a single DT.** Single DTs use the LAP to obtain a wireless connection to a LAN. The DT after connection emulates the behavior of a connection through dial-up networking. The DT has access to all services that are provided by the LAN.

◆ **LAN access by multiple DTs.** Multiple DTs use the LAP for a wireless connection to a LAN. The DT after connection emulates the behavior of a connection through dial-up networking. The communication between the DTs is through the LAP that facilitates access to all the services provided by the LAN.

◆ **PC-to-PC connectivity.** During a connection between two PCs, one of the devices takes up the role of the LAP and the other takes on the role of the DT. The connection between two PCs of the LAN Access Profile is similar to the direct cable connection between two PCs.

The following are the interactions that occur between the LAP and DT:

◆ First the DT uses the services of an application to identify a suitable LAP that is within its coverage area. The LAP selected for connection should provide PPP, RFCOMM, or L2CAP services.

◆ If there is no physical baseband link between the LAP and the DT, the DT requests a physical link with the selected LAP. After establishment of the link, the devices are authenticated and encryption is used on the link.

◆ After establishing a PPP, RFCOMM, or L2CAP connection, the LAP uses PPP procedures for authentication. During authentication, the LAP may challenge the DT to authenticate and prove its legality. If the DT fails to authenticate itself, the PPP link is terminated.

◆ The LAP and DT negotiate an IP address by using PPP procedures.

◆ The IP packets flow across the PPP connection. Both the LAP and DT can terminate the PPP connection at any time.

The User Interface

The LAN Access Profile is based on GAP. Therefore, the user interface specifications define the implementations for the following parameters:

♦ Security

♦ Generic modes

♦ Maximum number of users

Security Implementations

The wireless environment is prone to security breaches and requires security implementations to ensure that the transmitted data is not manipulated or misused. The LAP and DT encrypt the physical baseband link during the transmission of the PPP packets. Bluetooth pairing is implemented so that both the LAP and DT can refuse requests for disabling encryption.

The PIN code plays an important role for implementing security in this profile. The default PIN for LAN access is of zero length. Unpaired devices are prevented from accessing the services of the LAN.

Generic Modes

Table 8-10 lists the GAP-compliant modes of the LAN Access Profile as sourced from the Bluetooth Profile specification 1.0.

Table 8-10 The GAP Modes Supported by the LAN Access Profile

Service	LAP support	DT support
Discovery modes		
Non-discoverable mode	O	X
Limited discoverable mode	X	X
General discoverable mode	M	X
Connection modes		
Non-connectable mode	O	X
Connectable mode	M	X
Pairing modes		
Non-pairable mode	O	X
Pairable mode	M	X

The following two pairing procedures are defined for the LMP level:

◆ The user initiates bonding between two devices by entering a passkey.

◆ Alternatively, during the establishment of the link, the user is requested to enter the passkey. The devices in this case do not share a common link key.

Maximum Number of Users

The maximum number of users is a mandatory parameter for the LAP, which accommodates multiple user support for its procedures and are governed by different resources and limitations. The LAP administrator can choose to implement the following two modes to limit the number of simultaneous users:

◆ **Single-user mode.** In this mode the LAP or DT may assume the role of the master of the piconet. A single DT is able to access a LAP and, therefore, the maximum number of configured users to a LAN is automatically limited to a single user.

◆ **Multiple-user mode.** In this mode the LAP assumes the role of the master to gain access to a LAN. As a result, the maximum number of configured users in this case, is more than one.

The Application Layer

The Application layer procedures for the LAN Access Profile include initialization and shutdown procedures.

Initialization Procedures

The initialization procedures facilitate access to LAP services, creation of a LAN connection, and disconnection from a LAN connection.

◆ **LAP services.** Before a device assumes the role of the LAP, all its configurable parameters, required PINs and link keys, and PPP configuration options are set up.

◆ **Creating a connection.** The DT initiates the establishment of a connection to the LAN. A suitable LAP is selected by using one of the following ways:

The DT user is provided with a list of the LAPs and their services that are within its coverage area. The user then selects the LAP and its service from the list. The list of services provided by multiple LAPs is listed only once. The user selects the appropriate service and the DT automatically selects the corresponding LAP. This is an optional method used for selection of the LAP. In this method, the user is allowed to enter a Bluetooth PIN or link key that is supplied by the application.

The user enters the name of the required service. The DT then automatically selects the corresponding LAP. This is an optional method used for selection of the LAP. In this method, the user is allowed to enter a username and password for PPP authentication.

The DT searches and selects the required LAP and its service. The user or the application activates the connection by starting a PPP application. An attempt is then made to connect to the selected LAP.

Both the LAP and DT can disconnect from a LAN connection at any time.

Shutdown Procedures

The shutdown procedures of the LAN Access Profile stop the functioning of the LAP. To do so, one of the following steps is performed:

◆ The PPP server is shutdown.

◆ A product deletes the stored link keys to prevent unauthorized access to the LAP.

The File Transfer Profile

The File Transfer Profile facilitates exchange of objects (in the form of files and folders) between heterogeneous devices such as laptops, PDAs, and digital cameras. On examining the nature of the transfers between the devices, it is obvious that this profile uses the capabilities of OBEX and is, therefore, also based on GAP, SPP, and GOEP. The File Transfer Profile provides an unrestricted and robust mode of object exchange based on a bi-directional pushing and pulling of objects. Other than enabling object exchange, the File Transfer Profile provides browsing capabilities for navigation within the folders of the server's file system. This profile can be used to link two devices and enable operations such as scanning and printing. Figure 8-9 illustrates the distribution of the Bluetooth protocol layers for the File Transfer Profile as sourced from the Bluetooth Profile specification 1.0.

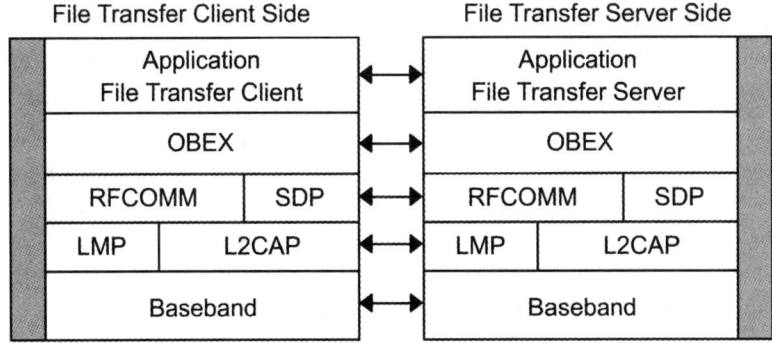

FIGURE 8-9 *The distribution of the Bluetooth protocol stack for the File Transfer Profile*

Like all other profiles, the LAN Access Profile also defines the following device roles:

◆ **Client.** The client device is the initiator of the operations that pushes or pulls objects to and from a server. It is mandatory for the client to comply with all interoperability requirements specified for the client of GOEP.

◆ **Server.** The server device is the target device that provides the exchange service so that objects can be pushed to or pulled from it. It is mandatory for the server to comply with all interoperability requirements specified for the server of GOEP.

Fundamental Features

The features of the File Transfer Profile are described in the form of the following usage scenarios:

◆ **Client browses the object store of the server.** If the client and the server support file browsing, the client is able to browse through the object store of the server. During browsing, the client should be able to understand and pull the Folder Listing Objects. The server at the other end should be able to respond to the requests for the Folder Listing Objects.

◆ **Client transfers objects to/from the server.** The objects transferred between the client and the server are in the form of the files and folders. The client should be able to push or pull files only, while the server should be able to push or pull both files and folders. In addition, the server should contain read-only folders and files so that the object pushes can be restricted.

◆ **Client creates and deletes objects from the server.** The client should not support creation and deletion of files and folders. The server should support read-only files and folders, so that the creation and deletion of can be restricted.

A device compliant with the File Transfer Profile should support client capability, server capability, or both. The fundamental features of the profile are similar to that of GOEP.

The User Interface

The user interface specifications define the implementations for the following parameters:

◆ **File transfer mode selection for servers.** Before a client performs the file transfer operation, the server should be in the File Transfer mode. When a server enters the File Transfer mode, it should set the device in the Limited Discoverable mode. In addition, the Object Transfer Bit should be set in the CoD and the service record should be registered in the Service discovery database (SDDB).

◆ **Function selection for clients.** The clients access file transfer functions through a user interface. For example, the file tree viewer is a common mechanism used to browse files and folders. The file tree view presents the files and folders on another PC in a network view so that they can be selected and manipulated.

The Application Layer

The Application layer procedures for the File Transfer Profile include the following:

- **Folder browsing.** After the client connects to the server, a file is transferred from the server's root directory to the client. During browsing, the contents of folders in the server's object store are displayed and the OBEX SETPATH command is used to set the current folder. The GET command is used to retrieve information from the root folder and the contents of the sub-folders.

- **Object transfer.** The client transfers objects to the server by using the OBEX PUT command. Similarly, the server transfers objects to the client by using the OBEX GET command. The files exchanged by the client and server is placed in folders that are created by using the SETPATH command.

- **Object manipulation.** The client can delete and create folders and files on the server by using the following commands:

  - The PUT command is used to delete a file from a folder. The name of the file is specified in the Name header and the Body header is left blank. The PUT command is also used to delete empty folders in the same way.

  - The PUT command is used to delete non-empty folders but the server may is restrict this operation. When the deletion of a non-empty folder is refused, the server returns the *Precondition Failed* response code. This response code is an indication for the client to delete the contents of the folder before opting for deletion of the empty folder.

  - The SETPATH command is used to create a new folder in the server's current folder. The name of the folder is added to the Name header. If the name of the new folder clashes with that of an existing folder, the new folder is not created.

Interoperability Requirements

The interoperability requirements for the File Transfer Profile are defined for the OBEX layer and includes specifications for OBEX operations, initialization, session establishment, browsing folders, pushing and pulling objects, and manipulating objects. The detailed definitions for the OBEX requirements is as follows:

- **OBEX operations.** The six mandatory OBEX operations for the client and server in File Transfer Profile include CONNECT, DISCONNECT, PUT, GET, ABORT, and SETPATH.

- **OBEX initialization.** The use of OBEX authentication is optional for devices that implement the File Transfer Profile.

- **OBEX session establishment.** The OBEX connections use a target header that is set to the File Browsing Universally Unique Identifier (UUID). This UUID is set in binary with 0xF9 sent first. OBEX authentication during session establishment is optional.

◆ **Browsing folders.** The current folder of the server is moved forward and backward to facilitate browsing within the folder hierarchy. After the completion of the OBEX Connect operation, the current folder of the server is set as the root folder.

◆ **Pushing and pulling objects.** When an object is pushed, files with Connection ID header are pushed. This feature of the File Transfer Profile is mandatory. Similarly, when objects are pulled, new folders are created and the corresponding files are pulled. When objects are pulled, files with the Connect ID header are pulled. When folders are pulled the folder hierarchy is browsed resulting in the pulling of the folder listing objects and the files.

◆ **Manipulating objects.** During manipulations objects (files and folders) are created and deleted by using the PUT operation. When the deletion of a folder is refused, the server returns the *Precondition Failed* response code. This response code is an indication for the client to delete the contents of the folder before opting for deletion of the empty folder.

Service Discovery

OBEX is the session protocol that is used during the bi-directional generic transfer of files. The service that belongs to the File Transfer Profile is the server. Table 8-11 lists the status and values of the file transfer service record as sourced from the Bluetooth Profile specification 1.0.

Table 8-11 The File Transfer Service Record of the File Transfer Profile

Item	Value	Status
Service Class ID List		M
Service Class #0	OBEX file transfer	M
Protocol descriptor List		M
Protocol #0	L2CAP	M
Protocol #1	RFCOMM	M
Parameter for Protocol #0	Server Channel number	M
Protocol #2	OBEX	M
Service name	displayable text name	O
BT Profile descriptor List		O
Profile #0	OBEX file transfer	-
Parameter for Protocol #0	Profile version	-

The Object Push Profile

The Object Push Profile is used with GOEP to send and receive objects and also define the interoperability requirements for the protocols used by the applications. Examples of this profile include exchange of business cards between the client and server, pulling of business cards from the server, or pushing limited objects to the server. Figure 8-10 illustrates the distribution of the Bluetooth protocol layers for the Object Push Profile as sourced from the Bluetooth Profile specification 1.0.

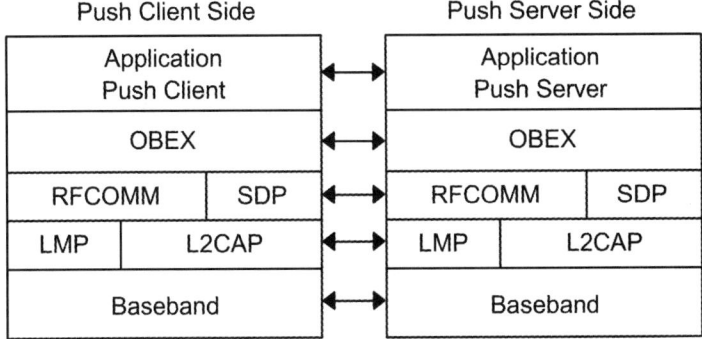

FIGURE 8-10 *The distribution of the Bluetooth protocol stack for the Object Push Profile*

The two roles defined for this profile are:

◆ **Push client.** This is the client device that pushes and pulls objects to and from the push server.

◆ **Push server.** This is the device that functions like an object exchange server.

Fundamental Features

The fundamental features of the Object Push Profile are:

◆ The push client is used to push objects such as business cards or appointments to the push server.

◆ The push client is used to pull objects (business cards) from the push server.

◆ The push client is used to exchange objects (business cards) with the push server.

The fundamental features of the Object Push Profile are similar to those of GOEP. OBEX authentication is not used, but support for link level authentication and encryption is mandatory. The server and client do not need to automatically move into discoverable or connectable modes.

The User Interface

The object exchange mode of this profile allows the push client to push and pull objects to and from the push server. The push server does not support object pulls and, therefore, responds to the pull requests with appropriate error messages.

The Object Push Profile performs the three functions that are activated by the user and not performed automatically without an interaction with the user. After the user selects one of the Object Push Profile functions, an inquiry procedures is initiated to produce a list of available devices within the coverage area. The three functions of the Object Push Profile are:

◆ **Object push function.** This function pushes one or more objects to the push server.

◆ **Business card pull function.** This function pulls the business cards from the push server.

◆ **Business card exchange function.** This function exchanges business cards with the push server.

The Application Layer

The object push, business card pull, and business card exchange capabilities are implemented by the application profile using GOEP. Of these, the object push function is mandatory for both the push client and push server. The business card pull and business card exchange functions are optional. The features of the Object Push Profile Application layer functions are:

◆ **Object push feature.** In this feature, the push server receives one or more objects from the push client. The application level interoperability is maintained by defining content formats for the object push. As a result, the push clients are expected to send objects in the proper format that is supported by the push server. The push servers should be able to receive multiple objects within an OBEX connection. The push clients, on the other hand, are able to send multiple objects in an OBEX connection. The push client uses the PUT operation to send objects.

◆ **Business card pull feature.** In this feature, the push client pulls a business card from the push server. This functionality is optional for the push client, but the push server should support the business pull card feature. The owner's business card is stored in the OBEX default GET object.

◆ **Business card exchange feature.** In this feature, the push client exchanges a business card with the push server. This functionality is optional for the push client, but the push server should support the business exchange card feature.

Table 8-12 lists the features of the application layer in the Object Push Profile as sourced from the Bluetooth Profile specification 1.0.

Table 8-12 The Features of the Application Layer for the Object Push Profile

Feature	Support in the Push Client	Support in the Push Server
Object push	M	M
Business card pull	O	O
Business card exchange	O	O

Interoperability Requirements

The six mandatory OBEX operations used in the Object Push Profile include Connect, Disconnect, Put, Get, Abort, and SetPath. The Object Push Profile does not support OBEX authentication and, therefore, OBEX initialization is also not supported. The push client always uses the Type header when pushing objects to the push server. The push client pulls objects from the push server only while getting the Default Get Object. In the absence of the Default Get Object, the push server responds with the *Not Found* error response code. The name header is not used with the Default Get Object. However, if the push client sends a non-empty Name header, the push server responds with the *Forbidden* error response code.

The Synchronization Profile

The Synchronization Profile defines programmatic decisions to choose the direction of the object transfers. This profile uses GOEP to define the interoperability requirements for the application protocols. Figure 8-11 illustrates the distribution of the Bluetooth protocol layers for the Synchronization Profile as sourced from the Bluetooth Profile specification 1.0.

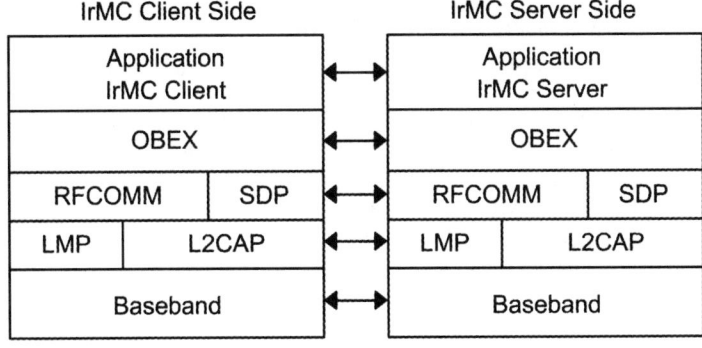

FIGURE 8-11 *The distribution of the Bluetooth protocol stack for the Synchronization Profile*

The two device roles defined for this profile are:

◆ **IrMC client.** This is the device, more specifically the PC, which pulls the PIM data to and from the IrMC server. The IrMC server complies with the interoperability requirements that are defined for GOEP.

◆ **IrMC server.** This is the device, more specifically the mobile phone or PDA, which provides the object exchange server. The IrMC client complies with the interoperability requirements that are defined for GOEP.

 NOTE

The IrDA specifications for Infrared Mobile Communications (IrMC) detail the methods used for exchange of data between telephony and mobile devices. This includes phone books, calendars, and messages.

In a typical synchronization model, the mobile phone functions like the IrMC server and the notebook serves as the IrMC client. The IrMC client pulls data from the IrMC server and synchronizes this data with the data stored in the IrMC client. The synchronized data is then returned to the IrMC server. The IrMC specifications define the IrMC client as an entity processing the synchronization, while the IrMC server is the server software.

Fundamental Features

The features of the Synchronization Profile define the following usage scenarios:

◆ The IrMC server can be used by the IrMC client to pull the PIM data that needs to be synchronized with the data on the IrMC client.

◆ The IrMC client can be used by the IrMC server to initiate previous scenarios by sending a sync command to the IrMC client.

◆ Automatic synchronization can also be initiated by the IrMC client.

The fundamental features of the Synchronization Profile are the same as that of GOEP. In addition, bonding, link level authentication, and encryption should be used for this profile. OBEX authentication is implemented at the application level and is supported by all devices of this profile. Both the IrMC client and server can act as clients and can also create physical links between the devices. The IrMC server or client does not need to move into the discoverable or connectable modes without any user interaction.

The User Interface

The specifications for the user interface are as follows:

◆ **Mode selection.** The two modes that are associated with this profile include the *Initialization sync* mode and the *General sync* mode. In the Initialization sync mode, the IrMC server is in the limited discoverable, connectable, and pairable modes. The IrMC client does not enter into these modes, but uses the limited discovery procedures to discover the IrMC server. In the General sync mode the IrMC server is in the connectable mode. In this mode, the IrMC server connects to the IrMC client and initiates the synchronization procedure after pairing.

◆ **Application usage.** The various scenarios for Synchronization and the Automatic Synchronization are determined by user interactions.

The Application Layer

The service capabilities of the application layer requires both the IrMC server and client to mandate support for the following synchronization scenarios:

◆ Synchronization of phonebooks
◆ Synchronization of calendars
◆ Synchronization of messages
◆ Synchronization of notes

It is also mandatory for the IrMC client to support the Sync command and optionally support the Automatic Synchronization. On the other hand, it is mandatory for the IrMC server to support the Automatic Synchronization and optionally support the Sync command. Table 8-13 lists the features of the application layer for the Synchronization Profile as sourced from the Bluetooth Profile specification 1.0.

Table 8-13 The Features of the Application Layer for the Synchronization Profile

Feature	Support in the IrMC Client	Support in the IrMC Server
Synchronization for one or more of the following	M	M
Synchronization of phonebooks		
Synchronization of calendars		
Synchronization of messages		
Synchronization of notes		
Sync command	M	O
Automatic Synchronization	O	M

The application level interoperability is maintained by defining content formats that are dependent on the application classes. The data stores present in the SDDB of the IrMC server identify the application classes supported by this profile.

The use of the Sync commands helps the IrMC client to temporarily function as the server. Similarly, the IrMC server receives the Sync command after which it temporarily functions like the IrMC client. After sending the Sync command and receiving an appropriate response, the IrMC server terminates the OBEX session and the RFCOMM data link connection.

The IrMC client initiates the synchronization process in the Automatic Synchronization, after the IrMC server enters the RF proximity of the IrMC client. As a result, at the baseband level, the IrMC client sends a page to the IrMC server at regular intervals and begins synchronization when it finds the IrMC server in its range. The support for automatic synchronization is optional for the IrMC client but mandatory for the IrMC server.

Interoperability Requirements

The six mandatory OBEX operations used in the Object Push Profile include Connect, Disconnect, Put, Get, Abort, and SetPath. The Synchronization Profile supports OBEX authentication. Table 8-14 lists the OBEX operation for the Synchronization Profile as sourced from the Bluetooth Profile specification 1.0.

Table 8-14 The OBEX Operation for the Synchronization Profile

OBEX Operation	Ability to Send (IrMC client)	Ability to Send (IrMC server)	Ability to Respond (IrMC client)	Ability to Respond (IrMC server)
Connect	M	O	M	M
Disconnect	M	O	M	M
Put	M	O	M	M
Get	M	X	X	M
Abort	M	O	M	M
SetPath	X	X	X	X

Summary

The usage profiles enable the implementation of the Bluetooth profiles in wireless scenarios. Just like the fundamental profiles, the usage profiles also ensure interoperability between devices from different manufacturers through a set of well-defined and standardized high-layer procedures that facilitate use of the lower layers of the Bluetooth protocol stack.

In this chapter, you learned about the nine usage profiles of the Bluetooth specification. Each of the profiles discussed in the chapter was define in terms of its fundamental features and the interoperability requirements.

The Bluetooth specification has helped to develop products for convenient, reliable, cost- and power-effective data communications. The volume 2 of the specification strengthens the applicability of the Bluetooth technology by defining profiles that describe the Bluetooth-enabled applications. The specification 1.0 also did initiate work on more profiles that were added to the next version. The specification 2.0 will, therefore, mentions new profiles that can be used in applications developed for homes and offices.

Check Your Understanding

Multiple Choice Questions

1. State whether the following statements are true or false.
   a. The two device roles defined for the Cordless Telephony Profile are the gateway and terminal.
   b. The CC states of TCS are park, unpark, sniff, and null modes.
   c. LAP is the device role for the Intercom Profile.

2. Which of the following are the call control TCS-BIN procedures for the Intercom Profile?
   a. Channel types
   b. Call clearing
   c. Call request
   d. Call confirmation
   e. In-band tones and announcements
   f. Call connection

3. Which of the following are the device roles for the Fax Profile?
   a. Client and server
   b. Audio gateway and headset
   c. Gateway and data terminal
   d. IrMC client and server

Short Questions

1. Define call request, call connection, call confirmation, and call clearing.
2. Define the roles of the IrMC client and server.
3. Define the roles of the client and server in the File Transfer Profile.

Answers

Multiple Choice Answers

1. a. True
    b. False
    c. False

2. b, c, d, and f. Call clearing, Call request, Call confirmation, and Call connection.
3. b. The gateway and data terminal.

Short Answers

1. The definitions for the call control terminologies are:

    ◆ **Call request.** A connection-oriented L2CAP channel is established between the devices before a request for an intercom call is made.

    ◆ **Call connection.** The mandatory SCO link establishment sub-procedure should be initiated before sending a CONNECT. The speech path between the units is connected only after receipt of CONNECT, or CONNECT ACKNOWLEDGE.

    ◆ **Call Confirmation.** When an incoming external call delivers the SETUP message on a connection channel, the incoming unit accepting the call should acknowledge the message by executing the call confirmation procedure.

    ◆ **Call clearing.** The call clearing procedures facilitate the release of the SCO connection by the lower protocol layers.

2. The roles of the IrMC client and server ca be defined as:

    ◆ **IrMC client.** This is the device, more specifically the PC, that pulls the PIM data to and from the IrMC server. The IrMC server complies with the interoperability requirements that are defined for GOEP.

    ◆ **IrMC server.** This is the device, more specifically the mobile phone or PDA, that provides an object exchange server. The IrMC client complies with the interoperability requirements that are defined for GOEP.

3. The roles of the client and server in the File Transfer Profile can be defined as:

    ◆ **Client.** The client device is the initiator of the operations that pushes or pulls objects to and from a server. It is mandatory for the client to comply with all interoperability requirements specified for the client of GOEP.

◆ **Server.** The server device is the target device that provides the exchange service so that objects can be pushed to or pulled from it. It is mandatory for the server to comply with all interoperability requirements specified for the server of GOEP.

Chapter 9

Bluetooth Security

The importance of security need not be emphasized. In the context of technology, more so in the world of computers, security implementations prevent unauthorized access to documents and networks. You'll agree that integrity and authenticity of transmitted data is of utmost importance in networking. The transmitted data traverses through numerous nodes and over vast distances before it reaches the intended destination. As a result, the risk of pilferage of vital and confidential data is increased. Network security models ensure safe transmission of data over intranets and the Internet. But what about security measures in the latest wireless communications?

Bluetooth technology does provide for a convenient mode of non-wired communication with unparalleled freedom of connectivity. The universal accessibility of Bluetooth-enabled devices adds to the possibility of security breaches and unauthorized access to confidential data. Many of the envisioned usage models of Bluetooth enable transfer of files, audio, videos, and business cards between disparate devices. Security in wireless communications is therefore an area of concern, which if not addressed can impede the mass adoption of this revolutionary technology.

This chapter discusses the security measures that are implemented in the Bluetooth to ensure the integrity and authenticity of transmitted data. However, before discussing security in the Bluetooth perspective, the initial sections of the chapter discuss the various modes of security implementations in the distributed technologies of the Internet and WAP.

Security in Distributed Technologies

Distributed systems consist of objects (represented by computers) scattered across different locations. As a result, threats to security of transmitted information exist in the form of disclosure threats due to unauthorized leakage of information, or integrity threats due to manipulation of data to alter the information, or denial of service threats that prevent access to a system. In this context, it's important to understand the mechanisms used for security implementation in the distributed systems of the Internet and WAP.

The Internet brought in the concept of information availability at anytime and anywhere. Information availability was further strengthened with the introduction of wireless communication using the *Wireless Application Protocol* (WAP) in mobile devices such as cellular phones, laptops, and PDAs. Next in the line is the facilitation of wireless communication between disparate devices using the Bluetooth technology. Although these three technologies are not parallel they do illustrate the application of distributed systems. This chapter, therefore, begins with a brief description on the models used for implementation of security in the Internet and WAP technology.

The Internet Security Model

With the increase in the popularity of the Internet, powerful solutions for the implementation of security were sought. However, it was only in the mid-90s that intense research led to a major breakthrough in security implementation, by using the mechanism of *Secure Sockets Layer* (SSL). SSL by itself is a topic beyond the scope of this book. However, to understand the basics of SSL, let's look at its role in a request-response cycle. When the browser requests a Web connection, the idea is to procure a connection that is secure and shielded from security threats. The server provides the browser with its server certificate, the validity of which is authenticated by the browser. The browser sends an encrypted shared secret key to the server that is used to encrypt the rest of the information, thereby making it inaccessible to threats. The SSL mode of security implementation provides a base for the *Wireless Transport Layer Security* (WTLS) favored by WAP applications.

The WAP Security Model

WAP is a communication protocol that connects wireless devices such as mobile phones, *Personal Data Assistants* (PDAs), and two-way pagers to the Internet. The WAP security model is based partly on SSL implementation and partly on WTLS implementation. The access to the information on the Internet calls for the implementation of the SSL model to ensure security of the transmitted data in WAP. Similarly, WTLS implementation ensures efficient and judicious use of power and memory in the small handheld devices without compromising on security issues.

The WAP security model includes a software component or the WAP Gateway that demarcates the functional areas of SSL and WTLS. The device communications over the wireless network are routed through the gateway using WTLS and the subsequent connection with the Web server is enabled using SSL. WTLS implementation enables super-secure transactions between devices by minimizing protocol overheads, using better compression techniques, and employing efficient encryption methods. The WTLS protocol layer and its functions were discussed in Chapter 3, "Architecture of Bluetooth."

After discussing the alternate and parallel mechanisms adopted for implementation of security in distributed systems, this chapter discusses the procedures used in Bluetooth to ensure secure transmission of data over Bluetooth links. However, Bluetooth connections form ad hoc networks, therefore the security issues faced by ad hoc networks are discussed first.

Security in Ad Hoc Networks

The concept of ad hoc networks in wireless communications facilitated impromptu connectivity between devices by eliminating the need for a fixed infrastructure. Individual devices in ad hoc networks function as routers relaying messages between devices that are separated by long distances. The topology of the network keeps changing with the change in connections that makes these networks vulnerable to attacks and security breaches. The key issues faced for security implementation in ad hoc networks include the following:

♦ The availability of devices for connectivity at all times is a non-essential factor of traditional networks. However, in ad hoc networks connections are impromptu and, therefore, availability is an important issue. In this context, routing protocols are the weakest and most vulnerable points in an ad hoc network.

♦ With the absence of a fixed infrastructure, users cannot be identified easily and this leads to issues concerned with user authorization. The genuineness of the user can be affirmed by good authentication mechanisms.

♦ Maintaining data confidentiality and integrity is another issue addressed by the use of encryption techniques. It is interesting to note that confidentiality of data is pointless in the absence of authentication. After all, you need to know whom you are connecting to before you talk or exchange information.

Bluetooth technology connects disparate devices and in the process, creates ad hoc networks called piconets or scatternets. The communication environment in Bluetooth is peer-to-peer facilitating data transmission over short distances. As a result, the security measures are implemented such that they are favorable for such an environment. You'll realize by the end of the chapter that security procedures in Bluetooth are actually implemented in the same way.

Bluetooth Security

Wired connections between devices are inherently secure due to the connecting cables. However, in the case of wireless communication, the air interface provides an open ground for unauthorized access to data. The Bluetooth specification defines various levels of security implementation to promote usage protection and information confidentiality. The security implementation is provided at the Application layer and the Link layer.

Every Bluetooth device uses a public address, two secret keys, and a randomly generated number to maintain link-level security. The two secret keys are confidential keys generated during the initialization process and are never disclosed. The detail of the four parameters used for maintaining link-level security is as follows:

♦ **The Bluetooth Device Address (BD_ADDR).** This is a 48-bit unique address defined and allocated by the Institute of Electronic and Electrical Engineers (IEEE). The BD_ADDR can be obtained publicly through Man Machine Interface (MMI) interactions, or automatically, during an inquiry process.

♦ **A private authentication key.** This is a 128-bit random number used as the secret key during device authentication.

♦ **A private encryption key.** This is 8 to128 bits in length and used as the secret key during encryption.

♦ **A random number (RAND).** This is a frequently changing 128-bit number generated by a pseudo-random process in the Bluetooth device.

The link level security parameters are used in the following security mechanisms:

- ◆ Random number generation
- ◆ Key management
- ◆ Device authentication
- ◆ Packet encryption

Random Number Generation

The random number generated by the random number generator in a Bluetooth device is used for security implementations for the creation of the authentication and encryption keys, or for drawing up the challenge-response scheme. The numbers used for security purposes are generated randomly and are non-repeating. Therefore, these numbers are not static, less predictable, and also do not repeat within the lifetime of an authentication key.

Key Management

Key management, more specifically link key management, defines an important aspect of security implementation between two Bluetooth devices. The link key can be a temporary key or semi-permanent key derived from a 128-bit random number and is used during the process of authentication and encryption. During authentication, the link key is used as an authentication key to verify the identity of Bluetooth devices. During encryption, the link key is also used as a parameter to derive the value of the encryption key.

A semi-permanent link key is stored in the non-volatile memory and can be used at the end of a current session to authenticate Bluetooth devices that share the same key. A temporary link key, on the other hand, is that which lasts only till the termination of a session and cannot be used thereafter. Temporary keys are used in point-to-multipoint connections to transmit the same data to multiple recipients.

The four different types of link keys that are used to ensure secure data transmission between devices include the following:

- ◆ The unit key (K_A) is a semi-permanent key that is generated in a single device during installation and rarely changed thereafter. The E21 key-generating algorithm is used to generate the unit key when a device functions or operates for the first time. A communicating device can use another device's unit key as a link key. Figure 9-1 illustrates the E21 algorithm that is used to generate both the unit and the combination keys.

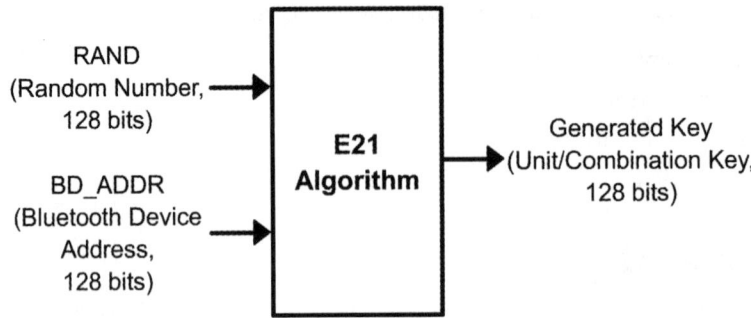

FIGURE 9-1 *The E21 algorithm for generating the unit and combination keys*

◆ The `combination key` (`KAB`) is created in the absence of a common link key, at the end of the pairing process by using the E21 algorithm. The random number and the 48-bit *Personal Identification Number* (PIN) from two devices are used to derive the combination key. As a result, this key is dependent on parameters from two units and is, therefore, derived for each new combination of Bluetooth devices.

 NOTE

The `PIN` code in Bluetooth devices is a short string of numbers, normally 4 digits in length, but can also vary from 1 to 16 octets. The `PIN` can either be a fixed number or can be selected by the user arbitrarily. If selected by the user, the `PIN` is entered in the two devices and then matched. The process of manually entering the `PIN` is safer and more secure than using a fixed `PIN`. A default value of zero is used if no `PIN` is available. However, if the length of the `PIN` code is long, exchange of the `PIN` between the two devices should use an application layer-based software support rather than the mechanical means of MMI interactions.

◆ The `master key` (K$_{master}$) is a temporary key that is used to replace the link key. The master key is used for point-to-multipoint communications when the master device wants to transmit information to more than two Bluetooth devices. The master device uses the E22 algorithm with two 128-bit random numbers to generate the master key. Figure 9-2 illustrates the E22 algorithm that is used to generate both the master and the initialization keys.

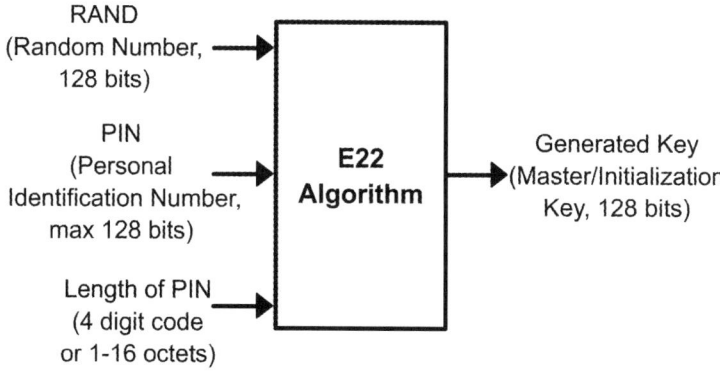

FIGURE 9-2 *The E22 algorithm for generating the master and initialization keys*

◆ The `initialization key` (`Kinit`) is used during initialization in the absence of a link or combination key. This key is used for a single session and created each time a unit is initialized. It protects the exchange of initialization parameters between devices. The E22 algorithm is used to generate the initialization key. The initialization key is derived from input parameters that include the `PIN` code, the `BD_ADDR`, length of `PIN`, and a 128-bit random number generated by the verifier. The initialization key thus created is used by both the devices for preliminary authentication prior to the generation of a permanent link key and discarded later on.

The initialization key is used to generate the current link key that is used for authenticating devices and also for the generation of the encryption key. An important aspect of key management involves setting up of the initialization key. During the initialization process, communicating devices exchange the initialization key. This phase or the initialization phase is implemented separately for units that want to implement authentication and encryption. The initialization process consists of the following five phases:

◆ Generation of the initialization key
◆ Authentication
◆ Generation of the link key
◆ Exchange of link keys
◆ Generation of the encryption key

At the end of initialization, the devices can communicate and exchange data. The process of generation of the link key was discussed in Chapter 5 "Link Manager Protocol." Therefore, I'll move on to discussing the events that take place during the processes of authentication and encryption.

Authentication in Bluetooth

The schema used for authentication in Bluetooth is based on the challenge-response strategy. The basis for the authentication is to check whether the other device has the same secret key. The secret key can either be a fixed key or a derived key. A fixed secret key is built in by the manufacturer while a derived secret key can be a link key or a key derived from the PIN code and a variable key. Authentication is successful if the keys of two devices are identical. The process of authentications consists of the following three stages:

1. The verifier sends a random number (the challenge or the AU_RAND$_A$) with the authentication code to the claimant for authentication.

2. The verifier and the claimant use the authentication function E1 along with the RAND, the claimant's BD_ADDR, and the current link key to generate a response (SRES).

3. The claimant sends the response (SRES) to the verifier to match its response (SRES).

It is not always that at the end of the verification the verifier becomes the master device. Often during a one-way authentication, the application decides on the device to be authenticated. If authentication fails, a new attempt at authentication is made only after the passage of a time period known as the *waiting period*. The duration of the waiting period depends on the results of previous authentication attempts. Figure 9-3 illustrates the process of authentication that takes place between two devices before a connection is set up.

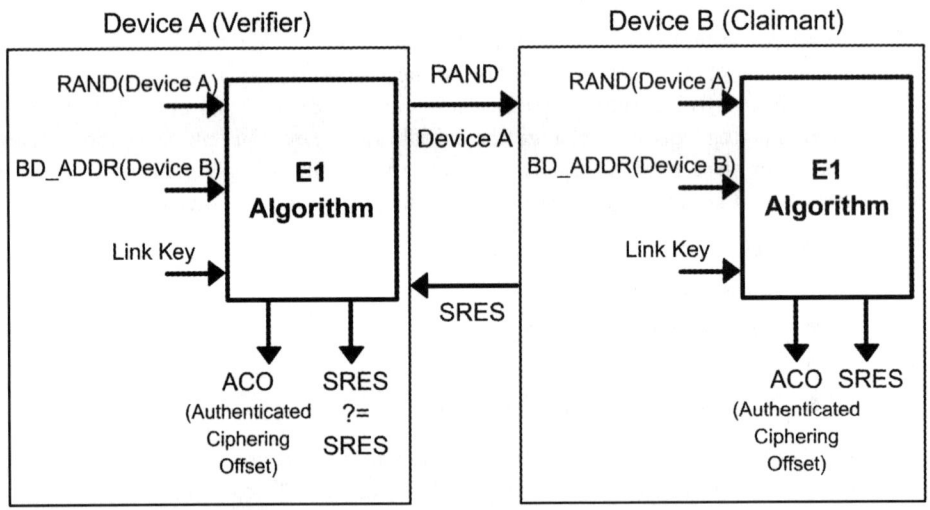

FIGURE 9-3 *The authentication process*

During authentication, the 128-bit unit key of each device that is stored in the non-volatile memory of the device is derived from the 128-bit RAND and the 48-bit address by using the mode 1 of the E2 algorithm. The unit key is used to generate the link key in the following two ways:

◆ If one of the two devices has limited memory, the unit of that device is encrypted with the initialization key to derive the link key.

◆ If both the devices agree upon a common key, the combination key is used to generate the link key. For this, both the devices independently generate a 128-bit random number using the E21 algorithm. The two random numbers are exchanged by encrypting them with the initialization key. The random number of the remote device is then XORed with that of the device to generate the link key. The initialization key is discarded after the generation of the link key.

 NOTE

The E algorithms are created by the system using the *Linear Feedback Shift Registers* (LFSRs). The output of the LFSR is combined with 16 states by using a simple finite state machine, which is called the *summation combiner*. The output of the summation combiner consists of the key stream sequence. During the initialization phase, the output of the summation combiner consists of the randomized initial start value. The algorithm is provided with an encryption key (K_C), a 48-bit Bluetooth address, the master clock bits CLK_{26-1}, and a 128-bit RAND value.

During authentication, the E1 algorithm is used to generate an Authenticated Ciphering Offset (ACO) that is stored in both the devices. This ACO value is indirectly used to generate the encryption key. The Link Manager Protocol (LMP) initiates encryption after a successful authentication between devices.

Encryption in Bluetooth

The process of encryption is initiated after authenticating the devices. As a result, in the interim the devices agree upon a link key. The encryption key is derived from the current link key, a 96-bit *Ciphering Offset number* (COF), and a 128-bit random number by using the E3 algorithm. The COF derivation is based on the type of the current link key. If the current link key is a master key, the COF is derived from the BD_ADDR of the master. On the other hand, if the link key is a unit key or a combination key, the value of COF is set to the ACO value that is calculated during authentication.

During encryption, the payloads of the packets are systematically encrypted into an unreadable format. For this, a stream cipher E0 is re-synchronized for each payload. The stream cipher consists of the following three parts:

◆ **The payload key generator.** The payload generator generates the payload key by combining the input bits in an appropriate order. After this the input bits are shifted to the four Linear Feedback Shift Registers (LSFRs) of the key stream generator.

◆ **The key stream generator.** The key stream generator is the main part of the cipher system that generates the key stream bits. A method derived by Massey and Rupel from the summation stream cipher generator is used to generate the key stream bits.

◆ **The encryption/decryption part.** The encryption/decryption parties are responsible for the encryption and decryption of the stream bits.

The encryption modes depend on the type of key used. As a result, in the case of a semi-permanent link key either a unit key, a combination key, or a master key is used for encryption. If the key used is a unit key or combination key, broadcast traffic is not encrypted. In addition, individually addressed point-to-point traffic can or cannot be encrypted. On the other hand, if the key used is a master key, the following three modes of encryption are used:

◆ **Encryption mode 1.** In this mode, nothing is encrypted.

◆ **Encryption mode 2.** In this mode, broadcast traffic is not encrypted. However, the master key is used to encrypt the individually addressed traffic.

◆ **Encryption mode 3.** In this mode, the master key is used to encrypt all traffic.

The encryption key used during the process of encryption is derived from the current link key and varies from 8 bits to 128 bits. Due to the varying size of the encryption key, communicating devices need to negotiate and arrive at an agreement regarding the size of the encryption key.

Negotiating the Size of the Encryption Key

The master and the slave devices propose, accept, or reject the suggestions for the size of the encryption key. Each device has a parameter that defines the maximum and the minimum length of the encryption key. During negotiations, the master device sends a suggestion for the size of the encryption key. The slave is at liberty to accept or reject the master's suggestion. A rejection from the slave device is followed by another key size suggestion from the slave to the master. This process continues till both the master and the slave reach a consensus about the size of the encryption key.

A key size that is less than the minimum set value results in the abortion of the negotiation and encryption is not performed. Malicious users use this parameter to force a device to choose a key size that is less than the predefined minimum size parameter so that encryption is abandoned. The procedure of encryption key size determination is discussed in Chapter 5.

The encryption key is generated each time a device enters the encryption mode. This encryption key generated by the E3 algorithm is used indirectly to encrypt data. This encryption key is actually used with the E0 algorithm to generate another key. The E0 algorithm uses the clock information of the transmitting device to generate the new encryption key. Figure 9-4 illustrates the process of encryption that takes place between two devices.

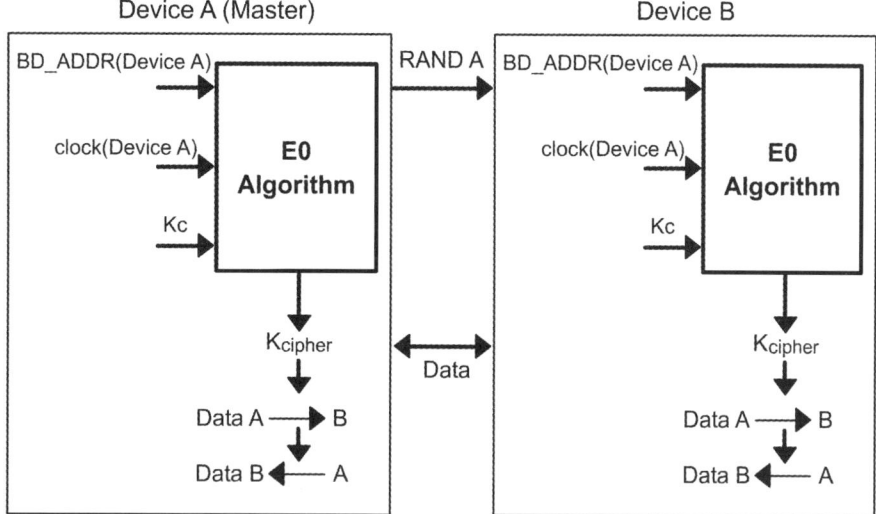

FIGURE 9-4 *The encryption process*

All through this chapter the processes of key management, authentication, and encryption use the E algorithms. Therefore, before ending the discussion on Bluetooth security implementation, I would like to tabulate the various algorithms used for security implementation in Bluetooth. Table 9-1 lists these E algorithms.

Table 9-1 The E Algorithms Used for Security Implementations in Bluetooth

Algorithm	Usage
E0	To create and apply the cipher stream to the bit stream data
E1	Used to encrypt and validate the keys generated by the E2 algorithm during the authentication process
E2	Creates keys used by the E1 algorithm for the generation of the authentication key. Depending on the key to be generated, the following two operational modes are used:
E21	Creates unit keys and combination keys by using a 48-bit **BD_ADDR**
E22	Creates initialization keys and the master key by using the user-supplied **PIN** code.
E3	Generates the ciphering key used by the E0 algorithm

The process of authentication and encryption does ensure security of transmitted data, but the architecture of Bluetooth has ample loopholes that can still be exploited. One such not-so-easy-to-implement loophole that is observed in most devices that rely upon key exchange systems is the stealing of identification and encryption keys. Being in its early stages of deployment, Bluetooth can conquer this weakness by supporting an authentication system that is based on digital certificates. A digital certificate is an electronic documentation similar to identification cards that is used for online verifications of individuals, organizations, and computers. Similarly, locking to device signals can be prevented by the use of unpredictable hopping patterns and intervals.

Bluetooth does require some serious security support that can implement security at higher levels. The Bluetooth SIG security white paper has documented suggestions for the implementation of security at higher levels that is based on the mode 2 security. The security architecture suggests that the implementation of security at higher levels can be achieved by the use of two databases—one to contain information about the authenticity and authorization of devices and the other to contain information about the required services. However, continuous endeavors of the SIG will surely ensure better and secure devices in the market in the years to come. For now, the current security implementations seem to be in control of the situations. So, intruders beware, Bluetooth data during transmission is a hard nut to crack.

Summary

Security is the stronghold of any technology. It is not surprising that the success of Bluetooth also depends on the security implementations to ensure that data traffic exchanged between devices is not violated. It is obvious that aided with the current security implementations, Bluetooth devices are in a position to transmit confidential data. However, these implementations are useful in small ad hoc networks such as that in a meeting. The advanced security implementation required in larger networks for money transfers and e-commerce transactions is an area that is still untouched. Despite all the hue and cry that put down Bluetooth security as a disaster area, security implementation in smaller Bluetooth networks is second to none. The SIG is on a wait and watch policy for stronger security recommendations.

In this chapter, you learned about the security implementations in Bluetooth that ensure that the transmitted data is received without any alterations. The security implementations at link level include the process of device authentication and data encryption. During authentication, a secret key is used to check and confirm the validity of the connecting device. After authentication, the devices use the link key to encrypt outgoing traffic on a link. The incoming traffic is decrypted at the receiver end. As a result, the data traffic is shielded from malicious attacks.

The Bluetooth security procedures ensure that only authorized and authenticated users are allowed to connect. Therefore, you know exactly whom you are talking to or who's accessing data on your device. Similarly, encryption codes the data into an unreadable format so that eavesdroppers have a hard time trying to make sense out of the transmitted data. For the time being the slow introduction of the devices seems like a boon in disguise. But Bluetooth security is an issue that will have to be addressed so that it is adequate for the transmission of highly confidential and sensitive data.

Check Your Understanding

Multiple Choice Questions

1. State whether the following statements are true or false.

   a. The WAP security model is based on the SSL mechanism.

   b. Every Bluetooth device uses a public address, three secret keys, and a randomly generated number to maintain link level security.

   c. The vulnerability of security breaches is higher in ad hoc networks.

2. Which of the following are used as parameters for implementing link level security in Bluetooth?

   a. The BD_ADDR

   b. The RAND

   c. The combination key

   d. The private authentication key

   e. An encryption key

   f. The current link key

3. Which of the following are the types of link keys created during security implementation in Bluetooth?

   a. The private authentication key

   b. The initialization key

   c. The unit key

   d. The combination key

   e. An encryption key

   f. The master key

4. Which of the following parameters are used to create the combination key?

   a. The private authentication key

   b. The BD_ADDR

   c. The RAND

   d. The K_{init}

   e. The PIN

5. Which of the following algorithms are used for the generation of the encryption key?

   a. The E0 algorithm

   b. The E21 algorithm

c. The E22 algorithm

d. The E3 algorithm

e. The E1 algorithm

Short Questions

1. List the three stages of the authentication procedure in Bluetooth.

2. Discuss the functions of the three parts of the cipher stream used for encryption of data.

3. Write short notes on:

    a. Random number generation

    b. The PIN in Bluetooth

Answers

Multiple Choice Answers

1. a. False
    b. False
    c. True

2. a, b, d, and e. The BD_ADDR, RAND, private authentication key, and an encryption key.

3. b, c, e, and f. The initialization key, unit key, combination key, and master key.

4. c and e. the RAND and the PIN.

5. a and d. The E0 and the E3 algorithms.

Short Answers

1. The three stages of the authentication procedure in Bluetooth include:

    The verifier sends a random number (the challenge or the AU_RAND$_A$) with the authentication code to the claimant for authentication.

    The verifier and the claimant use the authentication function E1 along with the RAND, the claimant's BD_ADDR, and the current link key to generate a response (SRES).

    The claimant sends the response (SRES) to the verifier to match its response (SRES).

2. The functions of the three parts of the cipher stream are:

    ◆ **The payload key generator.** The payload generator generates the payload key by combining the input bits in an appropriate order.

    ◆ **The key stream generator.** The key stream generator is the main part of the cipher system that generates the key stream bits. A method derived by Massey and Rupel from the summation stream cipher generator is used to generate the key stream bits.

    ◆ **The encryption/decryption part.** The encryption/decryption parties are responsible for the encryption and decryption of the stream bits.

3. a. The random number generated by the random number generator in a Bluetooth device is used for security implementations for the creation of the authentication and encryption keys, or for drawing up the challenge-response scheme. The numbers used for security purposes are generated randomly and are non-repeating. Therefore, these numbers are not static, less predictable, and also do not repeat within the lifetime of an authentication key.

b. The Personal Identification Number (PIN) in Bluetooth devices is a short string of numbers, normally 4 digits in length, which can vary from 1 to 16 octets. The `PIN` can either be a fixed number or can be selected by the user arbitrarily. If selected by the user, the `PIN` is entered in the two devices and then matched. As a result, manually entering the `PIN` is safer and more secure than using a fixed `PIN`. A default value of zero is used if no `PIN` is available. However, if the length of the `PIN` code is long, exchange the `PIN` of the two devices should use an application layer-based software support rather than the mechanical means of MMI interactions.

PART III

Bluetooth—
The Present and
The Future

Chapter 10

**Bluetooth
Potential**

Bluetooth guarantees high-speed wireless technology aimed to connect heterogeneous devices, such as mobile phones, laptops, PDAs, and other portable equipment with negligible user intervention. The current prototype circuit or the Bluetooth module can be either built into electronic devices or used as an adaptor (externally attached via the USB port) to provide a 1 Mbps link (up to 2 Mbps in the second generation of the technology) within the range of 10 cm and 100 m. As a result, one can predict a tremendous potential for this technology that provides convenient connections devoid of cumbersome wires at a cost that varies from $20.00 initially to $5.00 in a year or two, which is far lower than that of other equivalent and competing technologies.

Considering that Bluetooth is all set to hit the market and change our lives in the next few years, this chapter discusses the potential of the much-hyped Bluetooth wireless technology. This chapter begins with an insight into the challenges faced by this new technology. Next, it discusses the market expectations and developments that without a doubt will lead to further technological improvisations and open up new avenues for the implementation of Bluetooth.

The Initial Phase

As with any revolutionary technology, there is tremendous pressure and high expectations from the market. The homes of tomorrow will be able to boast of smart devices that are able to communicate with each other. What we are talking about here is a technology that will enable communication between devices as diverse as refrigerators, microwave ovens, and supermarket computer terminals. For example, can you visualize the relief at the thought that you no longer have to worry about the depleting supplies in your refrigerator? Bluetooth-enabled refrigerators will not only be able to check on low running supplies, but also will be able to contact the local supermarket to place an order to replenish the stock-level of specific items. Yes, that's exactly what I mean by the technological revolution brought about by Bluetooth. And it's not only homes that this technology is all set to revolutionize, but offices and day-to-day life too.

The low-complexity, robust, low-power, and low-cost features of the Bluetooth technology add up to tremendous market credit and interest each month. If analyst projections are to be believed, as many as a billion Bluetooth devices will enter the market in the next few years. Figure 10-1 illustrates the forecast for the sale and use of Bluetooth devices by 2006 as obtained from the online Bluetooth Industry Survey conducted at `www.arc-group.com` from May 15–21, 2001.

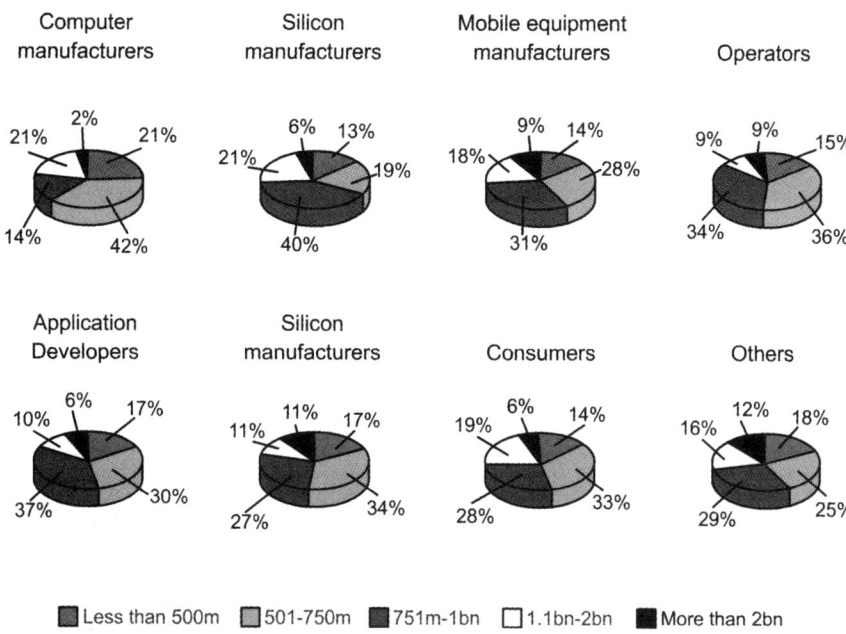

FIGURE 10-1 *The forecast for the global use of Bluetooth devices by 2006*

The fact that Bluetooth is all set to revolutionize connectivity in the near future is evident from the result depicted in Figure 10-2.

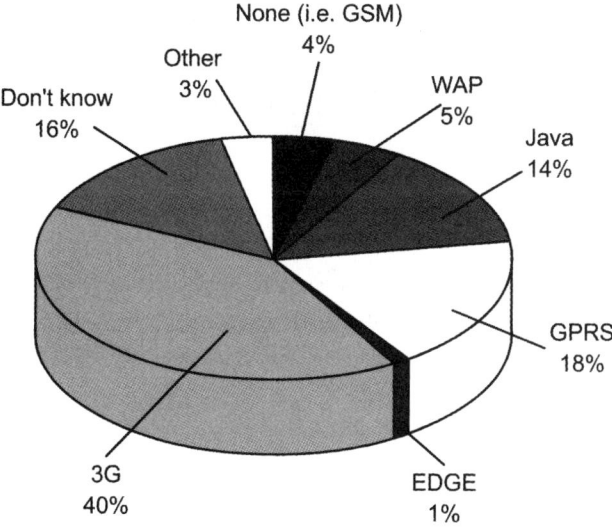

FIGURE 10-2 *The forecast for upcoming technologies created with Bluetooth*

In addition to system and technical challenges, Bluetooth is also pitted against two major non-technological concerns—excessive hype and corporate greed. These factors, by themselves, have weighed heavily against the technology. The fact that Bluetooth exudes potential in the future as an up-and-coming technology is the very basis for corporate greed.

In the early years, when Bluetooth technology was still in its inception, standardization was foreseen as the only way to ensure that the technology developed in the right direction. As a result, it was fruitless to have companies with an interest in the technology work separately with different standards and specifications leading to non-compatible market competition and loss of cross-operability. This was the very reason that initiated the formation of the Special Interest Group (SIG) by stalwarts of the computing and telecom industry. Others, such as Toshiba, 3Com, Motorola, and Lucent, joined the original members of the SIG later. The corporate greed to take the onus for the growth and forecasted potential of the Bluetooth technology became apparent from the initial much-publicized reluctance of Microsoft to join the SIG. The point of disagreement developed over the SIG-initiated rule that required the joining members to give up intellectual property rights to the technology developed by Bluetooth. In addition, during the time of its creation, the initial five members of the SIG (Ericsson, IBM, Intel, Toshiba, and Nokia) were used to accepting a 4-1 vote favoring a change in the specification. Microsoft wanted this precedent to be changed so that changes in the specifications could be made only if all the members consented to the change. Nevertheless, in keeping with the intent behind the favorite Shakespeare line, "All's well that end's well," Microsoft today is very much a part of the SIG.

That is just one of the challenges Bluetooth has to stand against. The others are the system and technical challenges that need to be appeased to ensure that Bluetooth devices are able to sustain themselves in and continue to rule the market.

The System and the Technical Challenges

Although Bluetooth was originally conceived to connect laptops, computers, and cellular phones, it was soon evident that this technology could take wireless communication to new heights by interconnecting a variety of equipment and devices. As a result, keeping in mind the growing expanse of Bluetooth implementation, it was important that this technology overcame all the system and technological limitations. The next sections look at the system and technical requirements that were addressed to ensure device functionality within the diversity of usage models.

System Challenges

Bluetooth has crossed over from being a mere cable replacement technology. The areas of Bluetooth implementation have grown and so has the pressure on system requirements. Following are a few system requirements necessary for the success of Bluetooth technology:

♦ The wireless link between the devices has to use a universal framework to enable a variety of devices to connect and exchange information.

♦ The connections between heterogeneous devices have to work within the functional capabilities of particular devices and also provide additional services from the collaboration between devices. For example, a connection between two devices has to use the inherent functions of each device by tuning to its individual capabilities in terms of its form, interface, cost, and the power. Besides the additional services resulting from the synergy of the collaboration has to be considered.

♦ The device connections have to be ad-hoc, or available at any time and anywhere. As a result, the devices within proximity can connect without having to undergo lengthy procedures involving user interaction.

♦ The standard specifications have to be open to introducing new usage models.

♦ Data security has to be maintained despite the switch in technology from cable connections to wireless connectivity.

Technical Challenges

Technical challenges involve complexity because they call for not only better functionality of the devices but also the efficient use of device size and battery power. The following are a few technical requirements necessary for the success of Bluetooth technology:

♦ The system has to be robust to handle interference from not only the royalty-free ISM band but also from interference arising from microwave ovens, which also use the ISM band. In addition, the transmitter has to use less power, ensuring that the device itself is not a source of noise for other devices.

♦ The intent of Bluetooth is to ensure connectivity at all times, which includes mobile connections. As a result, the transceiver has to be adaptable to both mobile and immobile environments. In the case of mobile connections, problems such as multi-path fading have to be addressed.

♦ The connectivity and routing protocols have to change according to the dynamic change in the number, the location, and the types of Bluetooth devices in an environment.

♦ The Bluetooth chip that holds the secret to wireless connectivity has to be small enough to be able to fit into small handheld and mobile devices.

♦ The power consumption has to be proportional to the capability of the host device into which the chip is fitted.

◆ Technological interoperability has to ensure that different types of devices with different power and memory resources can connect and exchange information.

◆ The connection between devices has to be automatic because of the change in the number and identity of proximal devices. Constant and frequent changes in the number and identity of the devices in the vicinity of each other otherwise calls for manual connections with the user having to remember or search for the other device's address.

◆ The confidentiality and integrity of the data exchanged between devices during a connection has to be secured. As a result, some form of encryption has to be used to provide data security.

◆ Bluetooth has to operate along with existing wireless services such as IrDA and OBEX. Interoperability with these and other such technologies would ensure the complete integration of Bluetooth with all classes of applications.

The Bluetooth specification 1.0B did address all these challenges, the result of which is quite evident from the popularity and interest that Bluetooth has created in the world of computing and telecommunications.

The following section touches upon the developments in the consumer electronics market. The discussion includes an insight into the market expectations and requirements in relation to the technology developments. As a result, you will be able to judge the proportionality of the market pull (requirements) to the market push (developments).

Comparing the Market Requirements and the Technological Developments

The industry has always performed according to the demand and supply phenomenon, which can be directly related to the market pull and push. It is this very phenomenon that initiated the concept of availability of information irrespective of time and location. The market pull for information availability at any time and anywhere was satisfied by the acceptance and growth of mobile telecommunications. There was also a simultaneous turn toward commercializing the potential of the Internet by promoting e-commerce. As a result, the next expectation from the market called for information availability on demand. Therefore, the introduction of Bluetooth-enabled devices will provide users with options to surf the Net for information and also trade, buy, or sell on the Net using the concept of e-cash.

The telecommunication industry is poised for the big event when services such as General Packet Radio Services (GPRS) and Enhanced Data Rate for GSM (EDGE) roll out with the first enhanced rate packet data services for customers. These two services, aptly called the 2.5-generation cellular services, are soon to be followed by the third-generation

Universal Mobile Telephony Services (UMTS) that provides a high data rate cellular WAN for voice and data. As a result, customers will be able to connect without any dial-up delay because the new generation services will operate at data rates of 144 kbps to 2 mbps and will totally support Internet multimedia traffic.

In keeping with these developments, the last paradigm of connectivity shapes up in the form of Bluetooth, which enables connectivity from the cellular terminal to mobile devices. A major competition that Bluetooth faces commercially is regarding its use. This assumption is based on the fact that most professionals, students, and people from various walks of life already use devices, such as PDAs or organizers, as information appliances. As a result, it is a bit too much to expect individuals to carry two devices for the same function. The great difference will come in the form of the wearable technology that will facilitate small Bluetooth devices fitting into accessories such as belts, earrings, and clips.

The developments in the cellular industry can simultaneously result in the cellular phone assuming the role of the information appliance that we now know as the smart phone. However, the chances of communication between this appliance and other devices such as PCs, headsets, handy cams, and printers are still grim. Bluetooth does stand a chance in this arena, because it does have the potential to quench this market requirement.

Market Segmentation

The mobile industry is already at the helm of its activity as the largest market segment in consumer electronics. However, with more appliances such as the headset, the mainstream customers will be segmented into the following three groups:

- **Mobile professionals.** The mobile professionals or the early adopters will pay for novel and convenient advancements in technology in the years to come. They will also contribute toward the demand for the evolution of better applications to facilitate mobile connectivity.

- **Business users.** The business users looking for the reliability and functional capability of applications will increase the volume of business. Bluetooth will definitely satisfy their business needs.

- **Home users.** The home users will initiate the new usage paradigm of Home Area Networking (HAN) only if Bluetooth is able to fit into the key performance parameters of ease of use, cost, and autonomy.

Keeping this segmentation in mind, it is obvious that ease of use, lower power consumption, and interoperability will provide Bluetooth with the advantage over all other competing technologies. Of these, interoperability is a major issue. It is obvious that with variations in market demands in terms of variety in choice and implementation, there will be different Bluetooth solutions from different vendors. As a result, the potential of Bluetooth will depend on guaranteed interoperability between heterogeneous devices. Bluetooth can learn from the drawbacks of IrDA to create applications that are able to work together in public domains.

The first two interops, or Un-plug fests (as they were called), to check for the level of interoperability in mid-1999 and early 2000s have shown a success rate of 70%. Studies have shown that Bluetooth will effortlessly gel with PAN, HAN, and also WLAN to offer better-integrated solutions. In the case of WLAN, there need not be a head-on technological collision, but Bluetooth can offer better printer- and disk-sharing options by providing small clustered inter-office piconets through LAN access points. Upcoming Bluetooth applications, including the single-chip, two-chip, and integrated modules along with products such as PC-based PCMCIA or USB adapters, cellular phone dongles, and headsets, will ensure a better generation of Bluetooth-enabled products and devices.

 NOTE

A dongle is a plug-in device that can be attached to a device externally. In the Bluetooth context, dongles can be used to exchange data between Bluetooth devices, access the Internet using Bluetooth access points on LANs, PSTNs, and ISDNs, and also synchronize heterogeneous devices inoerder to update address information.

Bluetooth will not only roll out a new range of products and applications but will also revolutionize networking. Before moving on, it's important to understand the trends and developments in the world of telecommunications after adapting to the wireless technology. The term "networking" is beginning to take a plunge into the newer concept of wireless connectivity. The next section looks at the advancements in the networking scene after the introduction of Bluetooth.

The Networking Scenarios

With the introduction of wireless technology, the networking scenarios will also be able to include wireless connectivity through modes such as Local Area Network (LAN) access, dial-up networking, small meetings, and ad-hoc mobile networking.

LAN Access

If you thought LAN access only catered to a wired mode for resource sharing, you're in for a surprise. LAN access can also be used without the hassles of connecting with wires in the following three modes:

◆ The first mode for LAN access uses a personal access point to access resources on the LAN, the Internet, and e-mail services. Such an access is a wireless access that provides freedom of movement within a specified radio range. Figure 10-3 illustrates LAN access that uses a personal access point.

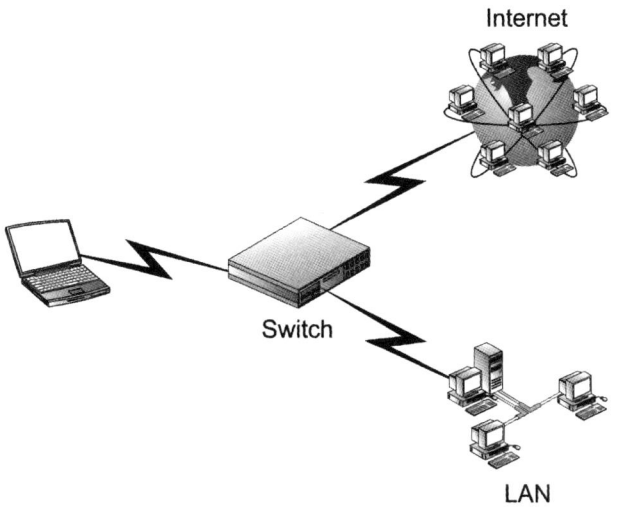

FIGURE 10-3 *LAN access through a personal access point*

◆ The second mode for LAN access uses a shared access point that is located within an organizational premise. It also facilitates access to the resources on the LAN, the Internet, and the e-mail services. This type of LAN access shares an access point and facilitates access to wireless users. Figure 10-4 illustrates LAN access that uses a shared access point.

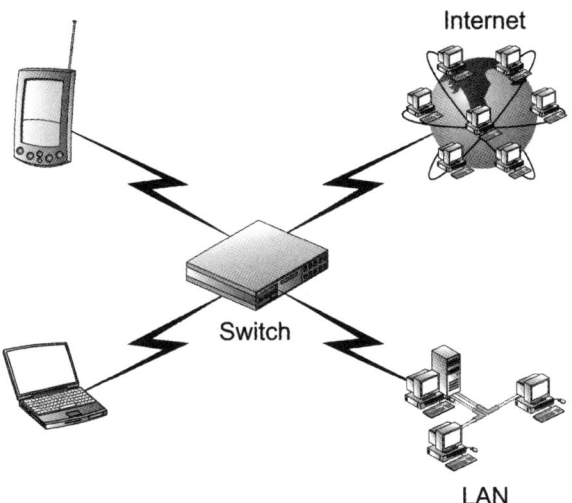

FIGURE 10-4 *LAN access through a shared access point*

◆ The third mode for LAN access uses public access points to provide services such as details about e-mail providers and flight departure information. Such LAN access points are situated in public places providing wireless access to information. Figure 10-5 illustrates LAN access that uses public access points for connectivity.

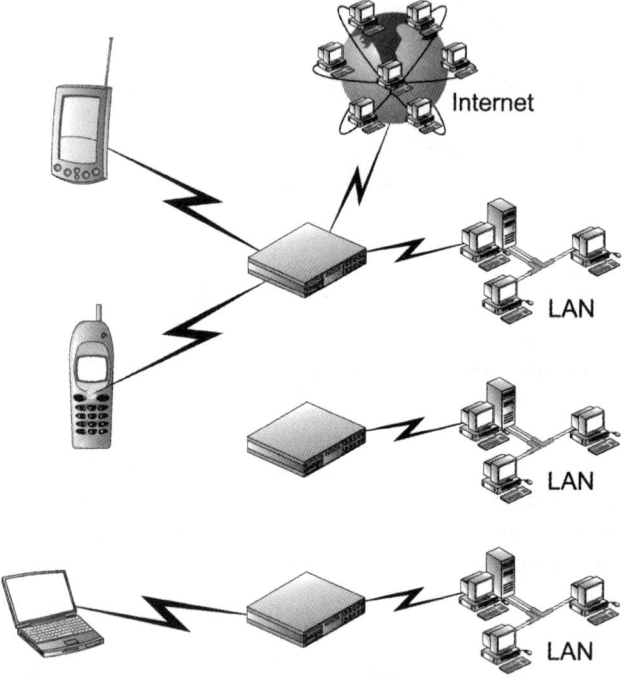

FIGURE 10-5 *LAN access through a public access point*

Table 10-1 lists the potential application of data and voice access points.

Table 10-1 Potential Applications of Data and Voice Access Points

Category	Application
LAN access	Web and e-mail services, e-commerce, and Virtual Private Networks (VPN)
DECT replacement	Cordless telephony services
Voice Over IP (VOIP)	Low-cost long distance calls via the Internet or LAN within a building.

The following sections discuss the other modes of wireless communication, including dial-up networking, small meetings, and ad-hoc networking. .

Dial-up Networking

Dial-up networking can be set up by using a cellular phone or a cordless modem. Both these modes use the existing software (Remote Access Software) to dial up a connection. The connection facilitates access to information on the network (such as the Internet) any time, anywhere. Figure 10-6 illustrates dial-up networking that uses a cellular phone.

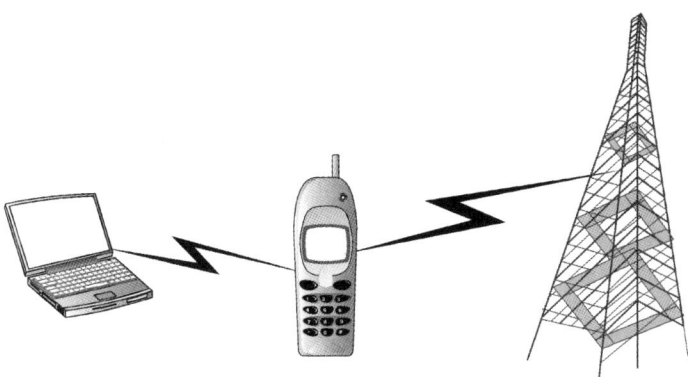

FIGURE 10-6 *Dial-up networking through a cellular phone*

Figure 10-7 illustrates dial-up networking that uses a cordless modem.

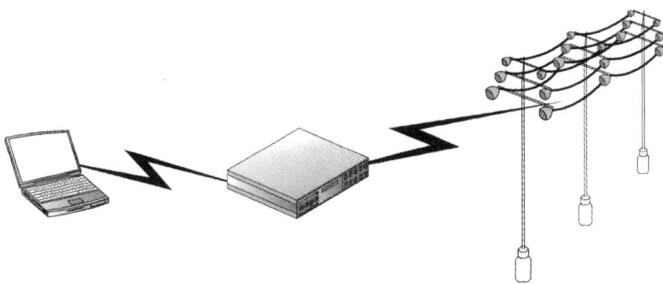

FIGURE 10-7 *Dial-up networking through a cordless modem*

Table 10-2 lists the potential applications of the cable replacement technology.

Table 10-2 The Potential Applications of the Non-cabled Dial-up Networking

Category	Application
The wireless desktop	PCs and their peripherals, printers, keyboards, and mouse. File transfers from one laptop to another and PDA synchronization
Wireless audio headsets	Cellular phones, portable cassette player, MP3 players, radio, and television
Mobile headsets and handsets	—
Remote control devices	—
Wireless connectivity within the premises for lighting and air conditioning	—

Small Meetings

Small meetings are a relatively new concept of wireless connectivity. It consists of PC-to-PC connectivity that will provide access to the allowed services on a device. The services include file transfers and sharing of peripherals such as CD drives and modems. The advantage is that such connectivity will not require additional equipment, access points, or wires. Figure 10-8 illustrates a PC-to-PC connectivity in small meetings.

FIGURE 10-8 *PC-to-PC connectivity*

Ad-hoc Networking

Connections in ad-hoc networking are more spontaneous and change with a change in the number and types of proximal devices. Connectivity in such a case will provide the same services as that in small meetings except that the connectivity will be between a variety of devices. Figure 10-9 illustrates ad-hoc networking that connects devices of different types.

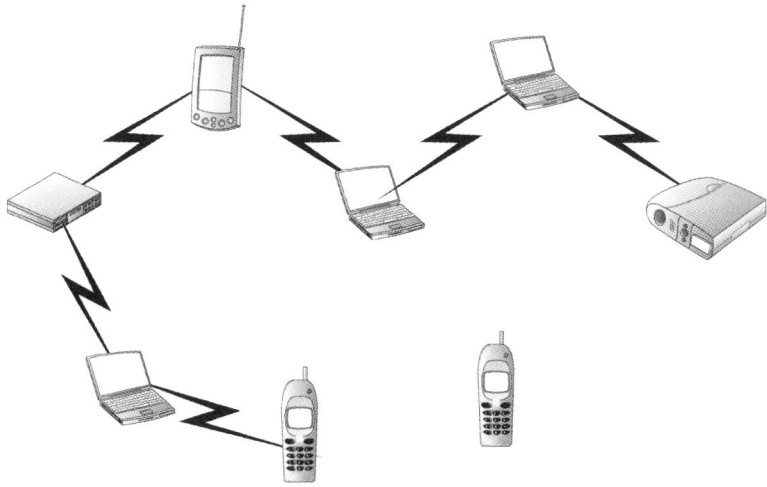

FIGURE 10-9 *Ad-hoc connectivity*

Table 10-3 lists the potential applications of ad-hoc networking.

Table 10-3 The Potential Applications of Ad-hoc Networking

Category	Application
Exchange of data	Peer-to-peer WLAN using TCP/IP. Services such as vending, Automated Telling Machine (ATM), ticket reservations and collections, and cashless transactions
Networking within homes	Connectivity between appliances such as fridges, freezers, Internet access points, and TVs
Tracking services	Services within a building or within a short range.
Voice Over IP (VOIP)	

The Coming Years and Bluetooth

Bluetooth technology has a lot to offer due to its strengths, which have helped it to gain an edge over other competing but similar technologies. The following is a list of the strengths of Bluetooth:

◆ Minimum hardware dimensions

◆ Low price of components

◆ Lower power consumption

◆ Point-to-point and point-to-multipoint links

◆ Voice and data links

◆ Error correction

◆ Robust frequency hopping

◆ Data security ensured through frequency hopping, encryption, and authentication

◆ Application-level interoperability with the use of profiles

◆ Non-licensed ISM band used for data transmission

As with any technology there are also limitations, and Bluetooth is no exception. The following is a list of the limitations of Bluetooth:

◆ Restricted piconet size of eight devices with limited scatternet extension

◆ Maximum data rate of 723.2 Kbps

◆ Occupies the already crowded ISM band

◆ Slow connection setup

◆ No handover facility

 NOTE

Handover or handoff is a mechanism that maintains continuity of connection between the slave and master devices of a piconet, by transferring the link to a master device in another piconet. Currently, Bluetooth devices do not support handover facility. .

The strengths of Bluetooth contribute to the adaptability of this technology, which offers support to a wide variety of devices at a much lower price. In addition, the concept of wireless data transmission at approximately 723.2 Kbps can also be used in other forms of cable replacement implementations such as a LAN and other networking solutions. The strengths of Bluetooth can be used to create different types of solutions. The potential of Bluetooth in providing solutions according to the market needs can be classified as follows:

◆ **Bluetooth-enabled technologies.** Bluetooth can also be implemented by creating single- and two-chip solutions. Toys and electronic controls within a building can use the wireless Bluetooth technology in a simple, quick, and easily deployed single-chip solution. The two-chip solution, on the other hand, can be used in WLANs for RF digital link controls and the baseband, providing a flexible RF source for a powerful, high-quality radio system. Currently, as many as 2000 companies have announced licensing partnerships for the development of single- or dual-chip solutions.

◆ **Bluetooth-enabled components.** Bluetooth can be effortlessly embedded into existing Application Specific Integrated Circuits (ASIC) for System on Chip (SOC) implementations that include a microprocessor, memory, external interfaces, and system-specific functional blocks. Such implementations can be used for multiplayer game pads, earrings with Bluetooth headsets, and other forms of wearable wireless jewelry. Licenses are becoming available for development kits, radio test analysis equipment, and protocol analysis equipment. The current trend of component solutions can definitely add value to the fast growing number and range of Bluetooth consumer products.

◆ **Bluetooth consumer products.** Bluetooth consumer products will initially be in the form of external add-on modules. For example, cellular phones can provide add-on accessories in the form of dongles, which can be plugged to the bottom of a handset. Another form of a Bluetooth add-on module is the compact flash device for PDAs, laptops, and some palmtops with PCMCIA cards. These add-on devices do not affect the design of the host product but provide additional simple and low-risk Bluetooth functionalities. However, add-on modules can provide the initial boost required for the acceptance of the Bluetooth technology. As a result, methodologies have to be adapted to evolve PCB-integrated modules that can be finally integrated in silicon so that the built-in modules are less costly, more convenient to use, and better-integrated solutions.

The potential of Bluetooth-enabled devices is apparent from the projected volumes sourced from **www.bluetooth.com**, as shown in Figure 10-10.

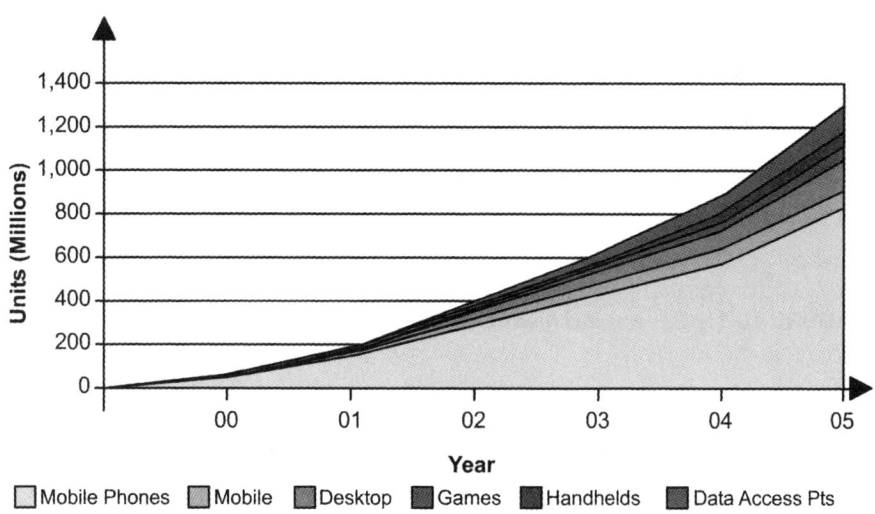

FIGURE 10-10 *The projected volumes of Bluetooth-enabled products from 2000 to 2004*

It is inevitable that the introduction of GPRS and UMTS will have a tremendous impact on Bluetooth. However, considering the projected timeline for the rollout of the services and Bluetooth, the world can expect to see voluminous changes in the way we communicate and exchange information today. Figure 10-11 illustrates the projected timeline for the rollout of Bluetooth, GPRS, and UTMS.

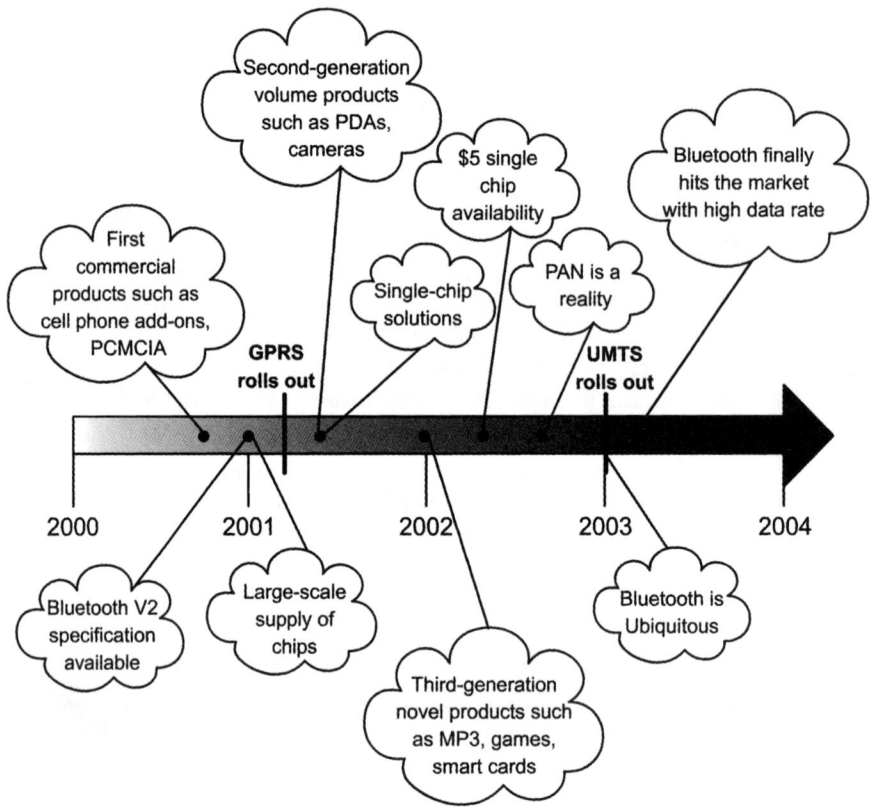

FIGURE 10-11 *The projected timelines for the rollout of Bluetooth, GPRS, and UTMS*

Bluetooth is a global venture providing a singular version of information access and connectivity that is compliant with the global emission rules. Supported with strong software goals, Bluetooth should be able to provide a good out-of-box experience by adding value to existing applications.

However, some analysts put forth a rather pessimistic view about Bluetooth. These analysts argue that although Bluetooth may provide easy solutions for HAN, it would still be a consumer choice rather than a preference. The point is whether the customer needs to use Bluetooth for refrigerator-oven communications or to use the mobile phone to switch on the lights of his/her home. Consumer comfort with gadgets is another assumption that needs to be addressed. The older generation will have to learn to program devices before they can actually utilize the Bluetooth technology. This, I dare say, will call for a lot of convincing, which will add to the promotional activities of the manufacturers and dealers.

Summary

Bluetooth seminars advertise the way our lives will change by using Bluetooth-enabled easy solutions for networking home and offices. Ericsson predicts that within a couple of years, the potential for Bluetooth will be somewhere near a billion devices per year. In addition, almost one-third of the mobile phones, desktops, and home appliances produced annually will be Bluetooth-enabled products. I'm sure you'll agree that this does speak of Bluetooth as a major revolution in the world of electronic communications. Hollywood movies such as *Mission Impossible 2* have already reflected the use of Bluetooth for message exchange using a wireless computer display fitted into a pair of sunglasses. Ericsson has envisioned cameras with Bluetooth features that will facilitate sending instant digital picture postcards to friends and relatives. Similarly, Motorola hopes to release a car kit with Bluetooth applications to telephonically control the car's air, heat, and radio. The list can go on and on. From homes to airports, offices, and other social setups, Bluetooth is here to stay.

This chapter discussed the potential of Bluetooth as a wireless solution to facilitate better and faster communication between different types of devices. In the course of the discussion I have tried to highlight the coming years that will build on the Bluetooth potential, the market and the networking scene after Bluetooth products finally roll in, and the views of pessimistic analysts.

It's only a matter of time before we know how consumers react to this ubiquitous standard for wireless communication. For now, it's wait and watch to find out whether the consumer will prefer to use Bluetooth-enabled products.

Check Your Understanding

Multiple Choice Questions

1. State whether the following statements are true or false.

   ◆ Bluetooth connections have to be ad-hoc so that proximal devices can easily connect.

   ◆ Bluetooth addresses multi-path fading problems in mobile environments and not in immobile environments.

   ◆ The routing and connectivity protocols in Bluetooth change according to the change in the number, location, and types of devices within an environment.

   ◆ Bluetooth devices do not operate with wireless services such as IrDA and OBEX.

2. Which of the following are limitations of Bluetooth?

   ◆ Slow connection setup

   ◆ No handover facility

   ◆ Use of profiles for application-level interoperability

   ◆ Maximum data rate of 723.2 Kbps

   ◆ Use of ISM band for data transmission

3. Which of the following services are included in the 2.5 generation?

   ◆ OBEX

   ◆ GPRS

   ◆ IrDA

   ◆ UMTS

Short Questions

1. Explain the segmentation of the mainstream customers in the mobile industry in brief.

2. Which are the different modes of wireless connectivity through LAN access?

3. Write short notes on:

   a. Bluetooth-enabled technologies

   b. Bluetooth-enabled components

Answers

Multiple Choice Answers

1. a. True

    b. False

    c. True

    d. False

2. a, b, and d. Slow connection setup, no handover facility, and maximum data rate of 723.2 Kbps

3. b and d. GPRS and UMTS

Short Answers

1. The mainstream of customers will be segmented into the following three groups:

    ◆ Mobile professionals. The mobile professionals or the early adopters will pay for novel and convenient advancements in technology in the years to come. They will also contribute toward the demand for the evolution of better applications to facilitate mobile connectivity.

    ◆ Business users. The business users looking for the reliability and functional capability of applications will increase the volume of business. Bluetooth will definitely satisfy their business needs.

    ◆ Home users. The home users will initiate the new usage paradigm of Home Area Networking (HAN) only if Bluetooth is able to fit into the key performance parameters of ease of use, cost, and autonomy.

2. LAN access can also be used without the hassles of connecting with wires in the following three modes:

    ◆ The first mode for LAN access uses a personal access point to access resources on the LAN, the Internet, and e-mail services.

    ◆ The second mode for LAN access uses a shared access point that is located within an organizational premise.

    ◆ The third mode for LAN access uses public access points to provide services such as details about e-mail providers and flight departure information.

3. a. Bluetooth-enabled technologies: Bluetooth can also be implemented by creating single- and two-chip solutions. Toys and electronic controls within a building can use the wireless Bluetooth technology in a simple, quick, and easily deployed single-chip solution. The two-chip solution, on the other hand, can be used in WLANs for RF digital link controls and the baseband, providing a flexible RF source for a powerful, high-quality radio system. Currently, as many as 2000 companies have announced licensing partnerships for the development of single- or dual-chip solutions.

b Bluetooth-enabled components: Bluetooth can be effortlessly embedded into existing Application Integrated Circuits (AIC) for System on Chip (SOC) implementations that include a microprocessor, memory, external interfaces, and system-specific functional blocks. Such implementations can be used for multiplayer game pads, earrings with Bluetooth headsets, and other forms of wearable wireless jewelry. Licenses are becoming available for development kits, radio test analysis equipment, and protocol analysis equipment. The current trend of component solutions can definitely add value to the fast growing number and range of Bluetooth consumer products.

Chapter 11

*Future of
Bluetooth*

The past years were the years of cable connections. Cable connections restricted the movement of devices, appliances, and equipment. In addition, they were cumbersome and prone to damage. I'm sure you noticed the tense of my previous sentence. Yes, cabled connections are passé! The present years and the years to come will pave the way for manageable connections that facilitate communication any time and anywhere. These are the years of infrared wireless connections between devices. The entire discussion of the preceding chapters talked in length about the revolutionary Bluetooth technology that has added versatility to device connections. In addition, this technology integrates perfectly into mobile devices, terminals, and peripherals at a cost as low as $10.00.

The previous chapter detailed the potential of Bluetooth and discussed the networking scenario in the years to come. However, the inevitable questions lurking in your mind about the future of Bluetooth will definitely need to be addressed. The Bluetooth specification has served to provide the regulatory standards for Bluetooth products to ensure their consistency. However, with newer profiles being created and with the radio and baseband enhancements, the specification will have to be revisited in the future. In addition to this, with the increase in members, the functions of the Special Interest Group (SIG) are increasing. As a result, the key performance areas have increased, leading to addition of new working groups to facilitate optimized implementation of this technology.

This chapter discusses the future of Bluetooth in terms of the future initiatives for the upgraded specification after version 1.0 and the reconstitution of the SIG. This chapter also provides a list of a few Bluetooth products that can be expected in the consumer market in the near future.

The SIG Then, Now, and in the Future

The SIG has played and will play a key role in developing the future of Bluetooth. As you know, the Bluetooth SIG was founded in 1998 and originally consisted of the five stalwarts of the computing and telecommunications industry, called the core promoters. Other members such as Microsoft, Lucent, 3Com, and Motorola joined the SIG in 1999. Today, the SIG consists of hundreds of associate and adopter member companies. The associate members are paying members who obtain early access to the specification and are free to provide input regarding the specification during its developmental stages. The adopter members, on the other hand, are non-paying members who are permitted to participate in certain meetings and obtain only the pre-published drafts of the specification.

The objective of the SIG is apparent from the mission statement, which states an intention *"To develop, publish, and promote the preferred short-range wireless specification for connecting mobile products and to administer a qualification program that certifies product interoperability for a positive user experience."*

The organizational board of the SIG is headed by the program management board, which is further divided into a number of working groups constituted by the employees of the member companies. The working groups focus on specific areas of operation such as marketing, product engineering, testing, and qualification. Figure 11-1 illustrates the structure of the SIG.

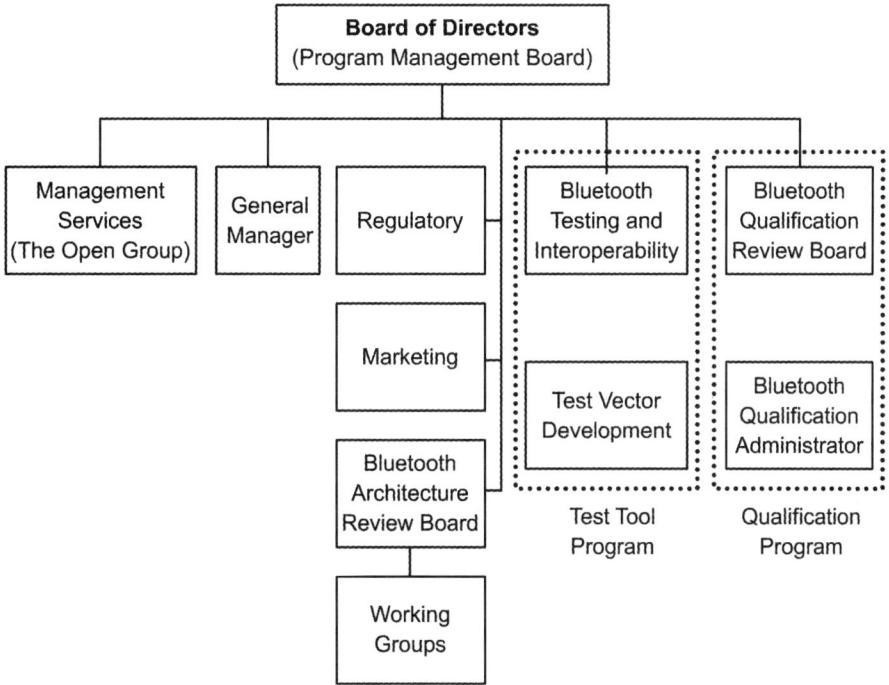

FIGURE 11-1 *The organizational structure of the Bluetooth SIG*

The main functional area of the SIG was the promotion and development of the Bluetooth specification. As a result, the SIG was segmented into a number of working groups that worked toward developing and refining the specification. With the publication of specification 1.0, the SIG charter almost expired technically. However, with the development of new profiles and the need to keep abreast of the enhanced radio and baseband developments, the SIG is now working toward defining the Bluetooth specification version 2.0.

As the development of the 2.0 version of the specification continues, many new usage scenarios have been identified, most of which were deferred from being included in specification 1.1. Therefore, in 2000, the SIG also announced the formation of new working groups to conduct further research on the new usage scenarios, resulting in new profiles. There is no significant change in the protocols detailed in the core specification except for the development of additional extensions where applicable. Thus, the new profiles will have to be made available without disturbing the existing content of the core specification. It is, therefore, apparent that most of the content in the latest specification will be related to the new profiles.

The new working groups announced by the SIG in 2000 include the following:

♦ The Radio 2.0 working group

♦ The Co-existence working group

♦ The Extensions and Enhancements working group

♦ The New Applications working group

Each of these new working groups, in turn, defines new profiles that address issues such as security, pairing, and mandatory features, and provides service records for the various profiles. The following sections discuss each of the new working groups, and also details the new profiles specified in each group.

The Radio 2.0 Working Group

The Radio 2.0 working group, which is managed by Ericsson and Nokia, explores the optional extensions that can be added to the Bluetooth 1.0 radio specification. The Bluetooth specification has already provided basic standards for data rates and the functioning of the baseband. Radio specification 2.0 aims for a data rate of 2 Mbps or even higher, maybe up to 10 Mbps. If the target data rate is achieved, Bluetooth will be able to transmit hi-fi quality audio and video that is equivalent to the features of third-generation (3G) cellular phones.

The need for the global availability of Bluetooth restricts its frequency band to the ISM band. As a result, radio innovations will have to include more complex modulation schemes to overcome the constraints of this overcrowded band. The cost restriction targeted at $10.00 (U.S.) remains undeterred and can, therefore, pose quite a challenge to radio manufacturers.

Compatibility between Bluetooth 2.0 and 1.1 devices is yet another area that can be included in the optional extension to specification 1.1. The 2.0 devices will, therefore, have to manage two modulation schemes to preserve backward compatibility with 1.0 devices. Similarly, alterations in the inquiry process and the handover facility are other changes under consideration. A change in the inquiry process can ensure faster connections by speeding up the process of device discovery. Both these changes complement each other. Handing over calls in Bluetooth can be better coordinated by handing over the connections between LAN access points instead of synchronizing the address books of the devices. This is because LAN access points feed into wider networks and provide a wide-area service as compared to the small and independent piconet of cell phones or PDAs. Speeding up the inquiry process complements the handover facility by providing faster connectivity between roaming devices.

Besides the additional inclusions in specification 2.0, other factors such as global operations, low cost, low power consumption, and short-range communication in specification 1.1 continue unaltered.

The Co-existence Working Group

The Co-existence working group is working toward ensuring the harmonious existence of Bluetooth and all the other 2.4-GHz technologies. As a result, it deals with issues such the performance and interference of parallel RF technologies within the same time and space. This group works along with other parallel associations such as the HomeRF™, the IEEE 802.11, and IEEE 802.15 working groups to give recommendations for the congruous working of all these technologies. An excellent example of such an association is the collaboration between the SIG and IEEE 802.15 working group in 1999. A proposal from the SIG in the summer of 1999 for the use of the then published specification 1.0 as an IEEE 802.15 standard was worked upon and finally drafted by spring 1999. The draft proposal of the IEEE 802.15 standard is, therefore, based upon the Bluetooth transport protocol.

 NOTE

The IEEE 802 standard relates to only the two lowest protocol layers, namely, the physical layer and the data link layer. As a result, the IEEE 802 standard requirement applies to the Bluetooth transport protocol. It has, therefore, been used as a basis for drawing up the draft proposal for the IEEE 802.15 standard specification.

The Extensions and Enhancements Working Group

The Extensions and Enhancements working group is responsible for completing the development of the deferred usage scenarios of specification 1.0. Although some amount of preliminary work was initiated in each of the usage cases, the work was left incomplete. The work of the Extensions and Enhancements group has continued the unfinished work on the usage scenarios and derived new profiles for the next version of the specification. The profiles identified so far include the following:

◆ The Personal Area Networking (PAN) profile
◆ The Printing profile
◆ The Still Image profile
◆ The Human Interface Devices (HID) profile
◆ The Extended Service Discovery Profiles (ESDP)

The Personal Area Networking Profile

The working group responsible for deriving a new protocol for PAN is co-chaired by Microsoft and Intel. The Bluetooth specification 1.1 defines networking standards that are based on dial-up networking and LAN access using PPP instead of a more generic IP-based ad hoc networking. In addition, security is a major concern because PANs in the future may be used for public access too. The comprehensiveness of this profile needed more time than was available before the publication of specification 1.0. As a result, the initial work was abandoned and continued later after the formation of the PAN working group.

The primary focus point of the PAN working group is to define an IP-based PAN profile to set up ad hoc networks using a more simplified security model. This new profile aims to create a PAN networking system that is platform-, device-, and language-independent.

This profile is targeted for the potentially huge market of multiplayer games. In addition, this profile also supports collaborative applications used for file sharing in offices, device collaborations on electronic whiteboards, instant messaging within a conference room, real-time viewing and group editing of presentations, and handling display devices.

The Printing Profile

In the world of computing, printing is a common task. Although many initial usage models discussed this task, sadly, none of them dealt with it directly. This was before the formation of the Printing working group co-chaired by Hewlett-Packard and Ericsson. The Printing profile group commands support from many printing experts.

The Printing working group aims to add the printer to the cordless computer usage model, thus facilitating printing over Bluetooth links. The success of this profile will enable Bluetooth devices to directly connect to and use the printing services of a Bluetooth-enabled printer. The Printing profile defines two levels of the printing facility. The first level of printing consists of a group of minimal functional features for devices such as cellular phones. The second level of printing consists of a set of comprehensive features, best suited for printing rich content from devices such as laptops. The printing of richer content is facilitated by the Universal Plug and Play (UPnP) specification that allows devices outside the PC environment to expose their capabilities to other devices.

The Still Image Profile

You'll recall that Chapter 1 talked of an example of Bluetooth usage that allows you to instantly share photographs and postcards with your family and friends. Well, that's exactly the purpose of the Still Image profile. Chaired by Nokia, the Still Image working group aims to formalize a profile that enables the manipulation and handling of still images.

As is obvious from the instant postcard usage model, this profile will facilitate the transfer of still images from a digital camera to other devices over a Bluetooth link. The Still Image profile will also enable image manipulation for display or printing.

The limited speed of data transmission in Bluetooth 1.1 created a hindrance in the formalization of this profile initially. However, with the promise of faster data rates in Bluetooth 2.0, it's just a matter of time before this usage scenario creates a stir among electronic camera manufacturers, especially due to the constantly increasing resolution of digital cameras. Figure 11-2 illustrates the structure of the instant postcard usage scenario that will enable the transfer of digitized photographs over Bluetooth links.

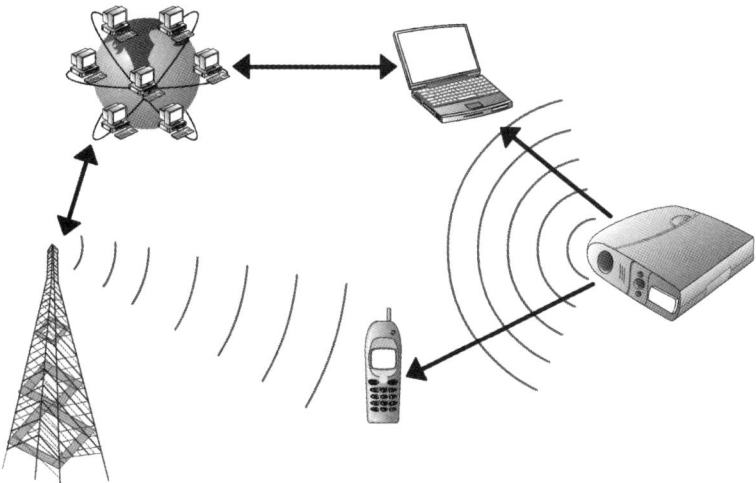

FIGURE 11-2 *The instant postcard usage scenario*

The Human Interface Devices Profile

The cordless computer usage model envisioned in Bluetooth 1.0 was abandoned due to time constraints and various other reasons. However, the deferment of this scenario was short-lived. The HID working group, chaired by Microsoft, is considering a profile definition in the Bluetooth specification 2.0 and is based on the cordless computer usage model.

The core of Bluetooth wireless communication lies in its cable replacement technology. The desktop computer is a vital part of the wireless peripheral device structure because it contains information that needs to be accessed from anywhere at any time. As a result, a cordless computer model was proposed that included unwired connections between the computer and its peripherals. The HID model includes peripherals such as mice, keyboards, joysticks, printers, scanners, and speakers. The HID profile offers freedom of use and placement that is independent of the length of the wire connecting the peripheral devices. Figure 11-3 illustrates the structure of the cordless computer usage scenario.

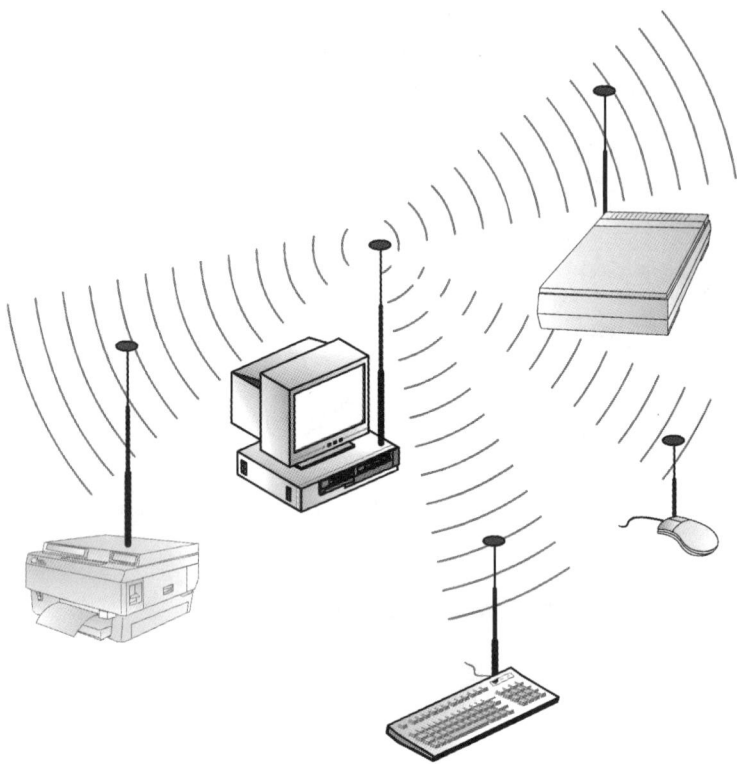

FIGURE 11-3 *The cordless computer usage model*

The Extended Service Discovery Profiles

The ESDP working group, co-chaired by Microsoft and 3Com, is responsible for defining a profile that permits co-existence and interoperability between the Bluetooth Service Discovery Protocol (SDP) and various other discovery protocols. The studies conducted by this group focused on the UPnP specification and the Salutation technologies (an off-shoot of Miller9) that describe specifications for informal Salutation mapping.

The New Applications Working Group

The Extensions and Enhancements working group has researched and completed the unfinished usage scenarios of Bluetooth 1.1. The profiles described in the Bluetooth 2.0 include deferred usage scenarios of specification 1.1 and some new profiles that were not developed for the previous version of the Bluetooth specification. The New Applications working group is responsible for identifying new application domains for the implementation of Bluetooth wireless communication. The three groups of the New Applications group are:

- ◆ The Car profile group
- ◆ The Audio/Video profile group
- ◆ The Local Positioning profile group

Each of these new profiles deals with an application of the Bluetooth technology that is beyond the scope of the preliminary extension and usage models of the Bluetooth specification 1.1.

The Car Profile Group

As the name suggests, the Car profile working group aims to define applications of the Bluetooth technology for in-vehicle communication. This working group, chaired by Nokia, has generated immense interest from the automotive industry. The application profiles include interdevice communication within an automotive environment and access to the services provided by a car. Of course, it goes without saying that all communication within the automobile is between Bluetooth devices over Bluetooth links.

The scope of application of Bluetooth wireless communication within a car environment is unlimited. Consider the following scenarios, which suggest the use of the Car profile for in-vehicle Bluetooth communication:

- ◆ Automatic and personalized configuration is set up within a car. This includes personalizing the configuration of the air conditioning, seat and mirror positioning, and radio settings. The criteria for the selection of the settings could be based on the personal identity of a Bluetooth device.
- ◆ Portable devices are interfaced with the other devices in the car. For example, the car speakers can be connected to the mobile phones for hands-free voice reception.
- ◆ The car's audio system is used to read incoming mail messages from the cellular phone. This type of in-vehicle communication involves a cellular link between the car's Bluetooth network and the much larger network of the handheld device.
- ◆ The remote operation of car phones is enabled. For example, the voice activation mechanism can be used to initiate calls from a headset.

The Car profile can also be used to establish communication between a car and the surrounding environment. For example, it can be used to minimize the work of the traffic police. The Car profile will almost eliminate the need for a car chase to stop speeding drivers. In the Bluetooth 2.0 environment, a faster speed of connection will ensure wireless transfer of information to prevent a speeding car from crossing a subsequent toll booth. In addition, this mechanism will also help the police alert other police ahead of them about the speeder. Awesome, isn't it? In addition, the Bluetooth links in the future can be used to pay for a car, transfer the car diagnostics to mechanics during routine maintenance checks, or transfer tourist information to the car's navigation system to ensure hassle-free drives. The list of innovative uses of the Car profile could run into quite a few pages. In short, the application of the Car profile will undoubtedly make driving a better experience. Of course, for unruly drivers, the chances of escaping the long arm of the law diminish further, thanks to Bluetooth.

The Audio/Video Profile Group

The Bluetooth SCO channels use data links that have high bandwidth but are inadequate for carrying music. This is because the limitation in the data rate of Bluetooth 1.0 requires an additional compression technique to transfer hi-fi audio or video. Co-chaired by none other than Sony® and Phillips®, the Audio/Video working group aims to use the faster data rates of Bluetooth 2.0 to transfer high quality and richer audio/video.

The premier European consumer showcase of 2000, CeBit, demonstrated the transfer of compressed video over Bluetooth links. With the addition of multimedia capabilities in future Bluetooth devices, new usage models will facilitate the transfer of audio and video clips between devices during video conferencing. The Audio/Video group has already initiated work on the following profiles:

- Video distribution
- Video conferencing
- Surround sound scenarios
- Distribution of mono and stereo CD-quality sound

These profiles, built over the L2CAP layer, will provide security to ensure copyright protection of audio/video material.

The Local Positioning Profile Group I have often faced situations where, despite having a road map, I have been unable to reach a particular destination or have wasted time running in circles trying to find out the exact location of an office. The Local Positioning working group, co-chaired by Microsoft and Nokia, aims to use the Bluetooth technology to help individuals or devices to determine their exact location both indoors and outdoors. The information can then be used for many purposes, such as the selection of the best device to connect to, determining if the non-performance of a device is due to its placement in the basement or other such locations in a building, and for locating a host device.

The invention of new profiles does not end here. As the months roll by, it is natural that the different working groups will come up with new and better profiles for the implementation of Bluetooth technology. The SIG has formalized a process for the creation of new working groups. The next section looks at how a new working group is formed within the SIG.

The Scope for Additional Working Groups

Any adopter company of the SIG is permitted to initiate the formation of a new working group. The process of requesting permission to form a new group begins with the definition of the profile in order to judge its necessity in the Bluetooth environment. During this phase, the possibility of integrating the new proposal within an existing profile is judged. This process ensures maximum device support for available profiles for better interoperability between devices.

Once the requirement for a new profile proposal is substantiated, the market potential is researched. The applicability of a profile to a small market results in the proprietary implementation of the profile. If a larger market potential is foreseen, the new profile proposal is directed to other process definitions and submitted to the core promoters group before being incorporated into the specification. Figure 11-4 illustrates the process followed for the introduction of a new profile in the specification.

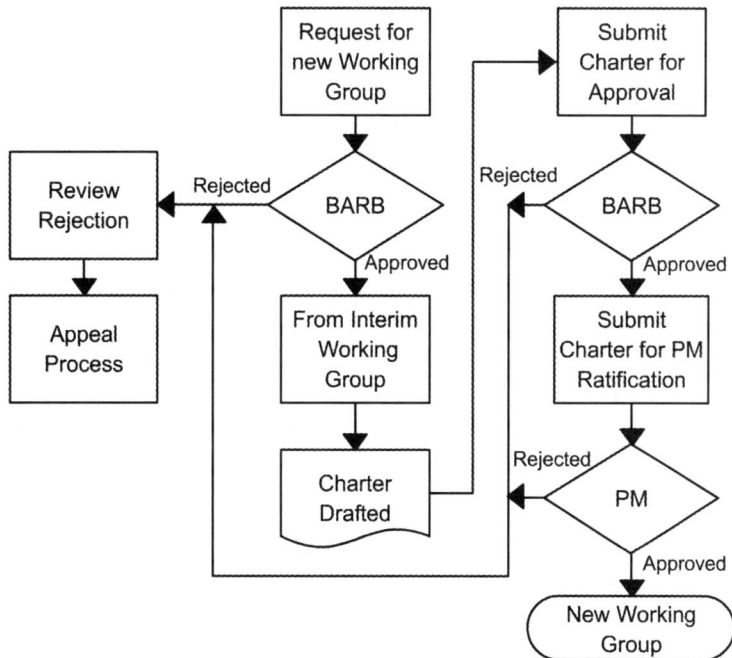

BARB: Bluetooth Architecture Review Board

FIGURE 11-4 *The flowchart depicting the process for introducing a new profile*

Future Bluetooth Products

The following section includes an insight into the future with Bluetooth-enabled products and devices. Assuming a universal acceptance of Bluetooth products, the pervasive computing scene in the near future can be segmented into the following networking categories:

- ◆ **E-business and mobile networking.** Bluetooth wireless communication will be able to benefit from the growth and popularity of e-business. The implementation of Bluetooth in e-business will include applications such as information kiosks and e-commerce transactions enabled through Bluetooth devices. Information kiosks can be used as walk-in centers to provide local information such as travel maps, shopping malls, hotel reservations, and airport/flight details. The Bluetooth kiosks would include features of wireless technology that are not available in the current standalone information kiosks. The features such as multi-user access through Bluetooth-enabled devices and the facility to download information from kiosks to personal devices would ensure availability of information any time and anywhere.

- ◆ **The home networking business.** Wireless communication between domestic appliances, such as refrigerators, washing machines, security systems, and entertainment systems, and personal devices such as PDAs, computers, automobiles, and smart phones, will be a part and parcel of every home and daily life. Future products such as the three-in-phone could be used as a cellular phone, cordless phone, or an intercom. A model such as this would reduce airtime by using a single telephone number for multiple purposes.

- ◆ **The automotive networking business.** As discussed earlier, the Car profile would enable the Bluetooth devices of the future conduct both in-vehicle and off-vehicle communication. Once again, the cable replacement technology will help to create a communication-rich environment inside the car without wiring its infrastructure.

The level of innovation that can be achieved for communication between disparate devices using the Bluetooth technology is immense. The future of Bluetooth seems bright with machine-to-machine interaction between even the smallest devices or appliances. Connectivity will be widespread and spontaneous due to the ad hoc networking function of Bluetooth. Here is a scenario of the easy and synchronized lifestyle of tomorrow's professional that includes Bluetooth-enabled devices and appliances. The morning would start with a melodious alarm from the Internet radio. At the breakfast table, swift connections between a handheld device and the Internet would retrieve the daily news and details about the weather and the traffic. In addition, the handheld device could retrieve the schedule from the office desktop and synchronize the calendar accordingly. Before leaving for the office, the handheld device (mobile phone) could be used to activate the alarm system and the garage door and reset the other appliances within the HAN.

While driving, client calls could be answered by using a headset. A synchronized navigation kit would ensure that the shortest and most uncongested route is taken to save traveling time. The journey log and mileage would be updated automatically. The car stereo could download the latest MP3 tracks and play them according to a personalized setting to suit individual music preferences.

In the office, the handheld device or the palmtop could serve as an identity pass to operate the security door and update the arrival/departure register. The day would include perfectly synchronized wireless meetings, conferences, and information exchanges between departments. Printing could be initiated from the laptop.

At the end of the day, on the way home from the office, the food stocks of the refrigerator could be assessed and restocked by connecting to the food store terminal. A cooking program could be initialized (in a microwave or an oven) to ensure that food is cooked to suit the individual's taste. Finally, the in-house settings could be activated to set the air conditioning at the right temperature and have music to welcome the person back home. That's just a small preview of life in the future. Of course, the basic requirement necessary for such a lifestyle is a substantial number of Bluetooth-enabled devices to ensure workable scenarios for this technology.

Summary

Bluetooth is here to stay. The market trends display a change in the approach of consumers from a conservative and cautious mode to a more open and inclusive mode. The concept of information availability moves from any time and anywhere to any time, anywhere, and on any device.

In this chapter, you learned about the importance of the SIG in carving the future of Bluetooth. You learned about the various new profiles of the Bluetooth specification 2.0 that will ensure better interoperability between the future Bluetooth devices. You also learned about the process followed by the SIG for the incorporation of newly developed profiles.

The opportunities for innovation in Bluetooth are incredible. The strength of this technology lies in the convenient wireless connectivity between disparate devices that helps to make life simpler for end users. The strong industry support, robust and detailed specification, market hype, and promise of dedicated service will no doubt ensure that the unification stand of King Harald is realized beyond the kingdoms of Denmark and Norway into the world of unified computing and telecommunication services.

Check Your Understanding

Multiple Choice Questions

1. State whether the following statements are true or false:
   a. Nokia, 3Com, and Ericsson initially constituted the SIG.
   b. The SIG announced the formation of five new working groups in 2000.
   c. The adopter members of the SIG participate in selective meetings and also suggest changes in the Bluetooth specification document.
   d. The Bluetooth SIG includes core promoters, associate members, and adopter members.

2. Which of the following are not new working groups (announced in 2000) of the Bluetooth SIG?
   a. The Radio 2.0 working group
   b. The LAN Access working group
   c. The Extensions and Enhancements working group
   d. The New Applications working group
   e. The Regulatory group

3. Which of the following profiles belong to the Extensions and Enhancements working group?
   a. HID profile
   b. Car profile
   c. PAN profile
   d. ESDP profile
   e. Local Positioning profile

Short Questions

1. Explain the Still Image profile in brief.
2. How will you categorize the Bluetooth products of the pervasive computing scenario in the future?
3. Write short notes on:
   a. Local Positioning profile

   b. The HID profile

Answers

Multiple Choice Answers

1. a. False

    b. False

    c. False

    d. True

2. b and e. The LAN Access working group and the Regulatory working group are not a part of the new working groups.

3. a, c and d. HID profile, PAN profile, ESDP profile, and Local Positioning profile

Short Answers

1. The Still Image profile will facilitate the transfer of still images from a digital camera to other devices over a Bluetooth link. The Still Image profile will also enable image manipulations for display or printing.

    The limited speed of data transmission in Bluetooth 1.0 created a hindrance in the formalization of this profile initially. However, with the promise of faster data rates in Bluetooth 2.0, it's just a matter of time before this usage scenario creates a stir among electronic camera manufacturers especially due to the constantly increasing resolution of digital cameras.

2. Assuming a universal acceptance of Bluetooth products, the pervasive computing scene in the near future can be segmented into the following networking categories.

    E-business and mobile networking. The implementation of Bluetooth in e-business will include applications such as information kiosks and e-commerce transactions enabled through Bluetooth devices.

    The home networking business. In the home networking business, Bluetooth will facilitate wireless communication between domestic appliances such as refrigerators, washing machines, security systems, and entertainment systems, and personal devices such as PDAs, computers, automobiles, and smart phones will be a part and parcel of every home and daily life.

    The automotive networking business. The car profile would enable Bluetooth devices of the future conduct both in-vehicle and off-vehicle communication. Once again, the cable replacement technology will help to create a communication-rich environment inside the car without wiring its infrastructure.

3. a. The Local Positioning working group aims to use the Bluetooth technology to help an individual or a device determine their exact location both indoors and outdoors. The information can then be used for many purposes such as selection of the best device to connect to, determining non-performance of a device due to its placement in the basement or other such areas of the building, and also for locating a host device.

    b. The Human Interface Devices (HID) working group is considering a profile definition in the Bluetooth specification 2.0 that is based on the cordless computer usage model. The core of Bluetooth wireless communication lies in its cable replacement technology. The desktop computer is a vital part of the wireless peripheral device structure because it contains information that needs to be accessed from anywhere at any time. As a result, a computer cordless model was proposed that included unwired connection between the computer and its peripherals. The HID model includes peripherals such as mice, keyboards, joysticks, printers, scanners, and speakers. The HID profile offers freedom of use and placement that is independent of the length of the wire connecting the peripheral devices.

PART IV

IV

Appendix

Appendix A

FAQs

Q. What is Bluetooth?

A. Bluetooth wireless technology facilitates spontaneous and effortless connections and data exchange between PCs, mobile phones, and other devices. It is a cable replacement technology promoting freedom of movement and has been developed to revolutionize communication methods in the coming years.

Q. How will Bluetooth Wireless Technology be used?

A. The Bluetooth technology will be implemented in the following scenarios:

   ◆ Internet sharing/wireless networking where several PCs and/or handheld PCs can share single point Internet or Network access through a Windows 98 PC or Windows 2000 PC without using wired connections.

   ◆ Work in hotel rooms will be easier due to Bluetooth. The need to find the right country connector for your modem, the right phone socket in your room, and working in the inconvenient corners of the room will be the scenarios of the past. Simple and wireless connections will facilitate connections to the hotel's Bluetooth network and help you to retrieve e-mails or access the Internet.

   ◆ Print documents at client sites by sending the file to their Bluetooth printer.

   ◆ E-mail collection will be an automated process where the mobile phone will receive e-mails and transfer them to your laptop while you're on the road.

   ◆ Automatic data synchronization will ensure that when you enter the office, your desktop, laptop, handheld PC, and mobile phone automatically synchronize e-mail, calendar, and address lists.

   ◆ Roaming network access will enable free movement with continued connections to access any files needed from the network.

Q. **How does Bluetooth work?**

A. Bluetooth uses a standard means for integrating wireless technology with a power-efficient and low-cost radio system. The Bluetooth wireless specification includes Link layer and Application layer definitions that support data, voice, and content-centric applications. The Bluetooth radio operates in the unlicensed, 2.4 GHz radio spectrum ensuring global communication compatibility. The radios use a spread spectrum, frequency hopping, full-duplex signal of 1600 hops/sec, where a single hop extends to 79 frequencies at 1-MHz intervals to give a high degree of interference immunity. The master and its seven slave devices establish and maintain a private network called the piconet.

The Bluetooth specification defines universal standards to ensure that diverse devices supporting the Bluetooth wireless technology can communicate with each other. The specification consists of two sections: a Core Specification (Volume I) and Profile Definitions (Volume II). A group of industry-leading promoter companies has constituted the Special Interest Group (SIG) that drives the specification forward. The success of Bluetooth lies in the fact that it is a cross-industry solution that amalgamates the vision of engineering innovation with business and consumer expectations.

Q. **What is the Bluetooth SIG?**

A. The Bluetooth SIG is a group promoted by 3Com, Ericsson, IBM, Intel, Microsoft, Motorola, Nokia, and Toshiba. It also includes many associate and adopter member companies. The Bluetooth SIG, Inc. has several employees including a general manager; but is primarily a volunteer organization that is run by the employees of the member companies. The SIG supports a number of working groups that focus on research and development in specific areas, such as engineering, qualification, and marketing. Interoperability is maintained by strict qualification procedures and regular testing of products that are undertaken at the various events (fests) sponsored by the organization.

Q. **How do you become a member of the SIG?**

A. The Bluetooth SIG provides a forum for companies to work together using short-range wireless technologies. Companies can join as associate or adopting members. To do so, you need to fill in a membership application. A registered member of the SIG receives the latest specifications, and is given the rights to use the Bluetooth Brand. `http://www.bluetooth.com/` is the official Bluetooth wireless information site that contains all the information about the SIG and its registration process.

Q. **What is the anticipated volume for Bluetooth wireless technology devices in the near future?**

A. According to Cahners-Instat, it is expected that by the year 2005 close to 700 million Bluetooth devices will be shipped annually.

Index

A

A (Answer) command, 268
A-party device, 218
ABORT operation, 285
abstraction primitives, 234
access, obtain access rights, 258
access code
    CAC (Channel Access Code), 105–106
    DAC (Device Access Code), 106
    defined, 104
    IAC (Inquiry Access Code), 107–108
acknowledgement Indication (ARQN), 108
ACL (Asynchronous Connectionless) link
    defined, 12
    master and slave units and, 103–104
ACO (Authenticated Ciphering Offset), 305
Active Member Address (AM-ADDR), 108, 115
active state, 263
ad hoc connection, 9
ad hoc networks, security in, 299–300
Adaptive Time Division Duplexing (ATDD), 65–66
adjacent signal frequency separation, 30
air interface, 8
AJ (Anti-Jam), 56–57
Alcatel OneTouch 700 GPRS, WAP, Bluetooth device, 14

AM-ADDR (Active Member Address), 108, 115
Answer (A) command, 268
antennas
    arrays, types of, 40
    on chip, 34
    dipole, 33
    efficient functioning processes, characteristics of, 34
    flat panel, 34
    gain of, 39
    Hertzian dipole, 33
    impedance, 35–36
    loss of, 39–40
    microstrip, 33
    polarization, 39
    radiation patterns, 37–39
    transmission lines, 35–37
Anti-Jam (AJ), 56–57
APIs (application programming interface), 229
application group (Bluetooth protocol stack), 72, 80
Application layer
    OSI Reference Model, 67–68
    WAP architecture, 82
architecture
    Bluetooth
        diagram of, 13
        hardware framework, 11–12
        software framework, 12–13
    WAP, 81

ARQN (Acknowledgement Indication), 108

arrays, antenna arrays, 40

Asynchronous Connectionless (ACL) link
defined, 12
master and slave units and, 103–104

AT command, 206, 267, 274

AT+CKPD command, 277

ATDD (Adaptive Time Division Duplexing), 65–66

ATM (Asynchronous Transfer Mode), 59

attributeList attribute, 234

audio communication, 13

Audio Gateway (AU) device role, 276

Audio/Video working group, 346–347

Authenticated Ciphering Offset (ACO), 305

authentication, 221
authentication failure, 134
device authentication, 132–138
pairing not allowed, 135
stages of, 304
waiting period, 304

AUX1 data packet, 112

AW (Audio Gateway) device role, 276

azimuth dimension, 37

B

B-party device, 218

balun interface, 36

band segregation in FFD, 62

Bandwidth Time (BT), 30

baseband, 95
Asynchronous Connection-Less (ACL) link, 103

functions, diagram of, 94
services, 93
Synchronous Connection-Oriented (SCO) link, 103

baseband layer, 75

BD_ADDR address, 99–100, 219

beacon channel, 146

bearer services, 83–84

binary modulation scheme, 30–31

Bluetooth
advent of, 4–5
air interface in, 8
computer devices, 13
defined, 7
domestic uses of, 15
features of, 16
forecast for global use of, 319
frequency hopping in, 8–9
future products, 348–349
hardware framework architecture, 11–12
history of, 5–6
link management in, 75–76
middleware protocol group, 77
networking in, 9–11
office uses of, 16
product demonstrations, 2000, 14
radios, link range of, 11
SIG (Special Interest Group), 6
software framework architecture, 12–13
standards, 7
system challenges of, 321

Bluetooth, Harold, 5

Bluetooth chip. *See* radio chip

Bluetooth clock
critical periods of, 101
offset, conceptual representation of relationship between, 102

overview, 100
types of, 101
Bluetooth device address (BD_ADDR), 99–100
Bluetooth-enable Nokia 9110, 14
Bluetooth Industry Survey, 318
Bluetooth profiles. *See* profiles
Bluetooth protocol stack, 71
   application group, 80
   for GAP profile, 217
   illustration of, 73
   protocol layers, list of, 72
   Transport protocol group, 72
Bluetooth radio
   control information in, 74
   data operations, 73
   ISM frequency availability, 73
   link range of, 11
   operational parameters of, 74
   technology behind, 24
Bluetooth Web site, 6
bonding, 223, 271
BrowseGroupList attribute, 208–209
browsing folders, 285
BT (Bandwidth Time), 30
business card exchange function, 288
business card pull function, 288

C

C (conditional) feature of LM, 238
&C (received line signal detector behavior) command, 268
cable emulation, 13
CAC (Channel Access Code), 105–106
call class, 257
call clearing, 258, 264

call confirmation, 258
call connection, 258
Call Control (CC), 259
call control communication, 13
call control procedures, 257–258
call information, 255
Call Line Identification Presentation (CLIP), 255
Call Line Identity, 259
call progress audio feedback, 269
Car profile working group, 345–346
CC (Call Control), 259
CDMA (Code Division Multiple Access), 84
CDMS, tri-mode hands free speaker phone, 14
CEPT (Conference of European Postal and Telecommunication Administration), 62
Cfm (Confirms) event, 186
challenge-response transaction, 132
challenges, of Bluetooth, 321
Channel Access Code (CAC), 105–106
channel establishment, 221
Channel Identifier (CID), 176
channel types
   L2CAP interoperability requirement, 227
channel types, L2CAP interoperability requirement, 227
channels
   beacon, 146
   CL (connectionless), 77, 175
   CO (connection-oriented), 174
   hop channels, 8–9
   LC (Link Controller), 127
   LM (Link Manager), 127

signaling, 77, 175
UA (User Asynchronous), 127
UI (User Isochronous), 127
US (User Synchronous), 127
CID (Channel Identifier), 176
Ciphering Offset (COF) number, 305
Circuit-Switched Data (CSD), 83–84
circuit-switched networks, 58
circuits, RS-232 interface, 196
circular waves, 39
CL (connectionless) channels, 175
Clear to Send (CTS), 196, 201
clients, roles of, 243
CLIP (Call Line Identification
    Presentation), 255
CLK (master clock), 101
CLKE (estimated clock), 101
CLKN (native clock), 101
clock
    baseband functions, 94
    critical periods of, 101
    off, conceptual representation of rela-
        tionship between, 102
    overview, 100
    types of, 101
clock offset request, 140
CLOSED state, 183, 185
closure procedures, 199–200
CO (connection-oriented) channels, 174
Co-existence working group, 341
coaxial transmission lines, 36
Code Division Multiple Access (CDMA),
    84
CODEC (coder/decoder) functionality, 85
COF (Ciphering Offset) number, 305
combination keys, 133, 302

Command not understood reason code,
    184
common mode, 36
communication
    audio, 13
    call control, 13
    compatibility between devices, 12
    peripheral, 13
CompId (CompanyId), 150
computers
    Bluetooth specifications, 13
    Windows CE-based Auto PC device,
        14
conditional (C) feature of LM, 238
Conference of European Postal and
    Telecommunication Administration
    (CEPT), 62
CONFIG state, 183–185
configuration distribution procedure, 258
Configuration Request command, 183
Configuration Response command, 183
Confirms (Cfm) event, 186
CONNECT operation, 258, 285
Connect Request, 204
connectable mode, 270
connection establishment, 94, 119–120,
    153
connection management, 255, 257
connection-oriented (CO) channels, 174
connection-oriented networks, 58–59, 77
connection state, 115
connection termination, 153
connectionless (CL) channels, 77, 175
connections
    ad hoc, 9
    piconets, 10
    point-to-multipoint, 9, 96–97

point-to-point, 9, 96

consortium, SIG (Special Interest Group), 6

Consumer Premise Equipments (CPEs), 64

content field, 129

Continuous Variable Slope Delta (CVSD) modulation, 276

control signals, 195–196

cordless phones, air interface and, 8

Cordless Telephony Profile, 215
   call control procedures, 257–258
   connection management, 257
   distribution of protocol stack for, 254
   features of, 256
   group management procedures, 258
   GW (Gateway) service role, 254
   L2CAP interoperability requirements for, 259
   LC interoperability requirements for, 260
   link loss detection by Gateway, 259
   LMP interoperability requirements for, 260
   overview, 253
   supplementary services, 259
   TL (Terminal) service role, 254

CPEs (Consumer Premise Equipments), 64

CRC (Cyclic Redundancy Checksum), 110

CSD (circuit-switched data), 83–84

CTS (Clear to Send), 196, 201

CVSD (Continuous Variable Slope Delta) modulation, 276

Cyclic Redundancy Checksum (CRC), 110

D

&D (data terminal ready behavior) command, 268

D (Dial) command, 268

DAC (Device Access Code), 106

Data call with audio feedback feature, 267, 274

Data call without audio feedback service, 267, 274

data calls, 267

Data Carrier Detect (DCD), 196

Data Circuit-Terminating Equipment (DCE), 196

Data High rate (DH1) data packet, 112

Data Link Connection (DLC), 198

Data Link Connection Identifier (DLCI), 196, 200

Data Link layer (OSI Reference Model), 67–68

Data Medium rate (DM1) data packet, 112

data objects, pushing/pulling, 244

data operations in Bluetooth radio, 73

data packets
   access code, 104–106
   device discovery and inquiry, 118
   header, 108–109
   L2CAP (Logical Link Control Adaptation Protocol), 179–181
   link connection, 114–118
   paging, 119–120
   payload, 109–110
   structure of, 104
   type fields of, 113–114
   types of, 111–112

Data Set Ready (DSR), 196

Data Terminal (DT) device role, 266, 272

Data Terminal Equipment (DTE), 196
Data Terminal Ready (DTR), 196
Data Voice (DV) packet, 109–111
dBc (decibel measure of power of signals), 30
dBi (decibel isotropic unit of power), 30
dBm (decibel miliwatt unit of power), 30
DCD (Data Carrier Detect), 196
DCE (Data Circuit-Terminating Equipment), 196
DECT (Digital Enhanced Cordless Technology), 17, 64
destination_CID field, 181
Device Access Code (DAC), 106
device authentication, 132–138
device discovery, 118
device discovery procedure, 223
DH1 (Data High rate 1) data packet, 112
DH3 data packet, 112
DH5 data packet, 112
Dial-Up Networking Profile, 215
    Application layer services, 266–267
    call progress audio feedback, 269
    commands, list of, 268–269
    DT (Data Terminal) device role, 266
    features of, 266
    GAP Idle mode and bonding procedures supported by, 271
    GAP modes supported by, 270
    GAP security aspects supported by, 270
    GW (Gateway) device role, 265
    interoperability requirements, 267
    overview, 264
    restrictions of, 266
Digital Enhanced Cordless Technology (DECT), 17, 64
dipole antennas, 33

Direct Sequence Spread Spectrum (DSSS)
    defined, 53
    generating PN sequences using, methods for, 54
    In-phase of, 54
DISC frame command, 202
disconnect indication, 263
DISCONNECT operation, 285
Disconnect Request, 205, 263
DLC (Data Link Connection), 198
DLCI (Data Link Connection Identifier), 196, 200
DM1 (Data Medium rate 1) data packet, 112
DM3 data packet, 112
DM5 data packet, 112
DSR (Data Set Ready), 196
DSSS (Direct Sequence Spread Spectrum)
    defined, 53
    generating PN sequences using, methods for, 54
    In-phase of, 54
DT (Data Terminal) device role, 266, 272
DTE (Data Terminal Equipment), 196
DTMF (Dual Tone Multiple Frequency) signaling, 255
DTR (Data Terminal Ready), 196
Dual Tone Multiple Frequency (DTMF) signaling, 255
duplexing
    ATDD (Adaptive Time Division Duplexing), 65–66
    defined, 60
    FDD (Frequency Division Duplexing)
    advantages of, 63
    allocation and bands to, 62
    band segregation in, 62

defined, 61
disadvantages of, 63
fixed channel allocation in, 63
TDD (Time Division Duplexing)
advantages of, 64
disadvantages of, 64–65
multiple access scheme of high peak
power in, 64
overview, 63
types of, 61
DV (Data Voice) packet, 109–111
dwell time, 56

E

E algorithms for security, 308
E (command echo) command, 268
E21 key-generating algorithm, 301–302
EDGE (Enhanced Data Rate) for GSM,
322
electric (E) field, 39
electromagnetic waves, 39
electronic conversion, 43
elevation dimension, 38
emulated serial ports, multiple, 196–199
emulation, cable emulation, 13
encryption, 85, 305–308
link encryption, 138–139
(WTLS) Wireless Transport Layer
Security, 85
Enhanced Data Rate for GSM (EDGE),
322
enumerateRemDev service primitive, 234
Ericsson Bluetooth GSM headset, 14
Ericsson Bluetooth Headset, 14
Ericsson Communicator device, 15
Ericsson Mobile Communications, 6

Ericsson R520
Bluetooth/WAP/RGPS/Triband, 14
Ericsson T36
Bluetooth/WAP/HSCSD/Triband
device, 14
error codes (HCI), 169
error handling, 128
errors
SDAP devices and, 239
SDP_ErrorResponse, 209
transmissions, jammed, 8
UIH (Unnumberbed Information with
Header) error check, 202
ERTX (Extended Response Timeout
Expired) timer, 190
estimated clock (CLKE), 101
ETSI (European Telecommunication
Standard Institute), 77–78
events
HCI, 169
L2CAP to L2CAP signaling, 188–189
lower layer to L2CAP, 187
upper layers to L2CAP, 188
excluded (X) feature of LM, 238
EXOR operation, 52
Extended Response Timeout Expired
(ERTX) timer, 190
Extended Service Discovery working
group, 344
Extensions and Enhancement working
group, 341–342

F

&F (set to configurations that are factory-
defined) command, 268

FAQs (frequently asked questions),
 358–360
fast-inter-member access, 258
Fax Profile, 215
  compliance with fundamental profiles,
   275
  dialing and control procedures, AT
   commands for, 274
  distribution of protocol stack for, 272
  DT (Data Terminal) device role, 272
  features of, 273
  GW (Gateway) device role, 272
  interoperability requirements, 274
  overview, 272
  restrictions of, 273
  services supported by, 274
fax service with audio feedback service,
 274
fax service without audio feedback service,
 274
FCC (Federal Communications
 Commission), 24
FDD (Frequency Division Duplexing)
  advantages of, 63
  allocation of bands to, 62
  band segregation in, 62
  defined, 61
  disadvantages of, 63
  fixed channel allocation in, 63
FEC (Forward Error Correction), 108,
 153–154
Federal Communications Commission
 (FCC) and, 24
FHS data packet, 111
FHSS (Frequency Hopping Spread
 Spectrum), 53
File Transfer Profile, 216

Application layer procedures, 285
client device role, 284
distribution of protocol stack for, 283
features of, 284
interoperability requirements, 285
overview, 283
server device role, 284
service records for, 286
user interface specifications, 284
flat panel antenna, 34
Flow Control (Flow), 108
flow control (HCI), 169
flow control methods (RFCOMM), 201
flow flag (payload header), 110
flush timeout option, 193, 238
folder browsing, 285
forecast for global use of Bluetooth, 319
Forward Error Correction (FEC), 108,
 153–154
frame commands, 202
frequency accuracy, 33
frequency band, ISM (Industrial-Scientific
 Medical) band, 8
Frequency Division Duplexing (FDD)
  advantages of, 63
  allocation of bands to, 62
  band segregation in, 62
  defined, 61
  disadvantages of, 63
  fixed channel allocation in, 63
frequency hopping
  defined, 8
  modulation and, 55
  per time division, 9
  spread spectrum frequency hopping
   technique, 42
  transmission, uninterrupted, 26

Frequency Hopping Spread Spectrum (FHSS), 53

frequency parameter (Bluetooth radio), 74

frequently asked questions (FAQs), 358–360

Fujifilm, Mobile Imaging Nokia 9110, 14

future Bluetooth products, 348–349

G

GAP (Generic Access Profile), 215
  A-party device, 218
  B-party device, 218
  bonding procedure, 223
  channel establishment, 221
  device discovery procedure, 223
  distribution of Bluetooth protocol stack for, 217
  features of, 218
  general inquiry procedure, 222
  idle mode procedures, 222
  limited inquiry procedure, 222
  link establishment, 220
  name request procedure, 223
  procedure levels, 219–220
  security aspects, 221
Gateway (GW) service role, 254, 265, 272
Gaussian Frequency Shift Keying (GFSK), 30
+GCAP (request for complete capability list) command, 268
general discoverable mode, 270
General Inquiry Access Code (GIAC), 219
general inquiry procedure, 222
General Packet Radio Switching (GPRS), 84, 322

general response management, 128, 130–131

General sync mode, 291

Generic Access Profile (GAP), 215
  A-party device, 218
  B-party device, 218
  bonding procedure, 223
  channel establishment, 221
  device discovery procedure, 223
  distribution of Bluetooth protocol stack for, 217
  features of, 218
  general inquiry procedure, 222
  idle mode procedures, 222
  limited inquiry procedure, 222
  link establishment, 220
  name request procedure, 223
  overview, 242–243
  procedure levels, 219–220
  security aspects, 221
Generic Object Exchange Profile (GOEP), 215
  distribution of protocol stack for, 243
  features of, 243–244
generic profiles, 216
GET operation, 285
GFSK (Gaussian Frequency Shift Keying), 30
GIAC (General Inquiry Access Code), 219
Global System for Mobile Communications (GSM), 254
+GMI (request for identification of manufacturer) command, 268
+GMM (request for identification of model) command, 268

GOEP (Generic Object Exchange
    Profile), 215
  distribution of protocol stack for, 243
  features of, 243–244
  overview, 242–243
GPRS (General Packet Radio Switching),
    84, 322
GroupID attribute, 208
GSM (Global System for Mobile
    Communications), 254
GSM headset, Ericsson and Bluetooth, 14
guard bands, 65
GW (Gateway) service role, 254, 265, 272

H

H (hook control) command, 268
H (magnetic field), 39
hardware framework, Bluetooth architec-
    ture, 11–12
HCI (Host Controller Interface), 72, 76,
    164
  defined, 12
  error codes, 169
  events, 169
  flow control, 169
  HCI driver, 166
  HCI firmware, 166
  Host Controller Transport layer, 166
  informational parameters, 168
  link control commands, 168
  link policy commands, 168
  overview, 165
  RS-232 Transport layer, 170
  status parameters, 168
  testing commands, 169
  UART Transport layer, 170

  USB Transport layer, 170
header
  defined, 104
  format, 108–109
Header Error Check (HEC), 108–109
Header Value 1 (HV1) data packet, 111
Headset (HS) device role, 276
Headset Profile, 215
  AW (Audio Gateway) device role, 276
  distribution protocol stack for, 275
  features of, 276
  fundamental profiles, compliance with,
    278
  HS (Headset) device role, 276
  interoperability requirements, 276–277
  overview, 275
headsets, types of, 14
HEC (Header Error Check), 108–109
Hertzian dipole, 33
HID (Human Interface Device), 14
hold mode, 115, 144
HomeRF, 17–18
hook flash, 255
hop channels, 8–9
hopping codes
  dwell time, 56
  FHSS implementation and, 55
hopping rate parameter (Bluetooth radio),
    74
horizontal interface, 186
Host Controller Interface (HCI), 72, 76,
    164
  defined, 12
  errors codes, 169
  events, 169
  flow control, 169
  HCI driver, 166

HCI firmware, 166
Host Controller Transport layer, 166
informational parameters, 168
link control commands, 168
link policy commands, 168
overview, 165
RS-232 Transport layer, 170
status parameters, 168
testing commands, 169
UART Transport layer, 170
USB Transport layer, 170
HS (Headset) device role, 276
HTTP protocol conversion, WSP
    (Wireless Session Protocol) to, 85
Human Interface Device (HID), 14
Human Interface Devices working group,
    343–344
HV1 (Header Value 1) data packet, 111
HV2 data packet, 111
HV3 data packet, 111
hybrids, 53

I

IAC (Inquiry Access Code), 107–108,
    118–119
IBM, 6
ID data packets, 111
idle mode procedures, 222
IEEE 802-11 standard specifications, 17
impedance, 35–37
in-band spurious emission, 32
in-band tones and announcements, 258
In-phase, of DSSS modulators, 54–55
incoming external calls, 255
Ind (Indications) event, 186
Industrial-Scientific Medical (ISM) band

Bluetooth radio and, 73
commercial use of, 25
frequency hopping factors, 26
overview, 8
range of, by country, 25
INFO ACCEPT message, 259
information exchange management
    LMP version, 149–150
    name request, 150–151
    supported features, 151–152
Infrared Data Association (IrDA), 17
initial frequency accuracy, 33
initialization key, 303
Initialization mode, 291
initialization procedures to LAN connec-
    tions, 282–283
initialization process of OBEX, 244
Inquiry Access Code (IAC), 107–108,
    118–119
Inquiry Complete Event, 169
inquiry procedures, 222
inquiry response state, 116
inquiry scan state, 115–116, 228, 241
inquiry state, 115
Integrated Services Digital Network
    (ISDN), 254
Intel, 6
intercom calls, 255
Intercom Profile, 215
    distribution of protocol stack for, 261
    features of, 261–262
    L2CAP interoperability requirements
        for, 263
    overview, 260–261
interfaces
    balun, 36
    HCI (Host Controller Interface), 76

interference
  evading techniques, 42–43
  interceptions in transmissions, 8
  ISM territory, 25
  protection against, 8
interference performance of receivers, 40
International Organization for
  Standardization (ISO), 207, 214
International Telecommunication Union
  (ITU), 17
International Telecommunications Union-
  Telecommunication (ITU-T), 78
Internet Protocol (IP), 59, 72
Internet Security model, 299
Invalid CID in request reason code, 184
invalid LMP parameters reason code, 157
IP (Internet Protocol), 59, 72
IrDA (Infrared Data Association), 17
IrMC client role, 290
IrMC server role, 290
ISDN (Integrated Services Digital
  Network), 254
ISM (Industrial-Scientific Medical) band
  Bluetooth radio and, 73
  commercial use of, 25
  frequency hopping factors, 26
  overview, 8
  range of, by country, 25
ISO (International Organization for
  Standardization), 207, 214
ITU (International Telecommunication
  Union), 17
ITU-T (International
  Telecommunications Union-
  Telecommunication), 78

K

key stream generator, 306

L

L-CH (logical channel), 109
L (loudness of monitor speaker) command, 268
L2CAP (Logical Link Control
  Adaptation Protocol), 12, 72, 76
  assumptions of, 172
  channels, list of, 174–175
  configuration parameter options,
    192–194
  connection primitive, 194
  connectionless traffic primitive, 194
  data packets, 179–181
  data primitive, 194
  functional requirements of, 173
  group primitive, 194
  information primitive, 194
  L2CAP to L2CAP signaling events,
    188–189
  L2CAP to lower layer actions, 190–191
  L2CAP to upper layer actions, 191–192
  layer interactions, 186
  lower layer to L2CAP events, 187
  overview, 171–172
  protocol multiplexing, 173
  signaling and data actions, 192
  signaling commands, 181–182
  state machine, 183–186
  timer events, 189–190
  upper layers to L2CAP events, 187–188
L2CAP_PDU_CL field, 180
L2CAP_PDU_CO field, 179

LAN Access Profile, 216
  Application layer procedures, 282
  distribution of protocol stack for, 279
  DT (Data Terminal) device role, 280
  DT interactions with, 280
  generic modes, 281
  initialization procedures, 282–283
  LAP (LAN access point) device role, 280
  overview, 279
  pairing procedures, 282
  PPP network scenarios, 280
  security implementations, 281
  shutdown procedures, 283
LAN (Local Area Network), 69
LAP (Lower Address Part), 99
layers
  Application, 82
  baseband layer, 75
  HCI (Host Controller Interface), 12
  HCI transport, list of, 170
  L2CAP, operation between, 177
  OSI Reference Model layers, 67–68
  Security, 83
  Sessions, 82
  TLS (Transport Layer Security), 83
  Transaction, 82
  Transport, 83
LC (Link Controller), 72
  baseband services and, 93
  connection state, 115
  defined, 11
  inquiry response state, 116
  inquiry scan state, 115–116
  inquiry state, 115
  interoperability requirements, for
        Cordless Telephony Profile, 260

page response state, 117
page scan state, 116
page state, 116
standby state, 117
LC (Link Controller) channel, 127
Least Significant Bit (LSB), 106
length field (payload header), 110
Level-2 Medium Access Control (MAC-2) layer, 171
LFSRs (Linear Feedback Shift Registers), 305–306
LIAC (Limited Inquiry Access Code), 118, 219
limited discoverable mode, 270
Limited Inquiry Access Code (LIAC), 118, 219
limited inquiry procedure, 222
linear arrays, 40
linear codes, 52
Linear Feedback Shift Registers (LFSRs), 305–306
linear waves, 39
Link Controller (LC), 72
  baseband services and, 93
  connection state, 115
  defined, 11
  inquiry response state, 116
  inquiry scan state, 115–116
  inquiry state, 115
  interoperability requirements, for
        Cordless Telephony Profile, 260
  page response state, 117
  page scan state, 116
  page state, 116
  standby state, 117
Link Controller (LC) channel, 127
link encryption, 138–139

link establishment, 220

link-level security, 300

    key management, 301–303

    random number generation, 301

Link Manager (LM), 12, 72, 75–76

Link Manager (LM) channel, 127

Link Manager Protocol (LMP), 75–76, 126

    functions, diagram of, 128

    interoperability requirements, for Cordless Telephony Profile, 260

    overview, 11

link supervision service, 155

link types, 94

links

    ACL (Asynchronous Connectionless), 12

    loss handling, 200, 226

    SCO (Synchronous Connection Oriented) link, 12

LISTEN ACCEPT message, 258

LM (Link Manager), 12, 72, 75–76

LM (Link Manager) channel, 127

LMP (Link Manager Protocol), 75–76, 126

    functions, diagram of, 128

    interoperability requirements, for Cordless Telephony Profile, 260

    overview, 11

LMP PDU Not Allowed error code, 169

LMP_accepted PDU, 134, 143, 145

LMP_au_rand PDU, 132

LMP_auto_rate PDU, 154

LMP_clock_offset_req PDU, 140

LMP_decr_power_req PDU, 149

LMP_detach PDU, 132, 134, 153

LMP_encryption_key_size_req PDU, 138

LMP_features_req PDU, 151–152

LMP_features_res PDU, 151–152

LMP_hold_req PDU, 144, 146

LMP_host_connection_req PDU, 153

LMP_incr_power_req PDU, 148–149

LMP_max_power PDU, 148–149

LMP_max_slot PDU, 155

LMP_max_slot_req PDU, 155

LMP_min_power PDU, 149

LMP_modify_beacon PDU, 147

LMP_name _req PDU, 150–151

LMP_name_res PDU, 150–151

LMP_not_accepted PDU, 133, 142–143

LMP_page_mode_req PDU, 156

LMP_page_scan_mode_req PDU, 156

LMP_park PDU, 146

LMP_park_req PDU, 147

LMP_PDUs (LMP Protocol Data Units)

    connection management, 152–153

    error handling, 157

    fields, list of, 129

    general response management, 130–131

    information exchange management, 149–152

    mode control and management, 142–148

    power management, 148–149

    security management, 131–139

    test mode, 156

    time management, 140–142

LMP_preferred_rate PDU, 154

LMP_quality_of_service PDU, 154

LMP_quality_of_service _req PDU, 154

LMP_remove_SCO_link_req PDU, 155

LMP_SCO_link_req PDU, 155

LMP_set_broadcast_scan_window PDU, 147

LMP_setup_complete PDU, 153
LMP_slot_offset PDU, 141
LMP_sniff_req PDU, 145
LMP_sres PDU, 132
LMP_start_encryption_req PDU, 139
LMP_stop_encryption_req PDU, 139
LMP_supervision_timeout PDU, 156
LMP_switch_req PDU, 143
LMP_temp_key PDU, 138
LMP_temp_rand PDU, 138
LMP_test_activate PDU, 156
LMP_timing_accuracy_req PDU, 142
LMP_timing_accuracy_res PDU, 142
LMP_unpark_BD_ADDR_req PDU, 148
LMP_unpark_PM_ADDR_req PDU, 148
LMP_unsniff PDU, 145
LMP_use_semi_permanent_key PDU, 138
LMP_version_req PDU, 150
LMP_version_res PDU, 150
Local Area Network (LAN), 69
LocDev (Local Device), 230–231
Logical Channel Identifiers (CID), 76
logical channel (L_CH), 109
Logical Link Control Adaptation Protocol (L2CAP), 12, 72, 76
    assumptions of, 172
    configuration parameter options, 192–194
    connection primitive, 194
    connectionless traffic primitive, 194
    data packets, 179–181
    data primitive, 194
    functional requirements of, 173
    group primitive, 194
    information primitive, 194
    L2CAP to L2CAP signaling events, 188–189
    L2CAP to lower layer actions, 190–191
    L2CAP to upper layer actions, 191–192
    layer interactions, 186
    lower layer to L2CAP events, 187
    overview, 171–172
    protocol multiplexing, 173
    signaling and data actions, 192
    signaling commands, 181–182
    state machine, 183–186
    timer events, 189–190
    upper layers to L2CAP events, 187–188
low power modes, RFCOMM, 202
Low Probability of Intercept (LPI), 56–57
Lower Address Part (MAC address), 99
lower protocols
    classification of, 92
    of transport protocol group, 93
LPI (Low Probability of Intercept), 56–57
LSB (Least Significant Bit), 106

M

M-ary signaling, 30
M (mandatory) feature of LM, 238
M (mode of monitor speaker) command, 268
MAC-2 (Level-2 Medium Access Control) layer, 171
MAC (Medium Access Control), 99
magnetic (H) field, 39
mandatory (M) feature of LM, 238
market requirements, comparing technological developments to, 322–323
master clock (CLK), 101
master key, 302

master-to-slave time slots, 98
master unit
  links between, 103
  in piconets, 9, 95
  switch of, 143–144
material loss in transmissions, 39–40
Maximum Transmission Unit (MTU),
    193, 237–238
media adaptation, 198
Medium Access Control (MAC), 99
Mega-Instructions Per Second (MIPS),
    166
message sequence charts, 235
microstrip antennas, 33
microwave ovens, air interface and, 8
middleware protocol group (Bluetooth
    protocol stack), 72, 77
military, SS (Spread Spectrum) technolo-
    gy and, 51
MIPS (Mega-Instructions Per Second),
    166
missing key reason code, 133
Mobile Imaging Nokia 9110 communica-
    tor, 14
mobile phones, 14
mode control management, 128
  hold mode, 144
  master/slave roles, switch of, 143–144
  overview, 142
  park mode, 146–148
  sniff mode, 145–146
modes
  common mode, 36
  connectable, 270
  general discoverable, 270
  General sync, 291
  hold, 115, 144

idle mode procedures, 222
Initialization, 291
limited discoverable, 270
non-connectable, 270
non-discoverable, 270
non-pairable, 270
pairing, 219, 270
park, 146–148
security, 270
sniff, 115, 145–146
modulation parameter (Bluetooth radio),
    74
modulation scheme, transmitters, 30–31
MTU (Maximum Transmission Unit),
    193, 237–238
Multiple-Terminal Support, 255, 260
multiple-user mode, 282
multiplexer control commands, 200–201
multiplexer startup procedures, 199–200

N

name discovery procedures, 222–223
name request, 150–151
name request procedure, 223
NAP (Non-significant Address Part), 100
native clock (CLKN), 101
Network layer (OSI Reference Model),
    67–68
networking, Bluetooth, 9–11
networks
  circuit-switched, 58
  connection-oriented, 58–59, 77
  packet-switched, 58
new application working group, 345–346
Nokia 9110 device, 14
Nokia Bluetooth Headset, 14

non-connectable mode, 270
non-discoverable mode, 270
non-linear codes, 52
non-pairable mode, 270
non-significant Address Part (NAP), 100
NULL data packet, 111
null mode emulation, 196
null state, 263

O

O (optional) feature of LM, 238
O (return to online data state) command, 268
OBEX (Object Exchange) protocol, 164
   functions of, 204–205
   initialization process, 244
   overview, 202–203
   requirements, 203
   session establishment in, 244
   transfer of objects in, 204
object manipulation, 285
object push function, 288
Object Push Profile, 216
   Application layer functions, 288
   features of, 287
   interoperability requirements, 289
   overview, 287
   push client role, 287
   push server role, 287
   user interface, 288
object transfer, 285
obtain access rights, 258
on chip antennas, 34
on hook, 255
opCode field, 129
OPEN state, 184–185

Open System Interconnection (OSI) Reference Model
   categories of, 69
   defined, 66
   inter-system communication using, 70–71
   layer wise flow of information in, 71
   layers, list of, 67
   protocols, 69
optional (O) feature of LM, 238
Organization Unique Identifier (OUI), 100
orthogonal, 55
OSI (Open System Interconnection Reference Model)
   categories of, 69
   defined, 66
   inter-system communication using, 70–71
   layer wise flow of information in, 71
   layers, list of, 67
   protocols, 69
OUI (Organization Unique Identifier), 100
out-of-band blocking, 41
out-of-band spurious emission, 32
outgoing external call, 255

P

P (select pulse dialing) command, 268
packet-switched networks, 59–61
packets. *See* data packets
page scan, 242
Page Scan Repetition Mode Change Event, 169
page scan state, 116

page state, 116

paging process, 119–120, 228, 241

paging scheme, 155

pairable mode, 270

pairing modes, 219, 232

pairing not allowed reason code, 135–136

PAN (Personal Area Network), 43

Parameter Negotiation (PN) command, 201

park mode, 146–148

payload body, 110

payload header, 104, 109–110

payload key generator, 306

PCB (Printed Circuit Board), 33

PDAs (Personal Data Assistants), 80, 252, 299

PDU not allowed reason code, 156

PDUs (Protocol Data Units), 104, 164, 195

peripheral communication, 13

Personal Area Network (PAN), 43, 342

Personal Data Assistants (PDAs), 80, 252, 299

Personal Handyphone Service (PHS), 64

personal identification number (PIN), 219, 281, 302

phones, cordless
air interface and, 8
Bluetooth specifications, 14

PHS (Personal Handyphone Service), 64

physical channel
TDD scheme, 99
time slots and, 98

Physical layer (OSI Reference Model), 67, 69

piconets

defined, 9

diagram of, 10

master unit in, 9, 95

overlapping, 10

point-to-multipoint links, 96–97

point-to-point link, 96

scatternet, topology of, 97

slave unit in, 9, 95

PIFA (Planar Inverted Antenna), 34

PIN (personal identification number), 219, 281, 302

pins, RS-232, 196

planar arrays, 40

Planar Inverted Antenna (PIFA), 34

Plug and Play (PnP), 209

PN code generator, 51

PN (Parameter Negotiation) command, 201

PN (Pseudo Noise) sequences
codes generated in, 52
overview, 51

PnP (Plug and Play), 209

point-to-multipoint connections, 9, 96–97

point-to-point connections, 9, 96

Point-to-Point Protocol (PPP), 78

polarization, 39

POLL data packet, 111

ports, remote port negotiation, 228

post-dialing, 255

power classes of Bluetooth radio transmitters, 29

power management, 128, 148–149

power mode, link loss handling and, 226

PPP (Point-to-Point Protocol), 78

preamble, 106

Precondition Failed response code, 285

Presentation layer (OSI Reference Model), 67–68
primitiveHandle attribute, 234
Printed Circuit Board (PCB), 33
printing working group, 342
procedure is terminated reason code, 157
products, Bluetooth, 14
profiles
  Cordless Telephony Profile
    call control procedures, 257–258
    connection management, 257
    distribution of protocol stack for, 254
    features of, 256
    group management procedures, 258
    GW (Gateway) service role, 254
    L2CAP interoperability requirements for, 259
    LC interoperability requirements for, 260
    link loss detection by Gateway, 259
    LMP interoperability requirements for, 260
    overview, 253
    supplementary services, 259
    TL (Terminal) service role, 254
  Dial-Up Networking
    Application layer services, 266–267
    call progress audio feedback, 269
    commands, list of, 268–269
    DT (Data Terminal) device role, 266
    features of, 266
    GAP Idle mode and bonding procedures supported by, 271
    GAP modes supported by, 270
    GAP security aspects supported by, 270
    GW (Gateway) device role, 265

    interoperability requirements, 267
    overview, 264
    restrictions of, 266
  Fax Profile
    compliance with fundamental profiles, 275
    dialing and control procedures, AT commands for, 274
    distribution of protocol stack for, 272
    DT (Data Terminal) device role, 272
    features of, 273
    GW (Gateway) device role, 272
    interoperability requirements, 274
    overview, 272
    restrictions of, 273
    services supported by, 274
  File Transfer Profile
    Application layer procedures, 285
    client device role, 284
    distribution of protocol stack for, 283
    features of, 284
    interoperability requirements, 285
    overview, 283
    server device role, 284
    service records for, 286
    user interface specifications, 284
  generic, 216
  Headset
    AW (Audio Gateway) device role, 276
    distribution protocol stack for, 275
    features of, 276
    fundamental profiles, compliance with, 278
    HS (Headset) device role, 276
    interoperability requirements, 276–277
    overview, 275

Intercom
distribution of protocol stack for, 261
features of, 261–262
L2CAP interoperability requirements for, 263
overview, 260–261
LAN Access Profile
Application layer procedures, 282
distribution of protocol stack for, 279
DT (Data Terminal) device role, 280
DT interactions with, 280
generic modes, 281
initialization procedures, 282–283
LAP (LAN access point) device role, 280
overview, 279
pairing procedures, 282
PPP network scenarios, 280
security implementations, 281
shutdown procedures, 283
list of, 215–216
Object Push Profile
Application layer functions, 288
features of, 287
interoperability requirements, 289
overview, 287
push client role, 287
push server role, 287
user interface, 288
overview, 214–215
serial, 216
Synchronization
Application layer features, 291–292
distribution of protocol stack for, 289
features of, 290
interoperability requirements, 292
IrMC client role, 290
IrMC server role, 290

overview, 289
user interface specifications, 291
telephony, 216
Protocol Data Units (PDUs), 104, 164, 195
protocol multiplexing, 76, 173
Protocol/Service Multiplexor (PSM), 259
protocol stack. *See* Bluetooth protocol stack
protocols
IP (Internet Protocol), 59, 72
L2CAP (Logical Link Control and Adaptation Protocol), 12
assumption of, 172
data packets, 179–181
functional requirements of, 173
L2CAP to lower layer actions, 190–191
layer interactions, 186
lower layer to L2CAP events, 187
overview, 171–172
protocol multiplexing, 173
signaling and data actions, 192
signaling commands, 181–182
timer events, 189–190
upper layers to L2CAP events, 187–188
LAN (Local Area Network), 69
LMP (Link Manager Protocol), 11, 75–76
lower
classification of, 92
of transport protocol group, 93
OBEX (Object Exchange), 164
functions of, 204–205
overview, 202–203
requirements, 203
transfer of objects in, 204

PPP (Point-to-Point Protocol), 78
RFCOMM, 12
SDP (Service Discovery Protocol), 12,
    78, 164
  overview, 206–207
  searching and browsing, 208–209
  service classes, 207–208
  service records, 207
TCP/IP (Transmission Control
    Protocol/Internet Protocol),
    59–60, 72
TCS (Telephony Control Protocol), 12,
    78–79, 164, 205–206
upper, 92
WAN (Wide Area Network), 69
WAP (Wireless Application Protocol),
    80–81, 298
WDP (Wireless Datagram Protocol),
    83
WSP (Wireless Session Protocol), 82
WTP (Wireless Transaction Protocol),
    82–83
Pseudo Noise (P.N.) sequences
  codes generated in, 52
  overview, 51
PST (Protocol/Service Multiplex), 259
PST (Public Switched Telephony
    Network), 7, 254
publicbrowserroot attribute, 208
pulling data objects, 244
pushing data objects, 244
PUT operation, 285

Q

Q factor, 35

Q (result code suppression) command,
    268
QoS (Quality of Service), 77, 154, 173,
    237–238
qualification process, SIG (Special
    Interest Group), 7

R

radiation patterns of antennas
  azimuth dimension, 37
  elevation dimension, 38
  uses of, 39
radio. *See* Bluetooth radio
Radio 2.0 working group, 340–341
radio chip, 6
radio frequency tolerance, 33
radio link. *See* physical channel
radio receivers
  Bluetooth device requirements, 42
  interference performance, 40
  out of band blocking, 41
  RSSI (Receiver Signal Strength
      Indicator), 41
  sensitivity levels of, 40
  usable level of operation, 41
radio transmissions
  gain in, 39
  loss in, reasons for, 39–40
  modulation scheme, 30–31
  radio frequency tolerance, 33
  radio wave equipment, list of, 26–27
  symbol timing, 31
radio transmitters
  Bluetooth, characteristics of, 29
  function of, 27
  power levels of, 29

sine waves, 28
square waves, 28
radio waves, 26–27
RAM (Random Access Memory), 56
random number generation, 301
RAS (Remote Access Server), 264
RD (Received Data), 196
readmission of parked devices, 146
Ready To Send (RTS), 201
reason codes
  authentication failure, 134
  Command not understood, 184
  Invalid CID if request, 184
  invalid LMP parameters, 157
  missing key, 133
  pairing not allowed, 135–136
  PDU not allowed, 156
  Precondition Failed reason code, 285
  procedure is terminated, 157
  Reserved, 184
  Signaling MTU exceeded, 184
  unknown, 157
  unsupported LMP feature, 142, 229,
    239
  unsupported parameter value, 144–145
Receive Signal Strength Indication
  (RSSI), 151
Received Data (RD), 196
receiver sensitivity parameter (Bluetooth
  radio), 74
Receiver Signal Strength Indicator
  (RSSI), 41
receivers. *See* radio receivers
register recall, 255
release request, 263
reliability, RFCOMM, 202
reliable one-way requests, 83

reliable two-way requests, 83
RemDev (Remote Device), 230–231, 234
Remote Access Server (RAS), 264
remote line status indication, 228
Remote Line Status (RLS) command, 201
remote port negotiation, 228
Remote Port Negotiation (RPN) command, 201
Req (Requests) event, 186
Request to Send (RTS), 196
requests
  clock offset request, 140
  disconnect, 263
  name, 150–151
  release, 263
  reliable one-way, 83
  reliable two-way, 83
  slot offset, 141
  unreliable one-way, 83
Requests (Req) event, 186
Res (Response) event, 186
Reserved reason code, 184
Response Timeout Expired (RTX) timer,
  189–190
RFCOMM, 12, 77–78
  control signals, 195–196
  emulated serial ports, 196–199
  flow control methods, 201
  low power modes, 202
  multiplexer control commands, 200–201
  null mode emulation, 196
  overview, 194–195
  reliability, 202
  TS 01.10 adaptions for
    DLCI allocation in RFCOMM serv-
      er, 200
    media adaption, 198

multiplexer startup and closure proce-
    dures, 199–200
  Type 1 devices, 198
  Type 2 devices, 198
RFCOMM transport protocol, 77
RI (Ring Indicator), 196
RING message, 277
RS-232 control signals, 227
RS-232 interface, pin and circuit names
    of, 196
RS-232 Transport layer, 170
RSSI (Receiver Signal Strength
    Indicator), 41, 151
RTS (Ready To Send), 201
RTX (Response Timeout Expired) timer,
    189–190

S

S0 (automatic answer) command, 268
S3 (command-line termination character)
    command, 269
S4 (response for formatting character)
    command, 269
S5 (command-line editing character)
    command, 269
S6 (pause before blind dialog) command,
    269
S7 (connection completion timeout) com-
    mand, 269
S8 (comma dial modifier time) command,
    269
S10 (automatic disconnect delay) com-
    mand, 268
SABM frame command, 202
SAR (Segmentation and Reassembly),
    173, 178–179

scatternet
  diagram of, 10
  topology of, 97
SCO (Synchronous Connection Oriented)
    link
  defined, 12
  master and slave units and, 103
SDAP (Service Discovery Application
    Profile), 215
  abstraction primitives, 234
  configuration options, 237–238
  distribution of protocol stack for, 230
  error behavior, 239
  features of, 231
  inquiry scan, 241
  LM capabilities, 238
  message sequence charts, 235
  mode selection, 232
  overview, 229–231
  pairing and, 232
  SrvDscApp_A, 232
  SrvDscApp_B, 232
  SrvDscApp_C, 233
  user requirements, 231
SDDB (Service Discovery Database), 284
SDP (Service Discovery Protocol), 12, 78,
    164
  overview, 206–207
  searching and browsing, 208–209
  service classes, 207–208
  service records, 207
SDP_ErrorResponse, 209
searchPattern attribute, 234
Secure Sockets Layer (SSL), 83, 299
security
  in ad hoc networks, 299–300
  authentication, 304–305

E algorithms, 308
encryption, 305–308
Internet security model, 299
LAN Access Profile, 281
link-level, 300
 key management, 301–303
 random number generation, 301
WAP gateway and, 85
WAP security model, 299
WTLS (Wireless Transport Layer
 Security), 299
Security layer (WAP architecture), 83
security management, 128, 131
 device authentication, 132–138
 link encryption, 138–139
Security mode 1: non secure, 221
Security mode 2: service level enforced
 security, 221
Security mode 3: link level enforced security, 221
security modes, 270
Segmentation and Reassembly (SAR),
 173, 178–179
sensitivity levels of receivers, 40
SEQN (Sequence Number), 109
Serial Port Profile (SPP), 215
 distribution of protocol stack for, 224
 features of, 224–225
 FRCOMM interoperability requirements of, 227–228
 L2CAP interoperability requirements,
  227
 Link Controller interoperability requirements of, 228
 Link Manager interoperability requirements of, 229
 overview, 223

 power mode and link loss handling, 226
 virtual connection, setting up, 225–226
 virtual serial connection, accepting and
  establishing, 226
serial ports, 196–199
serial profiles, 216
servers, role of, 243
service classes, 207–208
Service Discovery Application Profile
 (SDAP), 215
 abstraction primitives, 234
 distribution of protocol stack for, 230
 error behavior, 239
 features of, 231
 inquiry scan, 241
 LM capabilities, 238
 message sequence charts, 235
 mode selection, 232
 overview, 229–231
 pairing and, 232
 SrvDscApp_A, 232
 SrvDscApp_B, 232–233
 SrvDscApp_C, 233
 user requirements, 231
Service Discovery Database (SDDB), 284
Service Discovery Protocol (SDP), 12, 78,
 164
 overview, 206–207
 searching and browsing, 208–209
 service classes, 207–208
 service records, 207
service primitives, 234
service records, 207
service registry, 207
serviceBrowse service primitive, 234
ServiceClassIDList attribute, 208
serviceSearch service primitive, 234

session establishment in OBEX, 244
Session layer
    OSI Reference Model, 67–68
    WAP architecture, 82
SETPATH operation, 285
Short Message Service (SMS), 83–84
shutdown procedures, of LAN Access
        Profile, 283
SIG (Special Interest Group)
    components of, 6
    future of, 340
    middleware protocol group and, 72
    qualification process, 7
signaling
    DTMF (Dual Tone Multiple
        Frequency), 255
    L2CAP interoperability requirements,
        227
    M-ary, 30
signaling channels, 77, 175
signaling commands, 181–182
Signaling MTU exceeded reason code,
        184
signals
    RSSI (Receiver Signal Strength
        Indicator), 151
    SS (Spread Spectrum), 57
    weak, sending, 42
sine waves, 28
single-user mode, 282
slave-to-master time slots, 98
slave unit
    links between, 103
    in piconets, 9, 95
    switch of, 143–144
slot offset request, 141
SMS (Short Message Service), 83–84

sniff mode, 115, 145–146
software framework, Bluetooth architec-
        ture, 12–13
speaker phones, 14
Special Interest Group (SIG)
    components of, 6
    future of, 340
    middleware protocol group and, 72
    qualification process, 7
specifications, for Bluetooth radio para-
        meters, 74
SPP (Serial Port Profile), 215
    distribution of protocol stack for, 224
    features of, 224–225
    L2CAP interoperability requirements
        of, 227
    Link Controller interoperability require-
        ments of, 228
    Link Manager interoperability require-
        ments of, 229
    overview, 223
    power mode and link loss handling, 226
    RFCOMM interoperability require-
        ments of, 227–228
    virtual connection, setting up, 225–226
    virtual serial connection, accepting and
        establishing, 226
Spread Spectrum (SS) technology
    advantages of using, 57
    characteristics of, 56
    circuit-switch networks, 58
    DSSS (Direct Sequence Spread
        Spectrum), 53–54
    FHSS (Frequency Hopping Spread
        Spectrum), 55–56
    origin and growth of, 50–51
    packet-switched networks, 59–61

THSS (Time Hopping Spread Spectrum), 53, 56
spurious emission, 32
square waves, 28
SrvDscApp_A, 232
SrvDscApp_B, 232
SrvDscApp_C, 233
SS (Spread Spectrum) technology
  advantages of using, 57
  characteristics of, 56
  circuit-switched networks, 58
  DSSS (Direct Sequence Spread Spectrum), 53
  FHSS (Frequency Hopping Spread Spectrum), 55–56
  in military, 51
  origin and growth of, 50–51
  packet-switched networks, 59–61
  PN (Pseudo Noise) sequences, 51–52
  THSS (Time Hopping Spread Spectrum), 53, 56
SSL (Secure Sockets Layer), 83, 299
standby state, 117
still image working group, 343
Sub-version number (SubVersNr), 150
support features services, 151–152
symbol rate parameter (Bluetooth radio), 74
symbol timing, 31
sync word, 106
Synchronization Profile, 216
  Application layer features, 291–292
  distribution of protocol stack for, 289
  features of, 290
  interoperability requirements, 292
  IrMC client role, 290
  IrMC server sole, 290

overview, 289
user interface specifications, 291
Synchronous Connection Oriented (SCO) link
  defined, 12
  master and slave units and, 103

T

T (select tone dialing) command, 269
TCP/IP (Transmission Control Protocol/Internet Protocol), 59–60, 72, 78
TCS (Telephony Control Protocol), 12, 77–79, 164, 205–206
TD (Transmit Data), 196
TDD (Time Division Duplexing)
  advantages of, 64
  disadvantages of, 64–65
  master and slave devices, transmission between, 99
  multiple access scheme of high peak power in, 64
  overview, 63
TDMA (Time Division Multiple Access), 84
Telephony Control Protocol (TCS), 12, 77–79, 164, 205–206
telephony profiles, 216
terminatePrimitive service primitive, 234
test modes, 128
three-dimensional arrays, 40
THSS (Time Hopping Spread Spectrum), 53, 56
Time Division Duplexing (TDD)
  advantages of, 64
  disadvantages of, 64–65

multiple access scheme of high peak
power in, 64
overview, 63
Time Division Multiple Access (TDMA),
84
Time Hopping Spread Spectrum (THSS),
53, 56
time management, 128
clock offset request, 140
slot offset request, 141
timing accuracy information request,
141–142
time slots
master-to-slave, 98
RF hop frequencies, 99
slave-to-master, 98
TLS (Transport Layer Security), 83
Toshiba, 6
trailer, 106
Transaction layer (WAP architecture), 82
transactionID field, 129
transferring objects, 285
Transmission Control Protocol/Internet
Protocol (TCP/IP), 59–60, 72, 78
transmission lines, 35–37
transmissions
interceptions, 8
jammed, error correction algorithms, 8
radio
gain in, 39
loss in, reasons for, 39–40
modulation scheme, 30–31
radio frequency tolerance, 33
radio wave equipment, list of, 26–27
symbol timing, 31
Transmit Data (TD), 196

transmit power parameter (Bluetooth
radio), 74
transmitters, radio
Bluetooth, characteristics of, 29
function of, 27
power levels of, 29
sine waves, 28
square waves, 28
Transport layer
OSI Reference Model, 67–68
WAP architecture, 83
Transport Layer Security (TLS), 83
transport protocol group (Bluetooth protocol stack), 72
tri-mode CDMS hands free speaker
phone, 14
trusted devices, 234
TS 07.10 adaptions for RFCOMM
DLCI allocation in RFCOMM server
channels, 200
media adaption, 198
multiplexer startup and closure procedures, 199–200
Type 1 devices (RFCOMM), 198
Type 2 devices (RFCOMM), 198
Type Code (TYPE), 108

U

UA (User Asynchronous) channel, 127
UAP (Upper Address Part), 100
UART Transport layer, 170
UI (User Isochronous) channel, 127
UIH (Unnumbered Information with
Header) error check, 202
Ultra-Wideband Radio (UWB), 17
unit keys, 133, 301

Universal Serial Bus (USB), 76
Universally Unique Identifier (UUID), 207, 285
Unknown HCI Command error code, 169
unknown or new devices, 234
unknown reason code, 157
Unnumbered Information with Header (UIH) error check, 202
unreliable one-way requests, 83
unsupported LMP feature reason code, 142, 229, 239
unsupported parameter value reason code, 144–145
Upper Address Part (UAP), 100
upper protocols, classification of, 92
US (User Synchronous) channel, 127
USB adapter from TDK device, 15
USB Transport layer, 170
USB (Universal Serial Bus), 76
User Asynchronous (UA) channel, 127
User Isochronous (UI) channel, 127
user requirements, for SDAP, 231
User Synchronous (US) channel, 127
users, single-user mode, 282
UUID (Universally Unique Identifier), 207, 285
UWB (Ultra-Wideband Radio), 17

V

V (DCE response format) command, 269
vertical interface, 186
VesNr (version number), 149–150
virtual connections, setting up, 225–226
virtual serial connections, accepting and establishing, 226
virtual serial ports, 225

voice access, potential applications for, 326
voice calls, 267, 274
voice coding schemes, 151

W

W4_L2CAP_Connect_RSP state, 183
W4_L2CAP_Disconnect_RSP state, 184–185
WAE (Wireless Application Environment), 82
waiting period, 304
WAN (Wide Area Network), 69, 265
WAP Forum, 80–81
WAP gateway, 84–85
WAP (Wireless Application Protocol), 80–81, 298
    Application layer of, 82
    Security layer, 83
    Sessions layer of, 82
    Transaction layer of, 82
    Transport layer of, 83
waves
    circular, 39
    electromagnetic, 39
    linear, 39
    polarization of, 39
    sign waves, 28
    square, 28
WDP (Wireless Datagram Protocol), 83
weak signals, 42
Wide Area Network (WAN), 69, 265
Windows CE-based Auto PC, 14
Wireless Application Environment (WAE), 82
Wireless Application Protocol (WAP), 80–81, 298

Security layer, 83
Sessions layer of, 82
Transaction layer of, 82
Transport layer of, 83
wireless connection, 7
Wireless Datagram Protocol (WAP), 83
Wireless Lan (WLAN), 17
Wireless Session Protocol (WSP), 82, 85
Wireless Transaction Protocol (WTP),
    82–83
Wireless Transport Layer Security
    (WTLS), 83, 85, 299
wireless user groups, 206
WLAN (Wireless Lan), 17
WSP (Wireless Session Protocol), 82, 85
WTLS (Wireless Transport Layer
    Security), 83, 85, 299
WTP (Wireless Transaction Protocol),
    82–83

X

X (excluded) feature of LM, 238
X (result code selection and call progress-
    monitoring control) command, 269

Z

Z (reset to default configuration) com-
    mand, 269

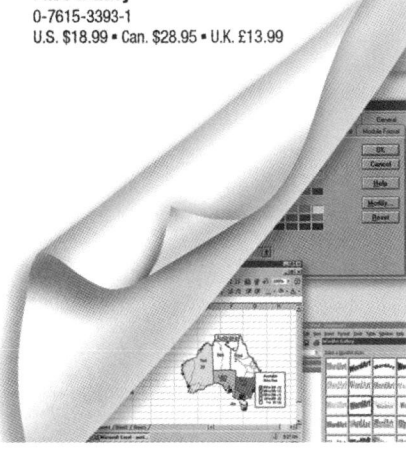